Let's Keep in Touch

Follow Us

Online

Visit US at

www.learnpersianonline.com

 www.facebook.com/PersiaClubCo

Call

 www.twitter.com/PersiaClub

1-469-230-3605

 www.instagram.com/LearnPersianOnline

Online Persian Lessons Via Skype

It's easy! Here's how it works.

1- Request a FREE introductory session.

2- Meet a Persian tutor online via Skype.

3- Start speaking Real Persian in Minutes.

Send Email to: info@LearnPersianOnline.com

Or Call: **+1-469-230-3605**

www.learnpersianonline.com

... So Much More Online!

- **FREE Farsi lessons**

- **More Farsi learning books!**

- **Online Farsi – English Dictionary**

- **Online Farsi Tutors**

Transliterated Dictionary of the Farsi Language

The Most Trusted Farsi-English Dictionary

By

Reza Nazari

&

Jalal Daie

ISBN-13: 978-1974363889

ISBN-10: 1974363880

Published by: Learn Persian Online Website

www.learnpersianonline.com

About Learn Persian Online Website

The *"Learn Persian Online Website"* was founded on the belief that everyone interested in Persian language should have the opportunity to learn it!

Established in 2012, the *"Learn Persian Online Website"* creates international opportunities for all people interested in Persian language and culture and builds trust between them. We believe in this cultural relations!

If you want to learn more about Persian, this beautiful language and culture, *"Learn Persian Online Website"* is your best starting point. Our highly qualified Persian experts can help you connect to Persian culture and gain confidence you need to communicate effectively in Persian.

Over the past few years, our professional instructors, unique online resources and publications have helped thousands of Persian learners and students improve their language skills. As a result, these students have gained their goals faster. We love celebrating those victories with our students.

Please view our website at:

www.learnpersianonline.com

About the Author

Reza Nazari is a Persian author. He has published more than 50 Persian learning books including:

- Learn To Speak Persian Fast series,

- Farsi Grammar in Use series,

- Persia Club Dictionary Farsi – English,

- Essential Farsi Idioms,

- Persian Verbs Dictionary

- Read and Write Persian Language in 7 Days

- Laugh and Learn Farsi: Mulla Nasreddin Tales For Intermediate to Advanced Persian Learners

- Top 50 Persian Poems of All Time

- Farsi Reading: Improve your reading skill and discover the art, culture and history of Iran

- and many more ...

Reza is also a professional Persian teacher. Over the past eight years, his online Persian lessons have helped thousands of Persian learners and students around the world improve their language skills effectively.

To participate in online Persian classes or ask questions about learning Persian, you can contact Reza via email at: reza@learnpersianonline.com or his Skype ID: rezanazari1

Find Reza's professional profile at:

http://www.learnpersianonline.com/farsi-tutor-reza

Guide to the use of the Dictionary

Designed for Farsi learners, this comprehensive and innovative dictionary of the Farsi-English languages makes Farsi language more accessible to students by removing the formidable barrier of the Farsi alphabet. Since it is alphabetized according to the transliterated English spelling, locating words is easy.

The Dictionary is fully updated with the latest lexical content. It's a unique database that offers the fullest, most accurate picture of the Farsi language today. Hundreds of new words cover technology, computing, ecology, and many other subjects.

More than 15,000 Farsi entries are organized phonetically according to their English verbalizations.

- A comprehensive Farsi to English dictionary
- Fully updated with the latest lexical content
- Offers more than 15,000 Farsi entries
- A unique database that offers the fullest, most accurate picture of the Farsi language today
- Hundreds of new words cover technology, computing, ecology, and many other subjects.

This dictionary was prepared for English people interested in Farsi language. It is dedicated to the Iranian history, culture, and mythology. With a stunningly array of more than 15,000 entries on words, phrases, names, titles, events, and places, it is an invaluable work of reference. And with a comprehensive review of words, it is guaranteed to intrigue, inform, and delight lovers of the Iranian literature, poetry, and culture.

The *Transliterated Dictionary of the Farsi Language* is intended to serve as a guidebook on the meanings of all words you are most likely to read, hear, and use. The authors attempted to include all the vocabulary you are likely to need. However, no single dictionary contains all words used in a language. New words are always being added to the continually changing language.

The main form of each word given in the dictionary is the accepted Iranian standard spelling. Although there is usually one way that most words can be spelled, sometimes other spellings are also acceptable. However, the spelling given as the headword is the most popular that most people use.

Finding words in the dictionary

The words that are listed alphabetically in the dictionary are called entry words. The entry word, which is printed in heavy black type, is the first part of the entry block. An entry block consists of the entry word, its type (noun, adjective, verb, adverb, pronoun and preposition) and the English meanings. It may be long, with many different meanings, or short, with only one meaning. Words may play different roles in different sentences, however, the most popular one is chosen as the type of the words.

In principle, entries are presented in the singular, except when usage indicates that the plural form is preferred. The plurals of most nouns are formed by adding "hâ" or "ân". These kinds of plural are not shown in the dictionary. Some popular irregular and difficult plural forms are shown as headwords, e.g. "ahvâl". Verbs are shown in infinitive format.

The entries, whether they are composed of single or multiple words, are arranged in absolute alphabetical order. (exepct for the symbol "â", that is provided in the beginning)

Pronunciation

This transliterated dictionary uses a simple spelling system to show pronunciation of Farsi words, using the symbols listed below.

Symbol	Example	Symbol	Example
a	hat /hat	m	move /muv
â	cut / cât	n	need /nid
âi	time /tâim	o	gorgeous /gorjes
ch	church /church	ô	coat/ côt
d	dog /dâg	u	mood /mud
e	men /men	p	park /park
ei	name /neim	r	rise /râiz
f	free /fri	s	seven /seven
g	get /get	n	nation /neishen
h	his /hiz	t	train /treyn
i	feet /fit	v	vary /vari
iyu	cute /kiyut	y	yet /yet
j	jeans /jinz	z	zipper /zipper
k	key /ki	zh	measure /mezher/
kh	loch /lakh	'	sounds like a slight pause between two letters.
l	loss /lâs	sh	shoes/shuz
gh	sound "r" in French word "Paris"		

Contents

Contents

â

â'di: adjective
usual - habitual - customary - ordinary - normal - common - regular

â'j: noun
tusk - ivory

â'si: adjective
sinner - sinful

â'tefe: noun
affection - sentiment

â'tel: adjective
idle - futile - vain - lazy

âb: noun
water

âb anbâr: noun
reservoir - cistern

âb bandi kardan: verb
To caulk

âb dâdan: verb
To water - To drench

âb kardan: verb
To dissolve

âb madani: noun
spa - mineral

âb raftegi: noun
shrinkage

âb shodan: verb
To melt

âb zirekâh: adjective
sneaky - pawky

âb âvardan (chashm): verb
To cataract

âb'band: noun
waterwheel - dam - dyke

âbaki: adjective
soupy - watery

âbdozdak: noun
squirt - syringe

âbdâr: adjective
succulent - juicy - aqueous - watery

âbdârkhâne: noun
pantry

âbe bini: noun
snot - snivel

âbe chizi ra gereftan: verb
To dehydrate

âbe dahân: noun
spit

âbe dahân partâb kardan: verb
To spit

âbe daryâ: noun
waterscape

âbe râked: noun
mere

âbe shur: noun
brine

âbe zolâl: noun
lymph

âbed: adjective
votary - devout

âber: noun
passer - passenger

âbeshkhor: noun
trough - destiny

âbestan: noun
pergnant

âbestan kardan: verb
To inseminate

âbestan shodan: verb
To pregnancy

âbfeshân: noun
geyser

âbgarmkon: noun
kettle - Water heater

âbgine: noun
glass

âbgir: noun
sluice - basin - pool

âbgusht: noun
chowder

âbi: adjective
blue - watery

âbiye tire: adjective
sloe

âbjo: noun
beer

âbjo: noun
beer

âbjosâz: noun
brewer

âbjosâzi: noun
brewery

âbkhori: noun
mug

âble: noun
pox - pock - smallpox

âble farangi: noun
syphilis

âbmive: noun
juice

âbmorvârid: noun
pearl

âbnabât: noun
candy

âbnamak: noun
saltwater - souse - brine

âbohavâ: noun
weather - clime - climate

âbohavâshenâsi: noun
climatology

âbpaz kardan: verb
To boil

âbpâsh: noun
pot - sprinkler

âbpâshi kardan: verb
To sprinkle

âbrumand: adjective
honorable - responsible - respectful - respectable

âbrurizi: noun
dishonor

âbrâh: noun
canal

âbse: noun
abscess

âbshâr: noun
fall - waterfall

âbtalâkâri: adjective
gilt

âbtani: noun
bathe

âbtani kardan: verb
To bath

âbyari kardan: verb
To irrigate

âbzi: noun
aquatic

âbâd kardan: verb
To inhabit

âbâdsâzi: noun
reclamation

âbâzhor: noun
lamp

âchâr: noun
wrench

âdam: noun
person - human

âdam barfi: noun
snowman

âdamak: noun
draw - manikin - dummy - robot

âdamake sare kharman: noun
scarecrow

âdami: noun
human

âdamkhâr: noun
cannibal

âdamkoshk: noun
cutthroat - assassin

âdat: noun
addict - accustom - custom

âdat: noun
habit

âdat dâshtan: verb
To accustom

âdat kardan: verb
To get

âdel: adjective
righteous

âdel: adjective
righteous

âdelâne: adverb
square

âdi kardan: verb
To habituate

âdine: noun
friday

âdâb: noun
ceremonial - rite - etiquette

âdât: noun
mores - manner

âfaride: noun
creature

âfaridegâr: noun
creator

âfarin: adjective
hurrah - bravo

âfarin goftan: verb
To applaud - To acclaim

âfarinande: adjective
creator - creative

âfarinandegi: noun
creativity

âfarinesh: noun
navigate - nature - creation

âfat: noun
pestilence - pest

âfrighâ: noun
africa

âfrighâyi: noun
african

âftâb: noun
sun

âftâb zadegi: noun
sunburn

âftâbe: noun
pitcher

âftâbi: adjective
shiny - sunny - bright

âgahi: noun
poster - caveat - notice

âgahi dâdan: verb
To announce - To advertise

âgahi fôt: noun
necrology

âghaze târikh: noun
era

âghebat: noun
sequal - end - outcome - finale

âghel: adjective
sane - sage - sagacious - sober - wise
âghelane: adverb
wise

âgheshtan: verb
To smear - To indoctrinate - To imbue

âghol: noun
corral - pound - pen

âghush: noun
embrace - arms

âghuz: noun
beestings

âghâ: noun
sir - gentleman - gent

âghâz: noun
start - beginning

âghâz kardan: verb
To initial - To begin - To commence

âghâz shodan: verb
To begin - To dawn

âgâh: adjective
conversant - conscious - cognizant - hep - aware

âgâh kardan: verb
To admonish - To acquaint - To inform - To warn

âgâhi: noun
cognizance - knowledge - advice - perception

âgâhi yâftan: verb
To learn
âgâhânidan: verb
To advise

âh: preposition
woe - alas - ah - ugh - sigh

âh goftan: verb
To pshaw

âh keshidan: verb
To sigh

âhak: noun
lime

âhaki: adjective
calcic

âhan: noun
iron

âhan forushi: noun
smithy - ironmongery

âhan âlât: noun
ironwork - ironware

âhang: noun
tune - tone - sonance - cadence - air - music - intonation

âhangar: noun
smithy - blacksmith

âhangari: noun
smithy

âhangsâz: adjective

composer

âhanin: adjective
steely

âhanrobâ: noun
magnet

âheste: adjective
slow

âheste kardan: verb
To slacken - To decelerate

âheste zadan: verb
To dab

âhu: noun
defect - asthma

âhâr: noun
starch - souse

âhâr zadan: verb
To size - To starch

âhây: preposition
hey - hallo - yoohoo

âjel: adjective
prompt

âjelâne: adverb
pronto

âjez: adjective
unable - incapable - determinant - cripple

âjez kardan: verb
To disable - To importune - To beset

âjil: noun
nut

âjor: noun
brick

âjudan: noun
adjutant

âkademi: noun
academy

âkh: preposition
ouch

âkhar: noun
end - finale - ultimate - last

âkhare hafte: noun
weekend

âkharin: noun
bottommost - last

âkherat: noun
hereafter - future

âkhor: noun
manger

âksford: noun
oxford

âlamgir: adjective
epidemic - universal

âlat: noun
tool - engine - organ - instrument

âlate dast: adjective
tool - stooge

âlate tanâsoliye mard: noun
phallus - penis
âlate tanâsoliye zan: noun
gash

âlem: adjective
scientist - universe - erudite - world

âli: adjective
excellent - supreme - superb - splendid -
spiffy - high - remarkable

âli: noun
excellent

âlijenâb: noun
eminence

âlimaghâm: adjective
dignitary - supreme

âlirotbe: adjective
supreme

âlmân: noun
germany

âlmâni: noun
jerry - germanic - german

âluche: noun
sloe

âludan: verb
To pollute - To smear - To spatter

âlude: adjective
spotty - septic - unclean

âlude kardan: verb

To defile - To infect - To muck - To mess

âlude konande: adjective
pollutant

âlude shodan: verb
To taint - To sully

âludegi: noun
alloy - pollution - impurity - sully - stain -
squalor

âlunak: noun
shed - hut

âlâchigh: noun
alcove - bower

âlât: noun
gear

âlâyesh: noun
stain

âm: adjective
ecumenical - generic

âmadan: verb
To come

âmadan va raftan: verb
To belabor

âmado raft: noun
trade

âmado shod: noun
traffic

âmbolâns: noun
ambulance

âme: noun
public - omnibus

âmel: noun
operative - element - agent

âmel: adjective
propellant

âmerâne: adverb
imperious - peremptory

âmi: adjective
layman - laic - illiterate

âmikhtan: verb
To compound - To incorporate - To interlard
- To mix

âmikhte: adjective
zygose - motley - medley

âmikhtegi: adjective
blend

âmiyâne: adverb
slangy - vulgar

âmizesh: noun
converse - mixture - intercourse - haunt -
hash

âmizesh kardan: verb
To associate

âmizeshi: adjective

coition

âmorzesh: noun
remission - pardon

âmorzidan: verb
To absolve - To remit - To forgive

âmpul zadan: verb
To shoot

âmrikâ: noun
America

âmrikâyi: adjective
American

âmukhtan: verb
To teach - To instruct

âmukhtani: adjective
teachable

âmuniyâk: noun
ammoniac

âmush va parvaresh: noun
education

âmushyâr: noun
instructor

âmuzande: adjective
instructive - informative - erudite

âmuze: noun
teachings - course

âmuzegâr: noun
teacher - instructor

âmuzegâr: noun
pedagogue

âmuzesh: noun
instruction

âmuzeshgâh: noun
academy - school

âmuzeshgâhi: adjective
scholastic

âmuzeshi: noun
didactic

âmuzeshkade: noun
college

âmuzândan: verb
To instruct

âmâde: adjective
ready - present

âmâde budan: verb
To be ready

âmâde shodan: verb
To prepare

âmâde sâkhtan: verb
To prepare

âmâdegi: noun
readiness - lurch - preparation - penchant

âmâdeye jang: adjective
warlike

âmâr: noun
statistics - census

âmârgar: noun
statistician

âmâri: noun
statistic

âmâse me'de: noun
gastritis

âmâtor: noun
unprofessional - amateur

ân: noun
moment - minute - it - instant - that - yond - yon

ân taraf: preposition
over

ânche: preposition
whatever - what

ânchenânke: preposition
wherever

ânfolânzâ: noun
influenza

ângah: adverb
then

ânghadr: adverb
enough - so

ânhâ: adverb
those - they

âni: noun
temporary - memnetary - immediate

ânjâ: adverb
yonder - thither - there - there

ânten: noun
antenna

ânzim: noun
enzyme

ânzimsâz: adjective
zymoplastic

ânâliz: noun
analysis

ânân: preposition
those - they

ânânâs: noun
pineapple

âparteman: noun
apartment

âramidan: verb
To rest - To repose

âranj: noun
elbow

ârd: noun
flour

ârd kardan: verb
To pound - To flour

âresu dâshtan: verb
To wish - To hope - To aspire

âresumand budan: verb
To thirst

âreze: noun
phenomenon

âreze: noun
accident - phenomenon

ârezu: noun
appetite - ambition - desire - wish

ârezu kardan: verb
To desire - To wish

ârezumand: adjective
wistful - desirous - avid - solicitous

âri: noun
bare - devoid

âri: noun
aye - yes - yea

âri az: noun
void

âri sakhtan: verb
To denude

âriye: noun
loan

ârm: noun
slogan

ârmân: noun
ideal

ârmângarâ: adjective
idealistic

ârmâni: noun
idealistic

ârugh: noun
burp - belch

ârugh zadan: verb
To burp - To belch

ârvâreh: noun
jib - jaw - mandible - chaw

ârâm: adjective
tranquil - taciturn - serene - calm - gentle -
moderate

ârâm kardan: verb
To calm

ârâm kardan: verb
To smooth - To cool - To conciliate - To
appease - To acquiesce

ârâm shodan: verb
To relax

ârâmesh: noun
serenity - equilibrium - calmness - peace

ârâmesh: noun
calm

ârâmesh dâdan: verb
To hush

ârâmgâh: noun
cemetery

ârâmi: noun
equanimity

ârâstan: verb
To attire - To arrange - To prune

ârâstan: verb
To inlay - To grooming - To attire - To
decorate

ârâste: adjective
natty - decorous - decent - brisk - prissy

ârâyesh: noun
polish - attire - array - garnish - décor

ârâyesh dâdan: verb
To decorate - To garnish - To beautify - To
adorn

ârâyesh kardan: verb
To embellish - To attire - To manicure

âsemân: noun
sky - height - heaven - loft

âsemân ghoresh: noun
thunder

âsemâni: noun
skiey - ethereal - empyreal - celestial -
heavenly

âsfâlt: noun
asphalt

âsfâlt kardan: verb
To pave - To blacktop

âshamidan: verb
To drink

âshegh budan: verb
To love

âshegh shodan: adjective
lover

âsheghâne: adverb
amorous

âshekâr kardan: verb
To display - To reveal - To unfold

âshekâr shodan: verb
To unfold - To revealing

âshekâr sâkhtan: verb
To manifest - To unveil

âshekârâ: adverb
clearly - obviously

âshenâ: noun
familiar - acquaintance

âshenâ kardan: verb
To introduce - To affiliate - To acquaint - To accustom

âshenâ shodan: verb
To accustom

âshenâyi: noun
acquaintance

âshenâyân: noun
acquaintance

âshiyân gereftan: verb
To nestle - To nest

âshiyân kardan: verb
To nest

âshiyâneh: noun
nest

âshiyâneh havâpeimâ: noun
hangar

âshkâr: adjective
palpable - apparent - evident - overt - obvious

âshkâr sâzi: noun
reveal - revelation

âshoftan: verb
To disturb - To perturb - To upset - To agitate

âshofte: adjective
upset - messy - disheveled - turbulent

âshofte kardan: verb
To embroil - To harrow - To mess

âshoftegi: noun
chaos - turmoil - consternation - disorder

âshpaz: noun
cook

âshpazi: noun
cookery

âshpazkhâneh: noun
kitchen - cookery

âshti: noun
reconciliation - peace

âshti dâdan: verb
To conciliate - To reconcile - To accord

âshti nâpazir: noun
irreconcilable

âshub: noun

turbulence - tumult - riot - revolution

âshubgar: adjective
agitator - rioter - troublemaker

âshâmidani: verb
To potable - To beverage - To drink

âsib: noun
damage - hurt - harm - injury

âsib resân: adjective
injurious - deleterious

âsib resândan: verb
To damage - To harm - To mar

âsib zadan: verb
To damage - To blemish

âsibnâpazir: adjective
invulnerable

âsiyab: noun
mill

âsiyayi: noun
asian - oriental

âsiyâb kardan: verb
To grind

âsiyâbe bâdi: noun
windmill

âsiyâbân: noun
miller

âsperin: noun

aspirin

âstar: noun
lining

âstar kardan: verb
To ceil
âstin: noun
sleeve

âstâne: adjective
threshold

âstâne: noun
threshold

âsudan: verb
To nubuckle - To nestle - To rest

âsude: adjective
tranquil - snug - easy - calm

âsudegi: noun
convenience - ease - relief - comfort - leisure

âsân: adjective
easy

âsângir: adjective
permissive - lenient - easygoing

âsânsor: noun
lift

âsâre adabi: noun
Literary works

âsâyesh: adjective
welfare - comfort - rest

âsâyeshe khâter: adjective
security - relief

âsâyeshgâ: noun
sanitarium

âsâyeshgâh: noun
sanatorium - nest

âtash afruzi: adjective
tinder - incendiary

âtash bazi: noun
bonfire

âtash gereftan: verb
To light - To inflame - To ignite

âtash zadan: verb
To fire - To burn - To ignite

âtashbâr: adjective
spitfire

âtashdân: noun
hearth - firebox

âtashfeshan: noun
geyser - volkano

âtashimezâj: adjective
passionate - irascible

âtashin: adjective
empyreal - igneous - hot

âtashteshâni: noun
volcanic - plutonian

âtashzane: noun
punk - silex - light

âvardan: verb
To fetch - To bring

âvikhtan: verb
To dangle - To hangout - To hang
âvikhte: adjective
pendant - hung - underhung - dropper

âvikhte budan: verb
To slouch

âvishan: noun
thyme

âviz: noun
earring - lobe

âvizeh: noun
lug - appendix - pendant

âvizân: adjective
suspension - dangle

âvizân budan: verb
To overhang - To dangle

âvizân kardan: verb
To hang - To dangle

âvizâni: noun
suspension - suspense

âvokâdo: noun
avocado

âvril: noun
april

âvâ: noun
sound - phone

âvâr: noun
collapse - debris

âvâre: adjective
adrift - immigrant
âvâre budan: verb
To wander

âvâre budan: verb
To tramp

âvâre kardan: verb
To stray

âvâre shodan: verb
To refugee - To rove

âvâregi: noun
tramp

âvâz: noun
song - sing

âvâz khândan: verb
To sing - To cant

âvâze: noun
fame - reputation - renown

âvâzkhân: adjective
songster - singer

âyande: noun
future - oncoming

âyandegân: noun
posterity

âyandenegar: adjective
provident

âyandenegari: noun
providence

âyat: noun
sign
âyedi: noun
revenue - income

âyedi dashtan: verb
To profit

âyedât: noun
proceeds

âyegh: adjective
damper - brake - insulator - impediment -
pawl

âyin: noun
religion - ordinance - order

âyin nâme: noun
bylaw - regulation

âyin va marâsem: noun
order

âyine: noun
mirror - glass

âyine ashâye rabâni: noun
communion

âyine dini: noun
sacrament - cult

âyine dâdrasi: noun
procedure

âyine mo'âsherat: noun
etiquette

âyine parastesh: noun
ritual

âyine tashrifât: noun
solemnity

âyâ: adverb
whether - if

âzarakhsh: noun
lightning - thunderbolt

âzarm: noun
pudency - shame - modesty

âzem: adjective
departing

âzem: adjective
bound

âzem shodan: verb
To depart - To embark - To leave - To pull
off

âzhang: noun
wrinkle

âzhir: noun
siren

âzmand: adjective
greedy - covetous - cormorant - avid -
avaricious

âzmandi: noun
avidity

âzmayesh: noun
test - try - trial - shy - experiment -
experience - examination

âzmayesh kardan: verb
To experiment - To gauge - To test
âzmayeshe mojadad: noun
retrial

âzmayeshgâh: noun
laboratory

âzmayeshi: noun
tentative - experimental - pilot

âzmudan: verb
To try - To examine - To grope

âzmude: adjective
tried

âzmun: noun
test - examination

âzmâyeshgâ: noun
lab

âzordan: verb
To distaste - To annoy - To hurt - To harry -
To irritate

âzordan: verb
To distress - To fash - To grip

âzorde: adjective
irksome - indignant

âzorde kardan: verb

To chagrin

âzorde shodan: verb
To writhe

âzordegi: noun
irritation - annoyance - chagrin

âzughe: noun
supply - provender

âzâd: noun
free - loose - exempt

âzâd kardan: verb
To ease - To release - To free - To liberate

âzâdeh: adjective
tolerant - noble - catholic - liberal

âzâdi: noun
independence - liberty - release - freedom

âzâdi khâh: adjective
liberal

âzâdibakhsh: adjective
liberator

âzâdiye amal: noun
scope - latitude

âzâdmanesh: adjective
tolerant

âzâr: noun
train - trade - torment - trouble - annoyance
- hurt - hindrance

âzâr dâdan: verb
To nag - To excruciate - To tease

âzâr dâdan: verb
To tease

âzâr kardan: verb
To badger - To persecute - To obsess

âzâr resândan: verb
To hurt - To molest - To plague

âzârdahandeh: adjective
irritant

a

a'dâde asli: noun
cardinal

a'dâde zôj: noun
even numbers

a'lâ: noun
supreme - golden

a'lâ: noun
supreme

a'lâ: noun
super

a'lâhazrat: noun
majesty

a'shâri: adjective
decimal

a'zam: noun
major

a'zâ: noun
staff

ab'âd: noun
dimension - girth

abad: noun
lifetime - perpetuity

abadan: adverb
never - whatsoever

abadi: adjective
everlasting - eternal - perpetual - permanent

abadiyat: noun
immortality - eternity - infinity

abarmard: noun
superman

abas: noun
vain - absurd

ablagh: noun
pied - piebald

ablah: noun
silly - fool

ablahane: adverb
idiotic

abr: noun
cloud

abrdâr kardan: verb
To overcast

abri: noun
cloudy

abri budan: verb
To of clould

abri shodan: verb
To cloud

abrisham: noun
silk

abrishame masnu'i: noun
rayon

abrishami: noun
silky - silken

abru: noun
eyebrows

abs: noun
horse

abus: adjective
rusty - morose - moody - peevish - sulky - stern

abus budan: verb
To gloom

abusâne: adverb
sullen - black

abzâr: noun
tool - implement - gadget

abâ: noun
cloak

adab: noun
curtsy - complaisance - gentry - manner

adab kardan: verb
To punish

adab va nezâkat: noun
attention

adabi: adjective
didactic - literary

adabiyât: noun
literature

adad: noun
digit - number

adade sahih: noun
integer

adade zôj: noun
even

adadi: adjective
numeral

adam: noun
nonentity - naught

adame rezâyat: noun
dissatisfaction

adasi: noun
Iraq

adasi: noun
glass - lens

adib: noun
bookman - literary - scholar

adibâne: adverb
literary

adl: noun
justice

adu: noun
foe - enemy

adviye zadan: verb
To condiment

adâ: noun
gesture

adâ kardan: noun
express - discourse

adâye deyn nemudan: verb
To acquit

af'i: noun
python - asp - adder

afif: adjective
clean - chaste - virtuous - virgin - honest

afkandan: verb
To shed - To throw - To upend - To cast - To give - To droop

afkâr: noun
thoughts

aflâtun: noun
Plato

afrukhtan: verb
To fire

afrâ: noun
maple

afrâshtan: verb
To fly - To erect

afrâshtan: verb
To unfurl

afrâshtegi: noun
supremacy - sublimity

afrâz: noun
tool - implement - gin - gear

afsar: noun
officer - pretor

afsare vazife: noun
noncommissionedoffic

afshân: noun
spray

afshândan: verb
To pour - To intersperse - To diffuse - To scatter - To spray

afshâne: noun
spray

afsordan: verb
To deject

afsorde: adjective
hypochondriac - gloomy

afsorde shodan: verb
To sadden - To gloom - To dampen - To languish

afsordegi: noun
depression - dejection - melancholia

afsun: noun
glamour - incantation - glamor - charm

afsun kardan: verb
To enchant - To witch - To bewitch - To voodoo

afsungar: adjective
charmer - mermaid - voodoo

afsungari: noun
charm

afsus: noun
remorse - regret - pity - alas

afsus khordan: verb
To sigh - To rue - To regret

afsâne: noun
tale - myth - legend - fiction - fable

afsâr: noun
tether - bridle - halter - rein

afsâr gosikhte: adjective
libertine

afv: noun
remission

afv kardan: verb
To forgive - To absolve

afyun: noun
hop - fix - opium

afzal: noun
trancscendent - supreme - superlative

afzudan: verb
To enhance - To amplify - To add - To
increase

afzudan: verb
To plus

afzudani: adjective
additive

afzude: adjective
adjunct - additional - addend

afzude shode: verb
To accrue

afzune: adjective
redundant

afzunegi: noun
redundancy

afzâyesh: noun
increase

afzâyesh: noun
summation - growth - gain - intensification -
increment - addition - addendum -
accretion - accession - access

agar: preposition
if

agarche: preposition
albeit - however - though

aghab: noun
rear - behind - back

aghab andâkhtan: verb
To postpone - To hinder - To defer

aghab mândan: verb
To lag

aghab neshândan: verb
To retreat - To drive

aghab oftâdegi: noun
leeway

aghabe: noun
sequel

aghabkeshidan: verb
To recede - To shrink - To setback

aghabmânde: adjective
laggard - behind - backward

aghabmândegi: noun
retardation

aghabneshini: noun
scuttle - retreat - recess

aghabtar: adjective
latter - posterior

aghaliyat: noun
minority

aghd kardan: verb
To espouse

aghide: noun
thought - opinion - belief - viewpoint

aghide dâshtan: verb
To have

aghigh: noun
agate

aghim: adjective
sterile - barren - abortive

aghim kardan: verb
To confute

aghl: noun
tact - sagacity - wisdom - intellect

aghle salim: noun
commonsense - gumption

aghlâm: noun
item

aghlâni: adjective
intellectual - rational

aghlâniyat: noun
rationality

aghrab: noun
scorpion

aghrabe: noun
hand - poniter

aghvâm: noun
kinfolk - relatives

aghziye: noun
food

aghâghiyâ: noun
locust

aghâjân: noun
dad - papa

ahamiyat: noun
significance - notability - importance

ahamiyat dâdan: verb
To emphasize

ahamiyat dâshtan: verb
To concern - To import

ahd: noun
promise

ahd kardan: verb
To engage

ahd shekastan: adjective
trespasser

ahdshekan: verb
To perjure

ahl: noun
inmate - inhabitant

ahle beit: noun
household - house - inmate

ahle belzhik: adjective
Belgian

ahle beritâniyâ: adjective
Briton

ahle berme: adjective
Burmese

ahle dânmârk: adjective
Dane

ahle fan: adjective
technician

ahle irân: noun
Iranian

ahli: adjective
tame - domestic - native - aborigine

ahmagh: noun
stupid - fool - inane

ahmaghâne: adverb
insane - infatuate - silly

ahriman: noun
demiurge

ahrimani: adjective
diabolic - devilish

ahrom: noun
lever - handspike

ahshâ: noun
viscera

ahshâm: noun
livestock - chattels

ahâliye shahr: noun
townspeople

ajab: noun
wonder - surprise

ajabâ: adverb
zounds - zooks

ajal: noun
ultimate

ajale: noun
haste - expediency - hustle - hurry

ajale kardan: verb
To hurry - To haste

ajdâd: noun
ancestor

ajib: adjective
extravagant - marvelous - strange

36

ajir: noun
hireling

ajir kardan: verb
To wage - To hire

ajnabi: noun
barbarian

ajul: adjective
hasty

ajuze: adjective
hag - trot - crone

ajz: noun
intolerance - insufficiency - insufficience -
inability - paralysis

ajzâ: noun
ingredient

akbar: adjective
major

akh khâb bidâr shodan: verb
To rouse

akhbâr: noun
news - information

akhir: noun
recent - latter - last

akhiran: adverb
late - new

akhlâgh: noun
morality - moral

akhlâghi: adjective
moral

akhm: noun
scowl - glower

akhm: noun
frown

akhm kardan: verb
To scowl - To glower

akhmu: adjective
moody

akhtan: verb
To unsheathe

akhtar: noun
star

akhtarshenâsi: noun
astronomer

akhte: adjective
eunuch - capon

akhte kardan: verb
To castrate - To emasculate

akhz: noun
grasp - catch

akhâzi: verb
To extort

akid: noun
strict

aknun: adverb
present - now

aks: noun
picture - photograph

aksariyat: noun
majority - bulk

aksbardâr: noun
photographer

aksbardâri: noun
photography

aksol'amal: noun
repercussion - reaction

akâs: noun
photographer

akâsi: noun
photography

al'lâh: noun
god

al'lâh kolang: noun
seesaw

alaf: noun
herb - vegetable - grass

alaf chidan: verb
To mow

alaf khordan: verb
To grass

alafchin: noun
haymaker - mower

alafe khoshk: noun
hay

alafzâr: noun
meadow - lawn - arbor

alak: noun
scalp - sift - sieve - harp

alak kardan: verb
To garble - To sift - To sieve - To screen

alaki: adjective
spurious

alam kardan: verb
To signalize - To fame

alangu: noun
bracelet - bangle - wristband

alani: adjective
aboveboard

alavi: noun
astral - ethereal - empyreal - celestial

albâghi: noun
rest

alefbâ: noun
alphabet

alefbâye nâbinâyân: noun
braille

alekol: noun
alcohol

alekoli: adjective
lush - alcoholic

algoritm: noun
algorithm

alil: noun
pimping

almosânâ: noun
double - replica - reduplicate

almâs: noun
diamond

alvâr: noun
lumber - timber

alvât: noun
waggish

alvâti kardan: verb
To debauch

alyâf: noun
yarn

alâ'ede: preposition
another - separate

alâghe: noun
tie - penchant - interest - bind

alâghemand: adjective
fond

alâghemand: adjective
enthusiastic - enthusiast

alâghemand budan: verb
To care

alâh: noun
god

alâj: noun
cure - remedy

alâj nâpazir: noun
incurable

alâjbakhsh: adjective
curative

alâlamtgozari: noun
demarcation

alâmat: noun
signal - sign - symptom - mark

alâmat: noun
sign - mark

alâmat gozâshtan: verb
To trig - To mark

alâmate ta'ajob: noun
ha - zooks

alâraghm: preposition
notwithstanding

alâraghm: preposition
nevertheless

alô: noun
excellency - predominance - ascendency

alô: noun
flame

amal: noun
act - function - operation

amal kardan: verb
To act - To exercise - To do

amal âmadan: verb
To ripen

amal âvardan: verb
To treat

amalan: noun
bodily

amale: noun
laborer - labor - worker

amale jarâhi: noun
surgery - operation

amali: adjective
practical - practicable - operable - workable

amali budan: verb
To practicability

amalkard: noun
turnover - work

amdi: adjective
studied - intentional - deliberate

ame: noun
aunt

ame zâde: noun
cousin

amigh: adjective
profound - recondite - deep

amin: adjective
trusty - trustworthy - trustee

amlâk: noun
estate

amn: noun
secure - safe

amniyat: noun
safety - security

amniye: noun
militia

amr: noun
order - ploy - imperious

amr kardan: verb
To command - To dictate - To order

amr kardan: verb
To direct - To order

amre mosalam: noun
certainty

amri: adjective
imperative

amriye: noun
order - prescription - prescript - precept

amu: noun
uncle

amud: noun
staple

amuzâde: noun
german

amvâl: noun
chattels

amâ: preposition
however - but

amâme: noun
sash - turban

amân: noun
security - respite - mercy

amân dâdan: verb
To safe-conduct

amân nâme: noun
safeconduct

amânat: noun
safekeeping - trusteeship

amânatdâr: adjective
trustee

amânatdâri: noun
trusteeship

amânate posti: noun
parcel

an'âm: noun
tip - bonus

anbor: noun
gadget - tong

anbuh: noun
gross - collective - dense - heap -
voluminous

anbuh kardan: verb
To clump

anbuhe mardom: noun
mob - crowd

anbâr: noun
store - depository - repository

anbâr: noun
storehouse

anbâr kardan: verb
To store - To stock - To warehouse

anbâr kardan: verb
To storage

anbârdâr: noun
storekeeper

anbâre ghale: noun
silo - granary - garner - barn

anbâre kâlâ: noun
storehouse - storage - warehouse

anbâre olufe: noun
hayloft

anbâshtan: verb
To stack - To accumulate

anbâshte: adjective
full - congeries - stockpile

anbâshte shodan: verb
To stockpile

anbâshtegi: adjective
amplitude - accumulation

andak: adjective
scarce - little - light

andak: adjective
scanty - little

andarun: noun
viscus - bowel

andarz: noun
sermon - counsel - advice - axiom - motto

andikâtur: noun
indicator

andishe: noun
thought - mentality - opinion

andishe kardan: verb
To deliberate - To cogitate - To ponder

andishidan: verb
To think - To contemplate

andishmand: noun
thoughtful - thinker

andishnâk: adjective
pensive - thoughtful

anduh: noun
grief - chagrin - dolor - dole - distress

anduhgin: adjective
stricken - ruthful - lugubrious

anduhgin kardan: verb
To grieve - To chagrin

anduhnâk: adjective
sad - penitent - remorseful - rueful - woeful

andukhtan: verb
To store - To save - To accumulate

andukhte: adjective
nestegg - hoard

andâkhtan: verb
To drop - To cast - To omit - To toss

andâkhtan: verb
To throw - To drop - To fell - To cast

andâm: noun
shape - member - organ

andâze: noun
size

andâze gereftan: verb
To measure - To gauge

andâzegiri: noun
measurement

andâzegiri kardan: verb
To meter

ang: noun
hallmark - brand

angabin: noun
honey

angal: noun
parasite - leech - guest

angharib: noun
soon

angikhtan: verb
To urge - To inanimate - To stimulate

angizande: adjective
monitor

angizeh: noun
stimulus - propellant - incentive - impetus - motive

angizesh: noun
provacation - incitement - urge

angizeye asli: noun
mainspring

angosht: noun
finger

angosht namâ: adjective
egregious - conspicuous

angosht zadan: verb
To finger

angoshtar: noun
ring

angur: noun
grape

anjoman: noun
society - council - congress - community

anjomane shahr: noun
duma - city council

anjâm: noun
implementation - implement -
accomplishment

anjâm dâdan: verb
To accomplish - To perform - To implement
- To do

anjâme vazife kardan: verb
To acquit

ankabut: noun
insect

ankabut: noun
spider

ansolin: noun
insulin

antar: noun
wanderoo

antegrâl: noun
integral

antern: noun
intern

anvâ'e: noun
species - types

anân: noun
rein - bridle

anâsor: noun
ingredient

ar'ar: adjective
bray

arab: noun
Arab - Arabian

arabi: adjective
arabian - arabic

aragh: noun
sweat - distillate

aragh: noun
sweat

aragh kardan: verb
To sweat

araghchin: noun
skullcap

araghgir: noun
pullover - sweater

araghgir: noun
undershirt

arbâb: noun
lord - boss - master

arbâbroju'e: noun
client

are: noun
yes

ariz: adjective
wide - broad

arize: noun
petition

arj: noun
value

arjmand: adjective
lofty

arkân: noun
pillar

arsh: noun
throne - sky - heaven - empyrean

arshad: adjective
superior - senior - major - eldest - elder - commander

arshadiyat: noun
seniority - primogeniture

arshe: noun
shipboard

artesh: noun
military - army

arteshbod: noun
general - marshal

arteshi: adjective
military

arus: noun
bride

arusak: noun
doll

arusakbâzi: noun
puppetry

arusi: noun
wedding - matrimony - marriage

arusi kardan: verb
To espouse

arz: noun
width - breadth

arzan: noun
millet

arze: noun
exposition - efficiency - offer - proffer - presentation

arze dâshtan: verb
To offer - To present - To submit

arzesh: noun
cost - price - value

arzi: adjective
territorial

arzi: adjective
transverse

arzyâb: noun
rater - assessor - appraiser - prizer

arzyâbi: noun
valuation - assessment - assess - appraisal - evaluation

arzân: adjective
cheap - inexpensive

arâbe: noun
wagon - cart

arâgh: noun
Iraq

arâghi: adjective
Iraqi

arâzel: noun
gangster

asab: noun
nerve

asabi: adjective
neurotic - overwrought

asabâni: noun
anger - rage

asabâni: adjective
mad - huffy - nervy

asabâni kardan: verb
To irritate - To madden - To enrage

asabâni shodan: verb
To aggression

asafnâk: adjective
woeful - deplorable - lamentable

asal: noun
honey

asar: noun
sign - trace - impression - vestige - affect

asar gozâshtan: verb
To trace

asare baghimânde: noun
hangover

asare sukhtegi: noun
burn

asare târikhi: noun
monument

asare zakhm: noun
scab

asare zakhm dâshtan: verb
To scar

asb savâr: noun
cavalier - horseman

asb savâri: noun
roadster - trooper

asbagh: noun
prior - predecessor

asbe chubi: noun
hobbyhorse

asbe âbi: noun
rhino

asbâb: noun
tool - instrument - gadget

asbâb bâzi: noun
toy - plaything

asbâbe safar: noun
caboodle

asbâbe zahmat: adjective
encumbrance - inconvenience

asghar: adjective
junior - minor - lesser - less

ash'âr: noun
poetry

asha'e iks: noun
xray

ashaeye gâmâ: noun
gamma

ashaeye leyzer: noun
laser

ashire: noun
tribe - phyle

ashk: noun
teardrop - brine - flood

ashk rikhtan: verb
To weep

ashkbâr: adjective
lachrymose

ashrâfi: adjective
patrician - plutocrat

ashyâ': noun
objects - things

ashâre dâshtan bar: verb
To imply

asil: adjective
noble - gentleman

asil: adjective
ingenuous - pure

asir: noun
slave - captive - prisoner

asl: noun
real - principle

aslahe: noun
weapon - arm

aslahe khâne: noun
armory

aslahe sâzi: adjective
weaponry

aslan: adverb
never

asle koli: noun
theory - generality

asli: adjective
seminal - basic - principal - prime - primary - main

asliyat: noun
reality - identity - paternity

aslo nasab: noun
lineage

asnâ ash'ari: noun
duodecimal

asnâdi: adjective
attributive

asr: noun
age - afternoon - period - era

asrâr âmiz: adjective
secret - numinous - mysterious

asâ: noun
cane - rod - wand - bat - stick

asâs: noun
furniture

asâs: noun
element - ground - root - basis

asâsi: adjective
vital - pivotal - basic - fundametal

asâsnâme: noun
statute

asâtir: noun
mythology

atash: noun
thirst

atf: noun
reference

atf be: noun
regarding

atigh: noun
early - old

atighe: adjective
antique - relic - curio

atigheshenâs: noun
antiquarian

atom: noun
atom

atomi: adjective
nuclear - atomic

atr: noun
smell - scent - odor - ambrosia - perfume

atre gol: noun
potpourri - attar

atrâf: noun
environment - milieu

atse: noun
sneeze

atse kardan: verb
To snuff - To sneeze

atâ: noun
grant

atâ kardan: verb
To grant

atâ kardan: verb
To vouchsafe

atâb: noun
pounce

atâr: noun
grocer - perfumer

aval: adjective
first - initial

avalin: adjective
initiatory - initial

avaliye: noun
early - rudiment - prime

avaz: noun
substitute - reparation - recompense

avaz kardan: verb
To exchange - To remodel - To change - To alter - To vary

avaz shodan: verb
To mew - To change

avazo badal: noun
alternate

avâgheb: noun
backwash

avâm: noun
community - popular - laity

avâmel: noun
ingredient

avâmonâs: noun
populace

avâmâne: adverb
common - vulgar

avârez: noun
toll - imposition - complications - charges

ay'âm: noun
time

ayub: noun
job

ayâdat: noun
visit

ayâdat kardan: verb
To visit

ayâl: noun
wife

ayâr: noun
carat - rover - alloy

ayâsh: adjective
jovial - pleasurable

ayâshi: noun
jollity - binge - debauchery - debauch

ayâshi kardan: verb
To riot - To revel

az: preposition
from

az bar kardan: verb
To memorize

az bar khândan: verb
To recite

az bein bordan: verb
To spoil - To annihilate - To washout

az bein raftan: verb
To waste

az che darigh: adverb
how

az dast dâdan: verb
To lose

az dast rafte: adjective
lost

az ebtedâ: adjective
uppermost

az ghalam andâkhtan: verb
To slip - To drop - To omit

az gheid rahâ shodan: verb
To unfetter

az gorosnegi mordan: verb
To starve

az ham bâz kardan: verb
To break - To untwine - To unravel - To unlink

az ham bâz shodan: verb
To unbraid

az ham jodâ kardan: verb
To split - To wedge

az ham pâshidan: verb
To disintegrate - To burst

az in jahat: adverb
hence

az in pas: preposition
hereinafter - hereafter - henceforth

az in ru: adverb
hence - since - therefore

az jâ dar raftan: verb
To transport - To outrage

az jâ jastan: verb
To bolt

az jâ paridan: verb
To jump

az jân gozashte: adjective
desperate - desperado

az khatar rahânidan: verb
To alarm

az khod bikhod shodan: verb
To transport - To ravish

az khod gozashtegi: noun
devotion

az khod râzi: adjective
overbearing - cocky - smug

az khâb barkhâstan: verb
To rise - To uprise

az khâb bidâr kardan: verb
To wake

az khâk dar âvardan: verb
To exhume - To excavate - To disinter

az kâr oftâde: adjective
lameduck - obsolete - effete - seedy

az kâr oftâdegi: noun
paralysis

az lahâze: preposition
of

az mabda'e: preposition
of

az miyân bardâshtan: verb
To surmount

az miyân bordan: verb
To wipe - To abrogate - To abolish - To
shunt

az miyâne: adverb
per - across - through

az nazdik: adverb
forby

az no: adverb
anew - again - afresh

az no sâkhtan: verb
To reconstruct

az pa dar âvardan: verb
To exhaust

az pish: adverb
preferment

az pâd darâmadan: verb
To tire - To consume - To peter

az ruye: preposition
aboard - off

az râhe khoshki: adjective
overland

az sar gereftan: verb
To resume - To renovate

az sar tâ pâ: adverb
capapie

az sargiri: noun
resumption

az tarafe: preposition
behalf - for - of

az tarighe: preposition
via - through

az vaghtike: adverb
since

az vasat: preposition
through - per - across - via

az yâd bordan: verb
To unlearn

az ânru: preposition
so, therefore

50

azab: adjective
bachelor

azal: noun
deposition

azali: adjective
everlasting - eternal

azaliyat: noun
eternity

azdâd: noun
paradox

azemat: noun
magneficence - greatness

azhdar: noun
torpedo

azim: adjective
tremendous - enormous - great - glorious - massive

azimat: noun
departure

azimat kardan: verb
To depart - To go

azimoljose: adjective
monster - gargantuan - whale

aziz: adjective
dear - darling - chary

aziz dordâne: adjective
minion

azjomle: preposition
among

azl kardan: verb
To dethrone

azm: noun
purpose - impetus - resolution

azme râsekh: noun
willpower

azole: noun
muscle

azolâni: adjective
muscular

azughe resândan: verb
To cater

azyat: noun
tease - annoyance - harm

azyat kardan: verb
To annoy - To tease

azâb: noun
torture - torment - tribulation

azâb dâdan: verb
To agonize - To lacerate - To torture - To torment

azâdâr: adjective
mournful - plaintful

azâdâri kardan: verb
To howl

b

ba'che: noun
infant - baby - kid - child

ba'che dozd: adjective
kinnaper

ba'che poru: adjective
saucebox

ba'd: adjective
then - next

ba'dan: adverb
afterwards

ba'dhâ: adverb
thereafter

ba'di: adjective
future - further - ulterior - subsequent

ba'zi: preposition
cretain - some

ba'zi ôghât: adverb
occasionally

babr: noun
tiger

bache bâzi: noun
sodomyh - pederasty

bachegi: noun
puerility - infantile - childhood

bachegâne: adverb
childlike - chilish - infantile

bad: adjective
bad - evil - ill

bad akhlâgh: adjective
reprobate - dissolute - moody - impatient - immoral

bad akhlâghi: noun
immorality - misconduct

bad andish: adjective
malicious

bad dahan: adjective
ribald - scurrilous

bad dahani kardan: verb
To blackgurad

bad nahâd: adjective
malign - malevolent

bad yomn: adjective
sinister - ominous - unlucky

bad zât: adjective
naughty - villainous - villain

badal: adjective
false - brassy - substitute - spurious

badali: noun
spurious - counterfeit - imitative - imitation

badan: noun
body

badanamâ: adjective
squawk - unsightly

badane: noun
framework - body - shaft - trunk

badaneye sâkhtemân: noun
shell

badani: noun
bodily - physical

badaz: adverb
since - posterior - behind - after

badazohr: noun
afternoon

badbakht: adjective
woeful - miserable - unhappy - unfortunate

badbakhti: noun
calamity - wrack - disaster - mishap - misery

badbakhtâne: adverb
unfortunately

badbin: adjective
pessimistic - pessimist

badbini: adjective
pessimism

badbu: adjective
gamy - reechy - frowzy - unsavory

badcheshm: adjective
envious

badghol: adjective
unfaithful - unfaith

badgomân: adjective
suspicious - defiant

badgomâni: noun
suspicion - mistrust - misgiving - distrust

badgu: adjective
vilifier

badi: noun
evil - disservice - vice

badi'e: adjective
novel - original - exquisite - picturesque

badihi: adjective
evident - natural - obvious - inevitable -
immediacy

badihiyât: noun
axiom

badjens: adjective
mischievous - mean

badjens: adjective
wicked

badkhim: adjective
virulent

badkhim: adjective
malignant - malign

badkholghi: noun
grouch

badkhu: adjective
bad - cranky - wicked

badkhâh: adjective
sinister - malignant - malevolent

badkâre: adjective
quean

badmaze: adjective
unsavory - brackish

badnâm: adjective
disreputable - infamous - infamous -
unpopular

badnâm kardan: verb
To blemish - To defame - To calumniate

badraftâri: noun
misuse - misdeed - misconduct

badraghe: noun
convoy - escort

badraghe kardan: verb
To convoy

badshegun: adjective
sinister - ominous - unlucky

badshânsi: noun
misfortune - mischance

badtar: adjective
worse

badtar kardan: verb
To exasperate - To exacerbate - To
deteriorate - To worsen

badtarin: adjective
worst

badtarkib: adjective
clumsy

badtinat: adjective
vicious - malignant

baghal: noun
bosom - armpit - sheaf

baghal kardan: verb
To embrace - To hug

baghâ: noun
survival - perpetuity

baghâl: noun
grocer

baghâli: noun
grocery

baghâyâ: noun
leftover - vestige - rest

baharkhâb: noun
terrace

bahman: noun
avalanche

bahr: noun
see

bahr: noun
quotient

bahre: noun
share - portion - lot

bahre dâshtan: verb
To partake

bahrebardâr: adjective
beneficiary

bahrâm: noun
mars

bahs: noun
agument - discussion - debate

bahso jadal: noun
toil - polemic - disputation

bahâ: noun
cost - worth - price - value - valuation

bahâdor: noun
valiant

bahâne: noun
plea - peg - excuse

bahâne kardan: verb
To dissemble

bahâne âvardan: verb
To pretext - To alibi

bahânegir: adjective
pernickety

bahâr: noun
spring

bahâri: noun
vernal

baid: adjective
far - unseemly - unlikely

bakhiye: noun
suture - stitch

bakhsh: noun
zone - segment - sector - section - part -
branch

bakhshandegi: noun
munificence

bakhshdâr: noun
demarche

bakhshesh: noun
profusion - mercy - grant

bakhshi: adjective
divisor - partial - parochial - sectorial -
sectional

bakhshidan: verb
To bestow - To pardon - To donate - To
grant - To forgive

bakhshidan: verb
To gift - To grant

bakhshidani: adjective
venial

bakhshide: adjective
donor - gracious - generous - merciful

bakhshnâme: noun
circular

bakhshudegi: noun
indemnity - impunity - immunity

bakhshâyande: adjective
clement

bakht: noun
chance - grace - luck

bakhtak: noun
incubus

bakhtiyâr: noun
auspicious - lucky

bal'e: noun
gulp - godown

bal'idan: verb
To swallow - To devour

bale: noun
aye - yes - yea

bali: noun
yes

balke: preposition
rather

balut: noun
chestnut

balva: noun
riot - uproar - uprising

balâ: noun
disaster - calamity - plague

bam: adjective
bass - grave

banafsh: adjective
violet

banafshe: noun
violet

band: noun
clause - dike - stanza

band zadan: verb
To tinker - To joggle - To garter - To leash

band âvardan: verb
To stop - To stem - To stanch - To block - To bloc

bandar: noun
seaport - wayside - port

bandargâh: noun
haven - harbor - port - strand

bande: noun
slave - servant - vassal

bande angosht: noun
knuckle - phalanx - phalange

bang: adjective
hemp - hashish - kef

banâ: noun
structure

banâ nahâdan: verb
To establish

banâvarin: preposition
hence - so - thus - thereupon - therefore

banâye yâdbud: noun
monument

bar: preposition
upon - against - in - on

bar bâd dâdan: verb
To squander - To misspend

bar bâd raftan: verb
To evaporate

bar hagh: noun
legitimate

bar hagh budan: verb
To legitimacy

bar ham zadan: verb
To unsettle - To disturb - To disorder

bar ruye: preposition
on - upon - incrust

bar shemordan: verb
To enumerate - To recount

bar tan kardan: verb
To don

bar zabân âvardan: verb
To tongue

bar zede: noun
versus - athwart - against

bar'aks: noun
unlike - vice versa - inverse

bar'rasi: noun
scrutiny - survey

bar'rasi kardan: verb
To peruse - To survey - To study

bar'âshofte: adjective
angry - wroth

barafrukhtan: verb
To inflame - To kindle - To provoke

barafrâshte: adjective
elate

barafshândan: verb
To raise - To hoist

barande: adjective
winner

barandâkhtan: verb
To subvert - To exterminate - To overthrow
- To abolish

barandâz: noun
glance

barangikhtan: verb
To provoke - To excite - To arouse - To
impulse

barangizande: adjective
provocative - irritant - impressive

barangizândan: verb
To provoke - To excite

barbari: noun
barbaric

barbariyat: noun
barbarism

barchasb: noun
ticket - tally - label

barchasb zadan: verb
To label - To tag

barchasbe: noun
to - unitage - at

barchidan: verb
To remove - To liquidate

barde: adjective
slave - serf - bondsman

bardegi: noun
slavery - servitude - bondage

bardâshtan: verb
To pickup - To remove - To delete

barf: noun
snow

barf bâridan: verb
To snow

barf pak kon: noun
wiper

barfak: noun
thrush

barfarâze: noun
over - upon

barfi: adjective
snowy

barfo bârân: noun
sleet

barg: noun
page - leaf

bargardân: noun
turnover - revers - refrain - lapel

bargardâni: noun
invert - revocation

bargasht: noun
return - regression - refluence

bargashtan: verb
To comeback - To return

barge: noun
form

bargh: noun
brilliance - electricity - glaze - flash - sparkle

bargh: noun
levin

bargh andâkhtan: verb
To gloss - To polish

bargh zadan: verb
To scintillate - To luster - To lightning - To flash

bargharâr: noun
indefeasible

bargharâr kardan: verb
To establish - To appoint

barghi: adjective
electric

bargozidan: verb
To elite - To elect - To pick

bargozide: adjective
selective - select - picked - favorite - chosen - choice

bargozidegi: noun
predilection

bargrizân: noun
autumn

barhazar dâshtan: verb
To premonition

barjaste: adjective
prominent - saleint - eminent - egregious -
dominant - outstanding

barjastegi: noun
eminence - notability - snob - prominence

barkat: noun
bliss - benediction - felicity

barkenâr kardan: verb
To relieve - To oust

barkhalâfe: preposition
unlike - athwart - with

barkhi: preposition
some

barkhi az: preposition
some

barkhord: noun
strike - smash - encounter - conflict

barkhord kardan: verb
To osculate - To collide

barkhordâr shodan: verb
To enjoy

barkhâst: noun
upheaval

barkhâstan: verb
To rise - To arise - To uprise

barliân: noun
diamond

barnâme rizi: noun
planning

barnâme rizi kardan: verb
To schedule - To plan

barnâmeye safar: noun
itinerary

barnâmeye âmuzeshi: noun
curriculum

barpâ kardan: verb
To establish - To erect - To raise

barpâ kardan: verb
To found

bartar: adjective
prevalent - premier - dominant - superior

bartar az: adjective
beyond

bartar budan: verb
To outrank

bartaraf kardan: verb
To surmount - To remove - To rectify - To
eliminate - To dispel - To loose - To acquit

bartari: noun
prominence - supremacy - primacy -
advantage

bartari jostan: verb
To best

bartari yâftan: verb
To transcend - To paragon

bartarin: adjective
paramount

barzakh: noun
limbo - isthmus

barzakh: noun
purgatory

barâbar: adjective
equal

barâbar: noun
parallel

barâbari: noun
equation - equality

barâdar: noun
brother

barâdari: noun
brotherhood

barâgh: adjective
splendid - silken - shiny - glossy - lucid

barâgh kardan: verb
To shine - To polish - To buff - To glaze

barâgh shodan: verb
To glitter

barâmad: noun
consequence - expense - result - outcome

barâmade: adjective
protuberant - bouffant

barâmadegi: noun
projection - nub - knob - mound

barâmadegi: noun
eminence

barâshoftan: verb
To embarrass - To ruffle

barâshoftegi: noun
distress

barâvard kardan: verb
To apprise

barâvord: noun
survey - calculation - estimate - assessment

barâyand: noun
consequent - resultant

barâye: preposition
sake - toward - pro

barâye hamishe: adverb
forever

barâye inke: preposition
for - because

barâye ânke: preposition
because

barâyeche: adverb
why - wherefore

barâzande: adjective
graceful

barâzandegi: noun
propriety

bas: adverb
enough

bas budan: verb
To suffice

basande: adjective
enough - adequate

basari: adjective
visual - optic - ocular

basd: noun
coral

bashar: noun
mankind

bashariyat: noun
humanity

bashâsh: adjective
jocund - riant - cheerful - roseate

basir: adjective
conversant - intuitive

basirat: noun
vision - insight - foresight - discretion

basirati: noun
discretionary

basit: adjective
extensive - comprehensive - large

bast: noun
girth - outrigger - spanner

bast: noun
extension - expansion - development - outspread

bastan: verb
To shut - To tighten - To tie

baste: noun
parcel - packet - package - bundle

baste bandi: noun
packer

bastegi: noun
dependency - bind

basâmad: noun
frequency

basât: noun
counter - layout - stall

batn: noun
womb - ventricle - abdomen

batni: adjective
uterine - umbilical - abdominal

batune: noun
putty - primer

bavâsir: noun
hemorrhoid

bayân: noun
statement - expression - explanation - declaration - quotation - remark - recitation

bayâne: noun
deposit

bayâne mobham: noun
enigma

bayâne mojadad: noun
restatement

bayângar: adjective
indicator - explanatory

bayâniye: noun
manifesto - manifest - bulletin

bazegu: adjective
humorist - witty - waggish - jolly - joker

bazl: noun
giveaway - munificence

bazle: noun
joke - jest - gambit - quip

bazle gu'l: noun
jest - wit - pleasantry

bazm: noun
party - banquet - shindig

bazr: noun
sperm - spawn - seed

be: preposition
to - in

be aghab: adverb
back - aback

be andâze: adjective
snug - enough - within

be anjâm resândan: verb
To complete - To process - To accomplish

be bahâye: preposition
for

be chang âvardan: verb
To grasp

be che kasi: preposition
whom

be dast âvardan: verb
To attain - To acquire - To earn - To obtain

be derâzâ keshidan: verb
To last

be eshtebâh andâkhtan: verb
To mislead

be estesnâ'e: noun
but - except

be estesnâye: noun
except

be etelâ': adjective
aware

be farzandi paziroftan: verb
To affiliate - To adopt

be ghata'ât taghsim kardan: verb
To parcel

be hadaf khordan: verb
To quiver

be ham rikhtan: verb
To disassemble

be hesâb âvardan: verb
To score

be hich vajh: adverb
whatsoever - no way

be injâ: adverb
hither

be jelo: adverb
on

be khod pischidan: verb
To agonize

be mahze: adverb
upon

be mirâs bordan: verb
To inherit

be mojarade: noun
upon

be mokhâtere andâkhtan: adverb
jeopard

be natije residan: verb
To aim

be nazar âmadan: verb
To seem

be nodrat: adverb
seldom

be ohde gereftan: verb
To undertake - To tackle

be peivast: adverb
therewith

be pishe: adverb
onward - on

be poshte: adverb
backward

be ramz neveshtan: verb
To cryptograph

be rasmiyat shenâkhtan: verb
To recognition

be rokh keshidan: verb
To boast

be ântaraf: adverb
thither

be âsâni: adverb
easily

be'alâve: adverb
moreover - plus - also - besides - beside

be'elate: preposition
due to

be'estelâh: adverb
socalled

be'ezâfe: noun
together - plus - beside

bechashm: adverb
well

bedard khordan: verb
To dow - To avail - To serve

bedard âvardan: verb
To sprain

bedegi: noun
debt - debit - liability

bedehkâr: adjective
yielder - indebted - debtor

bedehkâr budan: verb
To owe

bedin yomn: verb
To portent

bedinsân: adverb
thus

bedinvasile: adverb
hereto - hereby

bedonbâl: adverb
jackknife

bedune: preposition
without

bedush keshidan: verb
To horse

bedâhe: noun
offhand

bedân: preposition
thereto

bedân vasile: preposition
thereby

bedânja: adverb
there

bedânsu: preposition
thither

befarmâyid: verb
To please

beghadre: preposition
for - as

beghadre kefâyat: adjective
enough

beham bastan: verb
To join - To couple - To truss

beham bâftan: verb
To twine

beham chasbidan: verb
To hang together - To attach

beham chasbide: adjective
concrete - impacted

beham dukhtan: verb
To transfixion

beham ghofl kardan: verb
To interlock

beham khordan: verb
To knock - To collide

beham khordegi: noun
turmoil - revolt - collission

beham peivastan: verb
To link - To incorporate - To seam

beham peivaste: adjective
collective - conjunct - aggregate

beham pichidan: verb
To implicate - To interlock - To interlace

beham rikhtegi: noun
tumble

beham tâbidan: verb
To splice - To intersubjective

beham zadan: verb
To disarrange

beham zadan: verb
To disturb

beham âmadan: verb
To match

beham âmikhtan: verb
To fold - To commingle - To coalesce

beharhâl: adverb
however - anyway - anyhow - though

beharsu: adverb
about

behayejân âmadan: verb
To quake

behbud: noun
improvement

behbud nâpazir: adjective
incurable - incorrigible

behbud yâftan: verb
To recover - To ameliorate - To mend - To improve

behbudi: noun
recovery - health

behdâsht: noun
hygiene

behdâshti: adjective
sanitary - hygienic

behengâm: adjective
timely - opportune - pat

behesht: noun
zion - heaven - eden

beheshte barin: noun
paradise

beheshti: adjective
olympiad - heavenly

behichvajh: adverb
nix

behine: adjective
optimum

behsâz: adjective
reformer

behsâzi: noun
sanitation - improvement - reform

behtar kardan: verb
To improve - To ameliorate

behtar shodan: verb
To ameliorate - To improvement

behtarin: adjective
tiptop - pride - best

behush: adjective
sober - conscious

behush âmadan: verb
To revive - To respire - To recovery

behush âvardan: verb
To sober - To resuscitate

bei'at: noun
allegiance - homage

beine farhangi: noun
intercultural

beine ghâre'I: noun
intercontinental

beiragh: noun
flag - banner

beitol moghadas: noun
Jerusalem

beize: noun
testicle

bejib zadan: verb
To pocket

bejoz: preposition
than - bar - except

bejoz inke: preposition
save

bejush âmadan: verb
To simmer - To boil

bejush âvardan: verb
To stir

bejâ: adjective
timely - proper - right

bejâye: preposition
instead

bekhodiye khod: adverb
perse

bekhosus: adjective
particular - specific

bekhubi: adverb
truly

bekhâste: adjective
voluntary

bekhâter sepordan: verb
To memorize

bekhâter âvardan: verb
To remember - To recollect - To mingle

bekhâtere: noun
through - pro

bekoli: adverb
throughout - quite

bekr: adjective
mint - original

bekâr bordan: verb
To exert - To handle - To use - To apply

bekâr gereftan: verb
To serve - To answer

bekârat: noun
virginity

bel'aks: noun
conversely

belbedâhe: noun
impromptu

belderchin: noun
quail

belit: noun
ticket

beljiki: adjective
belgian

belof zadan: verb
To puff

belâ asar: adjective
null

belâ avaz: adjective
gratuitous

belâ estefâde: adjective
useless - haywire

belâ tasadi: adjective
vacant - void

belâ'taklifi: noun
uncertainty

belâderang: adverb
straightaway

belâfâsele: adverb
immediate

belâhat: noun
tommyrot - stupor

belâvâsete: adverb
immediate

bemanzure: preposition
sake - regarding

bemarâteb: adverb
in order

bemasâbehe: adjective
tantamount

bemoghe: adjective
timely - punctual - opportune

benaf'e: adverb
pro

benavâ: adjective
destitute - poor - unblest - unblessed

benazar residan: verb
To sound - To peer

benzin: noun
gasolene - gas

benzin: noun
petrol

benâchâr: adverb
perforce

benâm: adjective
namely - famous

beonvâne mesâl: noun
for example

bepâyân residan: verb
To peter - To expire - To end

bepâyân resândan: verb
To terminate - To consummate - To end

berehne: adjective
bald - untented - naked - nude

berehnegi: noun
nudity

berenj: noun
rice

bereshtan: verb
To roast

beritaniyâ: noun
britain

beritâniyâyi: adjective
British

berke: noun
pool - lake

beruz: noun
accession - outbreak

beryân: adjective
barbecue

berânkâr: noun
litter

berâsti: adverb
troth - indeed

besababe: adverb
of

besaf kardan: verb
To align - To string

besakhti: noun
sorely

besalâmati: noun
pledge - hobnob

besedâghat: adjective
insincere

beshedat: adverb
sorely - vengeful

beshomâr âvardan: verb
To enumerate

besotuh âvardan: verb
To beset - To annoy - To plague

bestar: noun
bed - kip

bestare daryâ: noun
ooze

bestânkâr: adjective
creditor

besuye: preposition
toward - to

besyâr: adjective
plenty - very - multifarious - much - many

besyâr khub: adjective
excellent - okay - well

besâdegi: adjective
simply

betadrij: adverb
gently - piecemeal

betakhir andâkhtan: verb
To hinder - To delay - To prolong

betarafe: noun
toward

betari: noun
bedridden - confined

beton: noun
concrete

betâlat: noun
vanity

betâzegi: noun
fresh

bevaght: adverb
timely

bevahshat andâkhtan: verb
To fright

bevaj âvardan: verb
To rapture

bevasileye: preposition
via - by - with

bevojud âmadan: verb
To engender - To creation

bevojud âvardan: verb
To make - To generate - To create

bevâseteye: noun
by - through

beyaghmâ bordan: verb
To sack

beytute kardan: verb
To roost - To lodge

beyzi: noun
oval

beyâd âvardan: verb
To remind - To recall

bezamime: adverb
together

bezehkâr: adjective
criminal - guilty - sinner

bezudi: noun
soon - early - anon

bi: preposition
without

bi adabi: noun
irreverence - discourtesy

bi adabi kardan: verb
To misbehave

bi adabâne: adverb
discourteous

bi aghl: adjective
insane - injudicious - unmeaning

bi ahamiyat: adjective
negligible - unimportant - inconsiderable

bi ajri: adjective
vageless

bi alâghe: adjective
nonchalant - unresponsive - uninterested

bi alâghegi: noun
apathy - lethargy - indifference

bi andâze: adjective
inordinate - infinite - indefinite - immense

bi asl: adjective
unfounded

bi asâs: adjective
unsubstantial - unfounded - idle

bi bâk: adjective
intrepid - heroic

bi bâkâne: adverb
audacious

bi e'tebâr kardan: verb
To disparage

bi e'tenâ: adjective
inattentive - reckless

bi ede'â: adjective
unassuming

bi efati: noun
unchastity - adultery

bi ehsâs: adjective
apathetic

bi ehterâmi: noun
insolence - disrespect - disrepute

bi ehterâmi kardan be: verb
To dishonor - To insult

bi ehtiyât: adjective
incautious - improvident - indiscreet

bi ehtiyâti: noun
imprudence - improvidence

bi eib: adjective
entire - unexceptionable - perfect - intact

bi eibi: noun
integrity

bi ekhtiyâr: adjective
spontaneous - involuntary

bi ensâf: adjective
unjust - unfair

bi ensâfi: noun
injustice - iniquity - inequity

bi eshtehâ: adjective
jadish

bi eshtiyâgh: adjective
lackadaisical - lukewarm

bi este'dâd: adjective
inapt - unintelligent

bi ete'lâ: adjective
unwitting - unknowing - unknowable - uninformed

bi ete'lâ budan: verb
To misknow

bi etebâr: adjective
bad - insecure

bi eteghâd: adjective
unbelievin - unbeliever

bi fekr: adjective
thoughtless - insensate - inconsiderate

bi fâyede: adjective
useless - vain - ineffective

bi fâyedegi: noun
drawback - disadvantage

bi ghâ'ede: adjective
foul - atypical - promiscuous

bi godâr: adjective
impassable

bi gonâh: adjective
innocent

bi hadaf: adjective
causeless

bi hamechiz: adjective
dishonest - shyster

bi hamtâ: adjective
unexampled

bi honar: adjective
inartistic

bi hâsel: adjective
lean - ungainly

bi imân: adjective
unbelievin - unbeliever - infidel

bi kale: adjective
blockhead - imbecile

bi kefâyat: adjective
incompetent - inefficient

bi kefâyati: noun
inefficiency - incompetence - inadequacy

bi kâre: adjective
inactive

bi liyâghati: noun
inaptitude - inability

bi mahâbâ: adjective
slambang - impavid

bi mantegh: adjective
inept

bi marz: adjective
spaceless

bi mas'uliyat: adjective
unresponsive

bi masraf: adjective
unemployed

bi meil: adjective
disinclined - resentful - reluctant - unwilling

bi mobâlât: adjective
perfunctory - remiss

bi moghadame: adjective
sudden

bi moghe': adjective
untimely - inopportune

bi molâheze: adjective
thoughtless - reckless - inconsiderate -
unconsidered

bi mored: adjective
inappropriate - inopportune

bi mânand: adjective
unprecedented - incomparable - unique

bi mâyegi: noun
superficiality

bi nahâyat: adjective
intolerable

bi natije: adjective
resultless - ineffectual - indeterminate

bi neshân: adjective
untitled

bi nezâkat: adjective
indelicate - indecorous - unceremonious - boorish - discourteous

bi orze: adjective
incapable

bi perdaro mâdar: adjective
orphan

bi sedâ: adjective
silent - quiet

bi taghsir: adjective
innocent

bi vafâ: adjective
disloyal - unfaithful - unfaith

bi vafâyi: noun
adultery - treason - treachery

bi vafâyi: noun
desertion

bi vojdân: adjective
wretch - unconscionable

bi âberu kardan: verb
To defamation

bi âlâyesh: adjective
open

bi âtefe: adjective
impassive - insensitive - unfeeling

bi âzâr: adjective
inoffensive

biadab: adjective
discourteous - coarse - unmannered - uncivilized - irrespective - impolite

biadabi kardan: verb
To dehydrate

biasar: adjective
nude - ineffective - inactive

biasar budan: verb
To ineffective

biasari: noun
inaction

bibahâ: adjective
inestimable

bibando bâr: adjective
profligate - unrestrained - loose

bibarkat: adjective
meager

bibi: noun
queen - dame

bibâk: adjective
ruthless - doughty - undaunted

bibâk: adjective
reckless

bibâki: noun
audacity

bibâki: noun
temerity

bichâre: adjective
incurable - destitute - desperate - wretched
- wretch

bichâre kardan: verb
To bust - To beggar

bichâregi: noun
calamity - misfortune - misery

bid: adjective
willow

bid: noun
moth

bidalil: adjective
unreasonable - uncaused

bidandân: adjective
toothless

bidavâm: adjective
brittle

bideghat: adjective
tentless - careless - negligent

biderang: adjective
therewith - thereupon - prompt - away -
outright

biderang: adverb
apace - immediate

bidin: adjective
irreligious - impious - paynim - ungodly

bidini: noun
adultery - perfidy - irriligion

bidmeshk: noun
pussy

bidâd: noun
cruelty - outcry - oppression - injustice

bidâdgar: adjective
cruel

bidâr: adjective
awake - vigilant - wakeful

bidâr kardan: verb
To raise - To waken - To arouse - To awaken
- To awake

bidâr mândan: verb
To awake

bidâr shodan: verb
To awaken - To awake - To waken

bidâri: noun
rouse - wake

bifarhang: adjective
lowbrow

bigharâr: adjective
variable - restless - fidgety - restive

bigharâri: noun
disquiet

bigheido band: adjective
unihibited - unihibit

bighâedegi: noun
irregularity

bighârâr budan: verb
To shuffle

bighârâri: noun
unrest - malaise

bigonâh: adjective
irreproachable

bigâne: adjective
stranger - exotic - abroad - barbarian

bigâne kardan: verb
To alienate - To estrange - To stranger

bigâne parast: adjective
xenophile

bigâne vâr: adverb
outlandish

bihamtâ: adjective
matchless - peerless - unique - unbeatable

biharkat: adjective
still - vapid - immobile - pat

bihayâ: adjective
brash - indecent

bihes: adjective
torpid - stolid - dead - vapid

bihes: adjective
senseless - numb - unfeeling - impassive - insensitive - insensible

bihes kardan: verb
To amortize - To paralyze

bihes shodan: verb
To nip

bihesi: noun
stupor - apathy - anaesthesia

bihesâb: adjective
untold - incalculable - quits

bihormat kardan: verb
To desecrate - To defile

bihormati: noun
irreverence

bihosele: adjective
impatient

bihoselegi: noun
impatience

bihude: adjective
trashy - ineffective - impracticable - idle - vain

bihude goftan: verb
To rant

bihude guyi: noun
rant

bihudegi: noun
vanity - inaction

bihush: adjective
comatose - unintelligent - unwitting

bihush kardan: verb
To anesthetize

bihush konande: adjective
anesthetic

bihushi: noun
trance - stupefaction - anesthesia

bihushi: noun
unintelligence

bihâl: adjective
torpid - supine - passive - lethargic -
insensate

bihâl shodan: verb
To languish

bijahat: adjective
unduly

bijavâb: adjective
unanswerable

bijâ: adjective
indecorous - unseasonable

bijâ: adjective
inappropriate - improper - inopportune

bijân: adjective
exanimate - inert - inanimate

bikarân: adjective
infinite - indefinite - immeasurable

bikh: noun
butt

bikhabar: adjective
abrupt

bikhabari: noun
ignorance - idiotism

bikhatar: adjective
safe - secure

bikherad: adjective
brute

bikherad: adjective
unreasonable - fool

bikheradâne: adverb
injudicious

bikhiyâl: adjective
carefree

bikhiyâli: noun
abandon

bikhod: adjective
unduly

bikhod: adjective
gratuitous - idle

bikhodi: noun
unreason

bikhâb: adjective
unsleeping - watchful

bikhâbi: noun
insomnia

bikâr: adjective
idle - vacant - unemployed

bikâre: adjective
vagabond - idler

bikâri: noun
sloth - unemployment - vacation

bil: noun
shovel - spade

bil zadan: verb
To hack - To spade - To shovel

bilche: noun
shovel - shim - spade - paddle

bim: noun
fear - scare - scrupulosity - dread - phobia

bimaghz: adjective
inane

bimahâbâyi: noun
unreserve

bimani: adjective
absurd - unmeaning - irrational - insensate - nonsense

bimarâm: adjective
shyster - unscrupulous - unprincipled

bimaze: noun
vapidity - platitude

bimaze: adjective
tame - colourless - arid - vapid

bime: noun
insurance

bime kardan: verb
To assure - To insure

bime nâme: noun
insurance

bimeili: noun
disaffection - reluctance

bimnâk: adjective
anxious - tremulous - careful - umbrageous

bimo vahshat: noun
fear - dread

bimobâlâti: noun
imprudence

bimâr: noun
sick - ill - patient - unhealthy - bedridden

bimâr kardan: verb
To sicken

bimâr sâkhtan: verb
To indispose

bimâre ravâni: noun
psychotic - psychopath - psyho

bimâre ravâni: noun
psychosis

bimârestân: noun
clinic - hospital

bimâri: noun
malady

bimâye: adjective
frail

binahâyat: noun
extreme

binande: adjective
viewer - spectator - seer

binavâ: adjective
pauper

binavâyi: noun
poverty

binazir: adjective
unique - unexampled - unbeatable -
incomparable

binazm: adjective
chaotic - amorphous

binesh: noun
intuition - intelligence - insight

bini: noun
nozzle - nose

biniyâz: adjective
needless

binâ: adjective
perspicacious - seeing

binâyi: noun
spectrum - sight - vision - eye - perspective

biogerâfi: noun
biography

bipanâh: adjective
shelterless

biparde: adjective
straightforward - straight - pert - blunt -
frank

biparvâ: adjective
slapdash - reckless - confident

biparvâyi: noun
audacity - impetuosity - temerity

bipedar: adjective
unfathered

bipul: adjective
broke - poor - impecunious

bipâye: adjective
unstable - unfounded - loose

bipâyân: noun
eternal - unending

birabt: adjective
impertinent - irrelevant

birahm: adjective
truculent - brute - brutal

birahm: adjective
cruel - dispiteous - relentless - unrelenting

birahmi: noun
savagery - sadism - atrocity - brutality

biramagh: adjective
lethargic

birang: adjective
colourless

birang: adjective
effeminate - neutral - gray

biraviye: noun
irregular

bireghbati: noun
distaste

biriyâ: adjective
sincere - heartfelt

biriyâ: adjective
unaffected

biruh: adjective
apathetic - namby

biruh: adjective
tame - pedestrian - vapid - meek - inert - arid - exanimate

birun: adverb
outside - outdoor - out - external - away - abroad

birun afkandan: verb
To jettison

birun andâkhtan: verb
To expel - To excrete - To eject - To sputter

birun az: adverb
away - forth - out

birun dâdan: verb
To exhale - To evolve - To emission

birun kardan: verb
To fire - To evict - To dispossess

birun oftâdan: noun
loll

birun rikhtan: verb
To vent - To emit

birun zade: adjective
saleint

birun âmadan: verb
To exude - To transpire - To pullout

birun âvardan: verb
To scoop - To unweave

birune shahr: noun
country

biruni: adjective
outward - outer - outdoor - out - external

birâh: adjective
astray - aberrant

birâhe: adjective
devious

bisabri: noun
impatience

bisamar: adjective
unprofitable - unfruitful

bisarosedâ: adjective
quietly - serene

bisarparast: adjective
derelict

bisavâd: adjective
illiterate

bisavâdi: noun
illiteracy

bisedâ: adjective
noiseless - whist - mute

bish: adverb
more

bisharaf: adjective
thug - blackguardly

bisharafi: noun
dishonor

bisharm: adjective
immodest - brazen - barefaced

bisharm: adjective
audacious

bisharmi: noun
brass - indecency

bisharmi: noun
effrontery

bishaz andâze: adjective
ample - excessive

bishaz had: adjective
inordinate

bishaz hame: adjective
most

bishe: noun
brushwood - brake - forest - grove - glade

bishebâhat: adjective
dissimilar - anomalous - unlike

bishekl: adjective
formless - amorphous

bishin: adjective
maximum - majority

bisho'ur: adjective
brutish

bisho'ur: adjective
insensible - numskull - numbskull - dunce

bishomâr: adjective
innumerable - unnumbered - uncounted

bishomâr: adjective
countless - populous - myriad - umpteenth

bishtar: adverb
rather - further - more - major

bishtarin: adjective
superlative - uttermost - utmost - most - maximum

bisim: noun
wireless

biskuit: noun
cooky - cookie - biscuit

bisobât: adjective
slippery - shifty - unstable - variable - impermanent

bisobâti: noun
jitter - instability - inconsistency - variation

bistom: adjective
twentieth

bistomin: adjective
twentieth

bisâbeghe: adjective
unprecedented - unheard

bisâbeghe: adjective
unexampled

bitadbir: adjective
brassy - imprudent

bitaghvâyi: noun
impiety

bitajrobe: adjective
raw - unskilled - immature - inexpert

bitaraf: adjective
neutral - dispassionate

bitaraf: adjective
neutral - unaligned

bitarafi: noun
neutrality - impartiality

bitarbiyat: adjective
underbred - uncivil - barbarous - impolite

bitarbiyati: noun
peasantry - discourtesy

bitardid: adjective
unmistakable - unerring - unassailable

bitavajohi: noun
inattention

bitâ: adjective
unrivaled - unique

bitâ: adjective
unmatched

bitâb: adjective
impatient

bitâbi: noun
impatience

bitâbi: noun
unrest

bive: adjective
lone - widow

bivâheme: adjective
undaunted

biyâbân: noun
desert

bizahmat: adjective
effortless

bizarar: adjective
inoffensive - innocuous - innocent

bizâr: adjective
tired - weary - loathloth - averse

bizâr budan: verb
To dislike - To hate

bizâr kardan: verb
To loathe - To repel - To weary - To disgust

80

bizâri: noun
aversion - hatred - disgust - grudge -
reluctance

bizâri: noun
aversion

biâberuyi: adjective
disrepute - disgrace

biâdab: adjective
thirsty - dry

boghche: noun
pack - bundle - truss

boghranj: adjective
intricate - obscurant - complex

boghz: noun
spite - hatred

boghz: noun
sob

bohrân: noun
tension - crisis

bohrâni: adjective
critical - climacteric

boht: noun
amazement

boht va heirat: noun
consternation

boht âvar: adjective
stupendous

bohtân: noun
vilification

bohtân zadan: verb
To vilify

bokhâr: noun
steam - gas - reek - haze

bokhâr: noun
steam

bokhâr shodan: verb
To vaporize - To evaporate

bokhâri: noun
heater

boks: noun
box

boksbâz: adjective
boxer

boland: adjective
upland - aloud - lofty - high - tall

boland ghad: adjective
tall

boland hemati: noun
magnanimity - ambition

boland kardan: verb
To heighten - To upraise - To enhance

boland parvâzi kardan: verb
To aspire - To soar

boland shodan: verb
To rise - To ascend - To arise - To upheave

bolandbâlâ: adjective
tall

bolandgu: noun
loudspeaker - microphone

bolandhemat: adjective
chivalrous - ambitious

bolandi: noun
supremacy - sublimity - eminence - height

bolandnazar: adjective
catholic

bolandpâye: adjective
high - lofty - sublime

bolantar kardan: verb
To heighten

bolbol: noun
nightingale

bolhavas: adjective
whimsical - capricious

bolugh: noun
puberty - maturity - maturation -
adolescence

boluk: noun
district - block - bloc

bolurin: adjective
crystalline

boluz: noun
jumper - blouse

bolvâr: noun

boulevard

bomb: noun
bombshell - bomb

bon: noun
root

bonakdâr: noun
wholesaler

bonbast: noun
deadlock - close

boneye safar: noun
outfit - kit - luggage

bongâh: noun
institution - institute

bonye: noun
stamina - gut

bonyâd: noun
substratum - institute - basis

bonyâd: noun
cornerstone

bonyâd nahâdan: verb
To establish

bonyâdi: adjective
fundametal

bonyân: noun
warpandwoof - root - basis - valence

bonyângozâr: adjective
originator

bor zadan: verb
To shuffle - To reshuffle

borande: adjective
cutting - cutter - trenchant

borandegi: noun
sharpness

borandegi: noun
sharpness

bord: noun
win - reach - range

bordan: verb
To win - To convey - To conduct - To drive -
To lead

bordbâr: adjective
tolerant - patient

bordbâri: noun
fortitude - patience - tolerance

bordâr: noun
vector - resultant

boresh: noun
slice - cutting - cut

borhân: noun
logic - theorem

boridan: verb
To chop - To cutoff - To cut - To slice

boridegi: noun
jag - cut - notch - gash - rift - hyphen

borj: noun
tower - month

borje kelisâ: noun
steeple

borje morâghebat: noun
watchtower

borje negâhbani: noun
watchtower

bornâ: adjective
young

boronze: adjective
tan

borum: noun
outside - without

borân: adjective
trenchant

boshghâb: noun
dish - plate - vessel

boshke: noun
barrel

bot: noun
juju - idol

botkade: noun
pagoda

botlan: noun
discomfit

botparast: adjective
pagan - idolatry - ilolater - heathen

botri: preposition
bottle

botshekan: adjective
iconoclast

boz: noun
goat

bozak: noun

bozdel: adjective
timorous - pusillanimous - coward

bozghâle: noun
kid - goat - yeanling

bozorg: adjective
sizable - great - enormous - big - vast - mighty - major - larg

bozorg: adjective
big - huge

bozorg jose: adjective
huge

bozorg kardan: verb
To amplify - To dilate - To enlarge

bozorg namâ: adjective
grandiose

bozorg shodan: verb
To grow

bozorgdâsht: noun
respect

bozorgi: noun
amplitude - magnitude - magneficence - dignity

bozorgrâh: noun
highway - freeway

bozorgtar: adjective
senior - major - elder

bozorgtarin: adjective
biggest

bozorgvâr: adjective
honorable - magnaimous

bozorgvâri: noun
magnanimity

bozâgh: noun
saliva - slobber - sputum - spit

bu: noun
aroma - whiff - scent - savor - smell

bu: noun
odor - smell

bu dâdan: verb
To smell - To singe - To scorch

bu kardan: verb
To smell - To respire

bu keshidan: verb
To scent - To sniff

bud: verb
To was

budan: verb
To stand - To exist - To like

budje: noun
budget

budâr: adjective
aromatic - redolent - smelly

buf: noun
owl

bufe: noun
buffet

bugh: noun
trumpet - horn - bugle

bugh zadan: verb
To hoot

bughalamun: noun
turkey

bujâr: noun
sifter

bum: noun
region - habitat

bumi: adjective
domestic - native

bur: adjective
auburn - blond

buriyâ: noun
straw - rush - matting

burs: noun
exchange

burân: noun
sleet - squall

bus: noun
kiss

buse: noun
kiss

buse gereftan: verb
To kiss

busidan: verb
To kiss

bustân: noun
garden

bute: noun
herb

butezâr: noun
shrubbery

buye khosh: adjective
perfume

buye tond: adjective
tang

buyidan: verb
To smell

buyâyi: noun
smell

buzine: noun
jackanapes - simian - ape - monkey

bvz: adjective
open - again

bâ: preposition
by - with

bâ adab: adjective
polite - housebroken - courteous - respectful

bâ ahamiyat: adjective
momentous - main

bâ ajale: adverb
rush - precipitant - posthaste

bâ arzesh: adjective
valuable - noteworthy - worth

bâ azemat: adjective
majestic

bâ chashme heghârat: noun
askance

bâ deghat: adjective
careful - attentive

bâ deghat didan: verb
To pore

bâ e'tebâr: adjective
prestigious

bâ e'tebâr: adjective
prestigious

bâ eghtedâr: adjective
sovereign

bâ ehtiyât: adjective
discreet - careful

bâ ensâf: adjective
just

bâ este'dâd: adjective
brilliant - clever - capable

bâ esteghâmat: adjective
standup - staminal

bâ farâsat: adjective
sage - sagacious

bâ fekr: adjective
thoughtful - brainy - considerate

bâ gheirat: adjective
zealous

bâ ghâ'ede: adjective
regular

bâ ham bâftan: verb
To interweave

bâ harârat: adjective
strenuous - warm - ebullient - earnest

bâ imân: adjective
believer

bâ in vojud: adverb
nonetheless - nevertheless

bâ inhâl: adverb
yet - nonetheless - never&eless

bâ inke: adverb
despite

bâ mohabat: adjective
kind

bâ shahâmat: adjective
plucky - bold

bâ talgh sâkhtan: verb
To talc

bâ tardid: adjective
waveringly - uncertainty

bâ tazalzol: adjective
waveringly

bâ toroshruyi: adjective
surly

bâ vojude inke: preposition
notwithstanding - though

bâb: noun
strait - portal - chapter

bâb kardan: verb
To introduce

bâbandegi: noun
radiance

bâbat: noun
regard - concern - behalf

bâbe dandân: adjective
toothsome

bâbe ruz: noun
chic - in - stylish

bâbâ: noun
papa - father

bâd: noun
wind - air

bâd: noun
wind

bâd kardan: verb
To inflate - To heave - To perk - To bulge - To brag - To bloat - To bag - To distend - To swell

bâdavâm: adjective
evergreen - hardy - lasting

bâdebân: noun
sail

bâdeh: noun
wine

bâdenjân: noun
eggplant

bâdgir: noun
funnel - windward - ventilator - louver

bâdiye neshin: adjective
bedouin

bâdkhor: noun
intermission - interlude - windy - windward

bâdkonak: noun
balloon

bâdpâ: adjective
clipper - fleet - speedster

bâdsanj: noun
anemometer

bâdshekan: noun
windbreaker - windbreak

bâdzan: noun
ventilator

bâdâm: noun
almond

bâdâmak: noun
cam

bâdârande: adjective
deterrent - intercepter

bâenzebât: adjective
orderly

bâes: noun
cause

bâes shodan: verb
To cause

bâfande: noun
weaver

bâfandegi: noun
weave - texture

bâfazilat: adjective
virtuous

bâfe: noun
sheaf

bâft: noun
tissue - texture - fiber-fibre - weave

bâftan: verb
To tine - To knit - To weave

bâftan: verb
To entwine

bâgh: noun
garden

bâghche: noun
garden - croft

bâghebâani: noun
horticulture

bâghebân: noun
gardener

bâghi budan: verb
To survive

bâghi gozârdan: verb
To impress

bâghimânde: noun
survivor - remainder

bâgozasht: adjective
lenient

bâham: adverb
together - intoto

bâhamdigar: adverb
together

bâhayâ: adjective
modest - squeamish

bâheysiyat: adjective
prestigious

bâhormat: adjective
deferential

bâhosele: adjective
meek

bâhosne niyat: adjective
bonafide

bâhush: adjective
keen - clever - bright - intelligent - smart - shrewd

bâikot: adjective
boycott

bâj: noun
imposition - toll - tax

bâjdâri: noun
tollgate

bâjgir: adjective
catchpoll

bâjgiri: noun
levy

bâjor'at: adjective
courageous - gritty - gamy - intrepid

bâkere: adjective
virgin

bâkhabar: adjective
aware - conscious - cognizant

bâkherad: adjective
discreet

bâkhoshunat: adjective
vengeful

bâkht: noun
loss

bâkhtar: noun
west

bâkhtari: adjective
western - westerner

bâl: noun
limb - pinion - wing

bâlegh: adjective
adult - adolescent - mature

bâlesh: noun
pillow - bolster

bâleshtak: noun
padding - pincushion

bâlidan: verb
To glory - To brag - To boast - To insult

bâlin: noun
bedside

bâlkon: noun
balcony

bâlon: noun
dirigible

bâlun: noun
balloon - zeppelin

bâlâ: noun
upside - up - ascendency - overhead

bâlâ andâkhtan: verb
To toss

bâlâ andâkhtane shodanâne: verb
To shrug

bâlâ barande: adjective
uplifter

bâlâ bordan: verb
To heighten - To amplify - To upraise - To uplift - To enhance - To raise

bâlâ jostan: verb
To bounce

bâlâ keshidan: verb
To raise

bâlâ raftan: verb
To soar - To climb - To aspire - To ascend - To boost

bâlâ âmadan: verb
To rise - To uprise - To upheaval

bâlâ âvardan: verb
To nauseate - To puke

bâlâkhâne: noun
upstairs - balcony

bâlâns: noun
handstand - balance

bâlâpush: noun
wrapper - quilt - coverlet - mantle

bâlârotbe: adjective
senior - upper

bâlâtane: noun
bust

bâlâtar: adverb
senior - superior - upper

bâlâtar budan: verb
To transcend

bâlâtarin: adjective
superlative - uppermost - upmost - maximum

bâlâyi: adverb
superior - over - upper

bâmaze: adjective
zestful (ty) - racy

bâmdâd: noun
morning - daybreak

bâme khâne: noun
housetop

bâmolâheze: adjective
considerate - wary - thoughtful - tender

bâmolâyemat: noun
gently

bâmorovat: adjective
humane

bânde forudgâh: noun
runway

bâneshât: adjective
racy - fresh - unwearied - vivacious - sprightly

bânezâkat: adjective
tactful - polite

bâng: noun
cry - call

bâng zadan: verb
To exclaim - To cry - To crow

bâni: noun
author - sponsor

bâni shodan: verb
To sparkplug

bâniye kheyr: adjective
benefactor

bânk: noun
bank

bânkdâr: adjective
banker

bânofuz: adjective
weighty

bânu: noun
madem - lady - gentlewoman

bâpâ zadan: verb
To kick

bâr: noun
burden - cargo - freight

bâr: noun
alloy

bâr kardan: verb
To pack - To burden - To load - To weight

bâr zadan: verb
To load

bâr âvardan: verb
To breed - To raise

bârandegi: noun
rainfall - rain

bârandâz: noun
jetty

bârband: noun
rack

bârbar: adjective
porter - backer

bârbari: noun
freight

bârdâr: adjective
heavy - pergnant - anticipant

bârdâr shodan: verb
To fur

bâre safar bastan: verb
To truss

bâreghe: noun
spark - twinkle

bâresh: noun
downfall - rainfall - rain

bârez: noun
sensible - manifest

bârgâh: noun
court

bârhâ: noun
often - freuqently

bâridan: verb
To rain

bârik: adjective
thin - strait - slender - slat - narrow

bârikbin: adjective
meticulous

bârike: noun
beam

bârkesh: adjective
wagon

bâru: noun
rampart - fortification - bulwark

bârut: noun
gunpowder

bârvar: adjective
prolific

bârân: noun
rain

bâsabât: adjective
stable - constant

bâsafâ: adjective
fun

bâsalighe: adjective
stylish

bâsavâdi: adjective
literacy

bâsekhâvat: adjective
bounteous

bâsere: noun
sight

bâshakhsiyat: adjective
personable

bâsherâfat: adjective
truly

bâshetâbi: adverb
summary - apace

bâshgâh: noun
club

bâshokuh: adjective
magnificent - stilted

bâsil: noun
bacillus

bâsor'at: adjective
swift

bâstâni: adjective
antique - antiquarian - ancient

bâstânshenâs: noun
archaeologist

bâtadbir: adjective
shifty - tactician - circumspect

bâtaghvâ: adjective
virtuous

bâtajrobe: adjective
thoroughbred

bâtarbiyat: adjective
mannerly - gentle

bâtarâvat: adjective
youthful

bâtel: adjective
invalid - inoperative - void - vain - null

bâtel kardan: verb
To cancel - To undo - To invalid

bâtel shodan: verb
To void - To dispense

bâtel sâkhtan: verb
To override

bâtele: adjective
useless - waste

bâten: noun
conscience - inside

bâteni: adjective
pectoral - intrinsic - internal - inner

bâteni: adjective
inward

bâtlâgh: noun
swamp - morass - marsh - bog

bâtlâghi: adjective
marshy - swampy

bâtri: noun
battery

bâtun: noun
bourdon

bâvafâ: adjective
fast - unfailing - loyal

bâvaghâr: adjective
superb - stately - ladylike - courtly - grand

bâvar: noun
belief - credence

bâvar: adjective
assistant - aid - adjutant - helper

bâvar kardani: adjective
credible - probable - plausible

bâvar nakardani: adjective
incredible - inconceivable - unbelievable

bâvar nakardani: verb
To disbelieve

bâvojud: adjective
notwithstanding - despite

bây'ganiye râked: noun
morgue

bây'gâni: noun
archive - record

bâyad: adverb
must - ought

bâyegân: adjective
recorder - archivist

bâyer: adjective
sterile - arid

bâyest: adverb
ought - must - shall

bâz dâshtan: verb
To proscribe

bâz shodan: verb
To unroll - To unlatch - To uncouple

bâzande: adjective
loser

bâzarbe zadan: verb
To quash

bâzargan: noun
trader - businessman - merchant

bâzargâni: adjective
commercial - commerce - mercantile - trade

bâzbini: noun
revision

bâzde: noun
turnover - output - revenue

bâzdid: noun
visit - revision - review - survey

bâzdâsht: noun
stoppage - deterrence

bâzdâshtan: verb
To deter - To detain - To block - To impede -
To prevent

bâzdâshtgâh: noun
lockup - detention

bâzgasht: noun
return - reference - recurrence - recession -
recess

bâzgashtan: verb
To untread - To comeback

bâzgoftan: verb
To unreel - To restate - To repeat - To
recount

bâzgrdândan: verb
To restoration

bâzgu: noun
repetition - repeat

bâzguyi: noun
restatement - repetition

bâzi: noun
game - play

bâzi kardan: verb
To play - To perform - To toy

bâzi kardan: verb
To act

bâziche: noun
toy - sport - plaything

bâzigar: noun
actor

bâzigush: adjective
wanton - playful

bâzikon: noun
player

bâziye nard: noun
dibs

bâziye varagh: noun
bridge

bâzjuyi: noun
quest - inquiry - inquest - crossquestion

bâzjuyi kardan: verb
To examine - To interrogate - To inquire

94

bâzkharid: noun
redemption

bâzkhâst: noun
interpellation

bâzmânde: adjective
survivor - hinder

bâzneshaste: adjective
retired - pensioner

bâzo baste shodan: verb
To wink

bâzpakhsh: noun
relay

bâzpardâkht: noun
refund - reimbursement

bâzpardâkht kardan: verb
To reimburse

bâzpors: noun
interrogator

bâzraz: noun
inspector - warden

bâzresi: noun
search - audit - detection - control -
examination

bâzresi kardan: verb
To examine - To inspect - To search

bâztâb: noun
reflex - reflection

bâztâbi: noun
reflexive

bâzu: noun
arm - grain

bâzuband: noun
brachial - bracelet

bâzyâbi: noun
detection - retrieval

bâzyâft: noun
resumption - recovery

bâzyâftan: verb
To gain - To retrieve - To resume - To regain
- To recover

bâzâr: noun
market - plaza - bazaar

bôl: noun
urine

ch

chah chahe zadan: verb
To twitter

chah chahe zadan: verb
To warble

chakhmâgh: noun
hammer

chakosh: noun
mallet - hammer

chakosh zadan: verb
To hammer

chakâme: noun
ode - poem

chakâme sarâ: adjective
poet

chakâvak: noun
warbler

chalghuz: adjective
guano

chaman: noun
grass - lawn - meadow

chamanzâr: noun
meadow

chamanzâr: noun
prairie - grassland

chamedân: noun
suitcase

chamush: noun
skittish - restive - outlaw

chamush: adjective
shier

chanbare: noun
torque - tassel

chanbare zadan: verb
To coil

chand: adjective
several

chand barâbar kardan: verb
To manifold

chand pahlu: adjective
multilateral

chandgushe: noun
polygon

chandgânegi: noun
plurality

chandi: adverb
some - quantity - quantitative

chandin: adverb
multiple - several

chandin: adverb
several

chandjânebe: adjective
multilateral

chandlâ: adjective
fold - multiple

chandsedâ: adjective
allophone

chandtâ: adverb
some - various - manifold

chandân: adverb
very - fold - so

chang: noun
grip - grapple - claw - harp

chang zadan: verb
To grasp - To grab - To harp

changak: noun
tach - prong - gaff - rake - uncus - hook - peg

changak: noun
crampon

changnavâz: adjective
harper

changâl: noun
fork - prong - pitchfork - paw

chante: noun
knapsack - pouch - bag

chap: noun
squint

chap: noun
left

chap chap: adjective

askew - askance - awry

chap dast: adjective
left-handed - soiuthpaw - gauche

chapândan: verb
To cram - To jam - To squeeze

chapânidan: verb
To frank

chapâvol: noun
plunder - raven - ransack

chapâvol kardan: verb
To ransack - To maraud

chapâvolgar: adjective
marauder - robber

charand: adjective
trashy - silly - nonsensical - crap - inane

charand goftan: verb
To twaddle

charb: adjective
oily - unctuous

charbi: noun
fat - oil - grease

charbidan: verb
To prevail - To predominate

charbkonande: adjective
lubricant

charbo narm: adjective
sleek - voluble - unctuous

97

charbzabân: adjective
glib

charbzabâni: noun
lard - bolubility - unction

charbzabâni kardan: verb
To coax

charidan: verb
To browse - To graze - To grass

charkh: noun
wheel - cycle - turquoise

charkh khordan: verb
To ring

charkh zadan: verb
To eddy - To gyrate - To pirouette

charkhak: noun
pulley - trundle - whirligig - caster

charkhande: adjective
revolving - rotative - rotary - whirler -
wheeler

charkhandegi: noun
bolubility

charkhe dande: noun
sprocket - gearwheel - gear - cogwheel

charkhesh: noun
swirl - twirl - troll - revolution - roll - wheel

charkhesh: noun
rotation

charkheshi: adjective

rotatory - gyration

charkhidan: verb
To troll - To whirl - To wheel - To revolve

charkhkâr: noun
machinist'smate - machinist

charkhofalak: noun
girandole

charkhân: noun
twister - rotor

charkhândan: verb
To pivot - To wind - To swivel - To spin

charkhânidan: verb
To whirl

charm: noun
leather

charmi: adjective
leathery

charândan: verb
To summer - To feed - To graze - To grass

chasb: noun
paste - gum - gluten - glue

chasb zadan: verb
To gum

chasbandegi: noun
tenacity - stick - cohesion - adherence

chasbdâr: adjective
adhesive

chasbidan: verb
To cohere - To cling - To stick - To attach

chasbide: adjective
innate - inherent - adhesive - gummy -
sticky - tenacious

chasbidegi: adjective
coherency - adhesion

chasbnâk: adjective
stick - goo - cohesive

chasbândan: verb
To stick - To cement - To attach - To paste

chasbânidan: verb
To affix

chashm: noun
eye - optic - sight

chashmandâz: noun
scenery - scene - prospect - lookout -
perspective - view - landscape

chatr: noun
umbrella

chatrbâz: noun
parachutist

chatre nejât: noun
parachute

che: preposition
whether - what - any

che andâze: preposition
what

che karirâ: preposition
whom

che kasi: preposition
whom - who

che khub: adverb
benedicite

che meghdâr: preposition
what

che no'e: preposition
what kind

che vaght: preposition
when

cheft: noun
snap - hasp - lid - latch

cheft kardan: verb
To slot - To hasp - To latch

cheft zadan be: verb
To lid

chefte dar: noun
slot

chefto bast: noun
lock

cheghadr: adverb
how much - what

chegune: adverb
how

chegunegi: noun
how - quality - circumstance - condition

chegâli: noun
density

chegâlisanj: noun
aerometer

chehre: noun
puss - visage - feature - face

chehâr na'I: noun
scamper - gallop - canter

chehâr zel'I: adjective
quadrilateral

chehârchub: noun
frame

chehârchube: noun
framework

chehârdaham: noun
fourteenth

chehârgholu: adjective
quadruplet

chehârgush: adjective
quadrilateral - quadrant - quadrangle

chehârgâne: adverb
quadruplet

chehârlâ: adjective
uradruple

chehârpâ: adjective
quadruped - beast

chehârshanbe: noun
wednesday

chek: noun
cheque

cheke: noun
drop - drip - sprinkle - seep - leakage - leak

cheke kardan: verb
To plash - To drip - To seep

chekidan: verb
To trickle - To drop - To drip - To plash - To lave

chekide: adjective
abstract - succinct - tabloid

chekideye kalâm: noun
resume

chekideye matlab: noun
precis

chekândan: verb
To distill

chekânidan: verb
To trickle - To drip - To dribble

chelchele: noun
swallow

chelik: noun
barrel - cask - drum

chelipâ: noun
cross

chelândan: verb
To squeeze - To wring - To crush

chenin: noun
thus - so - such - likewise

chenin: preposition
such

chenân: preposition
so

chenânche: preposition
if

chenânke: preposition
as - how

cherk: adjective
dirty - puss - sordid - slag - squawk - impure

cherk shodan: verb
To soil - To foul

cherkdâr: adjective
pussy - dirty

cherki: adjective
septic - pussy

cherkin: verb
To dirty - To lousy

cherâ: adverb
why

cherâgh: noun
light - lamp

cherâghe daryâyi: noun
lantern - beacon

cherâghe ghove: noun

torch

cherâghe khâne: noun
lighthouse

cherâghe râhnamâ: noun
traffic lights

cherâghâni kardan: verb
To illuminate

cherâgâh: noun
pasture

cherânidan: verb
To pasture

cheshidan: verb
To taste

cheshm bastan: verb
To blindfold

cheshm dukhtan: verb
To gaze

cheshm pezeshk: noun
oculist

cheshm pezeshki: noun
ophthalmology

cheshm pushi: noun
ignore - connivance - waiver

cheshm pushidan: verb
To ignore - To relinquish

cheshm sefid: adjective
impudent

cheshmak: noun
twinkle - blink - wink

cheshmak zadan: verb
To wink - To blink - To sparkle

cheshmak zan: adjective
blinker

cheshmband: noun
blind

cheshmbandi: noun
juggle

cheshmdâsht: noun
outlook

cheshme: noun
fountain - springhead - spring

cheshmgir: adjective
saleint

cheshâyi: adjective
taste

chetor: noun
how

chidan: verb
To pickup - To pick

chidan: verb
To crowd

chidani: adjective
ripe

chin: noun
China - plait - chitlings - fold - offset -

wrinkle

chin khordan: verb
To shrivel

chindâr: verb
To shirr - To wrinkle - To corrugate

chini: adjective
sinitic - chinese - china - porcelain

chinkhorde: adjective
crackly

chinkhordegi: noun
wrinkle

chino choruk: adjective
cockle - ruga

chire: adjective
proficient - dominant

chire shodan: verb
To overcome - To dominate

chiredast: adjective
dextrous - dexterous - adroit - master

chiredasti: noun
skill

chiregi: noun
effrontery - proficiency

chistân: noun
puzzle - conundrum - enigma

chiz: noun
thing - stuff

chogholi: noun
denunciation - rumble

chogholi kardan: verb
To inform

choghondar: noun
beet

cholâgh: adjective
cripple

cholâgh kardan: verb
To maim

chomâgh: noun
stick - cudgel - bat

chomâgh zadan: verb
To mace - To cudgel

chon: preposition
since - whereas - as

chonbâtme zadan: verb
To squat - To ruck

chonke: adverb
because

chonke: noun
because

chopogh: noun
pipe

chort: noun
snooze - slumber - nap - doze

chort zadan: verb
To nap

chorte khotâh: noun
catnap

chortke: noun
abacus

chortzan: adjective
drowsy

choruk: verb
To shrink - To constringe

choruk: noun
shrinkage - wrinkle - wizen - plica

chorukide: verb
To crimp - To wrinkle

chorukide shodan: verb
To wrinkle

chub: noun
timber - stick - stave - spunk - shaft - wood - rod

chub bast: noun
scaffold - framework

chub bor: adjective
lumberjack - logger

chub khat: noun
score

chub panbe: noun
stopper - cork

chub zadan: verb
To beat - To drub

chube: noun
shaft

chube afrâ: noun
maple

chube bâdavâm: noun
hardwood

chubeye dâr: noun
gibbet - gallows

chubi: adjective
woody - wooden - wood

chuchule: noun
clitoris

chuno cherâ: noun
dispute

chupân: noun
rancher - pastor

châbok: adjective
swift - speedy - nimble - agile - adroit - quick
- brisk

châbok: noun
slot - tear

châbokdast: adjective
swift

châboki: noun
alacrity - agility - activity - dexterity

châboksâvâr: adjective
jockey

châdor: noun

tent - veil

châdor zadan: verb
To encamp

châdor zadan: verb
To camp

châgh: noun
fat - overweight - obese

châgh shodan: verb
To blubber - To batten - To plump

châghi: adjective
overweight

châghu: noun
knife

châh: noun
shaft

châi: noun
tea

châk dâdan: verb
To unseam - To rift - To tear - To strip - To
slit

châk khordan: verb
To sliver

châker: adjective
menial

châkhân: noun
bluff - whiff

châkhân kardan: verb
To bluff - To vapor - To palaver

châl: noun
trench - cavern

châle: noun
pit

châle châle: adjective
pitted

châlâk: adjective
prompt - jimmy - dexterous - nimble - adroit

châne: noun
chin - haggle

châne zadan: verb
To bargain - To haggle

châp: noun
stamp - edition - press - impression

châp kardan: verb
To publish - To reproduce - To print

châpe mojadad: noun
reissue

châpidan: verb
To rob - To plunder

châplus: adjective
bootlick - servile

châplusi: noun
subservience - blarney - cajole - flattery - grease

châplusi kardan: verb
To wheedle

châplusâne: adverb
silky - greasy

châpâr: noun
mail - post

chârdivâri: adjective
enclosure

châre: noun
makeshift - remedy - recourse

châre kardan: verb
To ameliorate

chârghad: noun
kerchief

chârgush: noun
square

chârpâye: noun
stool

chârshâne: noun
stocky

châshinye ghazâ: noun
spice - ketchup

châshni: noun
flavor - sauce - condiment

châyi: noun
print

châyidan: verb
To cool

chôgân: noun
wicket - mallet - bat

chôgân bâzi: noun
polo

d

da'vat: noun
invitation

da'vat kardan: verb
To invite

da'vi: noun
claim - case - pretension - quarrel

da'vi kardan: verb
To quarrel - To pretend

da'vâ: noun
strife - squeal - quarrel - contest

dabe kardan: verb
To renege

dabestân: noun
prep - school

dabir: noun
teacher - instructor

dabirestân: noun
gymnasium - school

dabirkhâne: noun
secretariat

dabâgh: noun
tanner

dabâghi kardan: verb
To tan

dadmanesh: noun
brutish

daf': noun
expultion - repulse - repercussion - rebuttal
- rebuff

daf' kardan: verb
To eject - To dispel - To repulse - To repel

daf' shodan: verb
To void

daf'e hamle: noun
parry

dafn: noun
mortuary - interment - burial

dafn kardan: verb
To sepulcher - To grave - To bury

daftar: noun
bureau - notebook

daftarche: noun
booklet

daftardâr: noun
clerk

daftare kol: noun
ledger

daftare kâr: noun
office

daftare yad'dâsht: noun
notebook - folio

daftarkhâne: noun
bureau

daghal: noun
dishonest

daghalbâz: adjective
idol

daghigh: noun
punctual - subtle - scrutinizer - precise -
astute

daghigh shodan: verb
To attenuate

daghighe: noun
minute

daghighe: noun
minute

dah: noun
ten

dah chandân: adverb
tenfold

dahanbin: adjective
whimsical

dahande: adjective
donor - giver

dahane: noun
muzzle - gap

dahangoshâd: adjective
bigmouthed

dahankaji: noun
grimace - mug

dahe: noun
decade

dahom: noun
tenth

dahomin: adjective
tenth

dahr: noun
universe

dahsâle: adverb
decennial

dahân: noun
mouth - throat

dahâne: noun
spout - mouth - outfall

dake: noun
kiosk

dakhl: noun
pertinence - income

dakhme: noun
crypt

dale dozdi: noun
crib - cabbage

daledozd: noun
prig

dalghak: noun
jester - stooge - buffoon

108

dalil: noun
proof - sake - reason

dalil âvardan: verb
To argue - To allege

dalir: adjective
brave - intrepid - courageous

daliri: noun
courage - glamor - bravery

daliri: noun
valor

dalirâne: adverb
valiant - brave

dalsardi: noun
despondency

dalâl: noun
dealer - mediator

dalâli kardan: verb
To job

dam bar âvardan: verb
To expire - To exhale

dam be dam: adverb
blowbyblow

dam kardan: verb
To stew - To infuse - To brew

dam karde: adjective
infusion

dam keshidan: verb
To pant

damal: noun
boil - blotch - abscess - wen

damande: adjective
blower

damar: noun
prone

damar khâbidan: verb
To grovel

damdami: adverb
unpredictable - uncertain - ambivalent

damdami mezâj: noun
cyclothyme - erratic - capricious - pliant

dame: noun
vapor - steam

dami: noun
caudate

damidan: verb
To bop - To blow

damide shode: adjective
blown

damsâz: adjective
helpmate - confidant - compatible

damzadan: verb
To respire - To breathe

damâgh: noun
genius

damâghe: noun
headland - head - cape - nose

damâsanj: noun
thermometer

dande: noun
rib - gear

dande: noun
clobber

dandâ: adjective
greedy

dandân: noun
tooth

dandân darâvardan: verb
To teethe

dandândard: noun
toothache

dandâne: noun
dent - jag - tooth - tine - peg - cog

dandâne: noun
dent - cog

dandâne aghl: noun
wisdomtooth

dandâne dandâne: adjective
serrate - crinkle

dandâne pish: noun
cutter

dandâne âsiyâb: noun
molar - grinder - sectorial

dandânedâr: adjective
toothy - jagged - dentate

dandânpezeshki: noun
dentist

dandânshekan: adjective
unanswerable - irrecusable

dandânsâz: noun
prosthodontist - dentist

dar: preposition
door - inside

dar amân: noun
secure

dar atrâfe: preposition
around - about

dar avâyele: adverb
early

dar dastres: adjective
available - attainable - accessible

dar ekhtiyâr: adjective
disposal

dar emtedâde khat: preposition
along

dar entezâr: adjective
expectant - wistful

dar eshtebâh budan: verb
To err

dar ezâye: noun
in exchange for

dar ham rikhte: adjective
jakes

dar hamejâ: adverb
everywhere

dar har surat: adverb
ever - anyway - anyhow

dar harjâ: adverb
everywhere

dar jariyân: adverb
during - afoot

dar jostejuye: noun
after

dar kamin neshastan: verb
To ambush

dar kardan: verb
To discharge - To deny

dar khatar: adjective
subject

dar khelâle: adverb
meanwhile - meantime

dar khâk nahâdan: verb
To inter

dar ma'raze: adjective
disposable - subject

dar miyâne: preposition
midst - between - among - across

dar moghâbele: preposition
versus - against

dar nazar dâshtan: verb
To purpose - To contemplate - To envisage

dar nazar gereftan: verb
To spot

dar raftan: verb
To escape - To abscond

dar shegeft: adjective
agape

dar shorofe: adjective
eve - ace - about

dar tangnâ: adjective
strait

dar tangnâ gharâr dâdan: verb
To lockout - To sandwich

dar tardid budan: verb
To hover

dar zemn: adverb
meanwhile - meantime

dar âghush gereftan: verb
To hug - To cuddle - To embrace

dar âghush keshidan: verb
To caress

dar âvardan: verb
To render - To gouge - To wisp - To evolve - To erupt

darafsh: noun
banner

daraje: noun
mark - grade - gradation - degree

daraje bandi: noun
calibration - grade - gradation

daraje do: adjective
secondbest

daraje yek: adjective
topnotch - classy

darajedâr: adjective
noncommissionedoffic - gaduate

darajeye eftekhâri: noun
honorary

darande: adjective
fierce - predatory

darandekhu: adjective
rapacious

darb: noun
door - port

darband: noun
captive - canyon

darbar gereftan: verb
To encompass

darbarâbare: preposition
versus - against

darbast: noun
exclusive - enbloc

darbedar: adjective
gadabout - vagrant - vagabond

darbedari: noun
vagrancy

darbân: noun
doorkeeper - porter

darbâr: noun
court

darbâreye: noun
about - inre - regarding

darbâzkon: noun
doorkeeper

dard: noun
pain - agony - distress

dard: noun
pain

dard kardan: adverb
shoot - pain

dard keshidan: adverb
pain - twinge

darde dandân: noun
toothache

dardedel: noun
chat

dardesar: noun
inconvenience - headache

dardeshekam: noun
abdominal pain - cramp

dardnâk: adjective
angry - achy - painful - grievous

dardâvar: adjective
achy

dare: noun
valley

darebtedâ: adverb
early

darentehâye: noun
meanwhile - meantime

dargir: adjective
outbreak

dargiri: noun
involvement

dargozasht: noun
death

dargozashtan: verb
To passaway - To die - To decease

dargâh: noun
doorway

darham: adjective
shaggy - indistinct - mixed - mesh

darham keshidan: verb
To puchery

darham pichidan: verb
To taut - To tangle - To intersubjective

darham rikhtan: verb
To pie - To clutter

darham shekastan: verb
To smash - To breakdown - To vanquish - To
overwhelm

darham âmikhtan: verb
To conjugate - To interlace

darham âmikhtegi: noun
jumble

darhami: noun
compiexity

darharkat: adverb
underway - astir - agog - afloat

darheine: adverb
while

darhodude: adverb
about - within

darhâlike: adverb
whereas

dari vari goftan: verb
To tattle

dariche: noun
hatch - window

daridan: verb
To slit - To tear - To lacerate

daridegi: noun
rift

darigh: noun
pity

darigh dâshtan: verb
To spare - To withhold

darighâ: adverb
alas

darin hodud: adverb
hereabout

darinbâre: adverb
herein

darinjâ: adverb
there

darj: noun
interpolation

darjahate: preposition
of - with

darjevâre: adverb
besides

darjâyike: adverb
wherein

dark: noun
perception - uptake - realization

dark kardan: verb
To sapprehend - To understand - To
perceive - To coneive

darkhatâ: adjective
perverse

darkhor: noun
proportionate - appropriate - apposite

darkhâst: noun
solicitation - appeal - request - demand

darkhâst kardan: verb
To solicit - To request - To plead - To apply

darmân: noun
treatment - remedy

darmân: noun
therapy

darmân kardan: verb
To remedy - To treat

darmândegi: noun
insolvency

darmândâri: noun
government

darmângâh: noun
clinic - infirmary

darmânkade: noun
polyclinic - policlinic

daroftâdan: verb
To oppose

darpush: noun
blind

dars: noun
lesson - study

dars dâdan: verb
To teach - To educate

dars khând: adjective
studious

dars khândan: verb
To study

darsad: noun
percent

114

darsadad: noun
sought - about

darsadad budan: verb
To go - To figure on

darsuratike: adverb
while

darun: noun
inward - inside

daruni: adjective
subjective - esoteric - inward - internal -
interior - inner

daruni: noun
intestine

darvasat: adverb
midst

darvâghe: adverb
indeed

darvâze: noun
goal - gateway - gate - portal

darvâzebân: noun
goal - gatekeeper

daryâ: noun
sea - mere - mare - main - flood - channel

daryâche: noun
lake - laguna - pond - slew

daryâft: noun
comprehension - receipt - perception

daryâftan: verb
To discover - To comprehend - To realize -
To understand

daryânavard: noun
shipper - shipman - seagoing - seafarer

daryâsâlâr: noun
admiral

daryâyi: adjective
nautical - maritime - marine

darz: noun
gap - interstice

darz dâdan: verb
To seam

darz gereftan: verb
To chink - To caulk - To gasket - To seam

darze lebâs: noun
seam

darâmad: noun
revenue - income

darâmad: noun
income

darâmikhtan: verb
To commix

darânja: adverb
therein - there

dasht: noun
plain - moor - desert - flat - weald

dasise: noun
plot - machination - conspiracy

dasise kardan: verb
To angle - To intrigue - To cabal

dasise âmiz: adjective
insidious

dast: noun
hand

dast: noun
hand

dast andâkhtan: verb
To spoof - To kid - To ridicule - To fool - To hoax

dast derâzi kardan: verb
To encroach

dast dâdan: verb
To handclasp

dast dâdan: verb
To handshake

dast forush: noun
duffer - huckster

dast kaj: adjective
thievish

dast keshidan: verb
To desist - To cease - To resign

dast nakhorde: adjective
entire - whole - virgin - intact

dast tanhâ: adjective
barehanded

dast yâftan: verb
To attain - To achieve - To accede

dast zadan: verb
To plaudit

dast âmuz: adjective
pet

dastandâz: noun
ramp - puddle

dastband: noun
bracelet - wristband

dastband: noun
shackle - lei - cuff

dastband zadan: verb
To manacle

dastbord: noun
robbery - defalcation - larceny

dastbord zadan: verb
To steal - To rob

dastbord zadan: verb
To embezzle

dastbâf: adjective
handmade

daste: noun
stud - stem - stack - squad - team

daste bandi: noun
classification

daste bâlâ: adjective
upperhand - outside

daste shodan: verb
To shoal

dastebandi kardan: verb
To categorize - To rank - To grade

dastegol: noun
bouquet - posy

dastejam'I: noun
social - ensemble

dastekam: noun
leastwise

dastforush: noun
badger - vendor

dastgire: noun
catch - knob

dastgireye dar: noun
pin - pin

dastgiri: verb
To nab

dastgiri: noun
charity - capture

dastgiri kardan: verb
To assist

dastgâh: noun
system - set - machinery - machine

dasti: adjective
handy - handmade - manual - portable

dastkesh: noun
glove - gantlet - chevron

dastkhat: noun
handwriting

dastkhosh: noun
victim

dastkhosh shodan: verb
To undergo

dastkâri kardan: verb
To retouch - To manipulate

dastmozd: noun
wage - stipend

dastmâl: noun
napkin - kerchief - handkerchief

dastmâle gardan: noun
shawl - tie - handkerchief

dastmâle sofre: noun
napkin

dastmâli: noun
scrabble - grope

dastneshande: adjective
stooge - puppet

dasto delbâz: adjective
spendthrift

dastpokht: noun
cuisine

dastpâche: adjective
hasty

dastpâche: adjective
nervous - panicky

dastpâche kardan: verb
To shend - To baffle

dastpâchegi: noun
bafflement

dastpâchegi: noun
hurry

dastranj: noun
wage

dastres: noun
access - disposal

dastresi: noun
range - access

dastshuyi: noun
lavatory - basin - washstand

dastur: noun
rule - order

dastur dâdan: verb
To address

dasture kâr: noun
agenda

dasture zabân: noun
grammar

dasturi: adjective
grammatical - imperative - ministry

dasturol'amal: noun
recipe

dastyâr: noun
suffragan - assistant - ancillary

dastyâri: noun
assistance

dastâr: noun
turban

dastâvard: noun
consequence - result

dastâviz: noun
pretext - voucher

davande: noun
runny

davande: adjective
rsorial

davandegi: verb
To leg

davarân: noun
rotation

davarâni: adjective
revolving

davidan: verb
To trig - To race - To run - To leap

davâ: noun
medicine - medicament

davâm: noun
persistence - perpetuity - continuity - durante

davâm dâshtan: verb
To last

davâm yâftan: verb
To run

davâr: adjective
rotatory

davât: noun
inkwell - inkstand

davâzdah: noun
twelve

davâzdahom: noun
twelfth

davâzdahomin: noun
twelfth

dedune tardid: adverb
indubitable - undoubted

defâ': noun
advocacy - defence - defense

defâ' kardan: verb
To defence - To defense - To advocate

defâ'i: adjective
defensive - vindicative

defâ'iye: noun
defense

degarbâr: noun
again

degardisi: noun
metastasis - metamorphosis

degargun: noun
dissimilar - vicissitudinous

degarguni: adjective
change - alteration - variation

degh: noun
percussion

deghat: noun
attention - accuracy - precision

deh: noun
village

dehkade: noun
village

dehliz: noun
vestibule - corridor

dehshat: noun
terror - panic - horror

dehshatnâk: adjective
horrendous

dehât: noun
country

dehâti: adjective
boorish - villager - kern - rustic

dekhâlat: noun
hand

dekhâlat kardan: verb
To interfere

dekolte: noun
decollete - decolletage

dekor: noun
decor

del: noun
heart - midst - conscience

del be daryâ zadan: verb
To adventure

del dâdan: verb
To hearten - To heart

del kandan: verb
To abandonment

delbar: adjective
sweetheart - mistress

delbastegi: noun
interest

delbâkhte: adjective
lovesick

delchasb: adjective
hearty - meet

deldard: noun
bellyache

deldâr: adjective
sweetheart

delfarib: adjective
lovely - cute

delgarm: adjective
earnest - confident

delgarm kardan: verb
To encourage

delgarmi: noun
morale - assurance

delgir: adjective
pokey

delhore: noun
presentiment

delju: adjective
affable

deljuyi: noun
affability

delkesh: adjective
attractive

delkharâsh: adjective
irritant

delkhor: adjective
sulky

delkhori: noun
annoyance - offense

delkhâh: adjective
ideal - arbitrary - accord

delmordegi: noun
dejection

delnavâz: adjective
smooth

delojor'at: noun
pluck - heart

delpasand: adjective
exquisite - nice

delpazir: adjective
gracious - graceful - handsome - lovely - amiable

delrobâ: adjective
attractive

delrobâyi: noun
oomph - charm - mash

delsard: adjective
despondent

delsard kardan: verb
To dissuade - To dishearten - To discourage

delshekaste: adjective
heartsick

delshekaste: adjective
disconsolate

delshekastegi: noun
heartbreak

delsuz: adjective
sympathetic - piteous

deltang: adjective
sad - homesick - lone - nostalgic

deltang budan: verb
To gloom

deltangi: noun
melancholia - nostalgic

delvâpas: adjective
solicitous - anxious

delvâpasi: noun
anxiety

delvâpasi: noun
turpitude - worry

delvâpasi: noun
anxiety

delâlat: noun
implication

delârâm: noun
sweetheart - belle

delâvar: adjective
valiant

delâvari: noun
courage - gallantry - valor

delâvari kardan: verb
To gallant

demokrâsi: noun
democracy

denj: noun
snug

denj: adjective
cozy

derakhshandegi: noun
radiance - glitter - brilliance - blaze - luster

derakhshesh: noun
shine - sparkle - spangle - luster - glitter

derakhshidan: verb
To shine - To lighten - To luster - To glory

derakhshân: adjective
shiny - illustrious - luminous - lucid - bright

derakhshân kardan: verb
To irradiate

derakhshân shodan: verb
To brighten

derakhshân sâkhtan: verb
To illuminate

derakht: noun
tree

derakhtche: noun
shrub

derakhte bid: noun
sallow - willow

derakhte chenâr: noun
sycamore - plantain

derakhte khormâ: noun
date

derakhte zeitun: noun
olive

derang: noun
halt - pause

derang: noun
hesitancy

derang kardan: verb
To tarry - To linger - To let

dero kardan: verb
To reap - To scythe

derogar: adjective
reaper

derâm: noun
drama

derâyat: noun
tact

derâz: adjective
lengthy - oblong

derâz: adjective
long

derâz kardan: verb
To prolong - To extend - To lengthen

derâz kardan: verb
To crane

derâz keshidan: verb
To lie

derâz shodan: verb
To lengthen

derâzkesh: noun
prone

derâzâ: noun
longitude - length

deser: noun
dessert

deshne: noun
stiletto - sticker - bowieknife

deshne zadan: verb
To dirk - To stiletto

desâmbr: noun
december

deyn: noun
debt

dezh: noun
fort - castle - citadel

dezhkhim: adjective
hangman - deathsman

dibâche: noun
preamble

did: noun
seeing - lookout - vision - viewpoint - view

didan: verb
To observe - To look - To view - To see

didani: adjective
visual

didebân: noun
watch

didebân: noun
sentinel

didgâh: noun
standpoint - sight - viewpoint - lookout

didzadan: verb
To sight - To appraisal

didâr: noun
visit

difteri: noun
diphtheria

dig: noun
cauldron - pot

dig: noun
caldron

digar: preposition
other - another - alternative

digari: adjective
another - other

digarân: noun
rest

digche: noun
pot - kettle - skillet

dikte: noun
dictation

dikte kardan: verb
To dictate

diktâtor: noun
dictator

din: noun
religion - faith

dindâr: adjective
religious - devout - pious

dindâr: adjective
inward

dinâmit: noun
powder - dynamite

diplom: noun
diploma

diplome: noun
gaduate

diplomâsi: noun
diplomacy

diplomât: noun
diplomat

dir: noun
late

dir fahmidan: verb
To misconsture

dirak: noun
lug - mast

dirbâvar: adjective
unbelievin - unbeliever - incredulous

dirin: adjective
immemorial

dirine: noun
deepseated - old - chronic - ancient

dirtar: adjective
posterior - subsequent

diruz: noun
yesterday

dishab: noun
yestreen

disk: noun
discus

div: noun
spook - bogey - goblin - gnome

divsefat: adjective
infernal

divân: noun
bureau

divâne: adjective
mad - crazy

divâne: adjective
crazy

divâne kardan: verb
To derange - To craze - To madden

divâne shodan: verb
To madden - To rave

divâne vâr: adverb
maniac - demoniac

divânegi: noun
insanity - craze - rage

divânsâlâr: adjective
bureaucrat

divânsâlâri: noun
bureaucracy

divâr: noun
fence - wall

divâr: noun
wall

divâr keshidan: verb
To wall

divâre: noun
partition - parapet

divâre: noun
septum

diyâbet: noun
diabetes

diyâferâgm: noun
diaphragm

diyânat: noun
faith

diyâr: noun
land - country

dizel: noun
diesel

dizi: noun
cruse

do: noun
two

do pahlu harf zadan: verb
To prevaricate - To equivocate

do'â: noun
pray

do'â kardan: verb
To bless - To pray

dobeiti: adjective
couplet

dobâr: adverb
twice

dobâre: adverb
again - afresh

dochandân: adjective
reduplicate

dochandân kardan: verb
To redouble

docharkhe: noun
bike

dochâr: noun
afoul - stricken

dochâr kardan: verb
To trouble - To swamp - To embroil

dochâr shodan: verb
To catch

dodel: adjective
indecisive - hesitant

dodel budan: verb
To scruple - To waver - To vacillate

dodeli: noun
indecision - hesitancy - doubt

dogholu: adjective
twin - geminate

doghotbi: adjective
bipolar

dogushe: adjective
bicuspid - diagonal

dogâne: adjective
twosome - twofold

dojense: adjective
amphibious

dojânebe: adjective
bilateral - reciprocal

dokhtar: noun
girl - daughter

dokhtar bâzi kardan: verb
To wench

dokhtarak: noun
doll - chit - pussy - puss

dokhtarbache: noun
girl

dokhtarbâz: adjective
wencher

dokhtare dokhtar: noun
granddaughter

dokhtare sâde: noun
ingenue

dokhtari: adjective
girlhood

dokhtarâne: adverb
girlie

dokhul: noun
entry - entree - arrival

dokhâniyât: noun
tobacco

dokme: noun
button - knob

doktor: noun
doctor

dokân: noun
store

dolabe: adjective
bilabial

dolat: noun
state - government

dolati: adjective
state

dolatmand: adjective
wealthy - rich - affluent

dolme: noun
jelly - gelatin - clod

dolâ: adjective
geminate - dual - double

dolâ kardan: verb
To double - To bend - To ply

dolâ shodan: verb
To crouch - To stoop

dolâr: noun
dollar - buck

dolâyi: noun
duplicity - duplex - duple

dom: noun
moment - minute - breath - blast

dombal: noun
dumbbell

donafare: adjective
twosome

donbal: noun
abscess

donbâl: noun
rear - pursuit

donbâl kardan: verb
To trace - To pursue - To follow

donbâle: noun
sequel - stem - train - trail - appendix

donyavi: noun
terrestrial - mundane - worldly - earthy

donyâ: noun
universe - vale - macrocosm - world

dopahlu: adjective
equivocal - ambiguous

dor bardâshtan: verb
To rev

dorage: adjective
mulatto - hybrid

dorang: adjective
piebald

dorangi: noun
hyporisy - duplicity

doregard: adjective
peripatetic - badger

doreye tahsili: noun
course

dorosht: adjective
sturdy - harsh - large - abrupt - rough

doroshti: noun
amplitude - acerbity

dorost: adjective
true - correct - exact - right

dorost kardan: verb
To build - To make

dorosti: noun
truth - accuracy - precision - legitimacy - integrity - honesty

dorostkâr: adjective
upright - right

dorostkâri: noun
rectitude - honesty

doru: adjective
janusfaced - hypocritical - insincere

doru: adjective
reversible

dorud: noun
salute - salutation - regard - greet

dorudgar: noun
carpenter

dorudgari: noun
carpentry

dorugh: noun
lie - fiction - false - fable

dorugh goftan: verb
To belie - To lie

127

dorughgu: adjective
false - liar

dorughguyi: noun
lying - mendacity

doruyi: adjective
hyporisy - duplicity - guile

doshman: noun
foe - enemy

doshmani: adjective
odium - enmity - hatred - hate

doshmanâne: adverb
inimical

doshnâm: noun
abusive - curse

doshnâm dâdan: verb
To mistreat - To misname

doshvâr: adjective
hard - arduous - difficult - tough

doshvâri: noun
difficulty

doshâkhe: adjective
pitchfork - crotch

doshânbe: noun
monday

dotâyi: adjective
binary - duplex - dual

dovom: adjective
second

dovomi: adjective
latter - second

dozd: noun
burglar - robber - thief - stealer

dozdaki: adverb
slinky - stealthy

dozde daryâyi: noun
pirate

dozdi: noun
burglary - robbery - theft

dozdi kardan: verb
To thieve

dozdidan: verb
To steal - To thieve

dozdidan: verb
To steal

dozdiye adabi: noun
crib - plagiarism

dubl: noun
duple

dud: noun
whiff - smoke

dud kardan: verb
To smoke

dude: noun
grime - black - soot - smut

dude zadan: verb
To soot

dudemân: noun
progeny - genealogy - antecedent

dudi: adjective
smoky

dudkesh: noun
stacks - funnel

dudkhâne: noun
smokehouse

dudkonande: adjective
smoky

dughâb: noun
slush - whitewash

duk: noun
duke

dukhtan: verb
To sew - To suture - To steek - To bind

dun: adjective
poor - lowly - sordid - servile

dunpâye: adjective
understrapper - underling

dur: adjective
far - distant - away

dur: adjective
sightless - blind

durandishi: noun
foresight

durbin: noun
Camera

durdast: adjective
far away

duri: adverb
inaccessibility - improbability - distance

durkardan: verb
To distance - To dispossess - To oust - To remove

durnamâ: noun
prospect - outlook - lookout - vista

durshodan: verb
To scat - To recede

durtar: adjective
farther - beyond

durtarin: adjective
farthest

durâdur: noun
afar

dush: noun
showerbath - shower - shoulder

dush gereftan: verb
To shower - To douche

dushidan: verb
To milk

dushize: noun
girl - damosel - damsel - maiden

dust: noun
friend

dust dâshtan: verb
To like - To love

dust dâshtani: noun
amiable - lovely - lovable

duste pesar: noun
boyfriend

duste samimi: noun
crony - hailfellow - close friend

dusti: noun
haunt

dustân: noun
entourage

dustâne: adverb
friendly - blithe - amicable

dustâr: adjective
lover

duzakh: noun
inferno - hell - pandemonium

duzandegi: noun
sewing

dâ'l: noun
uncle

dâ'l: noun
motive

dâd: noun
shout - greet - ruction

dâd keshidan: verb
To roar

dâd zadan: verb
To shout - To roar - To bawl

dâd zadan: verb
To shout - To outcry

dâdan: verb
To grant - To give

dâdan: verb
To give

dâdgar: adjective
just

dâdgir: adjective
avenger - revenger

dâdgiri kardan: verb
To avenge

dâdgostar: noun
righter

dâdgostari: noun
justice

dâdgâh: noun
court

dâdkhâh: adjective
complainant - candidate - plaintiff

dâdkhâhi: noun
lawsuit - complaint

dâdkhâhi kardan: verb
To moot - To petition

dâdkhâst: noun
plea - petition - suit

dâdo bidâd: verb
To wrangle - To jangle

dâdo setad: noun
trade - bargain

dâdobidâd: noun
scrimmage - uproar - riot - rampage

dâdras: adjective
judge - magistrate

dâdresi: noun
judgment - trial

dâemi: adjective
perennial - eternal - continual - constant

dâemi kardan: verb
To perpetuate

dâfe': noun
eductor - repulsive - repellent - loathsome

dâgh: adjective
sultry - stigma - stain - hot - mark

dâgh kardan: verb
To singe - To brand - To cauterize

dâghdâr: adjective
scathing

dâgho derafsh: noun
brand

dâghân kardan: verb
To shatter

dâkhel: noun
inside

dâkhel shodan: verb
To enter

dâkheli: adjective
internal - inner - innate - indoor

dâkheli: noun
internal

dâlân: noun
corridor - porch - hall

dâm: noun
trap - net - grin - decoy - ambush - pitfall

dâm: noun
trap - snare - noose - decoy

dâman zadan: verb
To provoke

dâmane: noun
skirt - amplitude - amplitude - hillside

dâmaneye kuh: noun
hillside - skirt

dâmdâri kardan: verb
To ranch

dâmgâh: noun
stockyard - menagerie

dâmpezeshk: noun
veterinarian

dâmâd: noun
groom - birdegroom

dâne: noun
corn - seed

dâneh: noun
semen - seed - bean - bait - grain

dânesh: noun
science - scholarship - knowledge - wisdom

dânesh âmukhtan: verb
To educate - To study

dânesh âmuz: noun
student - pupil - grader

dâneshgâh: noun
university - college - academy

dâneshgâhi: noun
university - varsity - collegiate

dâneshju: noun
student

dâneshmand: noun
scientist - savant - erudite

dâneshnâme: noun
diploma

dâneshsarâ: noun
trainingcollege

dâneshvar: noun
scholar - master

dânestan: verb
To cognize - To know

dânestehâ: noun
knowledge

dâng: noun
toom - tone

dângi: noun
treat

dânmârki: adjective
Danish

dânâ: adjective
savant - sage - sagacious - astute - wise

dânâyi: noun
knowledge - wisdom

dâr: noun
scaffold - gallows

dârbast: noun
scaffold - trellis - stud

dârbast bastan: verb
To trellis

dârchin: noun
cinnamon

dârkub: noun
woodpecker

dârolta'dib: noun
penitentiary - reformatory

dâru: noun
cure - drug - medicine - medication

dârugar: noun
druggist - pharmacist

dârughe: noun
sheriff

dârukhâne: noun
pharmacy - drugstore

dârusâz: noun
apothecary - pharmacist - chemist

dârusâzi: noun
pharmacy

dâruyi: noun
medicinal - medic

dârâ: adjective
wealthy

dârâ budan: verb
To encompass - To own - To owe - To have

dârâye ebhâm: adjective
equivocal

dârâyi: noun
property - asset - possession

dâs: noun
sickle - scythe

dâshbord: noun
dashboard

dâshtan: verb
To bear - To relieve - To own

dâstân: noun
fable - tale - story

dâstân goftan: verb
To story

dâstâni: adjective
storied

dâstânsarâ: noun
storyteller

dâstânsarâyi: noun
narrative

dâvar: noun
arbiter - referee

dâvari: adjective
umpire - umpirage - decision

dâvtalab: noun
volunteer - entrant - candidate

dâvtalab shodan: verb
To volunteer

dâvtalabi: noun
candidacy

dâvtalabâne: adverb
voluntary

dâye: noun
foster - nursemaid - nurse

dâyer: noun
active - established

dâyere: noun
sphere - circle - roundel

dâyere'I: adjective
gyrate

dâyerolma'âref: noun
encyclopedia

dôr: noun
circuit - orbit - wheel -

dôr gereftan: verb
To encompass - To encircle - To embed

dôr zadan: verb
To twinge - To circle - To round - To revolve

dôre: noun
course

dôrân: noun
season - vertigo - era

e

e'dâm: noun
gallows

e'dâm kardan: verb
To administer - To execute

e'jâz: noun
miracle - marvel

e'lâm: noun
declaration

e'lâm kardan: verb
To notify - To exclaim - To enunciate - To herald - To acclaim

e'lâme jorm kardan: verb
To indict

e'lâme khatar kardan: noun
alert

e'lâmiye: noun
statement - manifesto - manifest

e'lâmiye dâdan: verb
To manifesto

e'lân: noun
notice - poster - placard

e'lân kardan: verb
To proclaim - To announce - To advertise

e'mâl kardan: verb
To apply - To exert

e'mâle nofuz kardan: verb
To impose

e'mâle zur: noun
exertion

e'tebâr: noun
credite - prestige - authority - authenticity - reputation - esteem

e'tebâr dâdan: verb
To authenticate

e'tebârnâme: noun
credential

e'tedâl: noun
sobriety - mean

e'teghâd: noun
belief - faith - trust

e'teghâd dâshtan: verb
To believe

e'telâf: verb
To pool

e'telâfi: noun
federal

e'temâd: noun
trust - belief - reliance - confidence

e'temâd benafs: noun
aplomb

e'temâd dâshtan: verb
To trust

e'temâd kardan: verb
To rely

e'tenâ: noun
heed

e'terâf: noun
avowal - admission - profession

e'terâf kardan: verb
To confess

e'terâz: noun
protest - defiance - objection

e'terâz kardan: verb
To protest - To object

e'tesâb: noun
strike

e'tesâb kardan: verb
To strike

e'tesâb kardan: noun
turnout

e'tiyâd: noun
addiction - addict

e'tâ: noun
grant - endowment

e'tâ kardan: verb
To grant - To admit - To confer

e'tâ': noun
conferment - concession

e'zâm kardan: verb
To detach

e'âneh: noun
contribution - bounty - benefit - handout - subvention

e'âneh dâdan: verb
To contribute

ebdâ'e: noun
innovation

ebdâ'e kardan: verb
To invent

ebgha: noun
retention

ebghâ kardan: verb
To maintain

ebhâm: noun
ambiguity - haze - obscurity - fog

eblagh: noun
prophecy

eblagh kardan: verb
To impart

eblaghe rasmi: noun
communique

eblis: noun
serpent

eblâghe rasmi: noun
bulletin

ebrat: noun
lesson - example - edification

ebrâm: noun
importance - persistence

ebrâz: noun
proposal - expression

ebrâz dâshtan: verb
To evince

ebrâze shâdi: noun
merriment

ebtedâ: noun
outset - start

ebtedâyi: adjective
primary - preliminary - initial - elementary - rudimentary

ebtekâr: noun
innovation

ebtezâl: noun
truism - triviality - platitude

ebtâl: noun
disproof - nullification - revoke - rescission

ebâ: noun
refusal

ebâdat: noun
worship

ebâdat kardan: verb
To worship

ebârat: noun
term - quotation - word - phrase

ebârat budan az: verb
To consist

ed'e: noun
quantity

ede'aye puch: noun
jactitation

ede'â: noun
purporst - claim - plea

ede'â: verb
To assert - To acclaim - To contend - To claim

ede'â: noun
recession - rebound

ede'â'e heisiyat kardan: verb
To rehabilitate

edghâm: noun
merger - ellipse

edghâm kardan: verb
To merge

edrâk: noun
realization - cognition - perception - understanding

edrâki: noun
conceptual

edrâr: noun
urine

edrâr kardan: verb
To stool - To urinate

edâlat: noun
justice

edâme: noun
continuation

edâme yâftan: verb
To resume

edâre: noun
office - bureau

edâre gomrok: noun
customhouse

edâre kardan: verb
To execute - To direct - To run - To manage

edâre konande: noun
director

edâri: noun
administrative - ministerial

edâvat: noun
hatred - enmity

efat: noun
purity - honor - virtue - modesty

eflij: adjective
paralytic

efrât: noun
superfluity - extravagance - excess - intemperance

efrât kardan: verb
To wanton - To lavish

efrâti: adjective
extrimist - intemperate

efshâ: noun
disclosure

efshâ: noun
exposure - disclosure - revelation

efte'tâh: noun
inauguration

efte'tâh kardan: verb
To inaugurate

eftekhâr: noun
attribute - honor

eftekhâr âmiz: adjective
honorific

efterâ: noun
defamation - obloquy - libel

efterâ zadan: verb
To calumniate - To blemish - To libel

efterâgh: noun
segregation

eftezâh: noun
debacle - ignominy - infamy - scandal

eftâr: noun
breakfast

efâde: noun
snobbery - pride

efâze kardan: verb
To impart

eghbâl: noun
fortuity - grace - luck

eghdâm: noun
action - ploy

eghfâl: noun
delusion - deception - allusion

eghfâl kardan: verb
To blind - To beguile - To entrap - To delude
- To deceive

eghlim: noun
continent - hemisphere

eghlimi: adjective
continental

eghlimshenâsi: noun
climatology

eghmâ: noun
comatose

eghmâz: noun
tolerance - connivance

eghmâz kardan: verb
To wink - To condone

eghnâ'e shodan: verb
To satiate

eghrâgh: noun
exaggeration - extravaganza

eghrâgh goftan: verb
To extol

eghrâgh âmiz: adjective
exaggerated - sententious

eghrâr: noun
profession

eghrâr kardan: verb
To admit - To confess

eghtebâs: noun
adoption - derivation - quotation

eghtebâs kardan: verb
To extract - To borrow - To adopt

eghtedâr: noun
power

eghteshâsh: noun
anarchy - turbulence

eghteshâsh kardan: verb
To tumult

eghtesâd: noun
economy

eghtesâdi: adjective
economic

eghtezâ: noun
pertinence - felicity - expediency

eghvâ: noun
seducement - temptation

eghvâ kardan: verb
To entice - To lure - To tempt - To seduce

eghvâ konande: adjective
tempter - hustler

eghâmat dâshtan: verb
To reside

eghâmat gozidan: verb
To dwell

eghâmat kardan: verb
To remain - To stay

eghâmatgâ: noun
home

eghâmatgâh: noun
residency - residence

eghâme kardan: verb
To pose - To allege - To advance

egzemâ: noun
eczema

ehdâ: noun
grant - present

ehdâ kardan: verb
To present - To donate

ehdâs: noun
construction

ehdâs kardan: verb
To generate - To build

ehmâl: noun
negligence - neglect - dodge

ehrâze mâlekiyat: noun
qualifying property

ehsân: noun
benefit - beneficence

ehsân kardan: verb
To benefit

ehsâs: noun
sense - sensation

ehsâs kardan: verb
To sense - To feel

ehsâse ghorbat: noun
nostalgia

ehsâsât: noun
emotion - affect - heartbeat

ehsâsâti: adjective
passionate

ehtekâr: noun
hoarding - hoard

ehtekâr kardan: verb
To speculate - To engross - To hoard

ehtemâl: noun
probability - possibility - likelihoood -
expectancy

ehtemâlan: adverb
maybe - presumably

ehtemâle voghu'e: noun
odds

ehtemâli: noun
probable - likely - eventual

ehtemâlât: noun
odds - possibilities

ehterâgh: noun
combustion - ignition

ehterâgh pazir: adjective
combustible

ehterâm: noun
curtsy - respect - regard

ehterâm: noun
deference

ehterâm gozâshtan: verb
To reverence - To defer

ehterâme nezami: noun
salute

ehtezâz: noun
swing - sway - vibration

ehtiyâj: noun
requirement - need - necessity - lack

ehtiyât: noun
precaution - caution

ehtiyât kardan: verb
To precaution

ehyâ: noun
revival

ehyâ shodan: verb
To revive

ehzâr: noun
citation

ehzâr kardan: verb
To evoke - To repeal - To remand - To call

ehzâre ghânuni kardan: verb
To summon

ehzâriye: noun
subpoena

ehâle: noun
reduction

ehânat: noun
disdain - contempt - offense - insolence

ehânat kardan: verb
To scorn

ehânat âmiz: adjective
contemptuous

ehâte: noun
siege - surround - environment

ehâte kardan: verb
To sphere - To circuit - To circle

ehâte shodan: verb
To surround

ei: preposition
hey

eib: noun
taint - defect - gall

eibju: adjective
cynical - nag

eibjuyi: noun
knock - denunciation - criticism

eibjuyi kardan: verb
To pick - To henpeck - To nag

eibjuyâne: adverb
censorious

eid: noun
tide

eide fetr: noun
passover

eide pâk: noun
easter

eikâsh: preposition
would - may

ein: noun
exact - self

einak: noun
glass - specs

einaksâzi: noun
optometry

einan: adverb
exactly

eini budan: verb
To objectivity

einiyat: noun
identity

eish: noun
luxury - mirth - pleasure

ejbâr: noun
constraint - compulsion - coercion

ejbâran: adverb
perforce

ejbâri: noun
compulsory - compulsive - mandatory

ejmâ'e: noun
consensus

ejmâl: noun
synopsis - conspectus

ejmâlan: adverb
unanimous

ejmâli: adjective
glancing - brief

ejrâ: noun
performance - implementation -
accomplishment

ejrâ kardan: verb
To exert - To execute - To enforce - To
perform

ejrâye namâyesh: noun
histrionics

ejrâyee: noun
executive

ejtemâ': noun
society

ejtemâ'I: noun
social - civic

ejtemâ'e kardan: verb
To congregate

ejtemâ'e mardom: noun
parade

ejtenâb: noun
shirk

ejtenâb kardan: verb
To avoid - To eschew

ejtenâbpazir: noun
inevitable - unavoidable

ejâbat: noun
compliance

ejâbat kardan: verb
To comply

ejâre: noun
hire - lease - rent

ejâre: noun
authority - permit - permission

ejâre dâdan: verb
To lease - To rent

ejâre kardan: verb
To rent - To tenant

ejâre'I: noun
rental

ejâredâr: noun
tenant - lessee

ejârename: noun
lease - rental

ejâreneshin: noun
lessee

ejâze: noun
leave

ejâzename: noun
charter

ejâzeye obur: noun
passage

ekbiri: adjective
crumby - crummy - lousy

ekhrâj: noun
ouster - expultion - eviction - ejection

ekhrâj kardan: verb
To fire - To oust

ekhrâj shodan: verb
To fire - To out

ekhtefâ: noun
secrecy

ekhtefâ': noun
hideout

ekhtelâf: noun
inequality - disparity - discord - difference

ekhtelâf dâshtan: verb
To differ

ekhtelâf peidâ kardan: verb
To diverge

ekhtelâfe aghide: noun
dissension

ekhtelâl: noun
disorder - tribulation

ekhtelâle ravâani: noun
neurosis

ekhtelâs: noun
defalcation - graft

ekhtelâs kardan: verb
To misappropriate - To embezzle - To defalcate

ekhtelât: noun
brew - mixture - mix

ekhtenâgh: noun
strangulation - choke - asphyxia

ekhterâ'e: noun
invention

ekhterâ'e kardan: verb
To invent

ekhtesâr: noun
brief

ekhtesâr: noun
reduction

ekhtesâri: adjective
summary

ekhtesâs: noun
specialty

ekhtesâs dâdan: verb
To allocate - To devote - To dedicate

ekhtesâsi: adjective
private

ekhtiyâr: noun
authority

ekhtiyâri: adjective
voluntary

ekhtâr: noun
alarm - notification - notice - signal

ekhtâr kardan: verb
To notify - To announce

ekrâh: noun
grudge - reluctance - duress

eksir: noun
panacea

ekteshâf: noun
discovery - detection

ekteshâf kardan: verb
To prospect - To explore

ektesâb: noun
inception

ektesâbi: adjective
acquisitive

elat: noun
trill - reason - cause - disease - motive

elekteriki: noun
electric

elekterod: noun
electrode

elekteron: noun
electron

elghâ: noun
inspiration - infusion

elghâ kardan: verb
To inspire - To infuse - To induct

elghâ'e: noun
revoke - revocation

elghâ'e kardan: verb
To quash

elgâgh kardan: verb
To stick

elhâd: noun
heresy - paganism - atheism

elhâgh: noun
juncture - joinder - adhesion - incorporation
- insertion

elhâgh kardan: verb
To insert - To append

elhâghi: adjective
extension - adjunct

elhâm: noun
sprite - revelation - apocalypse - inspiration

elhâm: noun
enthusiasm

elhâm bakhshidan: verb
To inspire

eliye: noun
against

elm: noun
science - knowledge

elme gheib: noun
prescience

elme nojum: noun
astronomy

elmi: adjective
scientific

elsâgh: noun
stick - adhesion - adherence

eltefât: noun
gratuity

eltehâb: noun
tumult - boil

eltemâs: noun
solicitation - entreaty - appeal

eltemâs kardan: verb
To beseech - To obtest - To supplicate

eltezâm: noun
obligation - requirement

eltezâmi: adjective
implicit

eltiyâm: noun
redress

eltiyâm dâdan: verb
To solder - To heal

elzâm: noun
tie - committal - commitment

elzâm âvar: adjective
obligatory - imperative

elzâmi: adjective
obligatory

elâhe: noun
goddess

elâhi: adjective
divine - celestial

elâhiyât: noun
theology - divinity

emdâd: noun
help

emdâdi: adjective
auxiliary

emkân: noun
possibility

emkân dâshtan: verb
To may

emkân nâpazir: adjective
impossible

emkân pazir: adjective
conceivable - possible

emlâ: noun
orthography

emlâ': noun
spelling - dictation

emlâyi: adjective
orthographic

emperâtur: noun
kaiser - emperor

emperâturi: adjective
imperial - emperor

emruz: noun
today

emruze: adverb
nowadays

emruzi: adjective
modern

emshab: adverb
tonight

emtedâd: noun
run - tension

emtedâd dâdan: verb
To stretch - To protract - To prolong

emtedâd yâftan: verb
To prolong

emtehân: noun
quiz - test

emtehân kardan: verb
To test - To examine

emtehân nashode: adjective
untried

emtehâni: adjective
tentative

emtenâ'e: noun
refusal

emtenâ'e varzidan: verb
To balk

emtiyâz: noun
privilege - precedence - upperhand

emtiyâz dâdan: verb
To handicap

emtiyâzi: adjective
patent - preferential

emzâ: noun
endorsement

emzâ kardan: verb
To signature - To sign

emzâ': noun
signature - sign

emzâ' kardan: verb
To endorse - To underwrite - To sign

emâmat: noun
pontificate

emârat: noun
edifice - construction - hall

en'eghâd: noun
coalescence - ratification

en'ekâs: noun
repercussion - reaction

en'ekâs: noun
reflection

en'ekâse sedâ: noun
echo

en'etâf: noun
plasticity

en'etâfpazir: adjective
flexible

enbesât: noun
pleasure - expansion

enbesâti: adjective
expansion

enerzhi: noun
energy

enfe'âl: noun
passivity

enfejâr: noun
explosion - bust - burst - blast

enfejâri: adjective
explosive

enferâdi: adjective
individual

enfesâl: noun
discharge - separate

enfeâli: adjective
passive

engelestân: noun
England

engelis: noun
Britain

engelisi: adjective
English - Briton - British

enghebâz: noun
retraction - shrinkage - traction

enghelâb: noun
revolution

enghelâb: noun
solstice

enghelâbi: adjective
revolutionary

engherâz: noun
extinct

enghetâ'e: noun
slack - cessation - curtailment

enghiyâd: noun
sufferance - submission - subjugation

engâre: adjective
tenet - sketch - idea

engâshtan: verb
To suppose - To imagine - To assume

enhedâm: noun
destruction - demolition - subversion

enhelâl: noun
breakup

enhenây: noun
deflexion - curvature

enherâf: noun
digression - deviance - detour - departure

enhesâr: noun
monopoly

enhesâri: adjective
exclusive

enhetât: noun
degeneration - decline - downhill - downfall

enjil: noun
gospel

enkâr: noun
denial

enkâr kardan: verb
To repudiate - To renounce - To deny - To dispute - To disclaim

enkârnâpazir: adjective
irrefutable - undeniable

enkârpazir: adjective
retractable

ensedâd: noun
obstruction - blockade - block

ensejâm: noun
solidarity

enserâf: noun
lapse

enshe'âb: noun
junction - tributary - divergence - ramification

enshe'âb yâftan: verb
To diverge

enshâ: noun
composition - essay - article

ensâf: noun
justice - equanimity

ensân: noun
human - man

ensângarâyi: adjective
humanism

ensâni: adjective
human

entebâgh: noun
coincidence - conformity

entebâghi: adjective
adaptive

enteghâd: noun
censure - gaff - criticism

enteghâd kardan: verb
To blame - To review - To criticize

enteghâdi: adjective
critical

enteghâdnâpazir: adjective
unexceptionable

enteghâl: noun
transmission

enteghâl dâdan: verb
To shift - To transmit - To remise

enteghâle bargh: noun
convection

enteghâle tadriji: noun
gradation

enteghâli: adjective
transitive - transfer

enteghâm: noun
revenge - reprisal - vengeance

enteghâm gereftan: verb
To wreak

enteghâmju: adjective
avenger - vengeful

entehâ: noun
terminal - end - extremity

entehâr: noun
suicide

entehâyi: adjective
terminal

entekhâb: noun
pickup - choice - election - draft

entekhâb kardan: verb
To select - To elect - To choose

entekhâbi: adjective
selective - elective

enteshâr: noun
publish - effluence - report - issuance

enteshâr: noun
diffusion - publish

enteshâr dâdan: verb
To propagate - To promulgate - To publish

entesâb: noun
appointment

entesâbi: adjective
dative - appointed

entezâ'l: adjective
abstract

entezâ'e: noun
secession

entezâr: noun
prospect

entezâr dâshtan: verb
To hope - To expect

entezâr keshidan: verb
To wait

enzebât: noun
discipline

enzejâr: noun
antipathy - abhorrence - phobia - disgust

enzevâ: noun
seclusion - retreat

enâd: noun
malice - animus

er'âb kardan: verb
To menace

erfâgh: noun
leniency

erfân: noun
theosophy - mysticism

erjâ'e kardan: verb
To assign

ers: noun
legacy - inheritance - heritage

ers bordan: verb
To inheriting

ersiye: noun
heritage

ersâl: noun
transmittal - transmission - dispatch

ersâl dâshtan: verb
To send

ersâl kardan: verb
To consign

erte'âsh: noun
shake - vibration

ertebât: noun
correlation - relevance - relation - liaison

ertedâd: noun
heterodoxy - heresy

ertefâ'e: noun
height

ertefâât: noun
height

erteghâ: noun
upgrade - raise

erteghâ dâdan: verb
To extol

ertejâ'e: noun
stretch - restitution

ertekâb: noun
perpetration - committal - commitment

erzâ: noun
satisfaction

erzâ kardan: verb
To satisfy

erâ'e: noun
show - presentation - exposure

erâ'e dâdan: verb
To exhibit - To present - To submit

erâde: noun
will - volition

erâde kardan: verb
To will

erâdi: adjective
voluntary

esbât: noun
proof

esbât kardan: verb
To prove - To affirm

esfanj: noun
sponge

esfanji: adjective
spongy

eshbâ' shodan: verb
To satiate

eshbâ' shode: adjective
impregnant - sodden

eshbâ'e: noun
saturation - glut

eshgh: noun
love

eshghâl: noun
occupation - occupancy - swill

eshghâl konande: noun
holder - occupier - occupant

eshkâl: noun
difficulty - drawback - disadvantage - impediment

eshte'âl: noun
ignition - combustion

eshtebâh: noun
mistake - wrong - error

eshteghâl: noun
employment - engagement

eshtehâ: noun
appetite

eshtehâr: noun
popularization - repute - reputation - renown

eshterâk: noun
subscription - unity

eshterâke manâfe': noun
union

eshterâke masâ'i: noun
synergy

eshterâke vajh: noun
parallelism

eshterâki: adjective
communal - collective

eshtiyâgh: noun
thirst - enthusiasm - avidity - appetite

eshtiyâgh dâshtan: verb
To hunger - To hanker - To aspire - To crave
- To yearn - To thirst

eshve: noun
coquetry

eshvegar: adjective
coquettish - coquette

eshvegari: noun
coquette

eshâ'e dâdan: verb
To broadcast

eshâl: noun
squirt

eshâl: noun
diarrhea

eshâre: noun
hint - mention - beckon - gesture

eshâreye mokhtasar: noun
cheep

eshâreye zemni kardan: verb
To connote

eskele: noun
pier - quay - wharf - waterfront

eskelet: noun
skeleton - frame

eskenâs: noun
money

eskeyt bâz: adjective
skater

eski: noun
ski

eskimu: noun
eskimo

eskort: noun
escort

eskâtlandi: adjective
scottish - scotchman

eslâh: noun
amendment - adjustment - revision - repair
- correction

eslâh kardan: verb
To modify - To ameliorate - To revise - To
remedy

eslâh konande: noun
corrector - corrective

eslâh nemudan: verb
To revise

eslâh nâpazir: adjective
incorrigible

eslâh shodan: verb
To repent - To reclaim

eslâh talab: adjective
reformer

eslâhe nezhâd kardan: verb
To grade

eslâhât: noun
reformation - reform

eslâm: noun
Islam

eslâmi: adjective
Islamic

esm: noun
noun - name - title

esme eshâre: noun
demonstrative

esme masdar: noun
gerund

esme mosta'âr: noun
pseudonym

esme obur: noun
password

esme ramz: noun
shibboleth

esme shab: noun
password - watchword

esmi: adjective
asthmatic - nominal - onomastic

espâniyâ: noun
spain

esrâ'il: noun
israel

esrâf: noun
profusion - squander - improvidence - prodigality

esrâf kardan: verb
To dissipate - To lavish

esrâr: noun
insistence - perseverance

esrâr: noun
insistence

esrâr kardan: verb
To persist

esrâr kardan: verb
To insist - To importune

esrâr varzidan: verb
To insist

establ: noun
stable

estakhr: noun
pool - lake

estakhre shena: noun
natatorium

este'dâd: noun
capacity - genius - brilliance - aptness - aptitude

este'dâd: noun
talent

este'dâde zâti: noun
natural

este'fâ: noun
breakaway - demission

este'fâ dâdan: verb
To resign

este'lâm: noun
inquiry

este'mâl: noun
use - usage

este'mâl kardan: verb
To apply - To handle

este'mâr: noun
colonialism

este'mârtalab: adjective
imperialistic

este'âre: noun
simile - metaphor - conceit

estebdâd: noun
autarchy

estebdâdi: adjective
reactionary - autocratic - absolute

ested'â: noun
plea - boon - entreaty

ested'â kardan: verb
To supplicate - To entreat

estedlâl: noun
logic - reasoning - ratiocination

estedlâl kardan: verb
To reason - To argue

estedlâl konande: noun
proponent

estedlâli: adjective
logical - discursive

estefhâm: noun
question

estefrâgh: noun
puke

estefrâgh kardan: verb
To vomit

estefsâr: noun
query

estefâ: noun
resignation

estefâ dâdan: verb
To abdicate

estefâde: noun
benefit - utilization - gain

esteghfâr: noun
retraction

esteghlâl: noun
independence - freedom

esteghnâ: noun
disdain

esteghrâ'i: adjective
deductive

esteghrâr: noun
pitch

esteghâmat: noun
perseverance

estehghâgh: noun
merit - deserve

estehghâgh dâshtan: verb
To deserve - To merit

estehkâm: noun
backbone - rigidity - consistency

estehkâmât: noun
fortifications

estehlâk: noun
depreciation

estehmâm: noun
bath

estehmâm kardan: verb
To bathe

estehzâ'e: noun
ridicule

estehâle: noun
permutation

estehâle kardan: verb
To transformation

estehâle yâftan: verb
To wax

estekhdâm: noun
recruitment - employment

estekhdâm kardan: verb
To employ

estekhlâs: noun
release

estekhrâj: noun
derivation

estekhrâj kardan: verb
To extract - To exploit

estekâk: noun
friction - attrition

estekâk dâshtan: verb
To overlap

estekâk peydâ kardan: verb
To rub

estekâki: adjective
spirant

estekân: noun
glass

estelâh: noun
idiom - term

estelâhe âmiyâneh: noun
slang

estelâhi: adjective
colloquial - idiomatic

estemhâl: noun
moratorium

estemrâr: noun
continuity

estemâ'e: noun
listen - audition

estenbât: noun
deduction - presumption

estenbât kardan: verb
To infer - To induct - To deduce

estenbât kardan: verb
To gather

estenshâgh: noun
inspiration - inhalation

estenshâgh kardan: verb
To inhale - To breathe - To aspire

estentâgh: noun
crossquestion

estentâj: noun
deduction - inference

estentâj kardan: verb
To infer - To induce - To derive - To conclude

estentâji: adjective
inductive

esterdâd: noun
refund - recovery - reclamation

esterâghe sam'e kardan: verb
To overhear

esterâhat: noun
rest - relaxation

esterâhatgâh: noun
retire - restroom

esterâtezhi: noun
strategy

esteshhâd: noun
affidavit

esteshmâm: noun
smell

esteshmâm kardan: verb
To inhale

estesmâr kardan: verb
To exploit

estesnâ'i: adjective
special - exceptional

estetâ'at: noun
ability

estetâat dâshtan: verb
To afford

estetâr: noun
camouflage

estizâh: noun
impeachment

estândârd: noun
standard

esâbat: noun
strike - onset - impact - access

esâlat: noun
gentry - originality - ism

esâlate khânevâdegi: noun
nobility

esâns: noun
essence

esârat: noun
captivity - enslavement

etefâgh: noun
accidence - occurrence - event

etefâgh oftâdan: verb
To occur

etefâghan: adverb
perhaps - peradventure

etefâghi: noun
accidental - chromatic - chancy - chance

etehadiyeye senfi: noun
syndicate

etehâd: noun
union - confederacy

etehâde movaghati: noun
coalition

etehâdiye: noun
union - confederacy

etehâdiyeye kardanârgari: noun
laborunion

etehâm: noun
denunciation - charge

etekhâz: noun
assumption - adoption

etekhâz kardan: verb
To pursue - To adopt

etekâ: noun
reliance

etelâ'e: noun
notification - notice - advice

etelâ'e dâdan: verb
To inform

etelâ'e nâme: noun
prospectus

etelâ'ât: noun
data - witting - information

eter: noun
ether

etesâ': noun
dilation - stretch

etesâ' dâdan: verb
To dilate

etesâl: noun
junction - linkage - connection

etesâl dâdan: verb
To bridge

etfâ'e: noun
quench

etiket: noun
label

etiket chasbândan be: verb
To tag

etil: noun
ethyl

etlâf: noun
destruction - wreckage - waste - wastage

etlâfe vaght: noun
dawdle

etminân: noun
confidence - certainty - cretain - assurance - trust

etminân bakhsh: adjective
safe - trusty

etminân dâdan: verb
To vouch - To assure

etmâm: noun
accomplishment - completion

etmâme hojat: noun
ultimatum

etâ'at: noun
submission - obedience

etâ'at kardan: verb
To obey

eybju: adjective
censorious - captious

eynak: noun
glasses

eynakforushi: noun
optometry

eynaksâz: adjective
optometrist - optician - oculist

ez hâr: noun
testimony - proposal - statement - remark

ez hâr dâshtan: verb
To state - To remark - To express

ez hâre eshgh: noun
assault - courtship - court

ez hâre nazar: noun
comment

ezat: noun
honor

ezdehâm: noun
crowd - throng

ezdehâm kardan: verb
To throng - To crowd - To overcrowd

ezdevâj: noun
marriage

ezdiyâd: noun
plethora

ezhdehâ: noun
dragon

ezhâre ta'asof: noun
condolence

ezhârnâme: noun
declaration

ezn: noun
permission - leave

ezterâb: noun
worry - anxiety

ezterâr: noun
constrait - coercion

ezterâri: adjective
emergency

ezâfe bahâ: noun
surcharge

ezâfe bâr: noun
overload

ezâfe hoghugh: noun
raise

ezâfe kardan: verb
To add - To aggravate

ezâfe kâr: noun
overtime

ezâfe nemudan: verb
To add

ezâfeh: noun
excess - access - increase - surplus

ezâfi: adjective
supplementary - supernumerary - extra -
additional

f

fa'âl: adjective
active - pragmatic - energetic

fa'âl shodan: verb
To activation

fa'âl sâzi: noun
activation

fa'âliyat: noun
activity

fadiye: noun
expense - ransom

fadiye dâdan: verb
To ransom

fadâ kardan: verb
To immolate - To devote

fadâkâri: noun
sacrifice

fadâkâri kardan: verb
To sacrifice

fadâyi: adjective
zealous - devotee - immolate - martyr

faghare: noun
episode - item

faghat: noun
only - just

faghih: noun
jurisconsult

faghir: adjective
poor - penurious

faghr: noun
depauperation - poverty

faghân: noun
shout - whine

fahm: noun
understanding - intellect - mind - grasp

fahmidan: verb
To understand - To grasp - To realize - To comprehend

fahmidan: verb
To understand

fahmidani: adjective
intelligible

fahmide: adjective
understanding

fahmândan: verb
To show - To purporst - To clear - To represent

fahâsh: adjective
blackguardly - vilifier - reviler

fahâshi: noun
scurrility

faji': adjective
tragic - calamitous - disastrous

faji': adjective
heinous

fajr: noun
dawn - aurora

fak: noun
chaw - jaw

fak: noun
jaw

fakhr: noun
glory - pride

fakur: adjective
thoughtful - thinker

fakur: adjective
ruminant

falaj: noun
paralysis - palsy

falaj kardan: verb
To paralyze - To mutilate

falaj shodan: verb
To freeze

falak: noun
sky - orbit

fals: noun
scale

falsafi: noun
philosophic

falâhat: noun
husbandry

falât: noun
plateau

fan: noun
art

fan: noun
technique - art

fanar: noun
spring - coil

fanari: adjective
elastic - bouncy - springy

fandak: noun
lighter

fandogh: noun
hazelnut

fani: adjective
technical

fanâ: noun
doom

fanâ kardan: verb
To ruin

fanâ nâpazir: adjective
undying - indestructible - immortal - eternal

fanâpazir: adjective
mortal

far': noun
sub - branch - outgrwth - offshoot

far'i: adjective
sideway - secondary - inferior

farahbakhsh: adjective
pleasurable

farahnâk: adjective
jocund

faraj: noun
pudendum

farangi: noun
european

farbe: adjective
fat - obese

fard: noun
odd - unit - unique - individual - singular - single

fardgarâ: adjective
individualist

fardi: adjective
subjective

fardiyat: noun
individuality

fardâ: noun
tomorrow

fargasht: noun
evolution

fargh: noun
vertex - inequality - odds - difference

fargh dâshtan: verb
To vary - To differ

farghe sar: noun
skull - scalp - crown - peak

farhang: noun
lexicon - dictionary - culture

farhangi: noun
cultural

farhikhtan: verb
To educate

farib: noun
defraud - deception - deceit - fiction - cheat

farib dâdan: verb
To cheat - To dissimulate - To delude - To deceive

farib khordan: verb
To beguile

faribande: adjective
deceptive - glamorous - captious

faribandegi: noun
charm - grace - glamor - glamour

faribkhordegi: noun
deception

faribkâr: adjective
japer - tortuous

faribkâri: noun
japery

faribâ: adjective
deceptive

fariftan: verb
To entice - To enchant - To decoy - To deceive

farjâm: noun
end

farkhonde: adjective
jubilant - happy - beatific - auspicious

farmudan: verb
To bid

farmân: noun
command - order

farmân dâdan: verb
To order - To command

farmânbordâr: adjective
subordinate - obedient

farmânbordâri: noun
obedience - submission

farmânbordâri kardan: verb
To obey

farmânde: noun
leader - commander - chief - governor

farmândegi: noun
command

farmândegi kardan: verb
To officer

farmândâr: noun
governor

farmânravâ: noun
lord - ruler

farmânravâyi: noun
rule

farmâyesh: noun
order - command

farokh: adjective
auspicious

farsh: noun
carpet

farsh kardan: verb
To spread - To pave - To rug

farsudan: verb
To fatigue - To rub off

farsude: adjective
effete - rusty - old - timeworn

farsude shodan: verb
To outwear - To fray

farsudegi: noun
exhaustion

farsâyesh: noun
scuff - erosion

faryâd: noun
shriek - shout

faryâd zadan: verb
To yell - To shout - To bawl - To howl

farz: noun
supposition - assumption - presumption

farz kardan: verb
To suppose - To assume - To imagine

farz nemudan: verb
To postulate - To imagine

farzandkhânde: adjective
stepson - stepchild

farzi: adjective
supposition - obligatory - hypothetical

farziye: noun
hypothesis

farzâne: adjective
wise

farzânegi: noun
wisdom

farâ khândan: verb
To evoke - To recall - To muster - To summon

farâ khâstan: verb
To summon

farâbanafsh: adjective
ultraviolet

farâgard: noun
process

farâghermez: noun
ultrared

farâgir: adjective
pervasive

farâham: noun
whorl - available

farâham kardan: verb
To prepare - To obtain

farâham âmadan: verb
To provide

farâham âvardan: verb
To assemble

farâkh: adjective
spacious - ample - wide

farâkhor: noun
worthy - proportionate - suitable

farâkhâni: noun
summon

farâmush kardan: verb
To forget

farâmushi: noun
amnesia - oblivion

farâmushkâr: adjective
forgetful

farâmushkâri: noun
negligence

farâr: noun
scape - evasive - escape

farâr: noun
volatile

farâr kardan: verb
To scape - To abscond - To escape

farâravi: noun
transgression - ultraism

farâri: adjective
runaway - refugee - escapee

farâru: noun
transgressor

farâsat: noun
sagacity - intuition - intelligence - insight -
perspicacity

farâsh: noun
lackey

farâvar: noun
productive - producer

farâvarde: noun
supply - production - product

farâvari: noun
production

farâvân: adjective
ample - copious - rampant - plenty - affluent

farâvân: adjective
abundant - plenty

farâvân budan: verb
To teem - To exuberate

farâvâni: adjective
superabundance - profusion - affluence -
abundance - plenty

farâyand: noun
process

farâz: noun
phrase - loft - ascent - accolade

fasih: adjective
eloquent - fluent - communicative

faskh: noun
revoke - revocation - repeal - recision -
waiver

faskh: noun
rescission

faskh kardan: verb
To terminate - To cancel - To dissolve - To
disannul

fasl: noun
term - season - article

fasl: noun
chapter - season

fasle bahâr: noun
springtime - springtide

fasli: adjective
seasonal

fatgh: noun
hernia

fath: noun
triumph - win - victory

fath kardan: verb
To conquer - To reduce

fatvâ: noun
sentence - judgment - verdict

fatvâ dâdan: verb
To arbitrate - To adjudicate - To judge

favarân: noun
eruption - outburst - spout

favarân kardan: verb
To spurt - To spout - To erupt - To geyser

favarân konande: adjective
effusive

favâre: noun
fountain - springhead

fazilat: noun
prepayment - accomplishment - excellence

fazle: noun
excrement

fazlo dânesh: noun
erudition

fazâ: noun
space - place - area - room - region

fazânavard: noun
astronaut - spaceman

fazâpeimâ: noun
spacecraft

fazâyi: noun
spatial

fe'l: noun
act

fe'l: noun
verb

fe'lan: adverb
now

fe'le lâzem: noun
intransitive

fe'li: adjective
verbal - present

fedelâlizm: noun
federalism

federâl: noun
federal

fegh'h: noun
jurisprudence

feghhi: adjective
juridical - juratory

fehrest: noun
list

fehrest kardan: verb
To tabulate - To list

feisale dâdan: verb
To evict

feiz: noun
grace

fekr: noun
thought - opinion - mind - idea

fekr kardan: verb
To think

fekre bekr: noun
mastermind

felez: noun
metal

felezkâri: noun
metallurgy

felfel: noun
pepper

felfel pâshidan: verb
To pepper

felfeli: adjective
pepper

felvâghe: noun
indeed

felâkat: noun
adversity - poverty

felân: noun
whatnot

felâsk: noun
thermos

fenjân: noun
calix - cupule

fenjân: noun
cup

fer: noun
splendor - curl

fer dâdan: verb
To curl

fer zadan: verb
To frizz - To spin

fer'ôn: noun
pharaoh

ferdôs: noun
paradise

ferekâns: noun
frequency

fereshte: noun
angel - intelligence

ferestande: adjective
transmitter - sender

ferestâdan: verb
To dispatch - To ship - To send

ferestâde: adjective
messenger - apostle - emissary

ferestâde: adjective
envoy

ferfere: noun
gig - whirligig - spin

ferferi: adjective
curly - kinky

ferghe: noun
sect - heresy

ferz: adjective
swift - spry - agile - quick - nimble

ferâghat: noun
opportunity - relief - leisure

ferâmâsiyon: noun
mason

fesgh: noun
debauchery

fesgho fojur: noun
vice

feshang: noun
cartridge

feshfeshe: noun
squib - rocket

feshordan: verb
To pressure - To crush - To squeeze - To tighten

feshorde: adjective
succinct - squeeze - massive

feshordegi: noun
jam

feshândan: verb
To erupt

feshâr: noun
pressure - press - constraint - stress - squeeze

feshâr dâdan: verb
To squeeze - To yerk - To hustle

feshâr âvardan: verb
To wrest - To press

feshâre khun: noun
hypertension

feshârsanj: noun
indicator

fesâd: noun
spoil - depravity - degeneration - decay - corruption

fetile: noun
wick - lint

fetne: noun
sedition - muitiny - insurrection

fetne'angiz: adjective
inflammatory

fetnejuyi: noun
sedition

fetrat: noun
interval - interregnum - recess

fetrat: noun
temperament - mould - mettle

fetri: adjective
natural - innate - ingrown - indigenous - inborn

fezâhat: noun
disgrace - scandalization

fibr: noun
fiber

filmbardâri kardan: verb
To shoot

filsuf: noun
philosopher

fimâbein: noun
interim

fin: noun
snivel

firuz: adjective
jubilant

fis: noun
vainglory

fish: noun
strap

fizik: noun
physics

fizikdân: noun
physicist

fiziki: noun
physical

fiziyolozhi: noun
physiology

foghdân: noun
loss - absence - lack

fohsh: noun
curse - cuss - darn - abusive

fohsh dâdan: verb
To insult - To cuss - To curse

fokâhi: noun
jocular - jocose - humorous

fokâhinevis: noun
humorist

folut: noun
pipe

folut zadan: verb
To pipe

fonun: noun
technology - tactics

forghân: noun
wheelbarrow

forje: noun
interval - respite - deadline

forje dâdan: verb
To respite

form: noun
form

formul: noun
frame

forsat: noun
opportunity - chance - vantage - leisure

foru bordan: verb
To swallow - To plunge - To aspire

foru kardan: verb
To embed - To inculcate - To implant

foru raftan: verb
To sink - To stick - To merge

foru raftan: verb
To dive

foru rikhtan: verb
To collapse - To crumble - To disintegrate -
To breakdown

forud âmadan: verb
To alight - To perch - To ground - To descend

forudgâh: noun
landingfield - airport - airfield

forugh: noun
shine - light - blaze

forugozâr: verb
To neglect

forugozâri: noun
silence - omission - neglect

foruhar: adjective
essence

forukesh: noun
refluence - ebb - deflation - letup

forukesh kardan: verb
To subside - To lower - To abate - To ebb

forukhtan: verb
To sell

forukhtani: noun
saleable - salable

forumândegi: noun
inability - intolerance

forumâye: adjective
currish - abject - vile

foruneshastan: verb
To abate - To sag - To slake - To subside

foruneshândan: verb
To tranquilize - To pacify - To appease - To relieve

forurafte: adjective
sunken

foruraftegi: adjective
dip - notch

forush: noun
sale

forushande: noun
vendor - dealer - salesman - seller

forushandegi: noun
solicitorship - salesmanship

forushgâh: noun
salesroom - store - shootinggallery

forutan: adjective
venal - meek - humble - courteous

forutani kardan: verb
To humble - To condescend

foruzân: adjective
luminous - ablaze

fosfordâr: adjective
phosphorous

fosfori: adjective
phosphorous - phosphoric

fosil: noun
fossil

fotokopi kardan: noun
photocopy

fotovat: noun
chivalry

fotur: noun
languor

fozul: adjective
voyeur - pry - blab - obtrusive

fozuli: noun
gallimaufry - impertinence - pry

fozuli kardan: verb
To rubberneck - To meddle - To presume

fozulât: noun
garbage

fozulât: noun
rejcet

fozuni: adjective
excess - extreme

fulâd: noun
steel

futbâl: noun
soccer

futo fan: noun
trick

fâ'egh: noun
paramount - prevalent

fâ'egh âmadan: verb
To surmount - To get

fâel: noun
doer - subject

fâeli: adjective
subjective - nominative

fâghed: adjective
without - toom

fâhesh: adjective
heavy - egregious - tremendous

fâheshe: noun
brothel - whorehouse - callhouse

fâheshe: noun
whore - wench - ribald

fâje'e: noun
tragedy - catastrophe - calamity

fâkher: adjective
fine - costly

fâktor: noun
invoice

fâl: noun
omen - auspices

fâlbin: noun
augur

fâlgir: noun
augur

fâmili: adjective
family

fâni: adjective
transitory - mortal - memnetary

fântezi: noun
extravaganza - phantasy

fânus: noun
louver - lantern - lamp

fâregh: noun
separator

fâreghotahsil: noun
gaduate - alumnus

fâreghotahsil shodan: verb
To gaduate

fârsi: noun
persian

fâsed: adjective
villainous - vicious - corrupt - sinister

fâsed kardan: verb
To spoil - To corrupt

fâsed shodan: verb
To spoil - To decay - To vitiate

fâsed shodan: verb
To disintegrate

fâsegh: adjective
goat - paramour - lover - lecher

fâsele: noun
distance - space

fâsele dâshtan: verb
To space

fâseledâr: adjective
distant

fâsh: adjective
overt

fâsh kardan: verb
To unfold - To disclose - To reveal

fâsh shodan: verb
To transpire - To out

fâteh: adjective
conqueror - winner - victorious - victor

fâteh shodan: verb
To win

fâtehe: noun
requiem

fâyede: noun
advantage - profit - fruit

fâyede bordan: verb
To gain - To benefit

fâyede resândan: verb
To profit - To benefit

fâzel: adjective
residue

fâzelâb: noun
sewerage - sewage

fâzelâb: noun
gutter

fôgh: noun
upon

fôghol'âde: noun
supernatural - extraordinary

fôgholzekr: noun
aforesaid

fôghâni: adjective
upside - uppish - upper - capital

fôran: adverb
immediately

fôri: adjective
immediate - urgent - sudden - spot -
spontaneous

fôriyat: noun
urgency - immediacy

fôt: noun
death - gust - puff - snuff

fôt kardan: verb
To die

g

gach: noun
stucco - plaster - chalk

gachbori: noun
tore

gachi: adjective
chalky

gahgâh: adverb
occasionally

gahvâre: noun
cradle

galangadan: noun
spanner

gale: noun
flock - herd

galu: noun
throat

galuband: noun
bangle

galudard: noun
sorethroat

galugâh: noun
gorge

galâviz shodan: verb
To wrestle - To grapple - To tackle

gamâne: noun
bore

gamâne zadan: verb
To sound

gand: adjective
stink - stench

gandidan: verb
To putrefy

gandidegi: noun
putrefaction

gandom: noun
wheat

gandâb: noun
bog - sewer - sewage

ganj: noun
treasury - treasure - hoard

ganje: noun
cupboard - closet

ganjine: noun
treasure

ganjur: adjective
treasurer

gap: noun
jaber - chat

gap zadan: verb
To gab - To chat

gar: preposition
if

garche: preposition
though

gard: noun
powder - flour

gardan: noun
neck

gardan nahâdan: verb
To submit

gardan zadan: verb
To decollate - To decapitate - To behead

gardanband: noun
collar - necklace

gardane: noun
neck - cervix - defile - stem

gardankesh: adjective
disobedient - refractory - unyielding

gardankeshi: noun
turbulence

gardankoloft: adjective
stodgy - dumpy - ruffian

garde: noun
pollen

gardesh: noun
jaunt - twirl - trip - operation - circuit - roll

gardesh: noun
turquoise

gardesh kardan: verb
To trip - To promenade - To revolve

gardeshgâh: noun
walkway - purlieu

gardeshi: adjective
rotatory - ambulatory

gardgiri: noun
whisk

gardgiri kardan: verb
To dust

gardidan: verb
To swirl - To revolve - To roam

gardokhâk: noun
dust

gardokhâki: noun
dusty

gardun: noun
sphere - heaven

gardune: noun
pass

gardânande: adjective
operator

gardândan: verb
To wheel - To manage - To turquoise

gardândan: verb
To turn - To manage - To direct

gardânidan: verb
To wield

garibân: noun
collar

garm: noun
hot - warm - ebullient - thermal

garm kardan: verb
To heat - To braise - To anneal - To warm

garm konande: adjective
warmer

garm shodan: verb
To thaw - To warm

garmak: noun
cantaloupe

garmi: noun
ardor - mettle - heat - warmth - glow

garmkhâne: noun
stove - greenhouse

garmo narm: adjective
snug - cozy

garmsir: adjective
tropic

garmsiri: noun
tropic

garmâ: noun
heat - therm

garmâbe: noun
bathroom - bath

garmâsanj: noun
thermometer

garmâyi: noun
thermal

garmâzadegi: noun
heatstroke

gas: adjective
astringent - acrid

gasht: noun
tour - veer

gasht zadan: verb
To cruise - To patrol

gashtan: verb
To search - To trundle - To troll

gashti: noun
patrolman - patrol

gashtâvari: noun
torque

gavazn: noun
stag

gazand: noun
harm - detriment

gazande: adjective
damage - piquant

gazandegi: noun
bite

gazesh: noun
bite

gazidan: verb
To select - To sting - To bite - To choose

gazne: noun
nettle

gazâf: noun
stupendous - extortionary - costly - vainglory

gazâfegu: adjective
braggart - braggadocio

gazâfeguyi kardan: verb
To rodomontade - To overstate - To exaggerate

gazâfguyi: noun
extravaganza - hyperbole - bounce

gazâfguyi kardan: verb
To bounce

gedâ: noun
beggar - pauper

gedâkhâne: noun
poorhouse - almshouse

gedâyi kardan: verb
To beg

gel gereftan: verb
To puddle

gelgir: noun
mudguard

geli: adjective
muddy - draggy

geli kardan: verb
To muddy - To rosy

geli shodan: verb
To drabble

gelâdiyâtor: noun
gladiator

gelâlud kardan: verb
To puddle - To mud

geravidan: verb
To gravitate

gerd kardan: verb
To round

gerdbâd: noun
tornado - hurricane - cyclone - whirlwind

gerdu: noun
walnut

gerdâb: noun
vortex - whirlpool - gulf - gourd

gerdâgerd: noun
around

gerdâmadan: verb
To flock - To gather - To herd - To assemble - To agglomerate

gerdâvardan: verb
To troop - To assemble - To amass - To compile - To collect

gerdâvari: noun
compilation - collection

gere: noun
knot - knob - tie

gere goshudan: verb
To unweave

gere khordan: verb
To knot - To snarl

gere zadan: verb
To twitch - To truss - To tie - To loop - To ruffle - To knot - To knit

geredâr: adjective
burly - knotty

gereftan: verb
To take - To hold - To cease - To catch - To capture

gereftegi: noun
melancholia - eclipse - congestion - obstruction

gereftâr: adjective
afoul - captive

gereftâr kardan: verb
To implicate - To hook - To involve

gereftâr sâkhtan: verb
To gin

gereftâri: noun
captivity - constraint - encumbrance

geregoshâyi: noun
relief

gerye: noun
tear - cry

gerye kardan: verb
To weep - To cry - To mourn

geryân: adjective
weepy - moist

gerâfik: noun
graph

gerâm: noun
phonograph

gerâmi: adjective
dear

gerâmi dâshtan: verb
To treasure - To value - To cherish

gerâmâfon: noun
gramophone - phonograph

gerân: adjective
expensive - exclusive - costly - heavy

gerânbahâ: adjective
valuable - inestimable

gerânbahâ: adjective
precious

gerânbâr: adjective
burdensome

gerânit: noun
granite

gerâyesh: noun
tendency - propensity - attitude

gerâyesh dâshtan: verb
To tend

gerâyidan: verb
To join

gerô: noun
deposit

gerô gozâshtan: verb
To pledge - To pawn

gerôgân: noun
hostage

geshniz: noun
coriander

gha'r: noun
depth

ghabghab: noun
lob

ghabih: adjective
objcetionable

ghabih dânestan: verb
To deprecate

ghabil: noun
type

ghabile: noun
phylum - clan - caste - tribe

ghabile'i: adjective
tribal

ghabl: adverb
former - ago - before

ghabl az: adverb
before

ghablan: adverb
beforehand - already

ghabli: adjective
prior - previous - predecessor

ghabr: noun
grave - sepulcher - tomb

ghabr kardan: verb
To grave

ghabrestân: noun
cemetery - graveyard

ghabul: noun
agreement - adoption - admission

ghabul: noun
accept

ghabul kardan: verb
To entertain - To matriculate - To adopt - To accord - To accept

ghabul shodan: verb
To pass - To accept

ghabuli: adjective
approbation - ratification

ghabz: noun
bill

ghabze: noun
hilt

ghabâ: noun
cassock

ghabâle: noun
deed

ghabâyel: noun
tribe

ghad: noun
length - size - stature

ghadah: noun
bowl

ghadam: noun
stride - step - foot - pace

ghadam bardâshtan: verb
To step

ghadam zadan: verb
To walk - To pace

ghadam âheste: noun
trudge

ghadamrô: noun
march

ghadar: noun
treason - treachery

ghadar: adjective
value - valence - magnitude - importance -
quantity - esteem - deal - significance

ghadboland: adjective
tall

ghadeghan: noun
interdict - injunction - prohibition

ghadeghan kardan: verb
To ban - To veto

ghadim: noun
primitive - aborigine

ghadimi: adjective
senior - timeworn - outdated - olden - old -
bygone - archaic - ancient

ghadrdâni: noun
gratitude

ghadrdâni kardan: verb
To value - To acknowledge

ghadre motlagh: noun
absolutevalue

ghadâm: noun
foreside

ghafas: noun
birdhouse - coop - cage

ghafase: noun
cupboard - cabinet - wardrobe

ghafaseye ketâb: noun
bookcase

ghafaseye sine: noun
kist - ribcage - chest

ghahghahe: noun
horselaugh - gaff

ghahr: noun
wrath - sulky - miff - tantrum

ghahr kardan: verb
To huff - To miff

ghahremân: adjective
champion - champ - knight - victor - hero

ghahremâni: noun
heroism

ghahremânâne: adverb
heroic

ghahti: noun
starvation - hunger

ghahtizadegi: noun
starvation

ghahve: noun
coffee

ghahve jush: noun
percolator

ghahve'i: adjective
brown

ghahvekhâne: noun
teashop - coffeehouse

ghal': noun
tin

ghal'e: noun
castle - fort - munition

ghalabe: noun
conquest - dominance - victory - beat

ghalam: noun
entry - pen - shaft - style

ghalam zadan: verb
To engrave - To enchase

ghalam'mu: noun
brush

ghalame: noun
slip - graft

ghalame zadan: verb
To propagate

ghalameye derakht: noun
sapling

ghalami: noun
slender

ghalamrô: noun
territory

ghalat: noun
error - foul - false

ghalat budan: verb
To err

ghalatgir: noun
reader

ghalb: noun
heart

ghale: noun
corn - cereal

ghalil: adjective
scarce - scant - slight - slender

ghaliz: adjective
caliginous - dense - thick

ghaliz: adjective
tantrum - wrath

ghaliz kardan: verb
To thicken

ghaliz shodan: verb
To thicken

ghalt: noun
tumble - slither

ghalt zadan: verb
To welter

ghaltak: noun
trundle - roller - roll

ghaltidan: verb
To wallow - To roll - To slither

ghaltândan: verb
To turnover - To trundle - To roll

ghalâf: noun
sheathe - sheath - casing - pod - vagina

ghalâf kardan: verb
To sheathe - To sheath - To scabbard

gham: noun
sorrow - rue - remorse - grief

gham khordan: verb
To grief

ghamangiz: adjective
tragic - somber - lugubrious - burdensome

ghamari: adjective
dove - lunar

ghamgin: adjective
sad - dyspeptic - woeful - melancholy

ghamgin shodan: verb
To anguish

ghamkhâr: adjective
sympathetic

ghamkhâri: noun
compassion

ghamnâk: adjective
sad

ghamo anduh: noun
sorrow - anguish - pine

ghandi: noun
sugary

ghani: noun
wealthy - rich

ghani kardan: verb
To enrich

ghani sâkhtan: verb
To enrich

ghanimat: noun
spoil - prize - plunder

ghanâ'em: noun
trophy

ghanâri: noun
canary

ghanât: noun
aqueduct

ghar'ye: noun
village

gharantine: noun
quarantine

gharantine: noun
quarantine

gharantine kardan: verb
To quarantine

gharaz: noun
peeve - intention - grudge

gharazvarzi: adjective
prejudice

gharb: noun
occident - west

gharbgarâyi: noun
westernization

gharbi: adjective
western - westerner

gharbâl: noun
screen - scalp - jigger - sieve - harp

gharbâl kardan: verb
To sieve - To screen - To winnow

ghargh: noun
shipwreck

ghargh kardan: verb
To flood - To deluge - To drown

ghargh shodan: verb
To merge - To drown - To sink

gharghâvol: noun
pheasant

gharib: adjective
stranger - extravagant - unusual

gharib: adjective
nigh - near - about

gharibe: noun
stranger - strange

gharibolvoghu: adjective
imminent

gharihe: noun
initiative

gharin: noun
tally - doublet - counterpart - correlate -
pendant - peer - like

gharine: noun
symmetry - proportion

ghariv: noun
outcry - uproar - boom

gharize: noun
instinct

gharizi: noun
innate

gharn: noun
century

gharniye: noun
corneal

gharz: noun
debt - loan - prest

gharz dâdan: verb
To lend

gharz gereftan: verb
To borrow

gharz kardan: verb
To loan

gharze: noun
prest - loan

gharâr: noun
set - agreement - accord - dictum - concord
- equanimity

gharâr dâdan: verb
To set - To put - To fix - To pose

gharâr gozâshtan: verb
To arrange - To stipulate

gharârdâd: noun
treaty - bond

gharârdâd: noun
contract

gharârdâdi: adjective
formal - arbitrary - bespoke

gharâvol: noun
sentry - sentinel - warden

ghasam: noun
type - speckle - species - sort - kind - genus -
gender - manner - persuasion

ghasam dâdan: verb
To swear - To adjure

ghasam khordan: verb
To avow - To oath

ghasame dorugh: noun
swearword

ghasb kardan: verb
To arrogate - To usurp

ghasd: noun
intention - purpose

ghasd dâshtan: verb
To purpose - To aim - To mean - To intend

ghasd kardan: verb
To design - To attempt

ghash: noun
fit - syncope - swoon

ghash kardan: verb
To swoon - To collapse

ghashang: adjective
beautiful - pretty

ghashô: noun
currycomb

ghashô kardan: verb
To currycomb

ghaside: noun
ode

ghasr: noun
castle

ghasâb: noun
butcher

ghasâbi: adjective
carnage

ghasâbi kardan: verb
To butcher

ghasâbkhâne: noun
slaughterhouse

ghat': noun
slack - cut

ghat' kardan: verb
To cut

ghat'e jariyân: noun
cutout - cutoff

ghat'i: adverb
decisive - cretain - irrevocable

ghat'iyat: noun
pragmatism

ghatl: noun
homicide - murder

ghatlgâh: noun
shambles

ghatloâm: noun
slaughter - genocide - carnage

ghatloâm kardan: verb
To massacre

ghatre: noun
drop

ghatre ashk: noun
teardrop

ghatrechekân: noun
dropper - drippan

ghatur: adjective
punch

ghatâr: noun
train

ghavi: adjective
vigorous - mighty - strong

ghavi budan: verb
To robustness

ghavi heikal: adjective
giant - robust - sturdy

ghavi kardan: verb
To strengthen - To able

ghavânin: noun
provision

ghavâre: noun
shape - lot - configuration

ghavâs: noun
diver

ghavâsi kardan: verb
To dive

ghayem: adjective
executor - guardian - protector

ghayem kardan: verb
To stake

ghayumiyat: noun
tutelage - protectorate - patronage -
mandate

ghayur: adjective
zealous - zealot - zeal

ghaza: noun
food - nutrition - nourishment - meat

ghazab: noun
usurpation - violence

ghazab: noun
anger - ire - rage - outrage - outburst -
wrath

ghazab kardan: verb
To rage

ghazabnâk: adjective
vehement - wroth

ghazabnâk kardan: verb
To anger

ghazal: noun
ode - sonnet

ghazal: noun
roan

ghazalkhâni: adjective
songster

ghaziye: noun
thesis - theorem - clause

ghazâ: noun
mishap

ghazâ: noun
food

ghazâ dâdan: verb
To nourish - To foster

ghazâ khordan: verb
To eat

ghazâl: noun
gazelle

ghazâyi: adjective
juridical - juratory

ghazâyi: noun
food

ghazâyi: noun
judicial

ghebte: noun
grudge

ghebte khordan: verb
To begrudge

ghebâhat: noun
obscenity

ghedmat: noun
archaism - antiquity

gheflat: noun
default - omission - negligence - neglect

gheflat kardan: verb
To passover - To neglect

ghei: noun
puke

gheib shodan: verb
To vanish

gheibat: noun
absence

gheibat kardan: verb
To backbite

gheibgu: adjective
python - necromancer - clairvoyant

gheibguyi: noun
divination - prophecy

gheichi: noun
scissors

gheichi kardan: verb
To snip - To shear - To share

gheichi konande: adjective
clincher

gheid: noun
reservations

gheimat: noun
price - value - worth

gheimat dâshtan: verb
To cost

gheimat gozâshtan: verb
To price

gheimat kardan: verb
To value - To apprise - To evaluate

gheimati: adjective
valuable

gheime: noun
executrix - mince

gheime kardan: verb
To mince

gheir: adjective
unlike - other

gheir ensâni: adjective
inhuman

gheirat: noun
zealotry - zeal - enthusiasm - mettle - ardor

gheiraz: adjective
than - except

gheire: adverb
whatnot

gheire erâdi: adjective
involuntary - automatic

gheire ghâbele faskh: adjective
irrevocable

gheire ghâbele hal: adjective
indissoluble

gheire ghâbele jobrân: adjective
irrecoverable

gheire moteraghebe: noun
unexpected

gheire mâdi: adjective
spiritual - immaterial

gheire rasmi: adjective
unofficial - informal

gheire tabi'i: adjective
unnatural - subnormal

gheire zaruri: adjective
unnecessary - unessential

gheireakhlâghi: adjective
unmoral

gheisar: noun
czar - kaiser

gheiz: noun
resentment

ghel khordan: verb
To trundle

ghelegh: noun
temper

ghelghelak: noun
tickle

ghelghelak dâdan: verb
To titillate - To tickle

ghelyân: noun
spout - seethe

ghelzat: noun
density

ghemat: noun
section - portion - share

gherghere: noun
spool - pulley - bobbin - hasp - hank

gherghere kardan: verb
To gurgle - To gargle

ghermez: adjective
red

ghermez kardan: verb
To crimson - To redden

ghermez shodan: verb
To glow - To redden

ghermezrang: adjective
ruddy

gherâbat: noun
propinquity - imminence

gherâbat: noun
singularity - singular - peculiarity - oddity

gherâmat: noun
fine - indemnity

gherâmat: noun
recompense

gherâmat pardâkhtan: verb
To recompense

ghese: noun
fiction - narrative - tale - story

ghesegu: adjective
storyteller

gheshlâgh kardan: verb
To winter

gheshr: noun
stratum - shell - crust - cortex

ghesmat: noun
division - chapter - portion - section

ghesmat kardan: verb
To sect

ghest: noun
payment

ghest: noun
installment - payment

ghesâs: noun
nemesis

ghesâvat: noun
atrocity

ghet'e: noun
segment - section - block - panel - plot - plat

ghet'e ghet'e: noun
sectional

ghet'e yakh: noun
icicle

ghey kardan: verb
To spew - To vomit - To regurgitate

gheybgu: adjective
augur

gheydi: noun
adverbial

gheymati: adjective
precious

gheyre behdâshti: adjective
insanitary

gheyre ghâbele e'temâd: adjective
unreliable

gheyre ghâbele estefâde: adjective
unprofitable

gheyre ghâbele estenâd: adjective
unpredictable

gheyre ghâbele esterdâd: adjective
irretrievable - irremediable

gheyre ghânuni: adjective
unlawful - illegal

gheyre herfe'i: adjective
amateur - unprofessional

gheyre jensi: adjective
asexual

gheyre vâghe'i: adjective
unreal

gheytân: noun
thread - lace - cordon

ghezel'âlâ: noun
salmon

ghezh ghezh kardan: verb
To creak - To whiz - To whir

ghezâvat: noun
witting - verdict - sentence - judge

ghezâvat kardan: verb
To judge - To advise

ghif: noun
hopper - funnel

ghir: noun
tar

ghir zadan: verb
To tar

ghiri: adjective
tarry

ghiy ghiyâm kardan: verb
To arise - To whomp up

ghiyâfe: noun
look - semblance

ghiyâm: noun
uprising

ghiyâs: noun
deduction - analogy

ghiyâsi: adjective
analogical - analog - inductive

ghobâr: noun
mist - dust

ghode: noun
tumor - wen - knot - gland

ghodghod: noun
cluck

ghodghod kardan: verb
To squawk

ghodrat: noun
zing - sovereignty - nerve - godown - rod -
authority - power - potency - posse - vis -
vim - might

ghodrat: noun
power - vigor

ghodrat dâshtan: verb
To be able to

ghodrate motlagh: noun
omnipotence

ghods: noun
sanctum

ghodus: noun
sacrosanct

ghofl: noun
lock - padlock

ghofl shodan: verb
To lock

ghoflsâz: noun
locksmith

gholdor: adjective
bully

ghole: noun
zenith - summit - vertex - peak - climax

gholeye yakh: noun
icicle

gholombe: adjective
snob

gholonbe: adjective
nub - lump - bombastic - baggy

gholonbegi: noun
protuberance

gholov: noun
hyperbole - overstatement

gholov kardan: verb
To overstate - To overestimate

gholve: noun
kidney

gholve sang: noun
cobblestone - rubble

gholâb: noun
hook - clasp - hank

gholâbduzi: noun
patchwork - crocket - crochet - embroidery

gholâbduzi kardan: verb
To crochet

gholâbi: adjective
adulterate - pasteboard - false

gholâbsang: noun
sling

gholâm: noun
bondsman - vassal - slave

ghomghome: noun
thermos - canteen

ghompoz: noun
bluff

ghomâr: noun
gamble - die - hazard

ghomâr kardan: verb
To gamble

ghomârbâz: adjective
gambler

ghomâsh: adjective
cloth - fabric

ghonche: noun
button - bud

ghonche kardan: verb
To purse

ghondâgh kardan: verb
To wrap - To swathe - To swath - To swaddle

ghondâghe tofang: noun
stock

ghonudan: verb
To repose - To nuzzle - To snug

ghor ghor: noun
mutter

ghor ghor kardan: verb
To grumble - To grudge - To growl

ghor zadan: verb
To bitch

ghor'e: noun
grace - lottery - lot

ghor'e keshi: noun
lottery - draw

ghor'e keshidan: verb
To ballot

ghor'ân: noun
koran - quran

ghorbâni: adjective
sacrifice - victim - prey

ghorbâni dâdan: verb
To sacrifice

ghorbâni shodan: verb
To immolate

ghore: noun
cocksure

ghoresh kardan: verb
To roar

ghorfe: noun
stall - booth - loge

ghorfeye namâyeshgâh: noun
pavilion

ghoridan: verb
To snort - To rumble

ghoroghchi: adjective
gamekeeper

ghoroland: noun
rumble

ghors: noun
tablet - cake - disk - pellet - brede

ghorse nân: noun
loaf

ghorub: noun
night - evening - sundown

ghorur: noun
pride - vanity - vainglory - conceit

ghorâani kardan: verb
To victimize

ghorâze: noun
rattletrap - scrap

ghose: noun
sorrow - rue - grief - woe

ghose khordan: verb
To pine

ghosedâr: noun
lachrymose

ghosl: noun
soak - ablution - wash - dip

ghosl dâdan: verb
To souse

ghosur: noun
shortcoming - delinquency - default - negligence

ghosur kardan: verb
To underdo

ghotb: noun
pole - hub - axis

ghotbe elektriki: noun
electrode

ghotbe jonub: noun
antarctic - southpole

ghotbe manfi: noun
cathode

ghotbi: adjective
polar

ghotbnamâ: noun
compass

ghotr: noun
diagonal

ghotri: adjective
diametrical

ghovat: noun
strength - nutrition

ghovat dâdan: verb
To invigorate - To nourish

ghove: noun
strength

ghoveye ebtekâr: noun
ingenuity - creativity

ghovâ: noun
force

ghozruf: noun
cartilage - gristle

ghuch: noun
buck - ram

ghul: noun
giant - ogre - hobgoblin

ghulpeykar: adjective
monstrous - gigantic - gargantuan

ghulâsâ: adjective
ogreish

ghurbâghe: noun
greenback - frog

ghuri: noun
pot

ghurt: noun
gulp

ghurt dâdan: verb
To poop - To englut - To gulp - To gobble

ghush: noun
hawk

ghute: noun
soak - plunge - duck

ghutevar shodan: verb
To dip

ghutevar sâkhtan: verb
To submerge - To overwhelm - To engulf -
To plunge

ghuti: noun
can

ghuti: noun
packet

ghuz: noun
hunch - hump

ghuz kardan: verb
To squat - To hump

ghuzak: noun
ankle

ghuzake pâ: noun
tarsus - ankle

ghâ'em: noun
upstanding - orthogonal - erect

ghâ'em'maghâm: noun
deputy - vicar - surrogate - successor

ghâb gereftan: verb
To frame

ghâbel: noun
good - capable - apt - able

ghâbele: noun
obstetrician - midwife

ghâbele e'temâd: adjective
trusty - trustworthy - authentic

ghâbele ehterâm: adjective
respectable

ghâbele esbât: adjective
provable

ghâbele estefâde: adjective
serviceable - utilizable - available -
instrumental

ghâbele etekâ: adjective
reliable

ghâbele etminân: adjective
reputable - reliable

ghâbele ghabul: adjective
tolerable - acceptable - receivable

ghâbeliyat: noun
sufficiency - ability - capability

ghâch: noun
plug

ghâch kardan: verb
To plug

ghâchâgh: noun
swindler - contraband - illicit

ghâchâgh kardan: verb
To smuggle

ghâchâghchi: noun
racketeer - smuggler

ghâchâghi: adjective
underthecounter - wildcat

ghâder budan: verb
To may

ghâdere mota'âl: noun
omnipotent

ghâede: noun
theorem - law - norm - rule - regulation -
frame

ghâedegiye zanân: noun
priod - menses

ghâfele: noun
convoy

ghâfelgir: adjective
surprise

ghâfelgir kardan: verb
To surprise

ghâfiye: noun
rhyme

ghâfiye: noun
rhyme

ghâfiyedâr: adjective
rhyme

ghâh ghâh: noun
guffaw

ghâh ghâh khandidan: verb
To guffaw

ghâher: adjective
violent

ghâl gozâshtan: verb
To walkouton

ghâleb: noun
mould - mold - model - case

ghâleb: adjective
dominant - conqueror - overbearing -
predominant

ghâleb: noun
pan - case

ghâleb gereftan: verb
To die

ghâleb zadan: verb
To form - To shove over

ghâleb zani: noun
snap

ghâleb âmadan: verb
To triumph - To prevail

ghâleban: adverb
some - freuqently

ghâlebe ôghât: noun
often

ghâli: noun
carpet

ghâliche: noun
rug

ghâmat: noun
stature

ghâmez: noun
unintelligible - abstruse - problematic -
knotty

ghâmus: noun
lexicon - thesaurus

ghâne' kardan: verb
To satisfy - To convince - To content

ghânun: noun
law - regulation - rule

ghânun shekan: adjective
scofflaw - lawbreaker - outlaw

ghânuni: adjective
juridical - legitimate - legal - lawful - valid

ghânuni budan: verb
To legitimacy - To legality

ghânunshekani: noun
offense

ghâp: noun
knucklebone

ghâp bâzi: noun
dib

ghâp zadan: verb
To snap

ghâp zani: noun
snatch

ghâpidan: verb
To yerk

ghâpidan: verb
To snatch - To snap - To seize - To raven - To grasp - To grab

ghâr: noun
cave - grotto - vault

ghâr ghâr kardan: verb
To croak

ghâr ghâr kardan: verb
To plunk

ghârat: noun
ravage - despoliation

ghârat kardan: verb
To reave - To raven - To harrow - To spoliate

ghâratgar: adjective
robber - predatory - marauder

ghâratgari: noun
sack - rapacity

ghârch: noun
mushroom

ghâre: noun
mainland - continent

ghâri: noun
reader

ghârneshin: noun
caveman

ghâseb: adjective
usurper - impostor - violator

ghâsed: noun
courier - herald - harbinger

ghâsedak: noun
dandelion

ghâser: adjective
short

ghâsh: noun
sliver - slice - plug

ghâsh kardan: verb
To sliver - To slice

ghâshangtar: adjective
natty

ghâshogh: noun
spoon

ghâte': adjective
decisive - conclusive - overbearing - incisive

ghâte' budan: verb
To predominate

ghâtel: noun
murderer - assassin - killer

ghâter: noun
mule

ghâti: adjective
mixed

ghâti kardan: verb
To mix

ghâyeb: noun
absence

ghâyeb: adjective
absent - away - away

ghâyeb: adjective
absent

ghâyeb shodan: verb
To disappear

ghâyegh: noun
boat

ghâyeghrân: noun
sculler - boatman

ghâyel: noun
teller

ghâyi: noun
ultimatum - ultimate

ghâz: noun
venue - goose

ghâz: noun
goose

ghâzi: noun
arbiter - pretor - judge

ghôghâ: noun
uproar - riot - rave - turmoil - scuffle

ghôghâ: noun
melee - turmoil - fray

ghôghâ kardan: verb
To jangle

ghôl: noun
promise - vow

ghôl dâdan: verb
To promise

ghôlanj: noun
colic - gripe - bellyache

ghôle mardâne: noun
parole

ghôm: noun
nation - race - people

ghôs: noun
archer - arch - arc - bow - chord

gij: noun
hazy - harebrained - giddy - wacky - dizzy

gij kardan: verb
To mystify - To puzzle

gij khordan: verb
To reel - To stagger

gij konande: adjective
hectic - problematic - stunner - stickler

gij shodan: verb
To dizzy

giji: adjective
stupor - stupefaction - stun - razzledazzle - muddle - quandary - bafflement

gilâs: noun
glass

gir: noun
trap - impediment - impasse - hitch

gir andâkhtan: verb
To entangle - To knot - To circumvent - To involve - To mesh

gir dâdan: verb
To engage

gir kardan: verb
To stymie - To stick

gir kardan: verb
To stammer

gir oftâdan: verb
To tangle - To strand - To stick - To pin

gir âvardan: verb
To grasp - To hook

girande: adjective
recipient - receiver - holder - prehensile

gire: noun
pin - bend - retainer - cleat - clamp - trigger

gire: noun
tach

gireye sar: noun
pin

girâ: adjective
impressive

girâyi: noun
charisma

gisu: noun
hair

giti: noun
universe - world

gitâr: noun
guitar

gitâr zadan: verb
To guitar

giyutin: noun
guillotine

giyâh: noun
vegetable - plant - herb

giyâhkhâri: noun
vegetarian

giyâhshenâs: noun
botanist

giyâhshenâsi: noun
botany

godâkhtan: verb
To thaw - To smelt - To melt

godâkhte: adjective
molten

godâkhte shodan: verb
To smelt

godâz: noun
melt

godâze: noun
lava

godâzeye âtashfeshâni: noun
slag

goft: verb
To said

goftan: verb
To say - To tell - To rehearse - To cite

gofto shenud: noun
dialogue

goftogu: noun
dialogue - conversation - discussion

goftoguyi: noun
colloquial

goftâr: adjective
speech - sermon

goh: noun
gad - cleat - slice - sprag

goh: noun
wedge

goharforush: noun
jeweler

gol: noun
flower - blossom

gol kardan: verb
To flower

gol zadan: verb
To goal

golbarg: noun
calycle

golbon: noun
shrub

golbul: noun
corpuscle - globule - glob

golbule sefide khun: noun
leukocyte

golchehre: noun
ruddy

golchin: noun
elite

golchin kardan: verb
To tab - To cull - To excerpt - To pluck

golchini: adjective
eclecticism

golduzi: noun
needlework

goldân: noun
jardiniere - urn - vase - pot

gole lâle: noun
tulip

gole mikhak: noun
clove

gole minâ: noun
aster

gole nastaran: noun
jonquil

gole ros: noun
bole

goler: noun
goalkeeper

golestân: noun
rosery - rosary

golgun: adjective
ruddy - rosy - roseate

golkhâne: noun
nursery - greenhouse - greenery -
glasshouse

golkâri kardan: verb
To flower

golokoz: noun
glucose

golsang: noun
lichen

golule: noun
shot - bullet

golule kardan: verb
To clow

golule shodan: verb
To conglobate

golâb: noun
rosewater

golâbatun: noun
purl - braid

golâbi: noun
pear

golâbpâsh: noun
sprinkler

gom kardan: verb
To lose - To miss - To mislay

gom shodan: verb
To scat

gomnâm: adjective
obscure - inglorious - unknown - scrubby

gomnâm kardan: verb
To obscure

gomnâmi: noun
anonymity - obscurity - oblivion

gomrok: noun
customs

gomrâh: adjective
devious - aberrant

gomrâh kardan: verb
To seduce - To mislead - To misinform - To
misguide

200

gomrâh konande: adjective
sinuous - sinister - seducer - screwy

gomrâh shodan: verb
To err - To pervert

gomrâhi: noun
slip - obliquity - loss

gomân: noun
supposition - thought - idea - belief -
assumption - guess

gomân bordan: verb
To conjecture - To surmise

gomân kardan: verb
To think - To suspect - To suppose - To
reckon

gomâsht: noun
duty - appointment

gomâshtan: verb
To charge - To designate - To assign - To
appoint

gomâshtan: verb
To designate - To assign - To appoint

gomâshte: adjective
agent

gomâshte: adjective
agent - assignee - batman - appointee

gonbad: noun
dome - cupola - vault

gonde: adjective
whopper - unwieldy - massive - huge

gong: adjective
incommensurable - mute - unvocal - whist

gong: adjective
speechless

gonjândan: verb
To inclusion - To jam

gonjânidan: verb
To lug

gonjâyesh: noun
capacity

gonjâyesh: noun
capacity

gonâh: noun
sin - guilt - misdeed - blame

gonâh: noun
sin

gonâhkâr: adjective
criminal - guilty - wicked - sinner - sinful

gor: adjective
scab - mangey - mangy - mange

gorbe: noun
pussy - puss - cat

gorbe sefat: adjective
catty

gorbeye vahshi: noun
wildcat

gorde: noun
kidney

gordân: noun
battalion - versatile - winch

gorg: noun
wolf

gorikhtan: verb
To escape - To runaway - To abscond

goriz: noun
evasion - escape

gorizân: adjective
runaway - evasive - elusive

gorosne: noun
hungry

gorosne shodan: verb
To hunger

gorosnegi: noun
hunger - starvation

gorosnegi dâdan: verb
To starve - To hunger

gorosnegi keshidan: verb
To starve

goruh: noun
team - group

goruhbandi: noun
grouping - regimentation

goruhbandi kardan: verb
To grouping

goruhi: noun
gregarious - republican

goruhân: noun
company

gorz: noun
maul - mallet - wand

gorz: noun
mace

gorâz: noun
hog - pork - pig

gosastan: verb
To tear - To disconnect - To rupture

gosastegi: noun
rupture

goshudan: verb
To untwine - To untie - To unfurl - To open

goshudan: verb
To unbolt

goshude: adjective
open - unbutton

goshâd: adjective
loose - broad - wide

goshâdan: verb
To solve - To evolve - To open

goshâde: adjective
patent

goshâdegi: noun
aperture

goshâyande: adjective
opener

goshâyesh: noun
inauguration

gosikhtan: verb
To tear - To snap - To cut - To fracture

gosikhtegi: noun
rupture

gosil: noun
dispatch

gosil dâshtan: verb
To send - To dispatch

gostardan: verb
To spread - To propagate

gostarde: adjective
widespread

gostarde kardan: verb
To explode

gostaresh: noun
spread - extension

gostaresh yâftan: verb
To spread - To outspread - To deploy

gostâkh: adjective
rude - insolent - indecent - impudent -
impertinent - immodest

gostâkhi: noun
audacity - arrogance

gostâkhi kardan: verb
To brazen - To blab

\govâh: noun
proof - voucher - evidence

govâhi: noun
testimony - testify

govâhi dâdan: verb
To testify

govâhi kardan: verb
To certify

govâhinâme: noun
certificate - diploma - affidavit

govâhinâme: noun
certificate

govâresh: noun
digestion

govâreshi: noun
digestive

govârâ: adjective
salubrious - tasty - digestive - digestible

gozar: noun
transit - passage - pass

gozargâh: noun
pathway - passageway

gozarnâme: noun
passport - pass

gozarân: adjective
maintenance

gozarân kardan: verb
To subsist - To fare

gozarândan: verb
To survive - To fare - To outwear - To while

gozasht: noun
remission - amnesty - pardon

gozasht kardan: verb
To remise

gozashtan: verb
To pass - To blowover - To elapse - To cross

gozashte: adjective
bygone - past

gozashte az in: noun
besides - also

gozashte zamân: noun
lapse

gozashtehâ: noun
bygone

gozinesh: noun
election

gozineshi: adjective
selective - elective

gozir: noun
remedy

gozârdan: verb
To set - To pose - To lay

gozâre: noun
predicate

gozâresh: noun
report

gozâresh dâdan: verb
To report

gozâreshgar: noun
reporter

gozâshtan: verb
To infiltrate - To place - To deposit - To stead - To shunt

gris: noun
grease

gristan: verb
To weep - To cry

gugerd: noun
brimstone

gul: noun
deception - cheat - cajole

gul zadan: verb
To hoax - To entrap - To dupe - To defraud - To deceive

gulzanande: adjective
deceptive

gune: noun
type - sort - species - kind

guni: noun
sacking - sack - gunny

guniyâ: noun
bevel

gunâgun: adjective
diverse - various

gunâgun sâkhtan: verb
To diversify

gunâguni: noun
variety - manifold - diversity

gur: noun
tomb

gur: noun
grave - tomb

gurekhar: noun
zebra

gurestân: noun
cemetery

guril: noun
gorilla

gurkan: noun
sexton - badger - pitman

gusfand: noun
mutton

gusfand: noun
sheep

gush: noun
ear

gush dâdan: verb
To listen

gush kardan: verb
To listen - To hear

gushbezang: noun
alert - vigilant - wakeful

gushbor: adjective
swindler

gushbori: noun
shark

gushe: noun
jest - angle - lobe - nook - quip - recess - corner

gushedâr: noun
poignant - piquant - angular

gusheneshin: adjective
solitudinarian - solitary - unsociable - recluse

gushi: noun
receiver - aural

gushiye telefon: noun
earphone

gushkharâsh: adjective
strident - loud

gushkhârâsh: adjective
earsplitting

gushmâhi: noun
scallop

gushmâl dâdan: verb
To punish

gushmâli: adjective
rebuke - scourge - punishment

gusht: noun
bully - brawn - viand

gushti: verb
To meaty

gushtkhâr: adjective
zoophagous

gushvâre: noun
earring - eardrop

gusâle: noun
veal - calf

guy: noun
sphere - orb - globe - ball

guyande: noun
speaker - announcer - narrator

guyesh: noun
dialect

guyâ: adjective
perhaps - communicative

guyâyi: noun
speech

guzh: noun
hunch - hump

guzhposht: noun
crookback - humpback

guzidan: verb
To poop

gâh: noun
period

gâhgâhi: adverb
sometime

gâhi: adverb
somewhen

gâhobigâh: noun
occasionally - sporadic

gâhshomâr: noun
timepiece

gâl: adjective
scabies

gâleri: noun
gallery

gâlon: noun
gallon

gâm: noun
step - pace - gamut - gait

gâm bardâshtan: verb
To gait

gâmâ: noun
gamma

gârd: noun
lifeguard - guard

gâri: noun
cart

gârânti: noun
warranty

gârâzh: noun
garage

gâv: noun
neat

gâve nar: noun
bull

gâvsandugh: noun
safedeposit - safe

gâvâhan: noun
plough - plow

gâyidan: verb
To fuck

gâz: noun
bite - gas

gâz: noun
gas - bite - fume

gâz gereftan: verb
To snap - To bite - To nip - To gnaw

gâz zadan: verb
To nibble

gâzanbor: noun
pincer - calliper - caliper

gâzdâr: adjective
gaseous

gâzeme'de: noun
gas

gâzi: adjective
gaseous

gâzsuz: adjective
gaslight

gôd: adjective
dished - deep - ring - arena

gôd kardan: verb
To scoop - To gull - To deepen

gôdi: adjective
lacuna - dent - delve - groove

gôdâl: noun
puddle - cavity - cavern - hole

gôhar: noun
essence - navigate - nature - jewel

gôje: noun
sloe - plum

h

habe: noun
bean - grain

habs: noun
jail - custody - durante - prison

habs kardan: verb
To jail - To incarcerate

habse abad: noun
life

had: noun
extent - limit

hadaf: noun
target - purpose - goal - aim

hadafgiri: noun
targeting

hade a'lâ: noun
uttermost - utter - culmination

hade aksar: noun
extreme - peak - uttermost - utmost

hade fâsel: noun
partition - median

hadevasat: noun
average - mediocre - mean

hadghe: noun
pupil - socket - orbit

hads: noun
surmise - aim - conjecture - guess

hads zadan: verb
To guess - To conjecture

hadsi: adjective
conjectural

hafr: noun
dig

hafr kardan: verb
To digging - To delve

hafr konande: adjective
excavator

haft: noun
seven

haft tir: noun
revolver - pistol

hafte: noun
week

haftegi: noun
weekly

haftom: adjective
seventh - seven

haftomin: adjective
seventh - seven

haftâd: adjective
seventy - septuagenarian

haftâdom: adjective
seventieth

haftâdomin: adjective
seventieth - septuagenarian

hafâri: noun
drilling

hagh: noun
right

haghe taghadom: noun
priority - preferment - precedence

haghighat: noun
truth - verity - reality

haghighatan: adverb
indeed

haghighi: adjective
real - actual - true

haghir shemordan: verb
To despise

haghshenâs: adjective
leal - grateful

haghâniyat: noun
legitimacy

hajim: adjective
large - voluminous - massive

hajm: noun
content - mass - volume - bulk

hajv: noun
libel - lampoon

hajv kardan: verb
To satirize - To lampoon

hajv nâme: noun
satire

hajv âmiz: adjective
caustic

hak: noun
erasure - hake

hak kardan: verb
To lithograph - To carve

hakamiyat: noun
umpire - umpirage

hakim: adjective
wise - sage

hakâki: noun
gravure

hakâki kardan: verb
To engrave - To inscribe

hal: noun
resolvent - resolution - solution

hal kardan: verb
To dissolve - To solve

halab: noun
tin

halabi: noun
tinfoil - tin

halazun: noun
mollusk

halazun: noun
snail

halgh: noun
gorge

halgh âviz: noun
gadarene

halghavi: adjective
convoluted

halghe: noun
loop - ring - curl

halghe: noun
ring

halghe kardan: verb
To curl

halghe zadan: verb
To encompass - To encircle

halghe'I: adjective
ring - gyrate

halgheye ghol: noun
garland - wreath

halim: noun
submissive - meek

halâk shodan: verb
To perish

halâl: adjective
solvent - resolvent - lawful

halâlzâde: adjective
legitimate

ham: preposition
too - both - likewise - even

ham mani: adjective
synonymous - synonym - equivalent

ham martabe: adjective
equal

ham mihan: adjective
patiot

hambastegi: noun
adhesion - correlation - solidarity

hambâzi: noun
playmate

hamchenin: adverb
too - also

hamchenân: adverb
so - likewise - like

hamchenânke: adverb
as

hamcheshmi: noun
competition - rival

hamcheshmi: noun
rivalry - vying

hamcho: preposition
so

hamchon: adverb
like

hamdam: adjective
jo - comate - cahoot - mate - billy

hamdam shodan: verb
To associate

hamdard: adjective
sympathetic

hamdardi: noun
pity - condolence - sympathy

hamdast: adjective
cooperator - partner - pal

hamdast: adjective
accessory

hamdasti: noun
cooperation - pally - assistance

hamdasti kardan: verb
To help - To cooperate - To collaborate

hamdore: adjective
contemporary

hame: adjective
all - everyone

hamechiz: adjective
everything

hamegi: noun
altogether - all

hamegân: noun
public - general

hamegâni: noun
general - public

hamejâ: adjective
everywhere - passim

hamekâre: adjective
jack of all trades

hameporsi: noun
referendum - plebiscite

hamesâle: adjective
perennial - every year

hamfekri: noun
sympathy

hamfekri kardan: verb
To consult

hamgarâyi: noun
convergence

hamgen: adjective
equal

hamghatâr: adjective
colleague

hamghatâr: adjective
teammate - brother - associate - confrere

hamhame: noun
tumult - ruckus - uproar

hamhame: noun
ruction

hamhame kardan: verb
To hum

haminghadr: adverb
so

hamintor: adverb
also - so

hamishe: adverb
always

hamishegi: noun
usual - perpetual - perennial - eternal -
continual

hamjavâr: adjective
adjacent

hamjensbâz: adjective
homosexual

hamkelâs: noun
classmate

hamkhu: noun
congenial - univocal

hamkhâbe: adjective
concubine

hamkhân: adjective
consonant

hamkâr: noun
colleague

hamkâri: noun
assist - cooperation

haml: noun
conveyance - portage - shipment

haml kardan: verb
To carry - To convey - To transport

hamle: noun
offense - rush - attack - assault

hamle kardan: verb
To assail - To layon

hamlonaghl: noun
transport - haul

hamnavâ: adjective
symphony - symphonic - unisonous

hamnavâyi: noun
conformity

hamnavâyi: noun
symphony

hamnavâyi kardan: verb
To conform

hamneshin: adjective
companion

hamnâm: adjective
namesake

hampeimân: adjective
confederate - ally

hamrâh: noun
participant - attendant - escort

hamrâhi: noun
companionship - camaraderie

hamrâhi kardan: verb
To squire - To accompany - To accompany -
To companion

hamrâhân: noun
attendance - entourage - retinue

hamsafar: noun
outfit

hamsar: noun
spouse

hamsedâ: adjective
homophone

hamsedâyi: noun
consonance - assonance - unison

hamshahri: noun
twonsman

hamshire: noun
sister

hamsân: adjective
isotope

hamsâni: noun
parallelism

hamsâye: noun
adjacent - neighbor

hamsâz: adjective
accommodate

hamtarâz kardan: verb
To equal

hamtâ: noun
counterpart - match

hamvâr: adjective
tabulate - smooth - flat - plane - plain

hamvâr kardan: verb
To grade - To shim

hamvâre: noun
always

hamzamân: adjective
simultaneous - simultaneity - synchronic -
contemporary

hamzisti: noun
symbiosis

hamzâd: noun
double

hamâhang: adverb
symphonic - consonant

hamâl: noun
porter - backer

hamâli kardan: verb
To porter

hamâm: noun
washroom - bathroom

hamâm gereftan: verb
To bath

hamân: adjective
same - very

hamânand: noun
similar - alike - equal

hamânâ: adverb
certainly - indeed

hamâse: noun
saga - epopee - epic

hamâsi: adjective
heroic - bardic - epic

hamâvard: adjective
antagonist - adversary - rival

hamâvâyi: noun
unison

hamâyel: noun
baldric

hamâyesh: noun
congress

handbâl: noun
handball

hang: noun
legion

hang: noun
regiment

hanjare: noun
larynx

hanjare: noun
chamber

hanjâr: noun
norm

hanuz: noun
still - nevertheless

hanâ: noun
henna

hanâyi: adjective
russet

har: preposition
any - every - each

har ghadr: noun
whatsoever

har ghadr ham: preposition
however

har kodâm: adverb
each - apiece

har kojâ: adverb
where - anywhere

har kojâke: adverb
wherever

har shab: adjective
nightly

harame motahar: noun
sanctuary

haras: noun
recision

haras kardan: verb
To prune - To lop - To rogue

harbe: noun
weapon

harchand: preposition
however

harche: adverb
whatsoever - whatever - whatever

harchiz: adverb
anything

hardambil: adjective
unprincipled - slovenly

hardo: adjective
both

harf: noun
speech - letter - word

harf: noun
letter - talk

harf zadan: verb
To speak - To say - To talk

harfe birabt: noun
rigmarole

harfe bisedâ: noun
consonant

harfe bozorg: noun
capital

harfe ezâfe: noun
preposition

harfe manfi: noun
not

harfe moft: adjective
tattle - guff

harfe moft zadan: verb
To prattle

harfe puch: noun
nonsense - moonshine

harfshenavi: noun
obedience

harfsheno: adjective
obedient

hargez: adverb
never

harghir: adjective
little - slight

hargune: adverb
any

hargâh: adverb
whenever

harif: noun
foe - rival - opponent

harif shodan: verb
To cope

harigh: noun
fire

harim: noun
sanctum

haris: adjective
greedy - fierce - avid - avaricious - voracious

haris: adjective
greedy

haris budan: verb
To greed

harjo marj: noun
anarchy - chaos

harjâ: adverb
anywhere - anyplace

harjâyike: adverb
wherever

215

harkas: adverb
anyone - everybody

harkasi: adverb
everybody

harkasike: adverb
whoever

harkat: noun
move - motion

harkat dâdan: verb
To propel - To move

harkate davarâni: noun
evolution

harkati: noun
dynamic

harke: adverb
every - whoever

harkodâmke: adverb
whichever

harvaght: adverb
whenever

harvaght ke: adverb
whenever

haryek: adverb
each - apiece

harz: adjective
weedy

harz dâdan: verb
To waste

harze: adjective
salacious - prurient - profligate

harzegi: noun
profligacy - incontinence - lechery - ribaldry

harâj: noun
auction - outcry

harâj kardan: verb
To auction

harâm: noun
unlawful - illegal - taboo

harâm kardan: verb
To waste

harâmzâde: adjective
spurious - unfathered - bastard

harâmzâdegi: noun
illegitimacy - bastardization

harânkas: adverb
whoever

harânke: adverb
whoever

harârat: noun
warmth - heat

harârati: adjective
thermal

harâs: noun
fright - feeze - panic

harâsidan: preposition
apprehend

216

harâsnâk: adjective
panicky

harâsân: adjective
frit - afraid

harâsânidan: verb
To fray - To affray

hasbe: noun
typhoid

hashare: noun
bug - insect

hasharekosh: noun
larva - insecticide

hasharâte muzi: noun
vermin - moth

hashish: noun
kef - hemp - marijuana

hashish: noun
hashish

hashtpâ: noun
octopus - devilfish

hashtâd: noun
eighty

hashtâdom: adjective
eightieth

hashtâdomin: adjective
eightieth

hasir: noun
matting - mat - straw

hasrat bordan: verb
To regret

hast: noun
existent

haste: noun
stone - kernel - nucleus - atom

hasti: noun
existence - reality - objectivity

hasud: adjective
jealous - envious

hasudâne: adverb
invidious

hasâs: noun
sensitive

hasâs shodan: verb
To sensitize

hasâsiyat: noun
sensitivity - sensibility

hatman: adverb
certainly - inevitable

hatmi: noun
indispensable - cretain

hatâ: adverb
even

hatâk: adjective
irreverent

hatâki: noun
affront

havas: noun
lust - fad - whim - fancy - caprice

havasbâz: adjective
capricious

havasrân: adjective
swinger

havasrân: adjective
sensual

havasâmiz: adjective
chimerical

havij: noun
carrot

havâ: noun
weather - air

havâ va havas: noun
vagary - whim

havâbord: noun
airborne

havâbord: noun
skyborne

havâdâr: adjective
pneumatic

havâkhâh: adjective
zealous - enthusiast - disciple

havâkhâhi: noun
zealotry - devotion - adherence

havâle: noun
order - assignment

havânavardi: noun
aviation

havâpeimâ: noun
plane - airplane - aircraft - aeroplane

havâs: noun
attention

havâsanj: noun
barometer

havâshenâs: noun
weatherman

havâspart: adjective
wacky

havâye nafs: noun
passion

havâyi: noun
atmospheric - airy

hayejân: noun
thrill - ignition

hayejân angiz: adjective
rip roaring

hayejânangiz: adjective
rapturous

hayejâni: adjective
emotional

hayulâ: noun
monstrous - monstrosity - monster

hayâhu: noun
hubbub - explosion - commotion

hayât: noun
life

hayât: noun
quirk - courtyard - patio

hayâti: adjective
vital - essential

haz: noun
joy - happiness

haz kardan: verb
To admire

hazf: noun
omission - ellipse - elimination - deletion

hazf kardan: verb
To omit - To eliminate - To delete

hazhir: noun
praiseworthy

hazimat: noun
defeat

hazin: adjective
desolate

hazl: noun
smut

hazm: noun
digestion

hazm kardan: verb
To digest

hazm shodan: verb
To digest

hazrat: noun
honor - holiness

hazyân: noun
delirium - maze

hediye: noun
present - gift

hediye dâdan: verb
To donate - To gift

hedâyat: noun
guidance - steerage

hedâyt kardan: verb
To steer - To direct - To lead

hefdahomin: adjective
seventeenth

hefz: noun
preservation - retinue - protection

hefz kardan: verb
To memorize - To preserve - To secure - To protect

hefâz: noun
shield - shell - safeguard

hefâzat: noun
conservation - keep - safekeeping

hegh hegh: noun
sob

heghârat: noun
scorn - demission - humility

hei: preposition
hey - hallo

heibat: noun
solemnity - awe

heif: noun
alack

heikal: noun
physique - person - statue

heirat: noun
surprise - wonder - amazement

heiratangiz: adjective
wonder

heiratzadegi: noun
transfixion

heiratzâ: adjective
wondrous

heiratâvar: adjective
marvelous - wondrous

heirâni: noun
perplexity

heisiyat: noun
prestige

heivân: noun
animal

heivâni: adjective
animal - brutish - bestial

heivânâte vahshi: noun
wildlife

hejdah: noun
eighteen

hejdahom: adjective
eighteenth

hejdahomin: adjective
eighteenth

heji: noun
spelling

heji kardan: verb
To spell

hejle: noun
bridechamber

hejâ: noun
epigram

hejâb: noun
veil

hejâb zadan: verb
To veil

hejâmat: noun
cup - leech

hejâr: noun
sculptor

hekmat: noun
doctrine - wisdom - motto

hektâr: noun
hectare

hekâyat: noun
story - tale

hekâyat goftan: verb
To fable

helhele: noun
yell - jubilation

helikupter: noun
helicopter

helikupter: noun
chopper

helâl: noun
roundel

helâli: noun
embowed

hemâghat: noun
stupidity - idiotism - idiocy

hemâyat: noun
support - shelter - aid

hemâyat kardan: verb
To support - To protect

hendel: noun
winch

hendesi: noun
numeral

hendevâne: noun
melon - watermelon

hendi: adjective
indic - indian

hendustân: noun
india

hengoft: noun
enormous - great

hengâm: noun
moment

hengâme: noun
scrimmage - tumult - uproar - rumpus

hengâmike: preposition
while - whenever

heram: noun
pyramid

herami: adjective
pyramidal

herfe: noun
profession - vocation - career - trade

herfe'l: adjective
professional

hero'in: noun
heroin

hers: noun
avidity - avarice - greed

hers zadan: verb
To raven

herâsat: noun
preservation

hes: noun
sense - sensation

hese sheshom: noun
sixth sense

hesi: adjective
sensory - sensational - intuitive

hesâb: noun
calculation - arithmetic - account

hesâb kardan: verb
To compute - To calculate - To count

hesâbdân: adjective
arithmetic

hesâbdâr: noun
accountant

hesâbdâri: noun
accounting

hesâbe bedehi: noun
debit

hesâbgar: adjective
calculator - arithmetic

hesâbi: adjective
arithmetic

hesâdat: noun
jealousy

hesân nashode: noun
unaccounted

hesâr: noun
fence - barrier - hedge

hey'at: noun
commission - panel

hezb: noun
party - sect - junta

hezbi: adjective
sectarian

hezâr: noun
thousand

hezâre: noun
millennium

hich: adverb
zero - nothing - none - nil

hich chiz: adverb
nothing

hichgune: adverb
no

hichgâh: adverb
never

hichkas: adverb
nobody

hichkas: adverb
nobody

hichkodâm: adverb
none

hichyek: adverb
none - neither

hidrolik: noun
hydraulic

hidrozhen: noun
hydrogen

hijdah: noun
eighteen (in spoken)

hile: noun
trick - foul - deceit

hile zadan: verb
To trick

hilebâz: adjective
cunning - gyp

hilegar: adjective
crafty - captious

hilegari: noun
quackery

hipnotizm: noun
hypnotism

his: noun
shush - goose

his: noun
whish

hite: noun
gamut - compass

hizom: noun
wood

hizomshekan: noun
woodman - woodcutter - woodchopper

hob: noun
pill - pellet

hobubât: noun
cereal - grain

hobâb: noun
bubble - boll - blubber - blob - globe

hodud: noun
range - limit

hofre: noun
hole - cavity - ditch

hofredâr: adjective
pitted - alveolar

hoghe: noun
trick - intake

hoghe bâz: adjective
trickster - snide - slicker

hoghe bâzi: noun
cog - underhand - quackery - legerdemain

hoghe bâzi kardan: verb
To spoof - To trick

hoghugh: noun
salary - pension - law - rights

hoghughdân: adjective
jurisconsult

hoghughe bâzneshastegi: noun
pension

hojat: noun
agument

hojum: noun
offense - invasion - inroad

hojum bordan: verb
To rush

hojum âvardan: verb
To swarm - To scrouge - To raid

hokm: noun
sentence - rule - dictum

hokm dâdan: verb
To judge - To doom - To determine

hokm kardan: verb
To adjudicate - To command - To rule

hokme bâzdâsht: noun
interdict - injunction

hokme dâdgâh: noun
court

hokme elâhi: noun
theosophy - theology

hokmfarmâ: noun
dominant - rampant - predominant

hokmfarmâ budan: verb
To dominate - To reign

hokmfarmâyi: noun
reign

hokmrâni: noun
reign

hokmrâni kardan: verb
To govern

hokumat: noun
government

hokumat kardan: verb
To rule - To govern

hol: noun
jostle - push - shove - cardamom

hol dâdan: verb
To poke - To haul - To push

hol dâdan: verb
To horrify

holand: noun
Netherlands

holandi: adjective
Holland

holandi: adjective
Dutch

holghum: noun
larynx

holu: noun
peach

holul: noun
reincarnation

homrân: noun
ruler - governor

homâyun: noun
imperial - august

honar: noun
art - craft

honarestâni: noun
vocation

honarkade: noun
studio

honarmand: adjective
handicraft - virtuoso - artist - craftsman

honarpishe: noun
artist - actor - craftsman

honarshenâs: noun
virtuoso

honarvar: adjective
artist - mechanic

hormat: noun
reverence - revere - sanctity

horufchin: noun
typesetter

horufe alefbâ: noun
alphabet

hoshdâr: noun
alarm

hoshdâr dâdan: verb
To warn

hoshyâr: adjective
wary - wakeful

hoshyâri: noun
watchful

hoshyâri: noun
sobriety

hosn: noun
virtue - advantage

hosul: noun
recovery - reach

hotel: noun
hotel - hostel

hoveidâ: noun
eminent - eidetic - obvious

hoviyat: noun
identity - personality

hozluli: noun
hyperbola

hozn: noun
sorrow - grief

hozn angiz: adjective
lugubrious - tragic - sepulchral

hozn âvar: adjective
pathetic

hozur: noun
attendance - presence

hozure zehn: noun
immediacy

hozuri: noun
personal

hozâr: noun
audience - attendance - grandstand

hume: noun
vicinity - outskirt - environs

humeye shahr: noun
suburb - countryside

huri: noun
nymph

hurâ: noun
bravo - cheer

hush: noun
intelligence - intellect - sagacity

hushmand: adjective
sagacious - intelligent

hushmandi: noun
sagacity

hushyâr: adjective
sober - cautious - observant - conscious -
astute - vigilant

hushyâr budan: verb
To sober

hushyâri: noun
quale - caution

hâ: preposition
plural sign

hâd: adjective
torrid - acute - acute - hot - keen

hâdese: noun
phenomenon - incident - accident

hâdeseye nâgovâr: noun
mischance - miscarriage - misadventure

hâdeseye târikhi: noun
epoch

hâdi: adjective
polestar - ductile - guide

hâel: noun
shutter - guard - louver - buttress - buffer

hâfbak: noun
halfback

hâfez: noun
keeper - retentive - patron

hâfeze: noun
memory - retention

hâg: noun
spore

hâjat: noun
chamberlain - porter

hâjat: noun
wish

hâkem: noun
governor

hâkem budan: verb
To govern

hâki: noun
expressive

hâki az: noun
representative - significant

hâki budan: verb
To portend

hâl: noun
health - mood - pep - status - state -
situation - self

hâl ânke: preposition
while

hâlat: noun
temper - situation - status - mood

hâlate tahavo': noun
nausea - qualm

hâle: noun
corona - halo

hâlu: adjective
hallo

hâlâ: noun
now

hâmel: adjective
carrier - conveyor - vehicle - porter

hâmel budan: verb
To comport

hâmele: adjective
pergnant

hâmele budan: verb
To expect

hâmelegi: noun
expectancy - gestation

hâmi: adjective
protector - sponsor - advocate

hâmun: noun
plain

hâr: adjective
rabid

hârmuni: noun
harmony

hâsel: noun
product - harvest - outcome

hâsel kardan: verb
To afford - To acquire - To get - To generate

hâsele jam': noun
sum - total

hâselkhiz: adjective
prolific - pergnant

hâselkhizi: noun
productivity

hâselzarb: noun
product

hâshiye: noun
margin - outskirt

hâshiye duzi: noun
sewing

hâshur zadan: verb
To hatch

hâshâ: adverb
denial - never

hâshâ kardan: verb
To deny

hâvi: noun
receptacle

hây: preposition
hey

hâyel kardan: verb
To thwart

hâyel shodan: verb
To intervene - To intercept

hâzegh: adjective
proficient

hâzeme: noun
digestive

hâzer: adjective
stock - present

hâzer kardan: verb
To ready

hô kardan: verb
To jeer - To hoot

hôl: noun
shock

hôle: noun
towel

hôlnâk: adjective
ghastly - terrific - terrible

hôlo hôsh: noun
environs

hôsele: noun
mood

hôz: noun
pool

hôze: noun
extent - district - zone

i

id'olozhi: noun
ideology

ideâl: adjective
ideal

ifâ: noun
performance

ifâ kardan: verb
To perform

ifâ kardan: verb
To implement

ifâ konande: noun
performer

ihâm goftan: verb
To quip

ijâb: noun
exigency - requirement

ijâd: noun
creation

ijâd kardan: verb
To engender - To create

ijâz: noun
brevity

il: noun
tribe

ilchi: adjective
envoy - embassador - ambassador

ilkhâni: adjective
patriarch

imen: adjective
secure - safe

imeni: noun
safety - security

imân: noun
belief - faith

imân âvardan: verb
To believe

in: preposition
this

inak: adverb
now - behold

inghadr: adverb
somush

inghadr: adverb
so

inhâ: adverb
these

injâ: adverb
where - hither

intor: adverb
such

intor: adverb
so - thus

229

inân: adverb
these

irlandi: adjective
Irish

irâd: noun
quotation - objection

irâd kardan: verb
To quote

irâdgir: adjective
prig - captious

irâni: adjective
iranian - persian

ishân: adjective
they

ist: noun
stoppage - stay - cease

istgâh: noun
stop

istâ: adjective
stationary - static

istâdan: verb
To stop - To stand - To cease

istâdegi: noun
persist - resistance

istâdegi kardan: verb
To resist - To abide

istâhe âtashneshâni: noun
firehouse

isâ: noun
jesus - christ

italiyâyi: adjective
Italian

iyâlat: noun
state - province

iyâlati: adjective
statehood - provincial

iyâlâte motahede: noun
United States

izad: noun
god

izâ: noun
ibidem - ditto

j

ja'be: noun
box - chest - case

ja'beye abzâr: noun
toolbox

ja'l: noun
fiction - fake

ja'l kardan: verb
To counterfeit

ja'li: adjective
counterfeit - imitation

jabr: noun
force - algebra

jabâr: adjective
taskmaster - unmerciful

jad: noun
predecessor - ancestor

jadid: noun
modern - novel - new

jadidan: adverb
new

jadidol ta'sis: adjective
recent

jadidol vorud: adjective
income - postulant

jadval: noun
list - groove - tableau - table - schedule

jadval: noun
chart

jafang: noun
trashy - rigmarole

jafâ: noun
misbehavior

jahanam: noun
inferno - hell - hades

jahande: adjective
springy - jumper - jumper - hopper

jahandegi: noun
resiliency

jahat: noun
sake - vector - point

jahat yâbi: verb
To orient

jahesh: noun
jump - caper

jahesh kardan: verb
To rebound

jahidan: verb
To bound

jahiziye: noun
dowry

jahl: noun
ignorance

jahâd: noun
jehad

jahâd kardan: verb
To crusade

jahân: noun
world - universe - macrocosm

jahân âfarin: adjective
demiurge

jahângard: noun
tourist - rubberneck

jahângardi: noun
tourism

jahângardi kardan: verb
To tourist

jahâni: adjective
universal - global

jahâni kardan: verb
To universalize

jahâz: noun
ship - system - appurtenance - apparatus - dowry

jak zadan: verb
To jack

jalase: noun
session

jalase: noun
meet

jalb: noun
jalap - invitation

jalb kardan: verb
To attract - To atone

jalbe rezâyat kardan: verb
To atone

jalgh zadan: verb
To masturbate

jalâ: noun
japan - gloss - polish - varnish - burnish - buff

jalâ: noun
veneer

jalâ dâdan: verb
To burnish - To polish

jalâd: noun
deathsman

jalâfe shar': adjective
unlawful

jalâl: noun
refulgence - kudos - glory - honest

jam': noun
total - tot - tale - summation - mass - plural - aggregate - rout

jam' bastan: verb
To tot

jam' kardan: verb
To total - To add - To gather - To collect

232

jam' shodan: verb
To gather - To constringe - To congregate

jam' zadan: verb
To add

jam' âvari: noun
muster - assemblage

jam' âvari kardan: verb
To reap - To rake

jam'I: adjective
plural - collective

jam'an: adverb
utter - wholly

jam'e kol: noun
entirety - gross

jam'iyat: noun
society - throng - crowd - group - gang -
flock - company - bike - army - party - herd -
heap - habitancy - mob - press - population
- people

jamâ'at: noun
passel - posse - stream - school

jamâl: noun
beauty

janbe: noun
aspect

janbi: noun
lateral

jang: noun
battle - warfare - war

jang afruz: adjective
warmonger

jang afzâr: noun
weapon

jangal: noun
forest - jungle

jangalbân: noun
woodsman

jangali: adjective
sylvan - wild

jangalneshin: adjective
forest dwellers

jangi: adjective
military - martial - warlike

jangidan: verb
To militate

jangju: adjective
belligerent - bellicose - comatant - warrior

jangjuyi: noun
militancy

jangâvar: adjective
warrior

janjâl: noun
tumult

janjâl kardan: verb
To jangle

janjâl râh andâkhtan: verb
To tumult

jaraghe: noun
arc - scintillation - sparkle - spark

jaraghe zadan: verb
To scintillate - To sparkle - To spark

jarh: noun
mayhem

jarihe: noun
wound

jarihedâr: adjective
raw

jarihedâr kardan: verb
To hurt - To harrow - To raw

jarime: noun
surcharge - fine - penalty

jarime kardan: verb
To fine - To assess - To penalize

jariyân: noun
outflow - stream

jariyâne havâ: noun
airflow

jaro bahs kardan: verb
To squabble

jarsaghil: noun
lift - derrick - crane

jarâh: noun
surgeon

jarâhi: noun
surgery

jarâyed: noun
press

jasad: noun
corpse - body

jashn: noun
celebration - carnival

jashne arusi: noun
marriage - bridal

jashne tavalod: noun
birthday party

jast: noun
leap - bounce

jast zadan: verb
To vault

jasto khiz: noun
spring - curvet - caper - bound

jasur: adjective
adventurer - boldface

jasurâne: adverb
perky

jav: noun
atmosphere

jav dâdan: verb
To oat

javande: adjective
hunter - acquisitive

javi: noun
atmospheric - weather

javidan: verb
To chewing

javidan: verb
To munch - To masticate - To chew - To chaw - To champ

javâb dâdan: verb
To answer

javâbe manfi: noun
nope - negative

javâbe rad: noun
recalcitrance

javâbgu: adjective
respondent

javâher: noun
jewel - treasure

javâherforush: noun
jeweller - jeweler

javâherforushi: noun
bijouterie - jewelry

javâheri: adjective
jeweler

javâhersâz: noun
jeweller - jeweler

javân: adjective
young

javâne: noun
bud - tiller - sprout

javâne: noun
youngling

javâne zadan: verb
To erupt - To ratoon - To grain - To spurt

javâni: adjective
youth - springtime

javânmard: adjective
chivalrous - sportsmanlike

javânmardi: noun
chivalry - magnanimity

javântarin: adjective
youngest

javânân: noun
youth

javâz: noun
permit - license - pass

jaza: noun
penalty

jazabe: noun
rapture - appeal - magnetism

jazaye keifar: noun
payoff

jazb: noun
suction

jazb: noun
next - side

jazb kardan: verb
To sponge - To attract - To absorb

jazire: noun
island

jazr: noun
ebb

jazr: noun
square

jazr: noun
pier

jazâb: adjective
lovable

jazâbiyat: noun
grace - spell

jazâmi: adjective
leper

jebhe: noun
deploy

jebre'il: noun
gabriel

jedi: adjective
serious

jediyat: noun
enthusiasm - gravity

jedâl: noun
controversy - battle

jedâl kardan: verb
To dispute

jedâl âmiz: adjective
controversial

jedâr: noun
septum - wall

jegar: noun
liver

jehâlat: noun
ignorance - idiotism

jeld: noun
cover - shell - sheathe - sheath

jeld kardan: verb
To cover - To case

jelde ketâb: noun
wrapper

jelf: adjective
gaudy - tawdry

jelighe: noun
underwaist - vest

jelve: noun
sight - showing - show - seeming - display -
flash - bravery - parade - luster

jelve dâshtan: verb
To luster

jelvegar: adjective
smart

jemâ': noun
copulation - coitus - coition

jemâ' kardan: verb
To meddle - To dight

jen: noun
sprite - urchin - bogey

jende: adjective
hack - townswoman - trollop

jeni: adjective
jenny

jenin: noun
chrysalis - germ

jens: noun
substance - stuff - gender

jense nar: noun
male

jensi: adjective
sexual - sex

jentelman: noun
gallant

jenâb: noun
honor - excellency

jenâghe sine: noun
sternum

jenâh: noun
shoulder - wing - side

jenâyat: noun
villainy - crime

jenâyatkâr: adjective
jailbird - criminal

jenâyatkâr: adjective
desperado

jenâyi: noun
criminal

jer zadan: verb
To cheat

jerâhat: noun
wound - sore - stricture

jesm: noun
substance - corpus - metal - material - body

jesme shenâvar: adjective
buoy - drift

jesmi: adjective
substantial - material - carnal

jesmâni: adjective
material - physical - earthen

jesârat: noun
temerity - audacity - presumption

jesârat: adjective
impertinence

jesârat kardan: verb
To obtrude

jet: noun
jet

jib: noun
tangent - purse - sinus - pocket

jib bor: adjective
cutpurse - dip - bung - pickpocket

jib bori kardan: verb
To purse

jib dâr: adjective
pocket

jibi: adjective
pocket

jigh: noun
shriek - shout - scream

jigh keshidan: verb
To zing - To screech

jigh zadan: verb
To scream - To yelp - To shout

jik jik: noun
chirp - peep

jik zadan: verb
To peep

jim shodan: verb
To scram - To nip - To guy

jin: noun
gin

jip: noun
jeep

jir: noun
chamoisleather

jir jir kardan: verb
To yip - To chirp - To cheep

jire: noun
stipend - allotment

jire: noun
ration - diet

jire bandi kardan: verb
To ration

jire dâdan: verb
To allowance

jirjirak: noun
cricket

jive: noun
quicksilver - mercury

jobrân: noun
amends - reprisal - recompense

jobrân kardan: verb
To compensate - To retrieve - To reciprocate

jobrân nâpazir: adjective
irreparable - irrecoverable

jobrâne khesârat: noun
redress

jodâ: adverb
apart - separate - segregate

jodâ kardan: verb
To unzip - To unlink - To chop

jodâ kardan: verb
To dismember

jodâ konande: adjective
insulator

jodâ shodan: verb
To part - To dissent

jodâ shodani: adjective
separable - detachable - dissoluble -
precipitant

jodâgâne: adverb
separate - aside - antiseptic

jodâshodani: adjective
irresolvable - inseparable

jodâsâzi: noun
detachment - severance - segregate

jodâyi: noun
segregation - divorce

jodô: noun
jiujitsu

joft: noun
couple - match - peer - even

joft kardan: verb
To twin - To accompany - To link - To
geminate

joftak: noun
buck

joftak andâkhtan: verb
To buck

joghd: noun
owl

joghrâfi: noun
geography

joghrâfidân: adjective
geographer

joghrâfiyâ: noun
geography

johud: noun
Jew

jolbak: noun
alga

jolge: noun
flat - plain

jolo: noun
ahead - beforehand - forward

jolo andâkhtan: verb
To antedate

jolo bordan: verb
To boost - To advance - To further

jolo raftan: verb
To comealong

jolo zadan: verb
To outgo

jolodâr: adjective
front - herald - harbinger - vanguard

jolodâr budan: verb
To van

jologiri kardan: verb
To prevent - To intercept

jolotar: adjective
further - previous

jolotar budan az: verb
To precede

joloye: noun
forward - former - fore - prior

jolus: noun
accession

jolus kardan: verb
To sit - To agree

jom'e: noun
friday

jomhur: noun
populace

jomhuri: noun
republic - commonwealth

jomhurikhâh: adjective
republican

jomjome: noun
cranium - pan - brainpan - skull - scalp

jomle: noun
sentence

jomud: adjective
solidity

jonbande: adjective
jiggly - wobbly - wiggler

jonbesh: noun
movement - motion

jonbidan: verb
To vibrate - To move - To shake

jonbojush: noun
motion - milling

jonbândan: verb
To wag - To bestir

jonub: noun
south

jonube khâvari: adjective
southeast

jonube sharghi: adjective
southeast

jonubi: adjective
southerner - southern - south

jonun: noun
insanity - psychosis

jor'at: noun
courage

jor'at dâdan: verb
To abet - To hearten

jor'at kardan: verb
To dare

jor'e: noun
sip - shot - swig - quaff

jor'e jor'e nushidan: verb
To dram

jorm: noun
spawn - misdeed - mass - crime - guilt

jose: noun
bulk

joshan: noun
mail - armor - armature

jostan: verb
To scoot - To jump - To leap - To hip

jostoju: noun
search - research - rummage - quest

jostoju kardan: verb
To seek - To search

jostoju kardan: verb
To search

jostojugar: adjective
explorer

jostâr: noun
inquiry - inquest - query

joz: preposition
but - retail - forby

joz: preposition
except

joz in: adverb
else

joz inke: adverb
unless

joz'iyat: noun
detail - elaboration

jozveh: noun
leaflet - brochure - booklet

jozyi: adjective
little - inconsiderable - retail

jozâm: noun
leprosy

jud: adjective
soon - early

juje: noun
squab - chick - bird

jujekeshi: noun
incubation

jujetighi: noun
urchin - hedgehog

juju: noun
bug

jukhe: noun
squad

jur: noun
sort - compatible

jur: noun
tyranny

jur budan: verb
To comport - To adhere - To accordance

jur budan: verb
To match

jur dar âmadan: verb
To sort

jur kardan: verb
To sort - To assort - To adapt

jur shodan: verb
To piece - To mesh

jurab: noun
gaskin - hose

jurvâjur: adverb
variety

jurâb: noun
reply - answer

jurâb bâfi: noun
hosiery

jurâbe kutâh: noun
vamp

jurâjur: noun
various

jush: noun
spout - rash - weld - boil

jush dâdan: verb
To solder - To shut - To weld - To vulcanize

jush zadan: verb
To breakout - To effervesce

jushe sarsiyâh: noun
blackhead

jushidan: verb
To seethe - To gurgle - To bubble - To perk

jushkâr: adjective
welder

jushkâri kardan: verb
To weld

jushân: adjective
ebullient

jushândan: verb
To seethe - To bubble - To decoction

jushânde: adjective
sodden

juy: noun
creek - stream - dike

juybâr: noun
stream

jâ: noun
situation - site - stead - station

jâ andâkhtan: verb
To set

jâ dâdan: verb
To settle - To stead - To insert - To infix - To incorporate - To embed

jâ gozâshtan: verb
To mislay

jâ kardan: verb
To fold

jâ oftâde: adjective
mellow - ripe

jâ pâshidan: verb
To inquire - To ask

jâbejâ kardan: verb
To displace - To replace

jâbejâ shodan: verb
To supplant - To metastasis

jâber: adjective
violent

jâde: noun
path - way - track

jâdu: noun
magic

jâdu kardan: verb
To conjure - To enchant

jâdugar: adjective
wizard

jâdugar: adjective
conjurer - wizard

jâdugari: noun
wizardry - incantation

jâduyi: adjective
magical

jâdâr: adjective
spacious

jâgereftan: verb
To situate - To hold

jâgozashtan: verb
To misplace

jâh: noun
dignity - eminence - pomp

jâhed: adjective
studious

jâhel: adjective
ignoramus - unwise - fool

jâho jalâl: noun
purple

jâhtalab: adjective
ambitious

jâhtalab budan: verb
To ambition

jâhtalabi: noun
ambition

jâkesh: adjective
bawd - pimp

jâkesh: adjective
pander

jâkhâli: noun
dodge

jâleb: adjective
attractive - marvelous

jâleb tavajoh: adjective
notable - remarkable - lively

jâliz: noun
patch

jâm: noun
cupule - chalice - goblet - cup

jâme': noun
comprehensive

jâme'e: noun
society

jâme'e: noun
suit - costume - garment

jâme'e shenâs: noun
sociologist

jâme'iyat: noun
universality - universalism

jâmed: noun
rigid

jân: noun
spirit

jân dâdan: verb
To die - To enliven

jân kandan: verb
To grub - To durdge

jândâr: noun
animate

jâne kalâm: noun
gist

jânebdâr: adjective
partial

jânebdâri: noun
predilection

jânebi: noun
sidelong - lateral

jâneshin: noun
substitute

jâneshin: noun
successor

jâneshin kardan: verb
To swap - To substitute

jâneshin shodan: verb
To inherit - To surrogate - To supersede

jâneshin shodan: verb
To displace

jânevar: noun
animal - creature

jânevarshenâs: noun
zoologist

jânevarshenâsi: noun
zoology

jânfeshân: adjective
zealot

jânfeshâni: noun
zeal

jângodâz: adjective
piteous

jâni: adjective
criminal - convict - bane

jânpanâh: noun
shelter - parapet

jânsakht: adjective
diehard

jâr: noun
candelabrum

jâr keshidan: verb
To acclaim

jâr zadan: verb
To blaze - To blare - To proclaim

jârchi: noun
trumpeter - herald - blazer

jâri budan: verb
To flow

jâri sâkhtan: verb
To shed - To perfuse

jâru: noun
sweep

jârub: noun
broom

jârub kardan: verb
To wisp - To whisk - To broom - To scavenger - To sweep

jârukesh: adjective
sweeper

jâsus: noun
spy

jâsus budan: verb
To espy

jâsusi: noun
espionage

jâsusi kardan: verb
To spy - To espy

jâvid: noun
eternal - immortal

jâvidân: noun
immortal - forever

jây dâdan: verb
To place - To implant

jâye aks: noun
album

jâye khalvat: noun
solitude

jâye khâli: noun
lacuna

jâye moghadas: noun
shrine

jâye pâ: noun
trace - toe - vestige - rake

jâye shib: noun
pitch

jâye vizhe: noun
box - booth - bench

jâye zakhm: noun
sore

jâye zarbat: noun
dent

jâye'e: noun
injury

jâyez: noun
allowable

jâyez: noun
prize - bonus - award

jâygahe vizhe: noun
stall

jâygozin kardan: verb
To replace

jâygozin shodan: verb
To tabernacle

jâygozin sâkhtan: verb
To seat

jâygozini: noun
situation

jâygâh: noun
station - seat - place

jâygâhe moghadas: noun
sanctum - sanctuary

jâyi: noun
someplace

jâyike: adverb
where

jâzadan: verb
To fake

jâzeb: adjective
attractive - absorbent

jôhar: noun
quintessence - marrow - ink

jôhari: noun
inky

jôje: noun
spouse - wife - wedlock - lady

jôlâ: noun
weaver

jôlân: noun
parade

k

kabed: noun
liver

kabir: adjective
great - major - adult

kabk: noun
partridge

kabud: adjective
gray - livid

kabud shodan: verb
To bruise

kabudshodegi: noun
bruise

kabutar: noun
pigeon

kabutarkhâne: noun
loft - penthouse

kabâb: noun
barbecue

kabâb kardan: verb
To roast - To grid - To barbecue

kachal: noun
bald

kachali: noun
tinea

kadbânu: noun
dame - housewife - mistress - matron

kadkhodâ: noun
sheriff - reeve

kadu: noun
gourd

kadu: noun
squash - cucurbit

kadu tanbal: noun
pumpkin

kaf: noun
foam - bottom - apron - insole - slag

kaf kardan: verb
To foam

kaf zadan (tahsin): verb
To acclaim

kafan: noun
shroud

kafan kardan: verb
To shroud

kafbin: noun
palmist

kafe: noun
pan

kafe pâ: noun
foot

kafgir: noun
splatter - spatula

kafil: adjective
surety - sponsor - guarantor - bondsman

kafsh: noun
shoe

kaftâr: noun
hyena

kafâlud: adjective
sudsy - scummy

kafâre dâdan: verb
To atone

kahir: noun
bay - urticaria

kahkeshân: noun
galaxy

kahkeshân: noun
galaxy

kahrobâ: adjective
amber

kahâli: noun
ophthalmology

kaj: adjective
tilt - indirect - crank

kaj kardan: verb
To tilt - To slant - To inflect - To incline - To bend

kaj nahâdan: noun
cock

kaj shodan: verb
To lean - To careen - To tilt - To swerve

kaji: adjective
tilt

kajkholghi: noun
tiff - tantrum - distemper - irritability

kajo ma'vaj: noun
zigzag

kalak: noun
pen

kalam: noun
cabbage

kalame: noun
word

kalame: noun
word

kale: noun
head - brain

kale khar: adjective
dolt

kale shagh: adjective
stubborn - obstinate - bullheaded - pertinacious

kalimi: noun
jew

kalsiyom: noun
calcium

kalâf: noun
skein - hasp - hank

kalâf: noun
coil

kalâfe: noun
hank

kalâgh: noun
crow

kalâm: noun
language

kalân: noun
massive - immense - huge

kalânshahr: noun
metropolis

kalântar: noun
sheriff - reeve - marshal

kalântari: noun
policestation - commissariat

kam: noun
slight - scant - little - low

kam aghl: adjective
vacuous - fool

kam arzesh: adjective
cheap

kam davâm: adjective
memnetary - weak

kam dâshtan: verb
To lack

kam harf: adjective
laconic - taciturn

kam kardan: verb
To subtract - To reduce - To rebate - To weaken

kam kharj: adjective
inexpensive

kam shodan: verb
To slacken - To abate - To dwindle - To diminish

kamand: noun
noose - lasso - lariat - snarl - snare - tether

kamand andâkhtan: verb
To lasso

kamar: noun
back

kamarband: noun
belt

kamarband: noun
belt

kamardard: noun
backache

kamardard: noun
lumbago - backache

kambud: adjective
shortcoming - shortage - leakage - deficit - deficiency - dearth

kami: adjective
paucity - insufficiency - deficiency - rarity

kamin: noun
ambush

kamin kardan: verb
To stalk - To waylay - To lurk - To ambush

kamingâh: noun
den

kamiyat: noun
quantity

kamkhun: adjective
wan - anemic

kamkhuni: noun
anemia - anaemia

kamo bish: adverb
some

kamo kasti: noun
wane

kamposht: adjective
sparse - thin

kamrang: adjective
inconspicuous - pale - lunar

kamrang: adjective
colourless - wan - pallid

kamru: adjective
shy

kamru: adjective
shy - sheepish - timid

kamruyi: noun
timidity

kamruyi: noun
timidity

kamtar: adjective
lesser - less

kamtar az: adjective
less than

kamtar kardan: verb
To lessen

kamtarin: adjective
least

kamud kardan: verb
To bruise

kamyâb: adjective
rare - scarce

kamyâbi: noun
scarcity - paucity - poverty - infrequency - rarity

kamâb: adjective
shallow

kamâl: noun
perfection - maturity

kamân: noun
bow - arc

kamândâr: noun
archer

kamâne: noun
ricochet

kamâne kardan: verb
To ricochet

kandan: verb
To dig - To mine - To peel

kandan: verb
To dig

kandu: noun
apiary - beehive - hive

kanduye zanbure asal: noun
hives

kaniz: adjective
bondwoman

kankâsh kardan: verb
To deliberate - To consult

kapak: noun
mould - mildew

kapak zadan: verb
To mould - To mildew

kapar: noun
shed

kapsul: noun
capsule - cachet

kapur: noun
minnow - carp

kar: adjective
deaf - choir

karafs: noun
celery

karbâs: noun
burlap - sackcloth

kardan: verb
To do - To perform - To set

kardan: verb
To do

kargadan: noun
rhino - hippopotamus

kargadan: noun
rhinoceros

karih: adjective
detestable - nasty - unsightly - ugly

karkas: noun
vulture

karâne: noun
strand - shore

kas: noun
person

kasb: noun
trade - avocation - metier - vocation

kasb kardan: verb
To gain

kasbe taklif: noun
referendum

kashf: noun
detection - discovery - overture

kashf kardan: verb
To discover - To detect

kashfe ramz kardan: verb
To decode

kashk: noun
whey - curd

kasi: noun
someone - somebody - anybody

kasif: adjective
nasty - dirty - impure

kasif kardan: verb
To dirty - To soil

kasif shodan: verb
To dirty

kasike: verb
whom

kasr: noun
deficit - deficiency - deduction - diminution
- leakage

kasr: noun
fraction

kasr kardan: verb
To detract - To deduct

kasre darâmad: noun
deficit

kasri: adjective
shortage - leakage - lack

katibe: noun
epigraph - cornice - coping - inscription

katirâ: noun
tragacanth

katân: noun
linen - bombast

kazhdom: noun
scorpion

kazâyi: noun
socalled - eventful

ke: preposition
that - than - who - which

kebre: noun
crust

kebre bastan: verb
To crust

kebrit: noun
match - lighter - light

keder: adjective
glum - opaque - turbid

keder kardan: verb
To tarnish

kefâlat: noun
bail

kefâyat: noun
sufficiency - autarchy - adequacy

kefâyat kardan: verb
To suffice

keif kardan: verb
To please

keifar: noun
retribution - penalty

keifar dâdan: verb
To punish

keifari: noun
pnitive - retribution - penal

keifiyat: noun
quality - how - kind - state

keihân: noun
universe - cosmos

keihâni: adjective
cosmic

keihânshenâs: noun
cosmographer

keihânshenâsi: noun
cosmology - cosmogony

keik: noun
cake

kelid: noun
key

kelisa: noun
church

kelishe: noun
stereotype

kelâj: noun
clutch

kelâs: noun
class

kelâse dars: noun
classroom

kenâr: noun
along - recess - rand - next

kenâr: noun
edge

kenâr keshidan: verb
To overrule - To reserve

kenâr keshidan: verb
To recede

kenâr raftan: verb
To sheer

kenâr âmadan: verb
To cope

kenâre: noun
edge - border

kenâre gereftan: verb
To resign

kenâregiri: noun
demission - retreat - resignation

kenâregiri kardan: verb
To secede - To abdicate - To retire

kenâye: noun
jest - allegory - metaphor - lampoon - innuendo

kenâye zadan: verb
To squib

kenâye âmiz: adjective
wry - snide - sardonic

kenâyedâr: adjective
sly - witty

ker kardan: verb
To deafen

kerdâr: noun
jest - act - issue - exploit - deed

kerekh: adjective
numbing - numb

kerem rang: adjective
cream

kerep: noun
crepe - crape

kerismas: noun
chrismas

kerk: noun
pubes - pile

kerm: noun
worm

kermak: noun
pinworm

kerme abrisham: noun
silkworm

kerme kadu: noun
jointworm - measles

kerme rude: noun
helminth

kernâ: noun
horn - trumpet

keroket: noun
croquet

kerâle posht: noun
backstroke

kerâmat: noun
munificence

kerâneye daryâ: noun
seaboard

kerâran: adverb
often - freuqently

kerâvât: noun
tie

kerâvât: noun
tie

kerâye: noun
hire - rent - fare

kerâye kardan: verb
To rent - To lease - To hire

kesel: adjective
weary - exanimate

kesh dâdam: verb
To protract - To stretch - To strain

kesh raftan: verb
To pilfer - To cabbage - To snitch - To snip

kesh âmadan: verb
To stretch

254

keshbâfi kardan: verb
To knit

keshdâr: adjective
supple - tensile

keshdâr: adjective
elastic

keshesh: noun
traction - twitch - haul

kesheshi: noun
tensional

keshidan: verb
To pull - To string - To weigh - To draw - To drag

keshidan: verb
To stretch

keshide: adjective
oblong - extensive - long - linear

keshidegi: noun
elongation

keshik: noun
sentry - sentinel - vigilance

keshish: noun
priest - cleric - clergyman

keshmesh: noun
raisin

keshmesh: noun
raisin

keshsân: adjective
elastic

kesht kardan: verb
To cultivate

keshti: noun
ship

keshtirân: noun
navigator

keshtirâni: noun
sailing

keshtirâni kardan: verb
To navigate

keshtkâr: noun
tiller - cultivator

keshtkâri: noun
husbandry

keshvar: noun
country

keshvardâri: noun
governance

keshvargoshâ: adjective
conqueror

keshâkesh: noun
struggle - strife - conflict

keshândan: verb
To drag

keshâvarz: noun
farmer

keshâvarzi: noun
agriculture

keshô: noun
drawer - slide - till

kesle konande: adjective
tedious - prosaic - irksome - drowsy - drab

kesrat: noun
multiplicity - intensity

kesvat: noun
garb

kesâd: adjective
slack - stagnant - insensitive - inactive

kesâd shodan: verb
To statgnate

kesâdi: adjective
depression - recession - stringency - slack

kesâfat: noun
dirt - impurity - pollution - muck - mire

kesâlat: noun
disorder

ketf: noun
shoulder - scapular - scapula

ketmân: noun
reservation

ketri: noun
skillet - pot - kettle

ketri: noun
kettle

ketâbat kardan: verb
To scribe

ketâbche: noun
cahier - booklet

ketâbdâr: noun
curator - librarian

ketâbe darsi: noun
textbook - text

ketâbe dâstân: noun
novel

ketâbe râhnamâ: noun
directory - guidebook - handbook - manual

ketâbforush: noun
bookseller - bookman

ketâbforushi: noun
library - bookstore

ketâbkhân: adjective
studious

ketâbkhâne: noun
library

ketân: noun
jacket - volume - book

kezb: noun
false - untruth

khabar: noun
news

khabar dâshtan: verb
To hear

khabar resâni: noun
information - news

khabari: adjective
news

khabarnegâr: noun
reporter

khabarnâme: noun
newsletter

khabs: noun
vice

khabâz: noun
baker

khafe: adjective
sultry - stuffy - pokey - muggy

khafe kardan: verb
To choke - To mute

khafe shodan: verb
To smother

khafe shô: verb
To shut up

khafegi: noun
asphyxia

khafekon: adjective
damper

khafif: noun
light - low - small

khafâ: noun
stealth - wrap

khajul: adjective
shamefaced

khal': noun
deposition

khal' kardan: verb
To dethrone - To depose

khal' selâh kardan: verb
To unarm - To disarm

khal' shodan: verb
To create

khal'e yad kardan: verb
To evict

khala': noun
vacuum

khalabân: noun
pilot

khalgh: noun
temperament - temper - kidney - humor -
mood - people

khalgh kardan: verb
To make

khalife: noun
caliph - vicar - prelate

khalij: noun
gulf

khalkhâl: noun
anklet

khalse: noun
trance - ecstasy - rapture

khalvat: noun
solitude - sanctum - privacy

khalvatgâh: noun
den - boudoir - sanctum

khalâf: noun
misdeed - foul - contrary

khalâf kâri: noun
misconduct

khalâfe orf: adjective
unconventional

khalâfe vâghe': noun
untrue

khalâfkâr: adjective
trespasser

khalâs kardan: verb
To rid

kham: noun
bend - curve

kham kardan: verb
To bend - To incline - To limber

kham shodan: verb
To bow - To lean - To recline

kham shode: adjective
bent

khamidan: verb
To retroflex - To bend

khamide: adjective
limber - embowed

khamide budan: verb
To slouch

khamide kardan: verb
To limber - To camber

khamide shodan: verb
To slump

khamidegi: noun
loop - bent - stoop

khamir: noun
duff - dough - paste - unguent

khamir dandân: noun
toothpaste

khamir kardan: verb
To mash - To levigate - To leaven

khamir mâye: noun
yeast

khamir zadan: verb
To paste

khamirmâye: noun
leaven

khamiyâze: noun
gape

khamiyâze keshidan: verb
To yawn - To gape

khamush: adjective
silent - hush - quiet

khandagh: noun
trig - trench - sike - ditch - graft - moat

khandan: adjective
smiling - laughing - riant

khande: noun
laugh

khande âvar: adjective
ludicrous - humorous

khandedâr: adjective
comic - hilarious

khandidan: verb
To laugh - To chortle

khaneghâh: noun
abbey

khanjar: noun
dirk - daggar - bowieknife - bodkin

khanjar zadan: verb
To jab

khanjar zadan: verb
To dirk - To stab

khar: noun
donkey

khar kardan: verb
To wheedle

kharak: noun
sawhorse

kharboze: noun
melon

kharchang: noun
cancer - crab

khardal: noun
mustard

khargush: noun
hare - rabbit

kharid: noun
buy - purchase

kharid kardan: verb
To shootinggallery

kharidan: verb
To buy

kharidâr: adjective
shopkeeper - purchaser - buyer

kharidâri: noun
purchase

khariyat: noun
stupidity

kharj: noun
cost - expense - expenditure

kharj kardan: verb
To expend - To disburse - To spend

kharji: noun
alimony - maintenance - spendingmoney

kharmagas: noun
gadfly - horsefly - maggot

kharman: noun
shock - stack - harvest

259

kharmohre: noun
bead

kharâb: adjective
ill - ruinous - rotten

kharâb kardan: verb
To devastate - To deteriorate - To destroy - To ruin

kharâbe: adjective
ruin

kharâbi: noun
destruction - decay - wreckage - ruination - ruin

kharâbkâr: adjective
subversive - saboteur

kharâbkâri: verb
To subvert - To sabotage

kharâbkâri: noun
obstructionism - subversion

kharâj: noun
tax - tribute - spendthrift

kharâmidan: verb
To stalk - To gait - To lope - To peacock

kharâsh: noun
scotch - abrasion - irritation

kharâshidan: verb
To graze - To scrape

kharâshândan: verb
To porcupine

kharât: noun
chipper

khashen: adjective
hoarse - harsh - boorish - blatant - coarse - rude

khashen: adjective
raucous

khashkhâsh: noun
poppy

khashm: noun
rage - wrath - anger - irritation

khashm va ghazab: noun
dander

khashmgin: adjective
irate - rabid - wroth

khashmgin kardan: verb
To irritate - To aggravate - To exasperate - To ensnare - To enrage

khashmgin shodan: verb
To boil

khashmgin sâkhtan: verb
To snarl

khashmginâne: adverb
high

khashmnâk: adjective
angry - irate

khashmnâk kardan: verb
To spleen

khashmnâk shodan: verb
To rage

khashmâlud: adjective
fierce

khasis: adjective
sordid - skimpy - stingy - ungenerous - hidebound

khasise: noun
trait

khasisi: noun
scotticism - miser

khasm: noun
enemy - opponent

khasmâne: adverb
inimical

khaste: adjective
spent - sear - tire - blown - weary

khaste: adjective
tired

khaste kardan: verb
To tire - To bore - To harass - To exhaust

khaste shodan: verb
To runout - To overweary - To irk - To bore

khaste va kufte: adjective
stump

khastegi: noun
exhaustion

khastegi nâpazir: adjective
indefatigable - inexhaustible

khastegi âvar: adjective
irksome

khat: noun
character - line

khat keshidan: verb
To line - To tick

khat'tât: noun
calligrapher

khat'tâti: noun
calligraphy

khatar: noun
jeopardy - risk - danger - peril - hazard

khatarnâk: adjective
jeopardous - disastrous

khatdâr: adjective
streaky

khate mash'y: noun
policy

khate momtad: noun
stretch

khate âhan: noun
track - railway - rail

khati: adjective
linear - lineal

khatib: noun
orator

khatir: adjective
serious - momentous

khatkesh: noun
liner - ruler

khatne kardan: verb
To circumcise

khatâ: noun
injustice - error - wrong - sin

khatâ kardan: verb
To sin - To bunlge - To miss - To err

khatâb: noun
address

khatâb kardan: verb
To address

khatâbe: noun
sermon - lecture - address

khatâkâr: adjective
transgressor - wrongdoer

khatâkâri: noun
wrongdoing

khavâs: noun
attribute

khayât: noun
tailor

khaz: noun
zibelline - fur

khazan: adjective
autumn - fall

khazande: adjective
creeper - crawly - worm

khazdâr: adjective
furry

khaze: noun
moss

khazidan: verb
To creep - To crawl - To glide

khazâne: noun
thesaurus - treasury

khebre: adjective
expert - critic - connoisseur

khedmat: noun
service - attendance - duty - office

khedmat kardan: verb
To minister - To serve

khedmatgozâr: adjective
server

khedmatkâr: adjective
server - servant - damsel

khef kardan: verb
To waylay

khefat: noun
disgrace - contempt

khefat dâdan: verb
To degrade

khefat âvar: adjective
derogatory

262

kheili: adverb
very - many

kheili khub: adjective
glorious - well - OK

kheime: noun
tabernacle - hovel - canopy

kheime shab bâzi: noun
puppetry

kheir: noun
no - nay - good

kheiriye: noun
welfare

kheirkhâh: adjective
propitious - gracious

kheirkhâhi: noun
benevolence - generosity - zeal

kheirât: noun
alms - charity

khejel: adjective
ashamed

khejâlat dâdan: verb
To shame - To embarrass - To abash

khejâlati: adjective
shy - shamefaced

khelghat: noun
creation

khelt: noun
mucus - phlegm

khelt: noun
phlegm

khelâl: noun
peel - interval

khelâle dandân: noun
toothpick - pick

kheng: adjective
stupid - dense

kher kher: adjective
snort - rattle

kher kher kardan: verb
To grunt - To rattle - To snore

kher khere: noun
larynx

kheradmand: adjective
wise - intellectual

kheref: adjective
wacky - idiot - senile - fool

kheref budan: verb
To senility

khereft: adjective
imbecile - doter

kherghe: noun
cloak - stole

kherghepush: adjective
cassock

khers: noun
bear

khersak: noun
badger

khes khes: adjective
wheeze

khes khesh kardan: verb
To wheeze

khesat: noun
parsimony

khesh khesh kardan: verb
To rustle

khesht: noun
adobe - brick - bat

khesârat: noun
damage - harm

khesârat: noun
loss

khesârat zadan: verb
To damnify - To damage

khete: noun
territory

kheyme barpâ kardan: verb
To encamp

kheyme zadan: verb
To pitch - To tent

kheyriye: noun
charitable

khire: noun
steadfast - agaze

khire shodan: verb
To stare

khiresar: adjective
obstinate - pertinacious - stubborn

khis: adjective
wet - soppy

khis kardan: verb
To douse - To swill

khis khordan: verb
To soak

khis shodan: verb
To sodden

khish: verb
self

khishi: noun
propinquity - kinship - kin - relationship

khishtan: noun
self

khishâvand: noun
relative

khishâvandi: noun
cognation - relativeness

khisândan: verb
To soak - To drench

khisândan: verb
To maceration

khiyalandishi: noun
idealism

khiyâbân: noun
street - road

khiyâl: noun
fiction - imaginary

khiyâl: noun
phantom - fiction

khiyâl dâshtan: verb
To intend

khiyâl kardan: verb
To deem

khiyâlbâf: adjective
woolgatherer - whimsical

khiyâlbâfi: noun
utopianism

khiyâle bâtel: noun
daydream

khiyâli: adjective
dreamy - romantic - unrealistic - imaginary -
visionary

khiyâli: adjective
phantasy - simulation

khiyânat: noun
treason - treachery - guile - betrayal

khiyânat: noun
infidelity

khiyânat kardan: verb
To sellout

khiyânatkâr: adjective
treacherous - traitor - conspirator

khiyâr: noun
cucumber

khiyâr torshi: noun
pickle - gherkin

khiz: noun
leap - dropsy - gradient

khod: noun
self - own - ego

khod: preposition
oneself

khod bekhod: noun
spontaneous

khod dâri kardan: verb
To withhold - To refrain - To contain

khod râ gereftan: verb
To prim - To perk

khod'dâr: adjective
undemonstrative - continent

khod'dâri: noun
restraint - refusal - abstinence

khod'e: noun
trick - deceit

khod'e kardan: verb
To cheat

khodam: preposition
myself - own

khodash: preposition
herself - himself

khodbasandegi: noun
autarchy

khodbin: adjective
smug - egocentric - presumptuous -
arrogant

khodemân: preposition
ourselves - us

khodemâni: adjective
homey - intimate - pally - unihibit - tame

khodeshân: preposition
themselves - their

khodi: adjective
relative - familiar - insider

khodkhâh: adjective
selfish

khodkoshi: noun
suicide

khodkoshi kardan: verb
To suicide

khodkâme: adjective
dictator

khodkâr: noun
automatic

khodmokhtâr: adjective
autonomous - independent

khodnamâ: adjective
ostentatious - blatant

khodnamâyi: noun
parade - ostentation

khodnamâyi kardan: verb
To parade

khodparast: adjective
selfish

khodparast: adjective
egotist

khodpasand: adjective
selfish

khodpasandi: noun
egocentric

khodro: noun
automotive - automobile

khodsar: adjective
stubborn - headstrong - intractable

khodsarâne: adverb
intractable

khodsetâ: adjective
vainglorious - bravado - bragger

khodsetâyi: noun
swagger - vainglory

khodsetâyi kardan: verb
To boast

khodâ: noun
god - lord

khodânegahdâr: noun
bye

khodâparast: adjective
theist - deist

khodâshenâs: adjective
theologian - theist - godly

khodâvand: noun
god - lord

khodâvand: noun
God - lord

khoftan: verb
To sleep

khofte: adjective
asleep

khofâsh: noun
bat

khojaste: adjective
blest - auspicious

khol: adjective
crackpot - offbeat - nut - halfbaked - light -
queer - screwy

kholf: noun
successor

kholus: noun
sincerity - purity - candour - candor

kholâse: noun
summation - summary

kholâse nemudan: verb
To sum

kholâse sâkhtan: verb
To minute

khompâre: noun
mortar

khomre: noun
crock - vat

khoms: noun
quint

khomâr: adjective
drunkard - languid

khonak: adjective
cool - chilly - breezy - icy

khonak kardan: verb
To cool - To refrigerate

khonak sâkhtan: verb
To fresh

khonsâ: noun
neutral

khonsâ kardan: verb
To neutralize - To negate - To annul

khonsâ nemudan: verb
To annihilate

khonâgh: noun
croup - asphyxia

khor: noun
inlet - cove

khoram: adjective
green - fresh

khord: adjective
retail - minuscule - little - inconsiderable

khord kardan: verb
To crushing

khord kardan: verb
To smash - To shatter - To hash - To crushing

khord shodan: verb
To crush - To crunch - To crumble

khordan: verb
To eat

khordan: verb
To eat - To corrode

khordani: adjective
comestible - edible - eatable

khorde: adjective
shred - particle

khorde: adjective
sub

khordegiri: noun
cavil

khordegiri kardan: verb
To cavil

khorderiz: adjective
tidbit - spall - snippet - shard

khordesang: noun
rubble

khordigir: adjective
censorious

khore: noun
leprosy - leper - canker

khorjin: noun
kyack - cantina - bag - valise

khormâ: noun
date

khormâlu: noun
persimmon

khormâyi: adjective
brown - russet

khornâs: noun
snort - snore

khornâs keshidan: verb
To growl

khoro pof: noun
snore

khoro pof kardan: verb
To snort - To snore

khorsand: adjective
content - glad - happy

khorshid: noun
sun

khorsâl: adjective
minor - child

khortum: noun
proboscis

khoruj: noun
exit - outgo - propulsion

khorus: noun
rooster

khorush: noun
slogan - roar

khorushidan: verb
To bubble - To rage - To roar

khorâfât: noun
superstition

khorâfâti: adjective
superstitious

khorâk: noun
nourishment - feed - nutrition - meat

khorâki: noun
edible - chow - larder - meal

khorâki: noun
comestible

khosh: noun
blissful - merry - happy

khosh aks: adjective
photogenic

khosh eghbâl: adjective
lucky

khosh ghalb: adjective
blithe

khosh ghiyâfe: adjective
handsome

khosh ghôl: adjective
punctual

khosh gozarân: adjective
sensual - jovial - luxurious

khosh heykal: adjective
statuesque - upstanding - buxom

khosh moshreb: adjective
sociable - genial - chummy

khosh ta'm: adjective
palatable - smacker - tasty

khosh yômn: adjective
lucky - propitious

khosh zabân: adjective
voluble

khosh'hâl: adjective
happy - merry - glad - jolly

khosh'hâl kardan: verb
To gladden

khosh'hâli: noun
jocosity - mirth - glee

khosh'hâli kardan: verb
To joy

khoshbakht: adjective
provident - blest

khoshbakhti: noun
serendipity - luck

khoshbakhti: noun
fortune

khoshbin: adjective
optimist

khoshbinâne: adverb
optimistic

khoshbu: adjective
rosy - aromatic - scented

khoshbuyi: noun
scent

khoshdel: adjective
happy - buxom - buoyant

khoshfekr: adjective
brainy

khoshgel: adjective
beautiful

khoshgeli: noun
beauty

khoshgozarân: adjective
luxuriate

khoshgozarâni: noun
revelry

khoshhâl shodan: verb
To rejoice

khoshi: adjective
joyance - joy - delight - cheer - pleasure

khoshi kardan: verb
To rejoice - To exult

khoshk: adjective
dry

khoshk: adjective
dry

khoshk kardan: verb
To desiccation - To dehumidify - To evaporate

khoshk shodan: verb
To shrivel - To atrophy

khoshkhim: adjective
benign

khoshkhu: adjective
comkpliant - affable

khoshkhuyi: noun
complaisance

khoshki: noun
drouth

khoshkide: adjective
sear - hidebound - wizen

khoshkândan: verb
To sear

khoshlebâs: adjective
dandy - gash - gallant

khoshmaze: adjective
humorous - taffeta

khoshmaze: adjective
zestful

khoshmazegi: noun
humor - banter - badinage

khoshnevisi: noun
calligraphy

khoshnud: adjective
acquiescent

khoshnud: adjective
content - glad

khoshnud kardan: verb
To satisfy

khoshnud kardan: verb
To agree - To gladden

khoshnud sâkhtan: verb
To please - To appease

khoshnudi: noun
satisfaction

khoshnâmi: noun
reputation

khoshraftâr: adjective
debonair

khoshru: adjective
glad

khoshru'l: noun
affability

khoshsalighe: adjective
stylist

khoshtip: adjective
handsome

khoshunat: noun
violence - rigor - truculence

khoshvaght: adjective
happy

khoshâmad: noun
welcome

khoshâmad goftan: verb
To welcome

khoshâyand: adjective
gracious - welcome

khoski: noun
welter - mainland - land - terrafirma

khosnevis: noun
calligraphist - calligrapher

khosrovâni: noun
majestic

khostâkh shodan: verb
To wanton

khosu' kardan: verb
To stoop

khosumat: noun
enmity - virulence

khosumat âmiz: adjective
hostile

khosusi: adjective
private - personal

khosusiyat: noun
quality - intimacy

khosusiyât: noun
features

khotbe: noun
sermon

khoteshaker: adjective
thankful

khotur: noun
haunt

khu: noun
temper - habit

khu dâdan: verb
To addict - To inure

khu gereftan: verb
To accustom

khu gereftan: verb
To wont

khub: noun
fine - good - well

khub kardan: verb
To heal

khub shodan: verb
To heal

khubi: adjective
good - grace

khubru: adjective
comely

khubtarin: adjective
best

khugiri: noun
naturalization

khuk: noun
pig

khuk: noun
pork - pig

khun: noun
blood

khun: noun
blood

khun rikhtan: verb
To bleed

khunbahâ: noun
ransom

khundamâgh: noun
nosebleed

khungarm: adjective
warm

khuni: adjective
sanguine - bloody

khunin: adjective
bloody

khunkhâh: adjective
avenger

khunkhâhi: noun
vengeance

khunkhâhi kardan: verb
To revenge - To avenge

khunkhâr: adjective
bloody - gory

khunriz: adjective
bloodthirsty

khunrizi: noun
hemorrhage

khunrizi: noun
slaughter - carnage - bloodshed

khunsard: adjective
cool - impassive - meek

khunsardi: noun
phlegm - unconcern - composure

khunâbe: noun
serum - plasma

khunâlud: adjective
bloody

khunâshâm: adjective
vampire

khushe: noun
cluster - beard

khushe khushe: adjective
gregarious

khushâb: noun
compote

khutahbin: adjective
sectarian

khutahfekr: adjective
lowminded - dogmatic - prude - provincial

khuy: noun
nature - grain

khâb: noun
nap - dream - asleep - sleep

khâb didan: verb
To dream

khâb mândan: verb
To oversleep

khâb raftan: verb
To sleep

khâbar dâdan: verb
To inform - To announce - To predicate - To delate

khâbe kutâh: noun
snooze

khâbgâh: noun
dormitory

khâbgâh: noun
dormitory

khâbidan: verb
To sleep

khâbide: adjective
torpid - sleeper - resting - recumbent - asleep

khâbâlud: adjective
sleepy - drowsy - dreamy

khâbândan: verb
To suppress - To embed - To appease

khâbândan: verb
To lay - To embed - To appease

khâbânidan: verb
To soften - To couch

khâbâvar: adjective
opiate - hypnotic

khâdem: adjective
servant

khâen: adjective
traitorous - traitor

khâenâne: adverb
treasonable - treacherous - traitorous

khâgine: noun
omelette - omelet

khâh: noun
or - whether

khâhar: noun
sister

khâhar: noun
sister

khâhar shohar: noun
sister in law

khâhari: adjective
sisterhood

khâharzan: noun
sister in law

khâharâne: adverb
sisterly

khâhesh: noun
wish - will - request

khâhân: noun
desirous - fond - wishful

khâj: noun
club - cross

khâje: noun
eunuch - neuter

khâk: noun
land - earth - dust - dirt - soil

khâkare: noun
sawdust

khâke ros: noun
pug - clay - bole

khâkestar: noun
ash - cinder - slag

khâkestari rang: noun
livid

khâki: adjective
terrestrial - mundane - earthy

khâki kardan: verb
To soil

khâkriz: noun
bulwark - moat - levee

khâkriz: noun
dike

khâkrube: noun
trash - rummage

khâkrube: noun
ross

khâl: noun
spot - speck - mole - blotch - dot

khâl kubidan: verb
To tattoo

khâle: noun
aunt

khâlegh: noun
demiurge - creator

khâles: adjective
genuine - pure - sheer

khâlesâne: adverb
sincerely - purely - candidly

khâlezâd: adjective
cousin

khâli: noun
vacant - mere - unoccupied - empty

khâli: noun
empty

khâli kardan: verb
To evacuate - To empty - To discharge - To vacate

khâm: noun
raw - rude - halfbaked

khâme: noun
cream

khâmi: noun
inexperience - crudity

khâmush: noun
silent - taciturn - tacit - quiet

khâmush kardan: verb
To stifle - To extinguish

khâmush shodan: verb
To snuff - To silence

khâmushi: noun
silence - mum

khâmushi: noun
reticence

khândan: verb
To spell - To reading - To invite

khândani: adjective
vocal - readable

khânde: noun
reader - singer

khândân: noun
house - clan - family

khâne: noun
house - home

khâne bedush: adjective
nomad - vagabond - tramp

khâne tofang: noun
groove

khânedâr: adjective
domestic - housekeeper - homemaker

khânedâri: noun
housekeeping - thrift

khânegi: adjective
domestic - indoor - household - homelike

khânemân barandâz: noun
ruinous

khânevâde: noun
family

khânevâdegi: noun
domestic

khâneye maskuni: noun
manse

khânom: noun
mademe - madem - lady - gentlewoman

khânâ: adjective
legible

khânâ budan: verb
To legibility

khânâ'yi: noun
legibility

khâr: noun
thorn - bur - barb

khâr: adjective
lowly - abject - wretch

khâr: noun
thistle

khâr kardan: verb
To insult - To reproach

khâr kardan: verb
To untwist

khâr shemordan: verb
To scorn - To disdain - To despise

khârdâr: adjective
barbed - picked - thorny

khâreghol'âde: adjective
extraordinary

khârej: noun
external - out - abroad - away

khârej az: noun
out - off

khârej kardan: verb
To evict - To emit

khâreje ghesmat: noun
quotient

khâreji: adjective
strange - alien - extraneous - external - exoteric - outsider

khâreji: adjective
foreign

khâresh: noun
itch - scabies

khâresh: noun
prurience

khâresh kardan: verb
To itch

khâri: adjective
contempt - ignominy

khâridan: verb
To itch - To tickle

khârobâr: noun
provender - grub - grocery - viand

khârposhte: noun
hedge

khârândan: verb
To scrape

khâs: noun
particular - specific - special

khâshe': adjective
submissive

khâshâk: noun
brushwood

khâsiyat: noun
navigate - nature - quale - virtue - property

khâst: noun
volition - wish - will - want

khâstan: verb
To ask - To desire - To wish - To want

khâstegâr: noun
wooer - suitor - bridegroom

khâstegâri: noun
woo

khâstegâri kardan: verb
To woo - To suitor - To suit

khâstâr: adjective
demanding - wishful - volunteer

khâstâr budan: verb
To solicit

khâtam: noun
cachet - signet

khâtamkâri: noun
inlay

khâteme: noun
end - closure

khâteme dâdan: verb
To terminate

khâteme yâftan: verb
To terminate

khâter: noun
mind - attention - remembrance - sake

khâtere: noun
souvenir - reminiscence - memoir - memento

khâterjam': adjective
sure

khâterkhâh: adjective
lover

khâterât: noun
note - memorabilia

khâti: adjective
trespasser

khâvar: noun
east - orient

khâvari: adjective
oriental - eastern

khâviyâr: noun
caviar

khâye: noun
testicle

khâze': adjective
submissive

khôf: noun
scare - horror

khôfnâk: adjective
macabre

ki: preposition
who

kif: noun
bag

kife pul: noun
purse - wallet

kilugaram: noun
kilogram

kilumetr: noun
kilometer

kiluvât: noun
kilowatt

kimiyâgari: noun
alchemy

kimiyâyi: noun
chemical

kine: noun
spite - enmity - hatred - peeve - vengeance

kineju: adjective
virulent - malignant

kinejuyi: noun
nemesis

kinejuyi kardan: verb
To revenge

kinetuz: adjective
spiteful - dispiteous - venomous - vengeful - implacable

kinetuzi: noun
implacability - malice

kinevarzi: verb
To spite - To despite - To hate

kip: noun
tight

kip kardan: verb
To tighten

kir: noun
phallus - penis

kise: noun
purse - bag - pouch

kise: noun
bag

kiseye pul: noun
purse

kish: noun
creed - religion - faith

kiyasat: noun
perspicacity

kodurat: noun
miff - tiff

kodâm: adverb
any - which - what

kofr: noun
blasphemy - atheism - infidelity - heresy -
profanity

kofrguyi: noun
swearword - profanity

kofrâmiz: adjective
profane - unholy - unhallowed - unhallow

kohan: adjective
hoary - ancient - olden

kohansâl: adjective
old

kohne: adjective
clout - old - obsolete - obsolescent - antique
- ancient

kohne: adjective
old

kohnegi: noun
archaism - obsolescence

kohnekâr: adjective
old - veteran

kohulat: noun
senility

kojâ: adverb
whither - where - where

kol: noun
total

kolang: noun
hack - pick

kolbe: noun
cottage

koleksiyon: noun
collection

koli: noun
general - total

koliyat: noun
totality

koliye: noun
kidney

koloft: noun
housemaid - chambermaid

koloni: noun
colony

kolorin: noun
chlorine

kolorofil: noun
chlorophyl

koluche: noun
cooky

kolukh: noun
clod

kolune dar: noun
slot

kolâh: noun
cap - hat

kolâh gozâshtan: verb
To welsh

kolâhak: noun
warhead - cupule - bonnet - lid

kolâhbardâr: adjective
swindler - crook

kolâhbardâri: noun
swindle

kolâhbardâri: adjective
rook - hustler

kolâhbardâri: noun
fraud

kolâhbardâri kardan: verb
To defraud

kolâhkhud: noun
helmet

komaj: adjective
shortbread

komak: noun
assistance - assist - aid - help

komak kardan: verb
To help - To aid

komakhazine: noun
allowance - subvention

komaki: adjective
secondary - subsidiary - auxiliary

kombâin: noun
combine

komisiyon: noun
committee - commission

komod: noun
dresser - commode

komodi: adjective
comedy

komonism: noun
communism

komonist: adjective
communist

komperesor: noun
compressor

komput: noun
canned - compote

kond: adjective
slow - tardy - dull - lazy

kond kardan: verb
To blunt - To letup - To dull - To clog - To rebate

kond sâkhtan: verb
To retard

konde: adjective
stub - stock - chump

kondzehn: adjective
imbecile - obtuse - dimwit - stupid

konesh: noun
action - act

koneshgar: adjective
active

konferâns: noun
conclave - colloquium - circuit - lecture

kongere: noun
jag - congress

konj: noun
corner - angle

konjed: noun
sesame

konjkâv: adjective
curious - prowler

konjkâvi: noun
pry

konjkâvi kardan: verb
To poke

konsert: noun
concert

konserv: noun
conserve

konservsâzi: noun
cannery

konsul: noun
consul

konsulgari: noun
consulate

konsuli: noun
consular

kont: noun
kenneth

konterât: noun
contract

konterât kardan: verb
To contract

kontor: noun
meter

kontorol: noun
rein - control

kontorol kardan: verb
To control

konuni: adjective
modern

konye: noun
epithet - nickname - title - surname

kope: noun
congeries - ruck - heap - pile - mass

kopi: noun
kepi

kopol: noun
buttock - butt - behind

kopon: noun
coupon

koravi: adjective
spherical

kore: noun
sphere - globe

koreye zamin: noun
earth

koridor: noun
hallway

kork: noun
boil - blotch - pimple

korsi: noun
stool

koruki: noun
top

koshande: adjective
murderous - mortal - deadly

koshtan: verb
To murder - To kill

koshti: noun
wrestle

koshti gereftan: verb
To wrestle

koshtâr: noun
carnage - murder - massacre

koshtârgâh: noun
slaughterhouse - shambles

kosinus: noun
cosine

kot: noun
coat

kotak: noun
smacker

kotak zadan: verb
To beat - To clobber - To thrash - To smack

kotlet: noun
cutlet

kovârtz: noun
quartz

kozâz: noun
tetanus

ku: preposition
where?

kubande: adjective
knocker - pounder - masher

kubidan: verb
To smite - To bruise - To beat - To hammer -
To knock

kubidan: verb
To pummel

kuch: noun
departure - migration

kuch dâdan: verb
To transplant - To transmigrate

kuch kardan: verb
To migrate - To immigrate

kuchak: adjective
small - short - teeny

kuchak shodan: verb
To shrink

kuche: noun
alley - lane - street

kuchek shomordan: verb
To underestimate

kuchektar: adjective
lesser - minor - beneath

kuchektarin: adjective
least

kuchidan: verb
To migrate

kuchneshin: noun
immigrant

kuchulu: adjective
tiny - kid - wee

kud: noun
dung - muck

kud dâdan: verb
To manure - To dung - To compost

kudak: noun
kid - child - baby - babe - infant

kudak: noun
stitch

kudakestân: noun
preschool - kindergarten

kudaki: noun
childhood - imfancy

kude giyâhi: noun
peat - mulch

kudetâ: noun
coup

kuft: noun
syphilis

kuftan: verb
To oppress

kufte: noun
lodged

kuh: noun
mountain

kuhestân: adjective
mountainous

kuhnavard: noun
cragsman

kuhpeimâ: noun
cragsman

kuhân: noun
hunch - hump

kuk kardan: verb
To crank

kul: noun
piggyback - pickaback

kul kardan: verb
To piggyback - To pickaback

kulebâr: noun
knapsack

kuleposhti: noun
swag - pack - knapsack

kuler: noun
cooler

kuli: noun
gypsy - gipsy - hungarian

kulâk: noun
storm - blizzard

kun: noun
ass

kupe: noun
compartment

kupâl: noun
mace

kur kardan: verb
To abacinate - To blindfold - To blind

kure: noun
stove - chimney - oven - kiln - manhole

kurerâh: adjective
byway

kurkurâne: adverb
Blindly

kuse mâhi: noun
shark

kushesh: noun
effort - attempt

kushesh kardan: verb
To attempt - To struggle - To strive

kushidan: verb
To strive - To endeavor

kushâ: adjective
industrious - diligent - studious - sedulous - trier

kutahfekri: noun
prudery

kutahnazar: adjective
hidebound - parochial - lowminded - smug

kutule: noun
stub - dwarf - grub - gnome - runt

kutâh: adjective
short - succinct - concise

kutâh kardan: verb
To abbreviate - To shorten - To stag

kutâh va mokhtasar: adjective
curt

kutâhghad: adjective
stump

kutâhi: noun
brevity - compendium - delinquency

kuze: noun
urn - pitcher - cruse - jug

kuzh: adjective
convex

kâbin: noun
cabin

kâbus: noun
incubus - mare - nightmare

kâbâre: noun
cabaret

kâdr: noun
cadre

kâenât: noun
universe

kâfar: adjective
unbelievin

kâfe: noun
restaurant - cafe - buffet

kâfer: noun
impious - heathen - pagan - ethnic

kâfi: noun
adequate - enough

kâfi budan: verb
To suffice

kâghaz: noun
paper

kâghazi: noun
pulpy - paper

kâh: noun
straw - pug - chaff

kâhande: adjective
reducer - ablative

kâhel: noun
laze - slothful

kâheli: adjective
sloth

kâhesh: noun
abate - decrease - decline - diminution - wastage - reduction - rebate - scaledown - slake

kâhesh dâdan: verb
To lessen

kâhesh yâftan: verb
To slake

kâheshe bahâ: noun
depreciation

kâhgel: noun
thatch

kâhidan: verb
To detract

kâhu: noun
lettuce

kâj: noun
pine

kâkh: noun
palace

kâkol: noun
topknot - scalplock - peak

kâktus: noun
cactus

kâkâ: noun
negro - brother

kâkâ'u: noun
cocoa - coca - chocolate - cacao

kâkâroni: noun
noodle - macaroni

kâl: adjective
raw - unripe

kâlbad: noun
framework - mould - mold - skeleton

kâlej: noun
college

kâleske: noun
coach - carriage

kâlibr: noun
caliber

kâlori: noun
heatunit - calory - calorie

kâlâ: noun
product

kâm: noun
desire - wish - palate

kâmel: noun
perfect - complete - whole - thorough

kâmel kardan: verb
To integrate - To complete - To complement

kâmel shodan: verb
To ripen

kâmelan: adverb
quite - wholly

kâmiyun: noun
truck

kâmkâr: adjective
prosperous

kâmkâr shodan: verb
To prosper

kâmkâri: noun
prosperity

kâmravâyi: noun
success

kâmyâb: adjective
prosperous - palmy

kâmyâb shodan: verb
To succeed - To thrive - To prosper

kâmyâbi: noun
prosperity - success

kândid: noun
candidate - nomination

kândid: noun
candidacy

kândid kardan: verb
To nominate

kângoro: noun
kangaroo

kâni: noun
inorganic - mineral

kânun: noun
club

kânâdâ: noun
Canada

kânâdâyi: adjective
Canadian

kânâl: noun
Channel

kâocho: noun
caoutchouc - rubber

kâpitân: noun
skipper

kâput: noun
preservative

kâr: noun
task - job - duty - work

kâr kardan: verb
To act - To go - To work

kârbari: adjective
practical

kârbari: noun
control

kârbord: noun
usage

kârbâr: noun
workload

kârchâghkon: verb
To jobber

kârd: noun
knife

kârdinâl: noun
cardinal

kârdân: noun
resourceful - deft - technician

kârdâni: noun
policy - resource - tact - skill

kârevân: noun
convoy - caravan

kârevânsarâ: noun
inn

kârfarmâ: noun
taskmaster - employer - master

kârgar: noun
worker - employee - labor

kârgardân: noun
director

kârgari: noun
proletarian

kârgoshâ: noun
entrepreneur

kârgâh: noun
workshop - studio

kârgâhe bâfandegi: noun
loom

kâri: noun
active - energetic - effective - drastic

kârikâtor: noun
cartoon - caricature

kârkerd: noun
function

kârkhâne: noun
factory - plant

kârkon: adjective
purge - purgative - workable

kârkonân: noun
personnel

kârmand: noun
employee

kârmozd: noun
wage

kârnâme: noun
workbook

kârnâvâl: noun
carnival

kârpardâz: noun
supplier

kârpardâzi: noun
jobprocessing

kârshenâs: noun
critic - expert - judge

kârt postâl: noun
postcard

kârte ozviyat: noun
membership card

kârte vizit: noun
card

kârton: noun
carton

kârâgâh: noun
sleuth - bloodhound

kârâmuz: adjective
trainee - apprentice

kârâmuzi: noun
novitiate

kârâyi: adjective
efficiency - proficiency

kâse: noun
bowl

kâseb: noun
tradesman

kâsebi: noun
trade

kâset: noun
cassette

kâsh: preposition
wish

kâshef: noun
pathfinder

kâsht: noun
implant

kâshtan: verb
To plant - To implant

kâshâne: noun
home

kâsket: noun
casquet

kâstan: verb
To subtract - To shorten - To decline

kâstan: verb
To reduce

kâsti: adjective
shortcoming - defect

kâteb: noun
ascribe - scrivener

kâtolik: noun
catholic

kâtâlog: noun
repertory - catalogue - catalog

kâvidan: verb
To rummage - To excavate - To drag

kâvoshgar: noun
excavator

kâzeb: adjective
liar

kâzino: noun
casino

kôdan: adjective
dull - fool

kôkab: noun
star

kônomakân: noun
universe

kôsan: noun
cushion - squab

l

la'l: noun
ruby - garnet

la'n: noun
imprecation - ban

la'nat: noun
damn - cuss - curse

la'nat kardan: verb
To damn

la'nati: adjective
darn - damnable

la'no nefrin: noun
commination

la'âb: noun
mucilage - glaze - slime

la'âb dâdan: verb
To glaze

la'âbi: adjective
overglaze

la'âbi kardan: verb
To glaze

lab: noun
lip

lab zadan: verb
To taste

labaniyât: noun
dairy - creamery

labe: noun
border - ledge - ridge - edge

labkhand: noun
smile

labkhand zadan: verb
To smile

labriz: adjective
replete - full - awash - large - profuse

labriz shodan: verb
To slop - To redound

labâlab: adjective
ivy

lafz: noun
particle - word

lafzi: adjective
textual - literal - verbal

lafâf: noun
padding - envelope - cover - wrapper

lafâfe: noun
shroud - mask - paraphernalia

lafâzi: adjective
rhetoric - verbiage

lafâzi kardan: verb
To verbalize

lagad: noun
kick - hurl

lagad kardan: verb
To tread

lagad zadan: verb
To boot - To poach - To hoof - To kickback -
To kick

lagadkub: noun
stampede

lagadmâli: noun
padding

lagadparâni: noun
wince

lagh: noun
wobbly - rickety - unsteady - loose

lagh budan: verb
To wobble

laghab: noun
epithet - label - title - surname - sobriquet

laghab dâdan: verb
To entitle - To title - To surname

laghv: noun
waiver - revocation - repeal

laghv kardan: verb
To annul - To abrogate - To cancel - To
repeal - To nullify

laghzande: adjective
slippery - slipper - slipover - slide - rattletrap

laghzesh: noun
slither - slippage - slip - slide

laghzesh khordan: verb
To trip

laghzidan: verb
To tumble - To stumble - To slip - To slide -
To skid

laghzân: adjective
slippery

lagân: noun
basin

lahestâni: adjective
Polish

lahje: noun
dialect - accent

lahje: noun
accent

lahn: noun
tone - tune

lahze: noun
moment

lahze'i: adjective
wee

lahzeye bohrâni: noun
zerohour

lahâf: noun
quilt - coverlet

lahâz: noun
viewpoint - phase - perspective - light

laj: noun
spite - grudge - grouch

lajanmâl: adjective
slimy

lajanzâr: adjective
bog - marsh - swampy

lajbâz: adjective
headstrong

lajbâzi: noun
pertinacity

lajuj: adjective
stubborn - headstrong - pertinacious - dogged - obstreperous

lajujâne: adverb
intractable

lajân: noun
slough - slosh - slobber - slob - mud - mire

lak: noun
stain - speck - smudge - blot

lak kardan: verb
To smudge - To blur

lake: noun
stain - spot - dirt

lake lake: adjective
mealy - splotchy

lakeye nang: noun
slur - stigma

lakhte: noun
lobe - clod

lakhte shodan: adjective
gory

lakhteye khun: noun
clot

lam: noun
trick - loll

lam dâdan: verb
To lounge - To loll

lamidan: verb
To recline - To lounge - To loll

lams: noun
handle

lams kardan: verb
To feel - To palpate - To stroke - To touch - To take

lamyazra': adjective
wasteland - arid - barren

lang: adjective
cripple - limp

lang budan: verb
To woke - To wobble

langar andâkhtan: verb
To anchor - To moor - To harbor

langargâh: noun
dock - levee - haven - harbor - port

langidan: verb
To stagger - To hobble - To halt - To limp - To lag - To clop

larz: noun
tremble - thrill - shiver - shake

larze: noun
vibration - quake - thrill - tremor - tremble - shiver

larzenegâr: noun
seismograph

larzesh: noun
quake - shake

larzesh: noun
tremor

larzesh dâshtan: verb
To quake - To shimmy

larzeshe sedâ: noun
trill

larzidan: verb
To vibrate - To hudder - To shiver - To shake

larzân: adjective
vibrant - unsteady - unstable - wobbly

larzânande: adjective
shaker

larzândan: verb
To jar - To tremble - To wangle

lase: noun
gingiva

lashgar: noun
army

lashkar: noun
corps

lashkar: noun
division

lashkargâh: noun
camp

latif: adjective
tender - subtle - soft

latife: noun
joke - jape - epigram

latifegu: noun
humorist - witty - japer

latme: noun
brunt - shock - stroke

lavand: noun
coquette

lavand: noun
coquette

lavât: noun
sodomyh - pederasty

lavâzem: noun
accessories - gear - paraphernalia - apparatus

laziz: adjective
delicious - delectable

lebâs: noun
clothing - dress - costume - attire - vestment

lebâs pushidan: verb
To dress

lebâs pushândan: verb
To attire - To able

lebâs pushânidan: verb
To garb

lebâse abrishami: noun
silk

lebâse mobadal: noun
disguise - guise - masquerade

lebâse rasmi: noun
tuxedo

lebâse zir: noun
underwear - underclothing - underclothes

lebâsforush: noun
clothier

lebâsshuyi: noun
laundry

leghâ: noun
visage

leghâh: noun
zygosis

leh: adjective
squash

leh kardan: verb
To scotch - To squeeze - To squash

leh shodan: verb
To crush

lehim: noun
solder

lehim kardan: verb
To solder

lei lei kardan: verb
To sikt - To skip - To hop - To hip

lejâjat: noun
pertinacity - obstinacy - obduracy

lejâjat kardan: verb
To grudge

lejâm: noun
rein - bit - line

lejâm gosikhte: adjective
ungovernable - unbridle

lenge: noun
bale - mate - match - pendant - leaf - doublet

lesân: noun
language

letâfat: noun
subtlety - elegance - rosewater

lezat: noun
joy - pleasure - pleasure - delight - gusto

lezat bordan: verb
To pleasure - To enjoy - To revel

lezatbakhsh: adjective
pleasurable

lezej: noun
slimy - slab

lif: noun
filament - brush

lif: noun
leif

life hamâm: noun
washcloth

liken / lâken: noun
but

limu: noun
lemon

limunâd: noun
lemonade - soda - sherbet

limutorsh: noun
lime - lemon

lire: noun
Pound

lis: noun
lick

lis zadan: verb
To lap

lise: noun
lick

lisidan: verb
To lick

list: noun
list

liste hoghugh: noun
payroll

lisâns: noun
bachelor

litr: noun
liter

livân: noun
tumbler - glass - mug

liyâghat: noun
merit - autarchy - aptitude

liz: adjective
glib - slippery - slimy - slick - slab

liz khordan: verb
To slip

liz khordan: verb
To slip

lobe kalâm: noun
gist

loghat: noun
verb - vocabulary - word

loghavi: noun
lexical

loghme: noun
morsel - bit - snap

logâritm: noun
logarithm

lokht: adjective
naked - nude - stodgy

lokht kardan: verb
To rob - To ransack - To harry - To pluck

lokht shodan: verb
To unclothe

loknat: noun
stutter - stammer

loknat dâshtan: verb
To stutter - To stumble

lokomotiv: noun
locomotive

long: noun
loincloth

lord: adjective
sir - lord

lotf: noun
boon - ethereal - kindness

lotf kardan: verb
To oblige - To indulgence

lotfan: adverb
please

lozh: noun
box - loge - stall

lozhe saltanati: noun
podium

lozum: noun
necessity - exigency - incumbency

lubiyâ: noun
bean

luch: noun
squint - crosseyed - cockeyed

luchi: adjective
squint

lul khordan: verb
To wriggle

lule: noun
cylinder - roll - pipe - spout - tube

lulekesh: noun
plumber - piper

lulekeshi: noun
canalization - pipeline

luleye tofang: noun
barrel

lulidan: verb
To hotch

lus: adjective
gaudy - chilish

lus: adjective
spoony

lus kardan: verb
To spoil

luster: noun
luster

luti: adjective
ruffian

lâbod: noun
must

lâf: noun
gash - brag - boast - vainglory

lâf: noun
jactitation (tattion)

lâf zadan: verb
To puff - To rodomontade - To brag

lâfzan: adjective
idol - bouncer

lâghar: adjective
scrannel - scraggy - toom - thin - spare -
slink - slim - slight - skinny - gaunt - wizen -
lean - angular

lâgharandâm: adjective
lithe

lâghari: noun
impotence - atrophy

lâjavard: adjective
azure

lâjavardi: adjective
azure

lâki: adjective
crimson

lâkposht: noun
turtle - tortoise

lâl: noun
speechless - mute

lâle: noun
tulip

lâlâyi: noun
lullaby

lâlâyi khândan: verb
To lullaby - To lull

lâmazhab: adjective
ungodly

lâmp: noun
tube - lamp

lâne: noun
nest - den - lair

lâne sâkhtan: verb
To nest

lâs zadan: verb
To mash - To pickeer - To philander

lâshe: noun
carcase - cadaver - corpse

lâshkhor: noun
buzzard - lammergeyer

lâstik: noun
tire - caoutchouc - rubber

lâstike charkh: noun
tire

lât: noun
scoundrel

lâtin: noun
latin

lây: noun
sludge - silt - sediment - in - ooze

lâyanfak: adjective
essential - innate

lâyanghat': adjective
incessant

lâyanhal: adjective
insoluble

lâyatanâhi: noun
infinite

lâye: noun
stratum - strand - padding - pad - layer

lâyedâr: adjective
zonate

lâyegh: adjective
competent - capable

lâyegh budan: verb
To deserve - To able

lâyeheye ghânuni: noun
bill

lâyerubi: noun
layer removal

lâyi: noun
wad - mattress

lâzem: adjective
needful - necessary - requirement

lâzem: adjective
obligatory

lâzem budan: verb
To require

lâzem dânestan: verb
To postulate - To require

lâzem dâshtan: verb
To want

lâzeme: noun
prerequisite

lâzemol'ejrâ: adjective
indispensable

lôde: adjective
clown

lôdegi: noun
badinage - tomfoolery

lôdegi kardan: verb
To droll

lôh: noun
brede - plate - tablet - table

lôhe: noun
plate - plaque - brede - tablet - slab - signboard

lôhe yâdbud: noun
memorial

lôlâ: noun
band - hinge - joint - joint

lôlô: noun
scarecrow - bugbear - bogeyman

lôs: noun
pollution

lôze: noun
tonsil

lôzi: noun
diamond - rhombic - lozenge

lôzi: noun
rhomboid - rhomb

lôzolme'de: noun
pancreas

lôzolmede: noun
sweetbread

m

ma'bad: noun
shrine

ma'bar: noun
pathway - road

ma'bud: noun
idol

ma'dan: noun
mineral - mine

ma'dane sang: noun
quarry

ma'dani: adjective
inorganic - mineral

ma'dud: noun
scant - paucity - poor - little

ma'dum kardan: verb
To ruinate - To obliterate

ma'ghul: adjective
sensible - sane - wise - reasonable - rational
- conscionable

ma'ishat: noun
livelihood

ma'jun: noun
confection

ma'khaz: noun
source

ma'kul: noun
edible - eatable

ma'kus: noun
reverse - upsidedown

ma'kus: adjective
converse

ma'lul: noun
effected - caused

ma'lum: noun
apparent - obvious - cretain - definite

ma'lum kardan: verb
To specify - To evince - To reveal

ma'lumât: noun
information - witting

ma'man: noun
stronghold - mine

ma'mul: noun
usual - usage - normal

ma'mulan: adverb
usually

ma'muli: adjective
commonplace - common - ordinary -
general - banal

ma'mur: noun
envoy - officer - agent

ma'mur kardan: verb
To launch

ma'muriyat: noun
duty - mission

ma'muriyat: noun
commission

ma'muriyat dâdan: verb
To detail - To commission

ma'navi: noun
spiritual - moral - immaterial

ma'naviyat: noun
idealism

ma'naviyat: noun
emolument

ma'naviyat: noun
manichaeanism

ma'ni: noun
definition

ma'ni dâdan: verb
To mean - To intimate - To intend - To
signify

ma'ni kardan: verb
To define - To translate

ma'nidâr: adjective
punctual - meaningful

ma'nus: noun
familiar - habitue

ma'nus shodan: verb
To acclimate

ma'raz: noun
open

ma'refat: noun
cognizance - cognition

ma'ruf: adjective
famous

ma'rufiyat: noun
renown - popularity

ma'shugh: noun
minion

ma'shughe: noun
sweetheart - ladylove

ma'siyat: noun
sin

ma'siyat kardan: verb
To sin

ma'sum: adjective
immaculate - innocent

ma'tuf dâshtan: verb
To lend - To divert

ma'yub: adjective
incorrect - incomplete

ma'yub kardan: verb
To damage - To impair - To mar

ma'yub shodan: verb
To maim

ma'yub sâkhtan: verb
To defect - To vitiate

ma'yus: adjective
chill

ma'yus kardan: verb
To disappoint

ma'yus konande: adjective
unpromising

ma'yus shodan: verb
To despair

ma'zerat khâstan: verb
To pardon - To apologize - To excuse

ma'zul: verb
To deprive - To depose - To eject

ma'zur dâshtan: verb
To excuse

ma'âsh: noun
sustenance - livelihood

mabda'e târikh: noun
epoch

mabhas: noun
topic - subject

mabhut: noun
agape - quizzical

mabhut kardan: verb
To transfix - To disconcert - To astound - To amaze

mablagh: noun
amount - sum

mabâdâ: preposition
lest

mabâdâ: noun
era - offspring - offset

madad: noun
reinforcement - help

madad resândan: verb
To help

madani: adjective
civil - civic - urban

madfu': noun
stool - excretion - excrement

madfun sâkhtan: verb
To inter

madh: noun
eulogy

madh kardan: verb
To laud - To eulogize

madid: adjective
long

madihe: noun
panegyric

madkhal: noun
gate - entry - entrance

madrak: noun
document

madrak: noun
document - evidence

302

madrese: noun
academy

madreseye ebtedâyi: noun
elementary school

madyun: noun
debtor - indebted

madyun budan: verb
To owe

madâhi: noun
eulogy

madâhi kardan: verb
To adulate - To eulogize

madâr: noun
zone - theme - circuit - orbit - pivot

maf'ul: noun
object

mafar: noun
exhaust - loophole

mafghud: adjective
lost - absent

mafhum: noun
purporst - context

mafruz: noun
putative - given

mafruzât: noun
information - data

maftuh: adjective
open - patent

maftuh shodan: verb
To open

maftul: noun
wire

mafâd: noun
context - content - intent

magar: adverb
except - but - unless

magar inke: adverb
unless

magas: noun
fly

magh'ad: noun
anus - rectum - croup

magh'ar: noun
dished - concave - cave

maghar: noun
seat - stead - domicile - chair

maghbare: noun
sepulcher - monument - mausoleum

maghbul: adjective
acceptable

maghdur: adjective
possible

maghferat: noun
pardon

maghhur sâkhtan: verb
To subdue

maghlub: adjective
anagram

maghlub kardan: verb
To lick

maghlub sâkhtan: verb
To overcome - To defeat - To vanquish

maghreb: noun
sunset - occident - west

maghreghi: adjective
oriental

maghrur: adjective
proud - snobbish - haughty

maghrur: adjective
uppity

maghrurâne: adverb
contemptuous - lofty

maghsad: noun
aim - goal - destination

maghshush: adjective
haywire

maghsud: noun
purpose

maghsum: noun
distributed - devided

maghsumo aleyh: noun
denominator

maghta': noun
segment - section

maghtul: noun
slain

maghule: noun
category

maghz: noun
brain - mind

maghzi: adjective
brain - mind

maghzubiyat: noun
disfavor

maghâle: noun
article - paper - essay

maghâm: noun
position - status - post - title

maghâze: noun
store - shop

magâvar: adjective
lethal - mortal

mahak: noun
shibboleth - criterion - examination

mahak: adjective
licorice

mahak kardan: verb
To stable

mahak zadan: verb
To assay - To test

mahal: noun
place - location

mahale: noun
neiborhood - parish - quarter

mahale obur: noun
passageway

mahali: adjective
autochthonous - residential - native -
territorial

mahbas: noun
prison - jail

mahbub: adjective
lovable - beloved - favorite - darling -
cuddlesome

mahbub: adjective
honey

mahbube: noun
lief - ladylove

mahbubiyat: noun
amicability - popularity

mahbubiyat: noun
decency

mahbus: adjective
jailbird - convict

mahbus kardan: verb
To stash - To confine

mahbus shodan: verb
To lock

mahdud: adjective
limited - narrow

mahdud sâkhtan: verb
To trammel

mahdude: noun
confine

mahdudiyat: noun
limitation - restriction

mahdudsâzi: noun
limitation

mahfaze: noun
lacuna

mahfel: noun
clique - circle

mahfuz: adjective
safe

mahfuz kardan: verb
To elate - To immune

mahib: adjective
horrible - hideous - grisly - tremendous -
terrific

mahjar: noun
fence - peel - parapet

mahjub: adjective
unobtrusive - diffident - decent

mahkame: noun
forum

mahkum: adjective
guilty - fey

mahkum kardan: verb
To sentence - To convict - To condemn

mahkum shodan: verb
To condemn

mahkumiyat: noun
condemnation - proscription

mahlul: noun
solvable - solution - soluble

mahmel: noun
litter

mahmule: noun
shipment - consignment

mahram: adjective
intimate

mahram sâkhtan: verb
To intimate

mahrame asrâr: adjective
secretary - confidant - privy

mahramâne: adverb
secret - esoteric

mahrum kardan: verb
To deprive - To evacuate - To divest - To disappoint

mahrumiyat: noun
proscription - reprobate - privation

mahshar: noun
doomsday - doom

mahsul: noun
product

mahsur: adjective
pent

mahsur kardan: verb
To yard - To compass - To close - To wall - To pale - To inclose

mahsus: adjective
tangible - sensible - phenomenal - patent

mahtâb: noun
moonlight - moon

mahv: adjective
pallid - nebulous - obscure - deletion

mahv kardan: verb
To blur - To eliminate - To efface - To obliterate - To washout

mahz: adjective
strict - downright - mere

mahzamâni: noun
simultaneity

mahzar: noun
registry

mahzun: adjective
somber - sad - tragic - despondent

mahâr: noun
stay - halter

mahâr kardan: verb
To restrain

mahârat: noun
artifice - ingenuity - skill

majahaz sâkhtan: verb
To prime

majale: noun
magazine - journal

majbur budan: verb
To have

majbur kardan: verb
To compel - To oblige - To enforce - To
bludgeon

majbur sâkhtan: verb
To impel

majhul: noun
unknown - unbeknownst

majles: noun
congress - parliament

majlese senâ: noun
senate

majlese shorâ: noun
parliament

majlesi: adjective
parliamentary

majma': noun
convention - meeting

majmu': noun
total - altogether

majmu'e: noun
collection - bundle

majnun: adjective
insane - maniac - demented

majruh: adjective
ulcerous

majruh kardan: verb
To wound - To lacerate

majrâ: noun
channel

majzub: adjective
spellbound - engross - rapt

majzub kardan: verb
To witch - To engage

majzub sâkhtan: verb
To attract

majzur: noun
square

majzur kardan: verb
To square

majâl: noun
leisure - opportunity

majâni: adjective
free

majârestâni: adjective
Hungarian

majâzi: noun
virtual

make: noun
Mecca

makesh: noun
suction

makhfi: adjective
secret - invisible - hid - undercover

makhfi kardan: verb
To hide - To camouflage - To huddle

makhfigâh: noun
sanctuary

makhfigâh: noun
blind - hideaway

makhlugh: noun
creature

makhlut: noun
mixture - mixed - hash - admixture - blend -
compost - composite

makhlut: noun
mishmash

makhlut kardan: verb
To mix - To meddle - To commix

makhmal: adjective
velvet

makhmali: adjective
velvet

makhmali kardan: verb
To velvet

makhmase: noun
predicament

makhraj: noun
denominator - outlet - outgo - vent

makhrut: noun
cone

makhruti: adjective
congurous

makhsus: noun
specific - special - particular - favorite

makhsusan: adverb
special

makhuf: adjective
gruesome - ghastly - ugsome - horrible -
hideous

makhzan: noun
storage - reservoir - depository

makhzane âb: noun
cistern - reservoir

makhârej: noun
expenditure

makhâreje koli: noun
overhead

makr: noun
ruse - guile - wile

makruh: noun
execrable - detestable

maks: noun
stay - breather - letup - halt - period - pause

maks kardan: verb
To pause - To halt - To letup

maktab: noun
school - academy - ism

makân: noun
location - place

makânshenâsi: noun
topology

makâr: adjective
cunning - pawky

mal'un: adjective
unblest - unblessed - execrable - cussed - cursed

malake: noun
rial - empress - queen - monarch

malakh: noun
quaker - grasshopper

malakh: noun
locust - grasshopper

malavân: noun
shipman - seaman - sailor - gone - gob - leatherneck

malavân: noun
jacktar

malbus: noun
clothes

malghame: noun
amalgam

malhafe: noun
bedsheet

malul: adjective
lukewarm - heartsick - glum

malus kardan: verb
To taint - To pollute - To infect - To deflower - To ntaminate

malâfe: noun
sheet - bedsheet

malâfe kardan: verb
To sheet

malâghe: noun
scoop - spurtle - ladle - dipper

malâlat: noun
humdrum - boredom - ennui - tedium

malâlatangiz: adjective
dismal

malâlatavar: adjective
tedious

malâmat kardan: verb
To upbraid - To blame - To calldown - To reprove - To rebuke

malâzemat kardan: verb
To gallant

mamar: noun
resource

mame: noun
tit - teat - pap

mamlekat: noun
realm

mamlov: noun
laden - rife

mamnu': noun
barred - illicit

mamnu' kardan: verb
To bar - To debar - To countermand - To prohibit

mamnu'iyat: noun
embargo - interdict

mamnun: adjective
thankful - indebted

mamzuj: noun
mixed

man: preposition
I

man darâvardi: adjective
mewfangled

man': noun
prohibition - stoppage - veto - obstruction - restraint

man'ba': noun
source - resource

manenzhit: noun
meningitis

manesh: noun
character

manfe'at: noun
benefit - profit - payoff - gain

manfe'at bordan: verb
To profit

manfi: noun
no - negation

manfur: adjective
outcast - obnoxious - unpopular - ungracious - hateful

mangane kardan: verb
To punch - To smash - To stamp - To perforate

mangene: noun
compressor - nip

manghale âtash: noun
brazier

manghush kardan: verb
To characterize - To engrave - To imprint - To stamp

mangule: noun
tuft - tassel - bob

manhus: adjective
disastrous

mani': noun
inaccessible

manjanigh: noun
catapult

mansab: noun
position - appointment

mansha': noun
offspring

manshur: noun
charter - prism

mansub: noun
nominee

mansub kardan: verb
To invest - To appoint

mansukh: adjective
abrogate - dead - outdated - obsolete -
obsolescent

mansukh shodan: verb
To outmode - To obsolesce

mansur: adjective
triumphant

mantaghe: noun
zone - zone - locale

mantarâz: adjective
yokefellow - justified - level

mantegh: noun
logic - frame

manteghi: adjective
logical - dialectician - dialectical - rational

manut budan: verb
To depend

manzar: noun
aspect - appearance - visage - face

manzare: noun
landscape - prospect - scenery - scene -
sight

manzel: noun
stage - abode - house - home - inn

manzelat: noun
altitude

manzelgâh: noun
dome

manzume: noun
epopee - poem - system

manzur: noun
sake - purpose - intention - prick

manâbe'e tabi'i: noun
natural resources

manâfe': noun
interests - revenue

manâfi: noun
foe - ignored

manâre: noun
minaret - pharos

maraz: noun
malady - disease

marbut: noun
relevant

marbut budan: verb
To depend - To pertain

marbut budan: verb
To pertain - To depend - To relate

marbute: noun
respective

mard: noun
man

mardi: noun
masculinity - manhood

mardom: noun
people

mardomake cheshm: noun
pearl - pupil

mardomi: adjective
humanity

mardomân: noun
people

mardud: adjective
failed

mardud shodan: verb
To fail

mardâne: adjective
masculine - mannish

mardânegi: noun
manhood - sportsmanship

maremat: noun
repair - upkeep

marg: noun
death - dying

margbâr: adjective
mortal

marghad: noun
tabernacle

marghub: adjective
desirable

marghzâr: noun
lawn - prairie

margomir: noun
mortality

marhabâ: noun
hurrah

marhale: noun
stage - grade - phase

marham: noun
balm - unguent - unction - ointment - chrism

marhamat: noun
grace - mercy

marhum: noun
late - decedent

marhun: noun
indebted

marhun budan: verb
To owe

mariz: noun
sick - morbid - patient

mariz kardan: verb
To indispose

mariz shodan: verb
To sick

marizâd: noun
bravo

marjah: noun
preferable

marjân: noun
coral

markaz: noun
center

markazi: adjective
central

marmari: adjective
jet - marble

marmi: noun
projectile

marmuz: adjective
exotic - mysterious

marsiye: noun
jeremiad - elegy

marsule: noun
consignment

marsum: noun
usual - prevalent - customary

marsum kardan: verb
To introduce - To standardize

marta': noun
tore - pasture - park

martabe: noun
stair - sphere - place - order

martub: adjective
muggy - moist - humid - wet

martub kardan: verb
To wet - To dank

martub shodan: verb
To moisten

martub sâkhtan: verb
To damp - To humidify

marz: noun
boundary - border

marzobum: noun
home - country

marzyâbi kardan: verb
To delimit

marâ: preposition
mine

marâm: noun
tenet - intent

marâsem: noun
ceremony - rite

mas'ale: noun
theorem - question - problem

mas'hur: adjective
spellbound - rapt

mas'hur kardan: verb
To bewitch - To bedevil - To charm - To ravish

mas-hur shodan: verb
To enchant

masal: noun
proverb

masalan: adverb
for example

masdar: noun
orderly

masdar: noun
infinitive

masdud: adjective
shut - barred

masdud sâkhtan: verb
To stockade

maserat: noun
joyance - joy

masghat: noun
abortive

mash'al: noun
torch

mash'uf sâkhtan: verb
To grace

mash'y: noun
tack - gang - demarche

mash'y: noun
policy

masheghat: noun
travail - hardship - pressure

mashgh: noun
homework - exercise

mashgh: noun
practise - homework

mashghul: noun
at - busy - engross

mashghul kardan: verb
To busy - To amuse

mashghuliyat: noun
engagement - avocation

mashhud: adjective
obvious - evident

mashhur: adjective
reputable - famous

mashiyat: noun
ordinance

mashiyate elâhi: noun
providence

mashkuk: noun
skeptic - suspicious - dubious - doubtful - uncertain

mashmul: noun
inclusive - liable

mashmul kardan: verb
To implicate

mashmuliyat: noun
incurrence - incidence

mashregh: noun
sunrise

mashru': adjective
legitimate - legal - lawful - rightful

mashru'iyat: noun
legitimation

mashrub: noun
drink - liquor - beverage

mashrubât: noun
moonlight

mashruh: adjective
punctual - unabridged - elaborative

mashrut: adjective
eventual - provisional - provided

mashrute: noun
conditional

mashverat: noun
advice - rede - counsel - consult

mashverat kardan: verb
To consult - To confer

mashverati: adjective
advisory

masih: noun
christ

masihan: noun
messiah

masihi: adjective
christian

masihiyat: noun
christianity - christendom

masir: noun
path

masjed: noun
mosque

maskan: noun
housing

maskhare: adjective
spoof - mower - dult - clown

maskhare kardan: verb
To clown - To buffoon - To mimic

maskharegi: noun
tomfoolery

maskhareâmiz: adjective
ridiculous - droll

maskuk: noun
money

maskukât: noun
coinage

maskuni: adjective
residential

maslakh: noun
slaughterhouse

maslehat: noun
interest - expedient

maslehati: adjective
advisable

maslub shodan: verb
To hang

masmu': noun
audible

masmum kardan: verb
To poison - To venom

masmum shodan: verb
To venom - To loco

masnad: noun
seat - substance - predicate

masnu': noun
manufacture - artifact

masnu'i: adjective
false - artificial

masraf: noun
expenditure - consumption - utilization

masraf: noun
expense

masraf kardan: verb
To consume - To expend - To use

masrafkonande: adjective
consumer

masrur: adjective
glad - vivacious

mast: adjective
drunken - drunk

mast kardan: verb
To befuddle - To fuzz

masti: noun
drunk - languor - inebriety

mastur: adjective
covered

masun: adjective
immune

masun kardan: verb
To immune

masun sâkhatan: verb
To defend

masuniyat: noun
security - immunity

masâfat: noun
distance

masâhat: noun
area - space

masâne: noun
cyst

masâne: noun
urinarybladder

matab: noun
clinic - policlinic

matalak: noun
josh

matarsak: noun
scarecrow

matbu': adjective
scrumptious - graceful - handsome - lief

matbu'ât: noun
press - literature

mate: noun
auger - bore - gimlet - drill

mate kardan: verb
To gimlet

mate zadan: verb
To drill

matin: adjective
sober - serene - sedate - placid

matin: adjective
staid

matlab: noun
subject - thought - theme

matlub: adjective
desirable - favorite - nice - lief - idealistic

matma'e nazar: adjective
scope

matn: noun
text

matni: adjective
textual

matrah kardan: verb
To introduce - To pose

matrud: adjective
abject - castaway - rejcet - outcast - despicable

matruk: adjective
desolate - derelict - bleak - lonely

matruke: adjective
obsolete - disuse

mavadat: adjective
amity

maviz: noun
currant

mavâj: adjective
undulatory - billowy

mavâjeb: noun
salary - stipend - emolument

mazane: noun
quotation

mazbur: noun
aforementioned

maze: noun
flavor - savor - taste

mazedâr kardan: verb
To flavor

mazeye tond: noun
tang

mazhab: noun
religion

mazhabi: adjective
religious

mazhar: adjective
showing

mazighe: noun
pinch - extremity

mazine: noun
expense - expenditure - cost

maziyat: noun
profit - privilege - advantage

maziyat dâdan: verb
To advantage

mazkur: noun
said

mazmaze: noun
sip - gust - assay

mazmaze kardan: verb
To sip

mazmun: noun
purporst

maznun: adjective
suspect - defiant

maznun budan: verb
To suspicion - To suspect

mazra'e: noun
champ - stead

mazrab: noun
multiple

mazrub: noun
multiplicand

mazâr: noun
sepulcher - bier

mazâyâ: noun
premium

maâser: noun
current - contemporary - contemporaneous

me'de: noun
stomach - tummy

me'de: noun
stomach - tummy

me'mâr: noun
architect

me'mâri kardan: verb
To architect

me'râj: noun
ascension

me'yâr: noun
scale - gauge - criterion

medâd: noun
pencil

medâdrangi: noun
colored pencil

medâl: noun
medal

medâmatgâh: noun
penitentiary

medâr: noun
orbit - circle

meftâh: noun
passkey - clef - opener

meghdâr: noun
quantity - scantling - sup

meghdâre kam: noun
morsel - snatch - spatter

meghdâre nâchiz: noun
trace - slight

meghnatis: noun
magnet

meghyâs: noun
gauge - measure - indicator - scale -
yardstick

meh: noun
vapor - mist - fog

meh gereftan: verb
To fog - To mist

mehmân: noun
guest - visitor

mehmân kardan: verb
To invite - To guest

mehmândâr: noun
lodger

mehmâni: noun
party

mehmânkhâne: noun
lobby - inn

mehmânsarâ: adjective
resthouse

mehnat: noun
pain - distress - tribulation - toil

mehr: noun
signet - love

mehrabân: adjective
kind - gracious - amiable - affable

mehrabâni: noun
amiability - affability - kindness

mehriye: noun
dowry

mehrâb: noun
altar

mehtar: adjective
senior - groomsman - groom

mehvar: noun
pivot - axle - axis

mehvare taghâron: noun
axis

mehvari: noun
rotate - pivotal

mehâlud: adjective
turbid - caliginous

mehâlud budan: verb
To fog

mei: noun
wine

meidân: noun
scope - purview - square

meidâne nabard: noun
battlefield

meigosâr: adjective
bibulous

meigosâri: noun
rouse - orgiastic - binge

meikade: noun
cabaret - bar

meikhâne: noun
tavern

meikhâre: adjective
drunkard

meikhâregi: noun
spree

meil: noun
zest - tendency - desire - delight - will

meimun: noun
ape - monkey

mek: noun
intake - suck

mek zadan: verb
To suck

mekidan: verb
To suck - To intake

mekzik: noun
Mexico

mekziki: adjective
Mexican

mekânik: noun
machanist - mechanics - mechanic

mekâniki: adjective
gadget - mechanic

mekânize: verb
To mechanize - To mechanization

mekânizm: noun
mechanism

melat: noun
state - people - nation

meli: noun
public - national - popular

meli kardan: verb
To nationalize

meli shodan: verb
To nationalize

meliyat: noun
nationality

melk: noun
territory

melki: noun
possessive - agrarian

melâk: noun
criterion

men men: noun
mutter

menbar: noun
rostrum - pulpit - tribune

menghâr: noun
bill - beak - rostrum - gouge

menhâ: noun
minus

meni: noun
sperm

menvâl: noun
rate

meri: noun
swallow - gullet

meri: noun
esophagus

mes: noun
copper

meshki: adjective
black

mesi: adjective
cuprous

meskin: adjective
poor

mesl: noun
example - adage - parable - like - instance

mesr: noun
Egypt

mesri: adjective
Egyptian

mesvâk zadan: verb
To brush

mesâl: noun
example - instant - instance

mesâle adabi: noun
locus

metod: noun
method - how

metr: noun
meter

metro: noun
subway

metâ': noun
commodity - article

metâbolizm: noun
metabolism

metânat: noun
sobriety - serene - equanimity

meydâne jang: noun
battlefield

meygosâri kardan: verb
To tipple - To carouse

meygu: noun
shrimp

meyl: noun
appetite - email

meyl dâshtan: verb
To desire

meyl kardan: verb
To tend

meymun: noun
monkey

mezâh: noun
prank - humor - wit

mezâh kardan: verb
To jest

mezâj: noun
temperament - temper

mezâji: adjective
quirk

mi'âd: noun
rendezvous

mi'âdgâh: noun
tryst - hangout - recourse

mifrofon: noun
saltshaker

migren: noun
migraine

mihan: noun
home - motherland

mihandust: adjective
patiot

mihanparast: adjective
patiot

mikh: noun
nail

mikhche: noun
picket - corn - spile

mikhkub kardan: verb
To transfix - To spike

mikrob: noun
microbe - germ

mikrofon: noun
microphone

mikroskop: noun
microscope

mile: noun
bar - rod - lever

mile: noun
bar

milimetr: noun
millimeter

miliyun: noun
million

miliyuner: adjective
millionaire

milâd: noun
birthday

min: noun
verily

min: noun
maine

miniyâtor: noun
miniature

minâ: noun
aster

mirâs: noun
heritage - legacy - inheritance

mirâsbar: adjective
heir

mirâsbari: noun
inheritance

misâgh: noun
pact - covenant - convention

misâgh bastan: verb
To stipulate - To covenant

mive: noun
fruit - blossom

mive dâdan: verb
To fruit

miyan: noun
centennial - waist - among - between -
meddle

miyo miyo kardan: verb
To mew

miyomiyo: noun
miaow

miyânbor: noun
crosscut

miyâne: noun
median

miyâne: noun
median

miyâneravi: noun
mean

miyânerô: adjective
sober - moderate

miyângin: noun
median - mean - average

miyâni: noun
mid - medial

miyânji: noun
mediator

miyânji shodan: verb
To interpose

miyânjigari: noun
intermediation - intercession

miz: noun
table

mizbân: noun
host - landlady

mize tahrir: noun
writingdesk - desk

mizikâl: noun
musical

mizân: noun
scale - yardstick - measure - criterion

mizân kardan: verb
To regulate - To adjust - To temper

mo'adel: noun
average - norm

mo'akad: noun
emphatic - accentual

mo'ayed: noun
subsidiary

mo'jeze: noun
token - miracle

mo'jeze âsâ: adjective
miraculous

mo'tabar: adjective
trusty - reliable - authoritative - valid

mo'tabar budan: verb
To dow

mo'tad kardan: verb
To habit

mo'tadel: adjective
modest - moderate - mild - medium

mo'taghed: adjective
believer

mo'taghedât: noun
belief

mo'talef: noun
confederate

mo'tamed: adjective
trustworthy

mo'taref: adjective
confessor

mo'tarez: noun
objecting - demurrer - demonstrator

mo'tâd: noun
addict - inveterate - habitual

mo'tâd shodan: verb
To accustom - To wont

mo'tâd sâkhtan: verb
To accustom

mo'âdel: noun
tantamount - equivalent

mo'âdele: noun
equation

mo'ârefe: noun
introduction

mo'ârez: adjective
opponent

moadab: adjective
respectful

moadab kardan: verb
To urbanize

moadabâne: adverb
courteous - urbane

moalagh: adjective
turntable - pendant

moalagh kardan: verb
To suspend

moalef: noun
compiler - writer - author

moalem: noun
teacher - instructor

moama: noun
enigma - mystery - puzzle

moanas: noun
feminine - woman

moaref: adjective
reagent

moarefi: noun
presentation - introduction

moarefi kardan: verb
To nominate - To introduce

moaser: adjective
effective - impressive - pivotal

moaser budan: verb
To adequate

moases: noun
father - originator - author

moasese: noun
institution - institute

moatal kardan: verb
To linger - To detain

moatal shodan: verb
To wait

moatar: adjective
redolent - nutty - aromatic - scented - spicy

moavagh: verb
To retard

moayan: adjective
specific - definite

mobadel: noun
converter

mobalas kardan: verb
To dight

mobaleghe mazhabi: noun
missioner

mobarâ: adjective
innocent

mobarâ kardan: verb
To exonerate - To absolve

mobham: adjective
obscure - ambiguous - vague - misty

mobham: adjective
hazy

mobham kardan: verb
To obscure - To adumbrate

moble kardan: verb
To furnish

mobram: adjective
sore - imperious - urgent - demanding

mobser: noun
monitor

mobtadi: noun
novice - beginner - youngling - tyro

mobtadâ: noun
subject

mobtaker: adjective
inventor - originator - ingenious

mobtalâ: noun
stricken - given

mobtazal: adjective
trivial - humdrum - vulgar

mobâdele: noun
exchange

mobâderat: noun
venture

mobâdi: noun
Ports

mobâdiye âdâd: adjective
tactful - polite

mobâhese: noun
disputation - discussion - controversy - agument

mobâhese kardan: verb
To dissert - To dispute - To debate

mobâhât: noun
brag - boast - pride

mobâleghe: noun
bombast

mobâleghe: noun
hyperbole

mobâlegheâmiz: adjective
superlative

mobârak: adjective
happy - auspicious - blest

mobârez: adjective
warrior - defiant

mobâreze: noun
battle - champion

mobâreze kardan: verb
To joust - To combat - To conflict

mobârezetalabi: noun
defiance

mobâsher: noun
steward - foreman - overseer

mobâsherat: noun
stewardship

mobâsherat kardan: verb
To steward

moch: noun
wrist

mochâle: adjective
crumple

mochâle kardan: verb
To rumple - To crumple - To tousle

mochâle shodan: verb
To snuggle

326

mod: noun
mode - highwater - vogue - chic

mod: noun
mode

moda'i: adjective
complainant - claimant

moda'i alayh: noun
defendant

moda'i budan: verb
To maintain

modarej: noun
gaduate - gradient - scaled

modares: noun
teacher - lecturer

modat: noun
time - term - duration - period

modati: noun
a while

modavar: adjective
circular - round

model: noun
reconstruction - model

modern: adjective
modern

modir: noun
director - manager

modiriyat: noun
management

modâfe': adjective
apologist - defender - contestant

modâfe'e: noun
plea - apology - advocacy

modâkhele: noun
intervention - intermediation - intermediary

modâkhele kardan: verb
To intervene - To interpose - To interfere

modâkhelegar: adjective
pryer - meddlesome

modârâ: adjective
tolerance - reserve - affability

modârâ kardan: verb
To tolerate

modâvem: noun
unremitting - perpetual

modâvem: adjective
continuous - ongoing

modâvemat: noun
perseverance - assiduity

modâvâ: noun
therapy - medicament

modâvâ kardan: verb
To medicate

mofarah: adjective
fun

mofasal: noun
spacious - joint - juncture - voluminous

mofasalan: adverb
quits

mofaser: noun
commentator - interpreter

mofid: adjective
profitable - beneficial - useful

mofid budan: verb
To advantage - To benefit - To stead

mofrad: noun
singular - odd

mofrat: adjective
intensive - extreme - extravagant -
excessive

moft: adjective
gratuitous - gratis

moftakhar: adjective
proud

moftakhar kardan: verb
To gratify

moftazeh: adjective
ignominious - infamous

moghadam: adjective
antecedent - prior - premier

moghadam budan: verb
To precede

moghadame: noun
introduction - preface - prologue

moghadamât: noun
preliminary

moghadamât: noun
rudiment

moghadamâti: noun
primary - elementary

moghadar: adjective
tacit - fey

moghadar shodan: verb
To fate

moghadas: adjective
holy - numinous - saint - sacrosanct - sacred

moghadas kardan: verb
To hallow

moghadas shemordan: verb
To sancify - To saint

moghadasnâma: adjective
sanctimonious

moghaleb: noun
yclept - ycleped

moghaled: adjective
imitator - clown - zany

mogharar: noun
regular - statutory - standard

mogharar dâshtan: verb
To doom - To assign - To adjudicate - To
adjudge

mogharari: noun
pension - emolument

moghararât: noun
institute - manual - precept

moghaser: noun
culprit - culpable - guilty - hangdog

moghaser dânestan: verb
To blame

moghavi: adjective
tonic - hearty - cordial

moghavâ: noun
carton - card

moghayad: adjective
pent - modal - bound - conditional

moghazi: noun
tonic - fortifying

moghe': noun
period - time

moghe'ike: preposition
when

moghe'iyat: noun
situation - position - location

moghe'iyate ejtemâ'i: noun
station

moghim: noun
resident - inmate - inhabitant

moghim shodan: verb
To reside

moghrez: noun
partial

moghtader: adjective
dominant - mighty - authoritative

moghtanam: noun
pleasurable

moghtanam shemordan: verb
To prize

moghâbel: noun
opposite - off - for - contrary - inverse

moghâbele: noun
contrast - collation - opposition

moghâbele kardan: verb
To beard - To repel - To check

moghâlete: noun
sophistry - sophism - chicanery

moghârebat: noun
intercourse - coition

moghârebate jensi: noun
gash - coitus

moghârebati: adjective
copulative - venereal

moghâren: noun
toward - against - into

moghâte'e: noun
contract - jobbery

moghâte'ekâr: noun
contractor

moghâvem: adjective
adamant - resister - resistant - refractory

moghâvemat: noun
defiance - resistance - opposition

moghâvemat kardan: verb
To pulloff

moghâyer: noun
adverse - discordant - offbeat

moghâyer budan: verb
To disagree

moghâyerat: noun
aversion - variance - contrast

moghâyese: noun
analogy - comparison - collation - resemblance

moghâyese kardan: verb
To compare

mohabat: noun
amour - love - glow

mohabatâmiz: adjective
tender

mohadab: noun
convex

mohaghar: adjective
humble - unpretentious

mohaghegh: noun
scholar

mohalel: adjective
resolvent

mohandes: noun
bachelor - engineer

moharek: adjective
motive - stimulus - stimulant - provocative - propellant

mohaval: verb
To relegate - To devolve - To vest

mohavate: noun
precinct - enclosure

mohayej: adjective
sensational - stimulant - dramatic

mohayâ: noun
prone - present - bound

mohayâ kardan: verb
To ready

mohayâ shodan: verb
To unlimber

mohayâ sâkhtan: verb
To prepare

mohbal: noun
cunt

mohbal: noun
vagina

mohbeli: noun
vagina

mohegh: adjective
rightful

mohem: adjective
significant - serious - substantial -
momentous - main - important

mohemtar: adjective
premier

mohemât: noun
ordnance - ammo - munition

mohemât: noun
arsenal

mohit: noun
environment - perimeter

mohite dâyere: noun
circumference - circle

mohkam: adjective
firm - tough - tight - sturdy - strict - steady -
stable

mohkam bastan: verb
To yerk - To cinch - To buttress - To brace

mohkam gereftan: verb
To gripe - To grip - To clutch

mohkam kardan: verb
To tighten - To consolidate - To fix

mohkam shodan: verb
To anchor

mohkam zadan: verb
To bang - To whack

mohlat: noun
respite - usance - break

mohlat: noun
break - respite

mohlat khâstan: verb
To demur

mohlek: noun
noxious - fatal - deadly - lethal - pernicious -
mortal

mohmel: noun
trashy - preposterous - nonsense

mohr: noun
seal - cachet

mohr kardan: verb
To signet - To seal

mohr zadan: verb
To stamp - To frank - To imprint - To
impress

mohr zadan be: verb
To imprint

mohre: noun
nut - vertebrate - vertebra - bead

mohtaker: adjective
speculator - hoarder

mohtaram: adjective
respectable - honorable

mohtaram: adjective
honor

mohtaram dâshtan: verb
To respect

mohtaramâne: adverb
deferential

mohtaregh: adjective
torrid

mohtareghe: adjective
igneous

mohtargh shodan: verb
To explode

mohtavi: noun
container

mohtavi budan: verb
To contain

mohtâj: adjective
dependent

mohtâj budan: verb
To want

mohtât: adjective
scrupulous - considerate - cautious

mohtât: adjective
prudent

mohâfez: adjective
preservative

mohâfezat: noun
shelter - preservation

mohâfezat kardan: verb
To keep - To guard - To shelter

mohâfeze kâr: adjective
stuffy

mohâjem: noun
aggressor - aggressive - invader - offensive

mohâjer: noun
immigrant - pilgrim - migrant

mohâjerat: noun
exodus - migration

mohâjerat kardan: verb
To migrate - To emigrate

mohâkeme: noun
trial

mohâreb: noun
warrior - comatant

mohârebe: noun
warfare - war

mohâsebe: noun
computation - calculation

mohâsebe kardan: verb
To calk

mohâsere: noun
siege - blockage - blockade

mohâsere kardan: verb
To surround - To siege - To encompass - To gird - To blockade

mohâvere: noun
colloquy - colloquium - conversation

332

mohâvere'i: adjective
colloquial

mojadad: noun
second - further

mojahaz kardan: verb
To equip - To furnish

mojalad: noun
tome - book

mojalal: adjective
sumptuous - illustrious - luxurious - glorious

mojalal: adjective
taffeta

mojarad: noun
bachelor

mojasam kardan: verb
To character - To depict - To embody

mojasam sâkhtan: verb
To image

mojasame: noun
image - idol - statue

mojasame sâzi: noun
imagery - plastic - sculpture

mojasamesâz: adjective
statuary

mojavez: noun
justification

mojazâ: adjective
separable - apart - discrete

mojazâ kardan: verb
To disassemble - To isolate

mojmal: noun
inconclusive - compendious - synopsis

mojmar: adjective
censer

mojrem: adjective
guilty - wrongdoer - convict

mojri: noun
executor - executive

mojtahed: noun
priest

mojtama': noun
complex

mojâb kardan: verb
To confute - To assure

mojâdele: adjective
toil - tussle - contention

mojâhed: noun
zealous - zealot - devotee

mojâhedat: noun
industry

mojâhedin: noun
militia

mojâver: adjective
contiguous - neighbor - adjacent

mojâver budan: verb
To bound - To border - To abut

mojâver budan: verb
To adjoin

mojâverat: noun
proximity - neighborhood - contiguity - vicinity - adjacency

mojâz: adjective
allowable - admissible - permissive - lawful

mojâz kardan: verb
To permit

mojâzât: noun
punishment - penalty - retribution - reprimand

mojâzât kardan: verb
To lynch - To punish

mojâzâti: noun
pnitive - penal - retribution

moka'ab: noun
cube

mokader: adjective
eerie

mokamel: noun
supplementary - supplement - complementary - complement

mokarar: adjective
bis - continual - eternity - eternal - repetitious

mokararan: adverb
freuqently

mokh: noun
brain

mokhader: adjective
narcotic - opiate

mokhamer: adjective
zymogenic - yeast

mokhareb: adjective
wrecker - destroyer - mortal

mokhber: adjective
informer - informant

mokhche: noun
cerebellum

mokhel: adjective
intruder

mokhles: adjective
sincere - devotee

mokhles: adjective
compendious - gist

mokhtal: adjective
teched

mokhtal kardan: verb
To disorganize - To disorder - To disarrange

mokhtalef: noun
diverse - dissimilar - disparate - various

mokhtales: adjective
grafter - peculator

mokhtalet: adjective
motley - medley

mokhtare': adjective
inventor - ingenious

mokhtasar: adjective
summary - succinct - concise

mokhtasar kardan: verb
To simplify - To shorten - To abridge - To abbreviate

mokhtaseran: adverb
nutshell

mokhtâr: noun
free

mokhtâsât: noun
coordinate

mokhâbere: noun
transmittal

mokhâbere kardan: verb
To dispatch

mokhâlef: adjective
defiant - contrary - opponent - adversary

mokhâlef budan: verb
To disagree

mokhâlefat: noun
defiance - opposition - objection - aversion

mokhâlefat kardan: verb
To controvert - To oppose - To object - To withstand

mokhât: noun
phlegm

mokhâtere: noun
jeopardy - risk - hazard - peril

mokhâtere âmiz: adjective
perilous

mokhâti: noun
pituitary - mucous

mokâleme: noun
colloquium - conversation

mokâleme kardan: verb
To parley

mokâshefe: noun
apocalypse

molavan: noun
colored

molghâ: noun
null - abrogate

molhagh shodan: verb
To join - To combine - To assist

molhed: adjective
atheist

moltafet: adjective
aware - attentive - conscious

moltafet budan: verb
To mind - To beware

moltames: adjective
supplicant - suppliant - wishful

moltazem: noun
sponsor

molukâne: adverb
royal

molâ: noun
mullah

molâghat: noun
visit

molâheze: noun
consideration - respect - regard - prudence

molâheze kardan: verb
To perceive - To consider - To observe - To remark - To regard

molâhezekâri: noun
canniness

molâyem: adjective
soft - smooth - kindly - moderate - mild - meek

molâyem shodan: verb
To smooth

molâyemat: noun
reproof - rebuke - snuff - tax

molâyemat: noun
equanimity - calmness - amenity - leniency

molâyematâmiz: adjective
reproachful

molâzem: noun
retainer - concomitant - attendant - adjunct

molâzemat: noun
attendance

momayezi: noun
survey - audit

momayezi kardan: verb
To verify - To survey

momken: noun
thinkable - conceivable - possible

momken ast: verb
To may - To perhaps

momtahen: noun
proctor - examiner - examinant - tester

momtane': noun
recusant

momtâz: adjective
superior - excellent

momâne'at: noun
prohibition - rein - blockage - annoyance

momâne'at: verb
To impede - To prevent

momâresat: noun
use - ure - practise - practice

momâresat kardan: verb
To practise - To practice - To ure

momâs: noun
tangent

mon'aghed kardan: verb
To conclude

mon'aghed shodan: verb
To coalesce

336

mon'akes kardan: verb
To resound

mon'akes shodan: verb
To rebound

monabatkâr: noun
woodcutter - woodcarver

monabatkâri kardan: verb
To splay

monajem: noun
astronomer - astrologer

monavar: adjective
illuminate

monazah: adjective
sacrosanct - sublimate

monazam: adjective
square - regular - orderly - ordered

monbaset: adjective
trig

monbaset kardan: verb
To extend - To explode - To expand - To
rarefy - To stretch

mondarajât: noun
content

mondares: adjective
seedy - threadbare - rundown

monfajer kardan: verb
To puff - To burst - To blowup - To dynamite

monfajer shodan: verb
To explode - To erupt - To detonate - To
blowout - To puff

monfajere: noun
obtuse

monfared: noun
solitaire - single

monfasel: noun
disjoin - discontinuous - free

monfasel kardan: verb
To expel

monghabez kardan: verb
To contract - To condense - To retract

monghabez shodan: verb
To twitch

mongharez: noun
extinct

monghate': adjective
discontinuous

monghazi kardan: verb
To terminate

monhadem kardan: verb
To ruinate - To exterminate

monhal kardan: verb
To dissolve - To disband

monhani: noun
round - cycloid - crump - bent

monharef: adjective
devious - deviant - hellbent - aberrant

monharef shodan: verb
To wander - To digress - To swerve - To stray

monhaser: noun
exclusive - limited

monhaser befard: adjective
unique - particular - exclusive

monhaser kardan: verb
To confine - To limit

monhaseran: adverb
exclusively

monhat: adjective
amiss - degenerate - decadent

monhat kardan: verb
To degrade

monjamed: noun
rimy

monjamed kardan: verb
To jell - To curdle - To ice

monjamed shodan: verb
To ice - To congeal - To freeze

monjar shodan: verb
To redound

monker: adjective
dissenter

monker shodan: verb
To repudiate - To controvert

monkere khodâ: noun
atheist

monsef: adjective
square - unprejudiced

monsefe: noun
panel

monsefâne: adverb
just - candid

monsha'eb shodan: verb
To ramify - To fork - To branch

monshi: noun
secretary - clerk

monsub: adjective
sib - relative

monsukh kardan: verb
To abrogate - To abolish

montabegh kardan: verb
To register

montafi kardan: verb
To liquidate

montaghel kardan: verb
To transmigrate - To transfer - To wend - To abalienate

montahi: noun
supreme

montakhab: adjective
chosen

montasab: adjective
germane

montasab kardan: verb
To relegate - To refer

montasher kardan: verb
To publish - To print

montasher kardan: verb
To diffuse - To publish

montasher shodan: verb
To spread - To circulate

montasher sâkhtan: verb
To release

montazer: adjective
wistful - anticipator - anticipant

montazer budan: verb
To await - To antedate - To expect

montazer shodan: verb
To wait - To hover - To abide - To await

monzajer budan: verb
To loathe

monzavi: adjective
hermit - recluse - solitudinarian - secluded

monzavi kardan: verb
To seclude

monâdi: adjective
front - precursor - herald - harbinger

monâjât: noun
chant - cant

monâseb: adjective
proper - suitable - appropriate - relevant - fit

monâseb budan: verb
To suit - To assort

monâsebat: noun
reason - rapport

monâze'e: noun
disputation - debate - plea - struggle - tilt

monâzere: noun
disputation - discussion - agument

monâzere kardan: verb
To debate

moraba': noun
square

morabi: adjective
visible

morabi: noun
mentor - corrector

morabâ: noun
jam

moradad: adjective
suspense - unready - uncertain - hesitant

moradad budan: verb
To vacillate - To linger - To hesitate

moraje'e kardan: verb
To confer - To refer

morakab: noun
composite - compound - ink

morakabdân: noun
inkwell - inkstand

morakabât: noun
citrus

moratab: adjective
ordered - neat - regular - tidy - trim

moratab kardan: verb
To arrange - To straighten - To serialize

morataban: adverb
away

mordan: verb
To dying - To perish - To pass away

mordani: adjective
dying - mortal

morde: adjective
dead

mordâb: noun
swamp - quagmire - morass - marsh - lagoon

mordâbi: adjective
paludal

mordâr: noun
carrion

mored: noun
occasion - instance

morede alâghe: adjective
beloved

morede etminân: adjective
trusty

morede etminân: adjective
dependable

morede hemâyat: adjective
support

morepasand: adjective
savory

morfin: noun
morphin

morgh: noun
hen - poultry

morghdâri: noun
aviculture

morghe eshgh: noun
lovebird

morghe mâhikhâr: noun
pelican - kingfisher

morghâbi: noun
duck

morghân: noun
bird

morid: noun
devotee - disciple

morkhasi: noun
vacation

morkhasi gereftan: verb
To recess - To vacation

moro mum kardan: verb
To seal - To lute

morovat: adjective
humanity

morshed: noun
mentor - master - preceptor

mortabet: adjective
correlate

mortabet kardan: verb
To correlate

mortad: noun
apostate - heterodox - heretic

mortad shodan: verb
To defect

mortaesh: noun
vibrant

mortaesh kardan: verb
To strum

mortaesh sâkhtan: verb
To tremble

mortafa': noun
high

mortafa' kardan: verb
To obviate

mortâz: adjective
ascetic

morur: noun
revision - review

morur kardan: verb
To turnover

morvârid: noun
pearl

morâ'ât: noun
consideration - regard

morâd: noun
gist - wish - aim

morâfe'e: noun
lawsuit

morâfe'e: noun
lawsuit

morâfe'e kardan: verb
To litigate

morâgheb: adjective
observer - observant - watchful - lookout -
vigilant

morâgheb budan: verb
To watch out

morâghebat: noun
surveillance - ovservation - watchful -
lookout - vigilance

morâghebat: verb
To care

morâje'at kardan: verb
To return

morâje'e: noun
referral - reference

morâsele: noun
letter

morâvede: noun
intercourse

mosabeb: adjective
inducement

mosade': noun
troublesome

mosaken: adjective
narcotic - calmative - palliative

mosalah kardan: verb
To equip - To weapon - To force

mosalam: noun
sure - cretain - incontrovertible -
incontestable

mosalam dânestan: verb
To presume

mosalaman: adverb
indisputable

mosalas: noun
triangle

mosalasât: noun
trigonometry

mosalat: adjective
dominant - preponderant - predominant

mosalat budan: verb
To predominate

mosalmân: noun
moslem - muslim

mosalsal: noun
machine gun - serial - consecutive

mosamam: adjective
stalwart

mosatah: adjective
flat - plane - plain

mosatah: verb
To flatten

mosavar: adjective
pictorial

mosbat: adjective
positive - plus

mosen: adjective
elderly - old

moser: adjective
demanding - precarious - insistent

moserâne: adverb
insistently

moshabak kardan: verb
To interweave - To interlace

moshakhas: noun
specified - determined - ditinct

moshakhas kardan: adverb
characterize - denote - delineate - specify

moshakhasât: noun
specs - specification - characteristic

mosharaf: adjective
dominant - verge

moshavash kardan: verb
To disconcert

moshavegh: adjective
incentive

moshkel: noun
problem - hard

moshreb: noun
grain - mood - habit

moshreb: noun
humor

moshrek: adjective
pagan - heathen

mosht: noun
punch - fist

mosht khordan: verb
To scuff

mosht zadan: verb
To box - To knuckle - To fist

moshtagh: noun
derivative - offshoot

moshtarak: noun
joint - joint - common

moshtari: noun
patron - customer - client

moshtzan: noun
boxer

moshtâgh: adjective
solicitous - studious - enthusiastic - earnest
- eager - fond

moshtâgh budan: verb
To yearn

moshtâghâne: adverb
intensive - intense

moshâ': noun
joint

moshâbeh: adjective
homogeneous - equivalent - similar

moshâbehat: noun
similarity - parallelism

moshâhede: noun
seeing - ovservation

moshâhede kardan: verb
To see - To observe

moshâjere: noun
dispute - scuffle

moshârekat: noun
partnership - participate

moshârekat kardan: verb
To participate

moshâver: noun
adviser - counselor - consultant

moshâvere: noun
council - consultation

mosibat: noun
tragedy - sorrow - disaster - catastrophe -
calamity

mosibatbâr: adjective
calamitous

mosleh: noun
righter - reformer - peacemaker

moslek: noun
sect

mosnef: noun
writer - composer

mosri: adjective
zymotic - infectious - epidemic

mosta'ed: adjective
susceptible - prone - apt

mosta'jer: noun
tenant - lodger - occupant

mosta'mere: noun
colony

mostabed: adjective
opinionated

mostabedâne: adverb
arbitrary - despotic

mostadal: adjective
arguable - reasonable - rational

mostafi shodan: verb
To resign

mostaghar: noun
put - deepseated

mostaghar shodan: verb
To set - To fix

mostaghbal: noun
future

mostaghel: noun
independent

mostaghelât: noun
tenement

mostaghim: noun
proximate - straight - upstanding - right

mostaghim: noun
direct - attributive

mostaghiman: adverb
sheer - straight - bolt - perse

mostahagh: adjective
worthy - meritorious

mostahjan: adjective
lurid

mostahkam: adjective
tenacious - redoubtable

mostahlak kardan: verb
To depreciate - To amortize

mostahlak shodan: verb
To merge

mostakhdem: noun
man - employee - retainer

mostakhdem: noun
employee - servant

mostalah: noun
yclept - ycleped - colloquial

mostalzem budan: verb
To implication - To implicate - To entail

mostamand: adjective
poor

mostame': adjective
auditor - listener

mostamer: adjective
continuum

mostamlekât: noun
colony

mostamsak: adjective
pretext

mostanad kardan: verb
To predicate

mostarâh: noun
toilet - restroom

mostashâr: noun
counselor

mostasnâ: noun
exempt

mostasnâ kardan: verb
To exclude

mostater kardan: verb
To occult

mostatil: noun
rectangular - oblong

mostoli: verb
To prevail

mosâ'edat: noun
help

mosâ'ede: adjective
auspicious - adjutant - propitious

mosâ'ede: noun
advance

mosâbeghate olampik: noun
olympiad

mosâbeghe: noun
match - contest - competition - game

mosâbeghe dâdan: verb
To race - To compete

mosâdef shodan: verb
To hurtle

mosâdem: noun
afoul

mosâdere kardan: verb
To sequester - To confiscate

mosâedat kardan: verb
To aid

mosâfer: noun
passenger - traveler

mosâfer: noun
passenger - traveler

mosâferat: noun
journey - tour

mosâferat: noun
travel - journey

mosâferkhâne: noun
inn

mosâheb: noun
consort - fere

mosâhebat: noun
companionship

mosâhebat kardan: verb
To accompany

mosâleh: noun
stuff

mosâlehe: noun
accord - reconciliation - compromise

mosâlehe kardan: verb
To compromise

mosâlematâmiz: adjective
peaceful

mosâmehe: noun
neglect

mosâmehe kardan: verb
To connive

mosâvi: noun
adequate - even - equal

mosâvi budan: verb
To equal

mosâvât: noun
equality

mota'âl: adjective
high - excelsior - eminent - sublimate

motafegh: adjective
confederate

motafegholghôl: adjective
unanimous

motaham: adjective
culprit

motaham kardan: verb
To impute - To accuse

motaham sâkhtan: verb
To charge

motahed: noun
allied

motahed kardan: verb
To unite - To unify

motahed shodan: verb
To band - To combine

motahedolghôl: adjective
unisonous (onal-onant

motahedolshekl: adjective
uniform

motaki: adjective
pending - reliant

motaki shodan: verb
To lean

motakâ: noun
slip - cushion - bolster - backrest - pillow

motamam: noun
complementary - supplementary -
supplement

motamem: noun
complement

motarjem: noun
translator - interpreter

motasel: noun
contiguous - conjunct - joint

motasel kardan: verb
To join - To connect - To link - To adjoin

motasel shodan: verb
To adjoin

mote'aded: adjective
multiple - several

mote'adi: noun
active

mote'afen: adjective
smelly - putrid - rancid

mote'ahed: adjective
undertaker - guarantor

mote'ahed shodan: verb
To plight - To pledge - To undertake

mote'ahel: noun
married

mote'ajeb shodan: verb
To swan

mote'ajeb sâkhtan: verb
To surprise - To admire

mote'akher: noun
recent

mote'alegh: adjective
dependent

mote'aleghât: noun
paraphernalia - appurtenance

mote'aseb: adjective
dogmatic - intolerant - bigot - zeal

mote'asef: adjective
sorry - afraid

mote'asefâne: adverb
unfortunately

mote'aser: adjective
sorry - regretful

mote'aser shodan: verb
To pity - To touch

mote'âdel: adjective
dominant

mote'âgheb: adjective
pursuant - subsequent

mote'âref: adjective
common - popular

moteadi: noun
transitive

motebaher: adjective
conversant - erudite

motebalver: adjective
crystalline

motebasem: adjective
riant

motebâdel: noun
alternate

motedâvel: adjective
ordinary - usual - uptodate - prevalent

motefaker: adjective
thoughtful - thinker

motefaregh kardan: verb
To intersperse - To scatter

motefaregh shodan: verb
To straggle

motefareghe: noun
sundries - miscellaneous

motefaresh sâkhtan: verb
To disperse

motefâvet: noun
away - different - other

moteghaleb: adjective
shark - swindler - dishonest - gyp

moteghayer: adjective
transitive - variable

moteghayer kardan: verb
To offend

moteghâ'ed kardan: verb
To ensure - To convince

moteghâbel: noun
reciprocal - polar

moteghâbel: noun
sponsor

moteghâren: adjective
concurrent - polar

moteghâren kardan: verb
To polarize - To proportion

moteghâren sâkhtan: verb
To time

moteghâte': noun
crossover - transverse

moteghâzi: noun
appropriate - expedient - due

moteghâzi: noun
suppliant - applicant

motehamel: noun
sufferer

motehamel: adjective
probable - plausible - likely

motehamel shodan: verb
To sustain - To defray - To incur

348

moteharek: adjective
versatile - mobile

motehaver: adjective
brash - audacious - venturer - intrepid

motehaver: adjective
daredevil

motehayer: adjective
astound - amaze - dumbstruck

motehayer sâkhtan: verb
To amaze

motejaded: adjective
ultramodern - mewfangled

motejanes: adjective
congruent

motejavez: adjective
transgressor - aggressor - violator -
offensive - offender - wrongdoer

motekaber: adjective
imperious - haughty - perky - arrogant -
proud

motekaberâne: adverb
high

motekalem: noun
speaker

motekhalef: adjective
offender - wrongdoer - transgressor -
trespasser

motekhases: noun
specialist - expert - adhoc - proficient

motekhâsem: adjective
hostile - party - belligerent - adversary

motel: noun
motel

motelâshi: adjective
disjointed - disjoin

motelâshi shodan: verb
To collapse - To decompose - To crackup

motelâtem: adjective
turbulent - unruly - lumpy - heavy

motemaden: adjective
civilized - cultivated - civil

motemaden kardan: verb
To civilize

motemaden shodan: verb
To civilize

motemalegh: adjective
sycophant

motemared: adjective
malcontent - intractable - disobedient -
rebellious - rebel

motemarkez: adjective
intensive - focus

motemarkez kardan: verb
To concentrate

motemasek shodan: verb
To truss

motemavej: adjective
wavy

motemâyel: noun
swept - tendentious - prone - like - apt - avid

motemâyez: adjective
diverse - different

motenabeh kardan: verb
To admonish

motenafer: adjective
irksome - averse

motenafer sâkhtan: verb
To nauseate

motenave': adjective
variety - varied

motenave' sâkhtan: verb
To vary

motenâghez: adjective
anomalous - incoherent

motenâseb: adjective
proportionate - commensurate

motenâseb budan: verb
To harmonize

motenâveb: adjective
periodic - alternate - continual

motenâveban: adverb
alternatively

moteraghi: adjective
progressive

moterâdef: noun
synonymous - equivalent

moterâkem: adjective
voluminous - dense - cumulous

moterâkem kardan: verb
To jam - To condense - To inflame - To amass

moterâkem shodan: verb
To agglomerate

motesadi: noun
operator

motesane': adjective
hypocrite

motesaref: adjective
possessor - proprietor

motesarefât: noun
realm

motesha'she: noun
radiant

moteshakhesh: adjective
magnate

moteshanej: adjective
nervous

moteshâbeh: adjective
analogous - homonym

motesâed: verb
To sublimate

motesâed shodan: verb
To reek

motevafiyât: noun
mortality

motevaghef kardan: verb
To gravel

motevaghef sâkhtan: verb
To layoff

motevajeh: noun
tendentious - heedful - attentive - wistful

motevajeh kardan: verb
To divert - To lend

motevajeh shodan: verb
To lend

motevajeh sâkhtan: verb
To address - To point - To direct

motevaled: noun
born

motevali: adjective
trustee - custodian - proctor

motevaregh: noun
sheet - laminate

motevarem: adjective
turgid - protuberant - gouty

motevasel shodan: verb
To resort

motevasel shodan be: verb
To recourse

motevaset: noun
medium - mediocre - medial - mean -
intermediate - average

motevâli: noun
continuous - consecutive

motevâze': adjective
humble - unselfish

motevâzi: adjective
collateral - parallel

motevâziyol azlâ': noun
parallelogram

motezalzel: adjective
shaky - ramshackle - unstable

motezalzel shodan: verb
To waver - To totter

motezamen: noun
pergnant - underlying

motezamen budan: verb
To entail - To embody - To include - To
presuppose

motezâd: noun
antonym

motezâher: adjective
hypocritical - ostentatious - ostensive

moti': adjective
understanding - hep

moti': adjective
submissive - submission - obedient - limber

motlagh: adjective
implicit - unconditional - absolute

motlagh: adjective
absolute

motlaghan: adverb
utterly

motma'en: adjective
secure - sure - confident

motma'enan: adverb
certainly

motmaen: verb
To be sure

motor: noun
motor - engine

motorkhâne: noun
powerhouse

motâbe'at: noun
follow

motâbegh: noun
respondent - relevant

motâbegh: verb
To modulate - To adjust

motâbegh budan: verb
To tally

motâbeghat: noun
accordance - compatibility - concord

motâle'e: noun
study - perusal - reading

motâle'e kardan: verb
To study - To conciliate

motâle'ât: noun
ovservation

motâlebe: noun
claim - demand

motâlebe: noun
charge

motâlebe kardan: verb
To demand

motâreke: noun
separate - quit

motâreke kardan: verb
To leaveoff

movafagh: adjective
prosperous - upbeat - successful

movafagh shodan: verb
To succeed - To prosper

movafaghiyat: noun
prosperity - success

movaghar: adjective
demure - grave - solemn - sober - sedate -
staid

movagharâne: adverb
solemn

movaghat: adjective
interim - provisional

movaghati: noun
temporary

movahed: adjective
theist

movahed: adjective
unitary

movahesh: adjective
redoubtable - horrible - lurid

movakel: noun
client - constituent

movakher: adjective
junior

movaled: adjective
reproductive - productive - birthplace -
active

movarab: noun
diagonal - crisscross

movarekh: noun
historian

movasagh: adjective
trustworthy - reliant - reliable

movazaf: adjective
bound

movâfegh: adjective
congruent - concurrent - agreeing

movâfegh budan: verb
To agree - To adapt

movâfeghat: noun
agreement - consent

movâfeghat: noun
congruence

movâjeh shodan: verb
To face

movâjehe: noun
affront - encounter

movâzeb: adjective
cautious - careful - watchful - aware -
attendant

movâzeb budan: verb
To tend - To watch

movâzebat: noun
attendance - vigilance - care

movâzebat kardan: verb
To mind - To attend - To assist

movâzene: noun
equilibrium - balance

movâzi: noun
parallel

movâzât: noun
parallelism

moyasar: noun
possible

moyasar sâkhtan: verb
To provide

mozafar: adjective
victorious

mozakar: noun
masculine - male

mozakhraf: adjective
trashy - tawdry - ludicrous - absurd - nonsense

mozayan: adjective
ornate

mozayan kardan: verb
To emboss - To dress - To furnish

mozd: noun
wage - hire - pension

mozdur: adjective
grub - grub - barrator

mozer: adjective
harmful - derogatory

mozhde dâdan: verb
To enunciate

mozhe: noun
eyelash

mozhek: adjective
ridiculous

mozhgân: noun
eyelash - lash

mozmen: adjective
chronic

moztareb: adjective
worried

moztareb kardan: verb
To upset - To distress

mozâ'af: noun
multiple - binary

mozâf: noun
addend

mozâhem: adjective
bothersome - tiresome - troublous - troublemaker

mozâhem: adjective
obtrusive

mozâhem shodan: verb
To annoy - To disturb

mozâhemat: noun
trouble - trade

mozâkere: noun
negotiation

mozâkere kardan: verb
To negotiate - To converse

mozâkere konande: adjective
negotiator

mozâyede: noun
outcry - auction - bid

mozâyeghe: noun
spare

moâf: noun
exempt

moâf kardan: verb
To exempt - To dispense - To dismiss

moâfiyat: noun
immunity - freedom - exemption

moâhede: noun
treaty - compact

moâlej: noun
therapeutic

moâleje: noun
treatment - therapy

moâmele: noun
deal

moâmele kardan: verb
To deal

moâned: adjective
dissident - dissenter - defiant - spiteful

moâsheghe: noun
courtship

moâsher: noun
socialite - sociable

moâsherat: noun
commerce - society

moâven: noun
assistant - adjunct - vicar

moâveze: noun
swap - exchange

moâveze kardan: verb
To change

moâyene: noun
examination

moâyene kardan: verb
To examine

mu: noun
hair

muchin: noun
tweezer

mudâr: noun
whisker

mughe' shenâs: adjective
tactful

muhebat: noun
gift - endowment

muhen: adjective
derogatory

mujed: noun
father - fathering

mujer: noun
renter - lessor - landlord

mujez: adjective
summary - succinct - laconic - concise

mum: noun
wax - beeswax

mumi shekl: adjective
wax

mumiyâyi kardan: verb
To embalmment

mur: noun
ant

mur mur: noun
horror

murche: noun
ant

muriyâne: noun
termite

murmur shodan: verb
To creep

mush: noun
mouse

mushak: noun
projectile - rocket - missile

mushekâfi: adjective
subtlety - splithair - scrutiny

mushekâfi kardan: verb
To analyze - To scrutinize

musighi: noun
music

musighidân: noun
musician

musighidân: noun
musician

musir: noun
scallion

muten: noun
home

muye damâgh: adjective
tagalong

muye sar: noun
head - hair

muyrag: noun
capillary

muzi: adjective
insidious - mischievous - baneful

muzik: noun
music

mâ: noun
we - kiss

mâbein: adverb
between - medial

mâbetafâvot: noun
margin

mâch: noun
smack

mâch kardan: verb
To kiss

mâdar: noun
mother

mâdari: adjective
motherhood - maternal

mâdarzâd: adjective
innate

mâdarzâdi: noun
congenital

mâdarâne: adverb
maternal

mâde: noun
material - substance - stuff - female

mâde: noun
matter - stuff - res - metal

mâdegi: noun
buttonhole - vulva - pistil - vigilance

mâdi: noun
material - physical

mâdiyân: noun
mare

mâdun: noun
subordinate - subject - sub - below

mâdâm: adjective
mademe - madem - while

mâdâmike: adverb
while

mâdâmol'omr: adjective
lifetime

mâfogh: adjective
superior - dominant - boss - supervisor

mâghabl: adjective
past - precedency

mâghabl: adverb
preceding

mâghable târikh: adverb
prehistory

mâh: noun
satellite - moon - month - acolyte

mâhe asal: noun
honeymoon

mâher: adjective
skillful - dextrous - proficient - adroit

mâherâne: adverb
workmanlike - subtle

mâhi: noun
lunar - fish

mâhiche: noun
brawn - muscle

mâhikhâr: noun
ichthyophagous - heron

mâhikhâr: noun
heron

mâhitâbe: noun
griddle - pan - saucepan

mâhiyat: noun
navigate - nature - essence

mâhiyâne: adverb
monthly

mâhtâb: noun
moonshine - moonbeam

mâhur: noun
knoll - dale - mound - barrow

mâhut: noun
broadcloth

mâhvâre: noun
sputnik - satellite

mâjarâ: noun
adventure - event

mâjarâju: adjective
venturer - adventurer

mâjarâjuyi: noun
adventure

mâkiyân: noun
hen - poultry

mâksimom: noun
maximum

mâl: noun
property - fortune - wealth

mâle: noun
trowel - malay

mâle che kasi: noun
whose

mâle ishân: noun
their

mâle man: noun
my - mine

mâle mâ: noun
ourselves - our

mâle shomâ: noun
yours - your

mâle to: noun
whose - its - her - his

mâle to: noun
thy - thine

mâle ânhâ: noun
their

mâlek: adjective
owner

mâlek budan: verb
To have

mâlekiyat: noun
ownership - possession

mâlesh: noun
scrub - friction - attrition

mâlesh dâdan: verb
To chafe

mâli: noun
financial - pecuniary

mâlidan: verb
To rub - To knead - To daub - To curry - To blob

mâlikhuliyâ: adjective
melancholy - melancholia - hypochondria

mâlikhuliyâyi: noun
hypochondriac

mâliye: noun
exchequer

mâliyât: noun
tax

mâlâriyâ: noun
malaria

mâm: noun
perfect - mother

mâmardi: noun
cowardice

mâmut: noun
mammoth

mâmâ: noun
obstetrician - midwife

mâmân: noun
mammy - mother

mânand: noun
similar - analogous

mânand budan: verb
To simulate - To similarity - To resemble

mânande ham: adjective
alike

mândan: verb
To stay - To remain

mândani: noun
permanent - viable

mânde: adjective
remainder - remain

mândegâr: adjective
indelible - immanent - indissoluble

mândegâri: noun
insolubility

mâne': noun
barricade - impediment - hurdle - hindrance
- obstacle - barrier

mâne': noun
curtain

mâne' shodan: verb
To prevent - To impede - To hinder

mânikor: noun
manicure

mânikor zadan: verb
To manicure

mânkan: noun
dummy - mannequin - manikin

mânovr: noun
manoeuvre

mânovr: noun
maneuver

mânovr dâdan: verb
To manoeuvre

mâr: noun
serpent - worm

mâr: noun
snake

mâre kobrâ: noun
cobra

mârgazidegi: noun
snakebite

mâri jo'vânâ: noun
grass - marijuana

mârk: noun
stripe - score - brand

mârmulak: noun
gecko - lizard

mârmulak: noun
lizard

mârmâhi: noun
lamprey

mârpich: adjective
spire - spiral - coil

mârpich: verb
To worm

mârpichi: noun
spiral - sinuous - whorl

mârshâl: noun
marshal

mâse: noun
gravel - sand

mâshe: noun
pincer

mâshin: noun
machine - car - automobile

mâshin tarâsh: noun
lathe

mâshine bokhâr: noun
steamer - engine

mâshine tahrir: noun
type

mâshine zarfshuyi: noun
dishwasher

mâshini: adjective
mechanic

mâsidan: verb
To jell - To congeal - To harden

mâsk: noun
mask - guise

mâsk zadan: verb
To mask

mâsure: noun
spool - reel - bobbin - hasp - hank

mâsâzh: noun
massage

mâsâzh dâdan: verb
To massage

mât: adjective
dumbstruck - quizzical - opaque - aghast

mât kardan: verb
To amaze - To checkmate

mâtam: noun
dole

mâtam gereftan: verb
To wail - To mourn

mâvarâye: noun
past - ultra

mâvarâye tabi'i: noun
supernatural

mâyahtâj: noun
needful

mâye: noun
nestegg - resource

mâye: noun
stock

mâye': noun
liquid - water

mâye' zadan: verb
To liquor

mâye'e ebrat: adjective
gazingstock

mâye'e ta'asof: adjective
unfortunate

mâyel: adjective
desirous - oblique - wilful - fond

mâyle budan: verb
To like

mâyle shodan: verb
To decline

mâyonez: noun
mayonnaise

mâzi: noun
past

mâziye ba'id: noun
pastperfect

mâzâd: noun
surplus - rejcet

mô'eze: noun
sermon

môghuf: noun
sacred

môhum: noun
superstitious - superstition

môhumât: noun
superstition

môj: noun
cockle - wave

môj zadan: verb
To shimmer - To surge - To wave

môjdâr: adjective
undulant - lumpy

môjdâr: adjective
storied - rippler

môjdâr budan: verb
To undulate - To surge

môjeb: noun
cause - inducement

môji: adjective
sinuous - undulatory

môjshekan: noun
pile - bulwark - breakwater

môjud: noun
existent - available

môjudi: noun
in stock

môjudiyat: noun
existence

môjudât: noun
creatures

môkul: noun
conditional

môkul: noun
dependence

môkul kardan: verb
To relegate - To postpone

môlud: noun
son

môludi: noun
natal

môrusi: adjective
inborn - congenital

môsuf: noun
noun

môsum: noun
yclept - ycleped

môsum be: noun
nee

môz: noun
banana

môze': noun
locality - position

môzu': noun
topic - theme - subject - point - issue

môzu'i: noun
thematic

môzu'ât: noun
topics

môzun: adjective
symphonic - level

n

na: noun
none - no

na'l zadan: verb
To calk

na'lband: noun
blacksmith - shoelace

na'nâ': noun
spearmint - mint

na're: noun
slogan - yell

na're keshidan: verb
To yell

na'shkesh: noun
hearse

na'shodan: noun
corpse

na'shodan: noun
cadaver

nabard: noun
conflict - fray - combat - battle

nabard kardan: verb
To militate

nabi: noun
prophet

nabovat: noun
prophecy

nabsh: noun
edge

nabshe ghabr: verb
To exhume

nabz: noun
pulse

nabât: noun
candy

nadim: noun
courtier

nadâneste: noun
unknowing

nadâri: noun
poverty - penury

naf': noun
gain

naf'y: noun
disavow - nope

nafaghe: noun
alimony

nafahm: adjective
stupid - incapable - hick

nafar: noun
person

nafas: noun
breath

363

nafas keshidan: verb
To respire - To breathe

nafis: adjective
precious - valuable - exquisite

nafkh: noun
bloat - emphysema

nafs: noun
oneself - ego

nafsâni: noun
sensual - carnal

naft: noun
petroleum - oil

naghab: noun
tunnel - burrow - hole - mine

naghab zadan: verb
To undermine - To burrow - To bore

naghd kardan: verb
To cash

naghde adabi: noun
literary criticism

naghdi: noun
cash

naghl: noun
story - transfer

naghl kardan: verb
To transcribe - To tell

naghlo enteghâl: noun
transfusion - locomotion

naghme: noun
song

naghme sarâ: adjective
songster - singer - vocalist

naghs: noun
deficiency - defect - incompetence

naghse ozv: noun
maim

naghsh: noun
role - pattern - figure - stamp

naghsh bastan: verb
To stamp

naghshe: noun
map - scheme - chart - plan

naghshe keshidan: verb
To map - To plot - To plan

naghshebardâr: noun
surveyor

naghshebardâri: noun
topography

naghshekesh: noun
tracer - draftsman - plotter

naghz: noun
reversal

naghâd: noun
critic

naghâl: noun
scop - storyteller

naghâli kardan: verb
To narrate

naghâsh: noun
painter - drawer

naghâshi: noun
portrait - picture

naghâshi kardan: verb
To picture - To paint

nagozâshtan: verb
To keep - To record

nahang: noun
whale

nahayat: noun
extremity - outrance

nahayi: adjective
terminal - ultimatum - ultimate - conclusive

nahif: adjective
skimp - scrimp - scant - meager

nahif shodan: verb
To peak

nahoftan: verb
To hide - To conceal - To closet

nahr: noun
slough - stream - dike - creek

nahs: adjective
infelicitous - inauspicious

nahy: noun
prohibition - prohibit - interdict - injunction

nahy kardan: verb
To interdict - To proscribe

nahâd: noun
character - institution - inclination

nahâdan: verb
To set - To invest

nahâdin: noun
characteristic

nahâl: noun
plant - slip - scion - sapling

nahâl zadan: verb
To plant

nahân: noun
stealth - secret - covert

nahân kardan: verb
To conceal

nahâni: adjective
surreptitious - secret - undercover

nahânkâri: noun
secrecy

najes: adjective
unclean

najes: adjective
polluted - untouchable - unclean

najib: adjective
decent - noble - gentle

najibzâde: adjective
magnate - patrician - nobleman

najm: noun
star

najvâ: noun
whisper

najvâ kardan: verb
To whisper

najâr: noun
carpenter

najâri: noun
woodcraft - carpentry

najâri kardan: verb
To carpenter

nakare: noun
theorem - indefinite

nakh: noun
thread - ribbon - string

nakhl: noun
date - palm

nakhle khormâ: noun
palm

nalbeki: noun
saucer

nam: noun
damp - moisture - humidity - humid

nam nevisi: noun
registration

nam zadan: verb
To sauce - To baste - To dabble - To dabber

namad: noun
wad - muffler

namak beharâm: adjective
ungrateful

namak zadan: verb
To corn

namakdân: noun
saltshaker - saltcellar - salt

namakin: adjective
briny - salty - saline

namakzâr: noun
salt

namdâr: noun
humid - moist

namname bârân: noun
drizzle

namnâk: adjective
dank - moist - humid

namâ: noun
surface - visage - diagram

namâyande: noun
indicator - agent - representative

namâyandegi: noun
representation

namâyandegi kardan: verb
To represent - To deputize - To depute

namâye: noun
index

namâyesh: noun
show - parade - presentation - exhibition - display

namâyesh dâdan: verb
To perform - To exhibit - To display

namâyeshgar: noun
display

namâyeshgâh: noun
exposition - exhibition - playhouse

namâyeshi: noun
expository - dramatic - scenic

namâyeshnâme: noun
drama - play

namâyân: noun
ostensible - visible

namâyân shodan: verb
To appear

namâyândan: verb
To represent

namâz: noun
prayer

namâz khândan: verb
To pray

nane: noun
mother

naneveshte: noun
unwritten

nang: noun
shame - scandal - reproach - dishonor - infamy

nangin: adjective
shameful - inglorious - infamous

nangâvar: adjective
ignominious - opprobrious

nar: noun
bull - masculine - husband

nard: noun
backgammon

narde: noun
rail - parapet - pale - balustrade

nardebân: noun
stairwell - stair - ladder

nareside: adjective
unripe

narges: noun
narcissus

narm: adjective
soft - smooth - lithe

narm: adjective
soft - smooth - fine

narm kardan: verb
To soften - To loosen

narm shodan: verb
To supple - To soften - To relent

narmi: adjective
amenity - plasticity - leniency - gloss

narmo molâyem: adjective
blithe

nasab: noun
parentage - genealogy - descent

nasanjide: adjective
unconsidered

nasb: noun
installation

nashib: noun
downhill - bent

nashr: noun
emission

nashr kardan: verb
To transpire - To infiltrate - To edit

nashriye: noun
journal

nasht: noun
leakage - leak

nasht: noun
session - meet

nasht kardan: verb
To permeate

nasht kardan: verb
To subside - To sink - To settle

nasib: noun
portion

nasihat: noun
advice

nasim: noun
breeze - breath - air - guff

nasiye: noun
credit

nasl: noun
slip - race - foster

nasr: noun
prose

nasuz: adjective
incombustible

nasâji: noun
loom

natije: noun
result - outcome

natijebakhsh: adjective
consequent

navad: adjective
ninety

navard: noun
roller - roll

navasân: noun
swing - undulation - lurch - pendulum - vibration

navasân dâshtan: verb
To undulate

nave: noun
grandson - granddaughter - grandchild

navid: noun
promise

navâ: noun
tone - tune

navâkhtan: verb
To sound - To execute

navâr: noun
tape - strip - ribbon - band

navâr zadan: verb
To tape

navâre chasb: noun
tape

navâzande: adjective
musician - player

navâzesh: noun
pat - caress

navâzesh kardan: verb
To cuddle - To coax

nazar: noun
thought - opinion - viewpoint

nazari: noun
visionary

nazariye: noun
theory

nazariye dâdan: verb
To counsel - To opine

nazd: noun
near - about

nazdik: adjective
proximate - near - close - besides - beside - adjacent

nazdik budan: verb
To abut

nazdik kardan: verb
To approximate

nazdiki: noun
proximity - contiguity - vicinity - approximation - adjacency

nazdiktarin: adjective
next

nazif: noun
clean

nazir: noun
comparable - analog - analogue - match

nazm: noun
rhyme - order - discipline

nazm dâdan: verb
To regularize

nazr: noun
bet - avow - vow

nazr kardan: verb
To avow

nazri: adjective
votive

ne'mat: noun
blessing - gift

nedâ: noun
calling

nedâmat: noun
repentance - remorse - compunction -
penitence

nefrat: noun
enmity - disgust - aversion - hatred - hate

nefrat dâshtan: verb
To despise

nefratangiz: adjective
horrid - odious - detestable

nefratâvar: adjective
dispiteous

nefrin: noun
gaff - curse - imprecation

nefrin kardan: verb
To cuss - To doggone

nefâgh: noun
dissension - discord - split

nefâgh andâkhtan: verb
To disunite

nefâgh dâshtan: verb
To dissent

negahbân: noun
lifeguard - escort - watchman

negahbâni: noun
sentry

negahbâni kardan: verb
To sentinel - To guard

negahdari: noun
maintenance - preservation - retinue

negahdari kardan: verb
To keep - To maintain - To protect

negahdâr: adjective
looker - keeper - tenter - protector

negahdâri: noun
maintenance

negahdâshtan: verb
To imprison - To hold - To restrain - To
sustain - To prop

negaresh: noun
theory

negaristan: verb
To regard - To look

negarân: adjective
apprehensive - gazing - solicitous - agog

negarân shodan: verb
To bother - To anguish

negarâni: noun
solicitude - anxiety - worry

negh zadan: verb
To nag

neghres: noun
gout

neghâb: noun
veil - mask

negâh: noun
look - glance

negâh dâshtan: verb
To retain - To refrain - To keep - To guard -
To hold

negâh kardan: verb
To see - To look

negâhdâr: adjective
preservative

negâre: noun
chart

negâresh: noun
record

negâshtan: verb
To write

nehzat: noun
crusade - movement

nei: noun
straw - sprit - junk

neil: noun
indigo

neirang: noun
trap - trickery - trick - artifice - deception

neishekar: noun
cane

neize: noun
dart - spear

nejâbat: noun
chastity - nobility - decency - honor

nejâsat: noun
excrement

nejât: noun
salvation

nejât dâdan: verb
To deliver - To reclaim

nejâte gharigh: noun
lifesaving

nekbat: noun
lousy - misery

nekhvat: noun
arrogance

nekuhesh: noun
reproof - remonstrance - criticism

nekuhesh kardan: verb
To reprove - To criticize

nekâh: noun
matrimony - wedlock

nemov: noun
development

nemov kardan: verb
To evolve

nemud: noun
aspect - appearance - phenomenon - growth

nemudan: verb
To show - To seem

nemudâr: noun
schema - diagram - conspectus - chart - graph

nemudâr shodan: verb
To outcrop - To rear

nemune: noun
sample - model - example

nemune budan: verb
To typify

nemâd: noun
symbolism - symbol

nemâdin: noun
symbolic

nepâli: adjective
Nepali

nerkh: noun
rate

nesbat: noun
proportion - scale - cognation - relationship - relation - ratio

nesbat dâdan: verb
To attribute - To attach - To ascribe - To impute

nesbatan: adverb
somedeal - enough - rather - partly

nesbi: adjective
comparative - respective - relative

nesbiyat: noun
relativity - ratio

nesf: noun
half

nesfe: noun
half

neshastan: verb
To sit

neshimangâh: noun
seat

neshân: noun
medal - mark - brand - signal - sign

neshân dâdan: verb
To show - To illustrate - To introduce - To indicate

neshân kardan: verb
To sight - To earmark

neshândahande: adjective
demonstrator - poniter

neshândan: verb
To imprint - To enchase - To embed

neshândan: verb
To inlay

neshâne: noun
sign - symptom - mark

neshâne gereftan: verb
To aim

neshâne raftan: verb
To train

neshâne vizhe: noun
trait - characteristic

neshângozari: noun
punctuation - impression

neshângozâr: noun
marker

neshângozârdan: verb
To check - To impress

neshâni: noun
address

neshâste: noun
starch

neshât: noun
vivacity - hilarity - alacrity

neveshtan: verb
To character - To write - To pen - To inscribe

neveshte: adjective
scrip - manuscript

nevisande: noun
author - writer

ney: noun
pipe

ney zadan: verb
To pipe

neyrang: noun
ruse - scheme

neyze zadan: verb
To lance - To pike

nezhâd: noun
race

nezhâdi: noun
ethnic - racial

nezhâdparast: adjective
racist - ethnocentric

nezhâdparasti: noun
ethnography - racism - racialism

nezâ': noun
dispute - warfare - quarrel - battle

nezâ' kardan: verb
To wrangle - To quarrel

nezâ' talabi: noun
militancy

nezâkat: noun
suavity - tact - propriety - comity - civility

nezâm: noun
system - military

nezâme ejtemâ'i: noun
society

nezâmi: noun
trooper - soldier - military

373

nezâmnâme: noun
bylaw - precept - manual

nezâmnâme: noun
workbook - code - manual

nezâmvazife: noun
service

nezârat: noun
supervision

nezârat: noun
helm - suppervision

nezârat kardan: verb
To supervise

nezâre kardan: verb
To behold

nik: adjective
good

nikel: noun
nickel

niki: adjective
beneficence

nikotin: noun
nicotine

niku: noun
good

nikukâr: adjective
upright - beneficent - benefactor - righteous

nikukâri: noun
charity - beneficence

nili: adjective
indigo - blue

nim: noun
half

nime: noun
mid

nimeshab: noun
midnight

nimetamâm: adjective
inchoate

nimkat: noun
sofa - seat - bench - couch

nimkat: noun
pew

nimpaz kardan: verb
To coddle - To underdo

nimrokh: noun
silhouette - sideview

nimruz: noun
noon - midday

nimruz: noun
meridian - noon

nimsâl: noun
term - semester

niru: noun
force - energy - vigor - power - strength

niru bakhshidan: verb
To nerve

niru dâdan: verb
To enliven - To invigorate

nirubakhsh: adjective
tonic

nirugâh: noun
powerhouse

nirumand: adjective
strong - prolific - vigorous - valiant - mighty

nirumandi: noun
strong - vigor - intensity

nish: noun
sting - tang - twinge - bite

nish zâdan: verb
To sting - To bite

nishdâr: adjective
poignant - sarcastic - punctual

nishdâr: adjective
snide

nishgun: noun
pinch

nishgun: noun
tweak

nishgun gereftan: verb
To pinch

nishkhand: noun
sneer

nishkhand zadan: verb
To snicker

nishtar: noun
harpoon - probe

nishtar zadan: verb
To lance

nisti: noun
nothing - naught

nitrozhen: noun
nitrogen

nitrâte petâsiyom: noun
saltpeter

niyat: noun
purpose - sentiment - intent

niyâ: noun
progenitor - stock

niyâm: noun
scabbard - legume - pod - vagina

niyâyesh: noun
adoration - veneration - praise - invocation

niyâyesh kardan: verb
To praise

niyâz: noun
need - necessity - requirement

niyâz dâshtan: verb
To require - To need

niyâzmand: adjective
needy - needful

niyâzmand budan: verb
To in need

niyâzmandi: noun
dependency - need

niz: noun
also - both - likewise

nobugh: noun
genius - ingenuity

nodrat: noun
paucity

nodratan: adverb
seldom - scarce

nofus: noun
population

nofuz: noun
influence

nofuznâpazir: adjective
inscrutable

nofuzpazir: adjective
permeable - penetrable - sensitive

noghre: adjective
silver

noghrekâr: adjective
silversmith

noghsân: noun
want - depletion

noghâle: adjective
grit - misfit - bran

noghâre: noun
timpani

noh: noun
nine

nohomin: adjective
ninth

nojumi: noun
planetary

nok: noun
top - tip - summit - peak - vertex

nok: noun
chimney

nokdâr: adjective
pointy

nokhbe: adjective
elite - flower

nokhod: noun
chickpea - gram

nokhodfarangi: noun
pea

nokhost: adjective
first

nokhostin: adjective
first - primary - premier - incipient

nokhostin: adjective
first - initial

nokhostvazir: noun
prime minister

nokte: noun
poniter - point

noktebin: adjective
particular

noktesanj: adjective
punctilious

noktiz: adjective
taper - pungent - picked - acute

nomre: noun
score - number - mark

norvezh: noun
Norway

norvezh: noun
Norway

norvezhi: adjective
Norwegian

noshkhâr: noun
cud - champ - quid

noshkhâr kardan: verb
To quid - To champ - To ruminate

noskhe: noun
prescription - version

noskheye asli: noun
manuscript

nosrat: noun
victory

nosyân: noun
oblivion - amnesia - lapse

not: noun
theme

notfe: noun
point - plot - dot

notfe: noun
sperm - semen

notgh: noun
speech - oration

novin: adjective
modern - new

novâmbr: noun
november

nozul: noun
discount - descent - fall

nozul kardan: verb
To sink - To comedown - To descend

nur: noun
light - glory

nurafkan: verb
To beam - To irradiate

nurafkandan: noun
spotlight - searchlight

nurafshândan: verb
To shine

nurafshâni: adjective
refulgence

nuremahtâb: noun
moonlight

nurâni: adjective
luminous

nurâni kardan: verb
To transfigure

nush: noun
pledge

nushdâru: adjective
panacea

nushidan: noun
potable

nushidan: verb
To imbibe - To bib

nushin: adjective
sweet

nushâbe: noun
beverage - drink

nâ âgâh: adjective
unwary

nâ ârâmi: noun
disquiet - unrest

nâ âshenâyi: noun
unfamiliarity - unfamiliar

nâ âzmude: adjective
clumsy - untried

nâ âzmudegi: noun
inexperience

nâ'amn: adjective
insecure

nâ'amni: noun
insecurity

nâb: adjective
pure - unalloyed - limpid

nâbalad: adjective
unperfect

nâbarâbar: adjective
disparate - unequal

nâbeghe: adjective
genius - wizard

nâbehengâm: adjective
untimely - precocious - immature -
inopportune

nâbejâ: adjective
aberrant - malapropos

nâbekhrad: adjective
unreasonable - brassy

nâbekâr: adjective
wicked - nefarious

nâbesâmân: adjective
unorganized

nâbinâ: noun
sightless - blind

nâbud shodan: verb
To go

nâbudi: noun
ruin - naught

nâbâlegh: adjective
immature

nâchiz: noun
teeny - trivial - negligible - meager - little

nâchâr: noun
inevitable

nâdem: adjective
penitent - repent - remorseful

nâder: adjective
rare - scarce

nâdide gereftan: verb
To dissemble - To disregard

nâdorost: adjective
false - erroneous - dishonest

nâdân: adjective
silly - fool

nâdâni: noun
puerility - ignorance - ineptitude

nâf: noun
belly button - navel

nâfarmân: adjective
insubordinate - disobedient - naughty

nâfarmâni: noun
disobedience

nâfe': adjective
beneficial - lucrative

nâfez: adjective
dominant - predominant - pervasive

nâfi: noun
umbilical

nâgahân: adverb
sudden - abrupt - bolt

nâgahâni: adverb
abrupt - precipitate - snap - sudden

nâghel: noun
transporter - conveyer

nâghel: adjective
conveyor - transporter

nâghes: adjective
rudimentary - imperfect

nâgholâ: adjective
shrewd - rogue - astute

nâghus: noun
bell - gong - ring

nâghâbel: adjective
trivial - inconsiderable - incapable

nâgoftani: noun
unspeakable - inexpressible

nâgofte: adjective
untold - unsaid

nâgovâr: adjective
horrible - harsh - burdensome - unpleasant

nâgovârâ: adjective
unwholesome

nâgozir: adjective
needful - incumbent

nâgozir budan: verb
To inevitability

nâgozir sâkhtan: verb
To necessitate

nâgâh: adjective
unexpected

nâhamgen: adjective
heterogeneous

nâhamvâr: adjective
jagged - rugged - ragged - bumpy

nâhamvâr kardan: verb
To ruffle - To ruffe

nâhamâhang: adjective
disharmonic

nâhanjâr: adjective
timber - nefarious - maladroit

nâhiye: noun
zone - region - district - area

nâhâr: noun
lunch

nâhâr khordan: verb
To lunch - To dine

nâji: noun
savior

nâjur: adjective
dissonant - dissimilar - disparate -
inconsistent - inappropriate

nâjur budan: verb
To mismatch - To discord - To jar

nâkes: adjective
villain - ignoble

nâkhodâ: noun
shipmaster - captain

nâkhodâgâh: noun
unconscious - unaware

nâkhon: noun
talon - nail - claw - ungual

nâkhosh: adjective
sick - unhealthy - ill

nâkhoshi: noun
disease - metastasis - malady

nâkhoshnudi: noun
unpleasantness - dissatisfaction - discontent

nâkhoshâyand: adjective
unsightly - uncomplimentary

nâkhânde: adjective
uninvited - uncalledfor

nâkhânâ: adjective
illegible

nâkhâste: adjective
undesirable - uncalledfor

nâkâm: adjective
unhappy

nâkâr: adjective
inert

nâkârâyi: noun
deficiency

nâle: noun
groan - whimper - moan

nâlidan: verb
To complain - To groan - To whine - To
whimper

nâlân: adjective
weepy

nâlâyegh: adjective
incompetent - incapable

nâm: noun
name - renown

nâm bordan: verb
To mention

nâm nahâdan: verb
To entitle

nâma'ghul: adjective
absurd - unreasonable - irrational

nâma'lum: adjective
unknown

nâmahdud: adjective
infinite - indefinite - unlimited

nâmar'i: noun
sightless - inconspicuous

nâmar'i budan: verb
To invisibility

nâmarbut: adjective
irrelevant

nâmard: adjective
coward - effeminate - caitiff

nâmarghub: adjective
inferior - raunchy

nâmashru': adjective
illicit - illegal - unlawful

nâmatbu': adjective
rancid - nasty - unpleasant

nâmatlub: adjective
unfavorable - undesirable - uncalledfor

nâmdâr: adjective
famous

nâme: noun
letter

nâme khânevâdegi: noun
surname

nâmeresân: noun
post - mail

nâmi: adjective
famous

nâmidan: verb
To entitle - To nominate - To name

nâmju: adjective
ambitious

nâmo neshân: noun
address

nâmobârak: adjective
inauspicious - unblest

nâmohayâ: adjective
unready

nâmolâyem: adjective
harsh

nâmonazam: adjective
erratic - acrostic

nâmonâseb: adjective
unsuitable - inappropriate - improper

nâmoshakhas: noun
indeterminate - unlimited

nâmosâed: adjective
unfavorable - bad - unfair

nâmosâed: adjective
uncomfortable

nâmosâvi: noun
disparate - unequal

nâmotejânes: adjective
incongruous

nâmotevâzen: adjective
skew - unbalanced

nâmovafagh: adjective
unsuccessful

nâmus: noun
honor

nâmzad: noun
nominee - candidate

nâmzad: adjective
candidate - troth - nominated

nâmzad kardan: verb
To engage - To nominate

nâmzadi: noun
engagement - candidacy

nâmôzun: adjective
unequal

nân: noun
bread

nânvâ: noun
baker

nâomid: adjective
gray - chill

nâpadid: adjective
invisible

nâpadid shodan: verb
To disappear - To vanish

nâpasand: adjective
absurd - incommensurate

nâpesari: noun
stepson

nâpokhte: adjective
crude - half-baked

nâpâidâr: adjective
transient - ramshackle

nâpâk: adjective
impure - dirty - squawk

nâpâki: adjective
impurity - pollution

nârangi: noun
tangerine

nâranjak: noun
bomb - canister

nâravâ: adjective
illegitimate

nârenj: noun
orange

nârenji: adjective
orange

nâres: adjective
premature - raw

nâresâ: adjective
inaudible - unfledged - unexpressive

nâresâyi: noun
incompetence - inadequacy - insufficiency

nârgil: noun
coconut

nâro zadan: verb
To foul

nârâhat: adjective
upset - uncomfortable

nârâhat kardan: verb
To annoy - To discomfort - To discomfit

nârâhati: noun
turmoil - irritation - inconvenience - ailment

nârâhati: noun
discomfort

nârâzi: adjective
tedious - peevish - malcontent

nârâzi: adjective
dissenter

nârô: adjective
treachery

nâseh: adjective
mentor

nâsezâ: noun
swearword - profanity

nâsezâ: noun
blasphemy

nâsezâ goftan: verb
To swear - To curse - To revile

nâshenavâ: adjective
indistinct

nâshenide: noun
unheard

nâshenâkhte: adjective
unknown

nâshenâs: adjective
strange - unknown

nâsher: noun
publisher

nâshi: adjective
muff - maladroit

nâshi: noun
dilettante

nâshi az: noun
due

nâshigari: noun
bunlge

nâshâyest: adjective
unrighteous

nâshâyeste: adjective
objcetionable

nâsâlem: adjective
unhealthy - insanitary

nâsâzegâr budan: verb
To conflict - To discord - To disagree

nâsâzegâri: adjective
discordant - irreconcilable - alien - adverse

nâsâzegâri: noun
discord - conflict - aversion - antipathy

nâtamâm: adjective
incomplete - imperfect - partial - unfinished

nâtavân: adjective
incapable - unable

nâtavân sâkhtan: verb
To incapacitate

nâtavâni: adjective
inability - infirmity

nâtegh: adjective
spokesman - speaker - orator

nâv: noun
ship

nâvdân: noun
spout - sike - tube - cullis

nâve jangi: noun
warship

nâvgân: noun
armada - fleet - navy

nâvshekan: noun
destroyer

nâyeb: noun
vice

nâyel shodan: verb
To gain - To attain

nâylon: noun
nylon

nâyâb: noun
unsuitable - unfit

nâyâb: adjective
rare

nâz: adjective
demur

nâzanin: adjective
nice

nâzer: adjective
overseer - supervisor - steward - spectator

nâzok: adjective
slim - frail

nâzok kardan: verb
To attenuate - To extenuate - To thin

nâzâ: adjective
sterile - barren

nâzâyi: noun
sterility

nô: adjective
scion - mint - novel - new

nô kardan: verb
To renovate - To renew

nô âvari kardan: verb
To innovate

nô': noun
type - sort - class - kind - gender

nô'i: noun
generic

nô'âmuz: adjective
novice

nô'âvar: adjective
innovator

nôbat: noun
turn - round - shift - period

nôbati: noun
tyupical - shift - periodic - intermittent

nôbe: noun
malaria

nôhe: noun
dirge

nôhe sarâyi: noun
jeremiad - dirge

nôjavân: noun
juvenile - juvenescent - adolescent

nôjavâni: noun
adolescence

nôkar: noun
server - servant

nôkari: noun
handyman

nôkise: adjective
upstart

nômidi: noun
despair

nôsâzi: noun
renovation - rehabilitation - reconstruction

nôsâzi kardan: verb
To reconstruct

nôzohur: adjective
mewfangled

nôzâd: noun
newborn - baby - babe

Ô

ô'ô: noun
bark

ô'ô kardan: verb
To yowl - To yip - To yap - To snap - To bay

ôbâsh: noun
gangster - hoodlum - hood

ôd: noun
reversion - relapse - regression - recurrence

ôdat: noun
relapse

ôghât talkh: adjective
stuffy - indignant - angry - glum

ôghât talkhi: noun
tantrum

ôj: noun
culmination - crescendo - climax - summit -
zenith - top

ôj gereftan: verb
To soar

ôlaviyat: noun
preference - precedence

ôlâd: noun
slip - breed - seeds

ôlâd: adjective
prior

ôrang: noun
throne

ôrâgh kardan: verb
To scrap

ôrâghchi: noun
wrecker

ôrâghe gharze: noun
bond

ôt: noun
August

O

obohat: adjective
grandeur

obur: noun
transmittal - transmission - transit - passage
- pass

obur kardan: verb
To traverse - To transit - To pass

oburo morur: noun
traffic

odul kardan: verb
To swerve - To backtrack

ofogh: noun
horizon

ofoghi: adjective
lateral - horizontal - straight

oftâdegi: noun
humility

oftân: verb
To tumble - To drop - To fall

oful: noun
sunset - wane - cadence

oful kardan: verb
To ebb

ofunat: noun
putrefaction

ofuni: noun
zymotic - infectious

ofuni kardan: verb
To infect

oghde: noun
knot

oghde: noun
complex - knot

oghde'i: adjective
obsessive

oghdeye ruhi: noun
obsession

oghyânus: noun
ocean

oghâb: noun
eagle

ohde: noun
responsibility

ohdedâr shodan: verb
To undertake - To emprise

ojrat: noun
wage - hire - pay

ojube: adjective
wonder - prodigy - monster

ojâgh: noun
oven

oksizhen: noun

oxygen

olgu: noun
sewer - sewage

olgu: noun
mould - pattern - sample - type - standard

olufe: noun
provender - feed

olum: noun
science

olume ensâni: noun
humanism

olâgh: noun
donkey

omat: noun
nation

omde: adjective
significant - major - main - principal - prime
- primary - dominant

omdeforush: noun
wholesaler

omdeforushi: noun
wholesale

omgh: noun
depth

omghi: adjective
deepseated

omi: adjective
maternal

omid: noun
expectancy - hope - trust

omidvâr: adjective
sanguinary - tantalize - anticipant - hopeful

omidvâr budan: verb
To hope

omr: noun
age - lifetime - life

omum: noun
public

omumi: noun
common - generic - general - public

omumi: noun
public - general

omumiyat: noun
generality

onf: noun
force

ons: noun
ounce

ons gereftan: verb
To accustom

onsor: noun
element

onvân: noun
title - headline

operâ: noun
opera

ordak: noun
duck

ordu: noun
camp

ordu zadan: verb
To encamp - To camp

ordugâh: noun
cantonment - camp

orf: noun
tradition - custom

orib: adjective
slant - sidle - oblique - diagonal

orib: noun
ryb

orkester: noun
band

orshalim: noun
jerusalem

oruj: noun
ascent

orupâ: noun
Europe

orupâyee: adjective
European

oryân: adjective
unaadorned - bare - bald - naked - nude

oryân: verb
To unclothe - To undress

orze: noun
arena - field

orzhâns: noun
emergence - emergency

orâniyom: noun
uranium

osghof: noun
bishop

oslub: noun
method

ostokhân: noun
bone

ostokhânbandi: noun
skeleton - anatomy - framework

ostokhândâr: adjective
bony

ostokhâni: adjective
bony

ostokhâni shodan: verb
To ossify

ostovâne: noun
roller - cylinder

ostovâne'I: adjective
cylindrical

ostovâr: noun
tenacious - sure - steady - stable - firm

ostovâr kardan: verb
To fix - To firm - To pitch - To stabilize

ostovâr shodan: verb
To stable

osture: noun
myth

ostâd: noun
professor - master - adept

ostâdâne: adverb
scholastic - deft - workmanlike - professorial

ostâni: noun
provincial

osul: noun
tenet - doctrine

osul: noun
principles

osule akhlâghi: noun
ethic

osuli: adjective
material - doctrinaire

osuli: adjective
underlying

osyân: noun
sin

osâre: adjective
extract - distillate - juice

osâre gereftan: verb
To extract

otobus: noun
bus

otobân: noun
superhighway

otomobil: noun
car - automobile

ototomobil: noun
automobile

otu: noun
iron

otu keshidan: verb
To launder

otâgh: noun
chamber - room

otâghak: noun
module

otâghak: noun
box - booth - cubicle

otâghe jarâhi: noun
surgery

otâghe khâb: noun
chamber

otâghe khâb: noun
bedroom

otâghe motâle'e: noun
study

otâghe neshiman: noun
sittingroom

otâghe nâhârkhori: noun
dining roum - spence

otâghe âsânsor: noun
car

out: noun
iron

out kardan: verb
To iron

out zadan: verb
To press - To iron

ozbak: adjective
Uzbek

ozrkhâhi: noun
apology

ozrkhâhi kardan: verb
To apologize

ozv: noun
organ - member

ozviyat: noun
membership

p

pachin sâkhtan: verb
To hedge

padide: noun
phenomenon

padidâr: adjective
visible - conspicuous

padidâr: noun
extant

padidâr shodan: verb
To emerge

padidâri: noun
visibility

padâfand: noun
defence - defense

padâfandi: noun
defensive

pahlavi: noun
at - by

pahlavân: noun
athlete - champion

pahlavâni: adjective
athletic

pahlu: noun
side

pahlu be pahlu: noun
collateral - abreast

pahlu gereftan: verb
To berth

pahlu zadan: verb
To emulate

pahluyi: noun
lateral - immediate

pahn: adjective
wide - flat - plain - broad

pahn kardan: verb
To broaden - To expand - To widen

pahne: noun
poll - palm - arena

pahnâ: noun
width - expanse - breadth

pahnâvar: adjective
immense - vast - broad - extensive

pakar: adjective
pensive

pakhsh: noun
prevalence - effluence - diffusion

pakhsh kardan: verb
To scatter - To spread - To distribute - To
dispread

pakhsh shodan: verb
To pervade

palang: noun
tiger

palang: noun
panther

palid: adjective
frowzy - foul

panbe: noun
cotton

panbe zani: noun
card

panbedâne: noun
cottonseed

panchar: noun
puncture

panchar shodan: verb
To blowout

panchar shodan: verb
To puncture

pand: noun
motto - advice

pand: noun
aphorism

pand dâdan: verb
To advise - To admonish

pand dâdan: verb
To counsel

panguan: noun
penguin

panir: noun
cheese

panj gholu: noun
quintuplet

panj gushe: noun
pentangle - pentagon

panje: noun
pitchfork - paw - claw - fork

panjere: noun
window - peeper

panjgâne: adjective
five - quintuple

panjomin: noun
quintuplicate

panjul zadan: verb
To scrape

panjzel'I: noun
pentagon

panjâh: noun
fifty

panâh: noun
safeguard - guard - bulwark

panâh bordan: verb
To harbor - To refuge

panâh bordan be: verb
To quarter

panâh dâdan: verb
To shelter - To fence - To refuge - To house

393

panâhandegi: noun
refuge

panâhandeye siyâsi: noun
political refugee

panâhgâh: noun
shelter - hovel - harbor

panâhgâh: noun
haven

par: noun
feather

par par zadan: verb
To flicker

parande: noun
bird

parandegân: noun
birds

parastesh: noun
adore - adoration - praise - devotion -
worship

parastesh kardan: verb
To worship

parastidan: verb
To idolize - To deify

parastu: noun
swallow

parastâr: noun
sister - foster - nurse

parastâre bache: noun
nanny

parastâri kardan: verb
To tend - To nurse - To minister

parch kardan: verb
To clinch - To clench - To rivet

parcham: noun
flag - banner

parcham: noun
flag - banner - stamen

parchamdâr: adjective
ensign

parchin: noun
fence - hedge

parde: noun
curtain - blind - veil - membrane - screen

parde zadan: verb
To upholster - To veil

pardebardâri: noun
unveil

pardedâr: noun
chamberlain

pardeye bekârat: noun
hymen

pardeye darbe vorudi: noun
portiere

pardeye sinamâ: noun
screen

pardâkht: noun
payoff - payment

pardâkht kardan: verb
To pay

pardâkhtan: verb
To disburse - To pay

pardâkhtan: verb
To pay

pardâkhtani: noun
solvency - due - payable

paresh: noun
jump - leap

paresh kardan: verb
To skip

pargâr: noun
compass

parhiz: noun
abstinence - diet

parhiz kardan: verb
To abstain

parhizgâr: adjective
pious

parhizgâri: noun
continence - piety

parhizkâr: adjective
righteous

pari: noun
glut - full - elf

parishân: adjective
disheveled - disconsolate - faraway -
heartsick

parishân kardan: verb
To stress - To nonplus - To distract - To
agitate

parishâni: noun
bother - remorse - woe - depression

pariyâ: noun
pteropod

parkhâsh: noun
invective - quarrel - ruffe

parkhâsh kardan: verb
To bicker

parkhâshgar: adjective
aggressor - aggressive

parkhâshgari: noun
agression

parobâl: noun
plumage

parse zadan: verb
To ramble - To roam - To swan - To scamp -
To prowl

part: noun
aback - faraway

part kardan: verb
To throw - To hurl

part shodan: verb
To overshoot - To cropper

partgPortugueseh: noun
crag - headland - precipice - bluff

parto: noun
shaft - beam - aegis - rayon - ray - radiance

parto afkan: noun
projector

parto afkandan: verb
To beam - To radiate

parto darmâni: noun
radiotherapy

parto âfshân: adjective
radioactive

partâb: noun
toss - throw

partâb kardan: verb
To shoot - To jaculate

partâb shodan: verb
To slat - To shove

parvande: noun
dossier - file

parvardegâr: noun
god

parvaresh: noun
nurture

parvaresh dâdan: verb
To inbreed - To develop - To foster

parvaridan: verb
To breed - To encourage - To feed

parvâ: noun
heed - solicitude - prudence

parvâne: noun
butterfly

parvâz: noun
wing - fly - flight - plane

parvâz: noun
fly - blastoff

parvâz kardan: verb
To kite - To fly - To flight

parvâze boland: noun
kite

parâkandan: verb
To transmit - To scatter - To cast

parâkande: adjective
diffuse - outspread - sporadic - sparse

parâkande kardan: verb
To intersperse - To meddle - To disperse - To dash

parâkandegi: noun
sprawl - dispersal

parâkonesh: noun
transmittal

parântez: noun
parenthesis - bracket

pas: adverb
thus - so

pas andâkhtan: verb
To sire

pas az: adverb
after - since

pas dâdan: verb
To giveback - To retort - To repay - To
refund

pas dâdan be: verb
To repay

pas gereftan: verb
To retrieve - To retreat - To recapture - To
withdraw

pas raftan: verb
To retrogress - To retrograde - To retire - To
recede

pas zadan: verb
To rebut - To rebound - To backlash

pasand: noun
choice - approbation

pasand kardan: verb
To approve - To admire

pasandidan: verb
To choose - To allow - To accept

pasandide: adjective
honorable - admirable - acceptable -
desirable

pasandâz kardan: verb
To save

pase gardan: noun
scruff - nape

pashe: noun
gnat

pashimân: adjective
contrite - regretful - penitent

pashimân shodan: verb
To repent - To relent

pashimâni: noun
remorse - regret

pashm: noun
wool

pashmâlu: adjective
shaggy - ulotrichous

pasin: adjective
subsequent - astern - hindmost - hinder -
last

pasmânde: noun
leftover - remainder

pasraft: noun
recession

pasravi: noun
retrogradation - regress

past: noun
ungenerous - humble - villain - peevish -
wretched

past budan: verb
To grovel

past fetrat: adjective
rascal

past kardan: verb
To abase - To humiliate - To mortify - To demean - To degrade

past shodan: verb
To bastardize - To grovel

past tar: adjective
beneath - lower

pasti: adjective
villainy - misery - postal

pasto haghir: adjective
knave

pastu: noun
closet

pasvand: noun
suffix

patu: noun
blanket

paymardi kardan: verb
To assist

payâm: noun
message

payâmbar: noun
prophet

payâpây: noun
cambium

pazhmordan: verb
To blight

pazhmorde: adjective
sear

pazhmordegi: noun
languor - welter

pazhmorede shodan: verb
To droop - To miff - To languish - To quail

pazhuhesh: noun
research

pazhuhesh kardan: verb
To research

pazhuheshgar: noun
researcher

pazhuheshname: noun
bulletin

pazhuhidan: verb
To research

pazirande: adjective
receptive

paziresh: noun
reception - admission - acceptance

paziroftan: verb
To admit - To accept - To embrace

paziroftani: adjective
admissible - acceptable - plausible

pazirâ: adjective
receptive - acceptable

pazirâyi: noun
reception

pazirâyi kardan: verb
To lodge - To entertain - To welcome

pech pech kardan: verb
To chatter - To whisper

pedar: noun
father

pedar ya mâdar: noun
parent

pedarbozorg: noun
grandpa - grandfather

pedari: adjective
patronymic - paternal

pedari kardan: verb
To sire

pedarsâlâr: noun
patriarch

pedarâne: adverb
paternal

pedâl: noun
pedal

pei: noun
foundation

pei bordan: verb
To discover

pei dar pei: adjective
continuum - continual - consecutive

peidâ: adjective
visible - apparent - transparent

peidâyesh: noun
birth - appearance - genesis - emersion

peidâyeshi: noun
genetic

peigard: noun
pursuit - prosecution

peighambar: noun
prophet

peighambari: adjective
prophecy

peighâm: noun
message - dispatch - word

peighâm dâdan: verb
To message

peighâm âvar: adjective
messenger

peighâmbar: adjective
mercury

peighâmresâni: noun
errand

peigiri: noun
pursuit

peik: noun
messenger

peikar: noun
statue - figure - effigy

peikare: noun
statue

peikân: noun
dart - arrow - barb

peikâr: noun
battle - combat

peimudan: verb
To pace

peimân: noun
contract

peimân bastan: verb
To stipulate - To promise - To pact

peimân nâme: noun
treaty - convention

peimâne: noun
measure - gauge

peimâyesh: noun
survey

peiravi: noun
imitation - follow

peiravi kardan: verb
To conform - To imitate

peirovân: noun
suit - clientele

peivand: noun
link - connection

peivand kardan: verb
To splice

peivand zadan: verb
To join - To connect

peivast: noun
appendix - annex - enclosure

peivastan: verb
To join - To attach - To annex - To connect

peivaste: adjective
continual - contiguous - allied

peivastegi: noun
juncture - unity - cohesion - continuity

pele: noun
step - stair

pele barghi: noun
escalator

pelekân: noun
step - stairway - ramp - pitch

peleye nardebân: noun
rung

pelk: noun
eyelid

pelâk: noun
plate

pelâstik: noun
plastic

pendâr: noun
supposition - image

pendâshtan: verb
To suppose - To assume - To imagine

penhân: adjective
surreptitious - cryptic - abstruse - latent

penhân kardan: verb
To secrete - To conceal - To dissemble - To cover - To mask

penhân sâzi: noun
irony

penhâni: adjective
privacy - potential

penhânshodan: verb
To burrow - To abscond - To hide

penhânsâzi: noun
wrap

penisilin: noun
penicillin

peres: noun
pressure

peres kardan: verb
To smash

persenel: noun
personnel - staff

pesar: noun
son - boy

pesarbache: noun
youngster - boy

pesare barâdar: noun
nephew

pesare dokhtar: noun
grandson

pesare khâhar: noun
nephew

pesare pesar: noun
grandson

pesare shohar: noun
stepson

pesare zan: noun
stepson

peshkel: noun
dung

peste: noun
pistachio

pestân: noun
breast

pestânak: noun
pacifier - teat

pestânband: noun
bra

pestândâr: noun
mammal

petansiel: noun
potential

petroshimi: noun
petrochemical

pey âmad: noun
consequence - result - outcome

peydâ kardan: verb
To find - To detect - To discover

peykarbandi: noun
configuration

peyrov: noun
pursuant

pezeshk: noun
medico - medic - physician

pezeshki: adjective
medicine - medic

pezeshki: noun
medical

pezhmân: adjective
dejecte - depressed

pezhvâk: noun
echo - reflection

pich: noun
screw - twist - meander

pich dâdan: verb
To hurtle - To flex - To wrench - To screw -
To tweak - To strain

pich khordan: verb
To loop - To wrench - To sprain

pich khorde: adjective
twisted

pichak: noun
arvense

pichdâr: adjective
swept

pichdâr kardan: verb
To twist

pichesh: adjective
deflexion - curvature - wrest - torsion

pichidan: verb
To twist - To twinge - To tweak - To enwrap
- To roll

pichide: adjective
intricate - complecated

pichide: adjective
complex

pichide kardan: verb
To entangle - To complicate

pichidegi: noun
compiexity - elaboration

pichkhordegi: adjective
screw - twist - turquoise - rick

picho tâb: noun
twist

pichokham: noun
maze

pichokham dâshtan: verb
To meander

pichândan: verb
To screw - To twitch - To curl - To crinkle

pichândan: verb
To tweak

pichânde: adjective
wound

pichânidan: verb
To trill

pif: preposition
ugh

piknik: noun
picnic

pil: noun
bishop - cell

pile: noun
cocoon

pine: noun
bunny - callus

pineduz: adjective
cobbler

pip: noun
pipe

pir: adjective
old

pir shodan: verb
To aging

piremard: noun
senile - oldster

pirezan: noun
witch

pirezan: noun
grimalkin

piri: noun
senility - aging

piruz: noun
triumphant - victorious - victor - palmary -
conqueror

piruz shodan: verb
To triumph - To outfight - To win

piruzi: noun
win - conquest - victory - success - triumph

piruzmandâne: adverb
triumph

pirâhan: noun
shirt

pirâhan pushidan: verb
To shirt

pirâmun: noun
around - circumference - outline

pirâmuni: noun
peripheral

pirâstan: verb
To decorate

pirâste: adjective
trim

pirâyeshgar: noun
trimmer

pish: adverb
beforehand - before - along - ahead

pish az: adverb
before

pish az in: adverb
hitherto - heretofore - already

pish barande: adjective
promoter

pish bordan: verb
To expedite - To further - To advance

pish darâmad: noun
prologue - overture - prelude

pish ghazâ: noun
appetizer

pish âmadan: verb
To beetle

pishbini: noun
prospect - precaution - foresight - expectancy

pishdâvari: noun
prejudice

pishdâvari kardan: verb
To prejudge

pishe: noun
trade - profession - vocation - job

pishe va shoghl: noun
job

pishepâ oftâde: adjective
ordinary - commonplace - common - banal

pishevar: noun
tradesman

pishevari: noun
trade

pishghadam: adjective
protagonist - pioneer

pishghadam shodan: verb
To pioneer

pishghadami: noun
initiative

pishgharâvol: noun
vanguard

pishgiri: noun
prevention

pishgiri kardan: verb
To prevent

pishgiri konande: adjective
prophylactic

pishgoftâr: noun
preface - prologue

pishguyi: noun
prophecy - oracle - omen - augury - prediction

pishgâm: adjective
trailblazer - van - pioneer

pishi: noun
puss - kitty - antecedent

pishi gereftan: verb
To outshine

pishi jostan: verb
To outstrip

pishin: adjective
antecedent - prior - primitive - previous - former

pishine: noun
record - history - past

pishkesh: noun
gift - present

pishkesh kardan: verb
To grant

pishkeshi: noun
present - gift

pishkesvat: noun
protagonist

pishkhedmat: noun
servant - bellboy

pishkhân: noun
counter

pishnahâd: noun
offer - bid - purpose - proposal

pishnahâd dâdan: verb
To suggest - To recommend

pishnahâd kardan: verb
To suggest - To purpose - To propose - To offer

pishnahâde ezdevâj kardan: verb
To propose

pishnevis: noun
draft - minute

pishniyâz: noun
prerequisite

pishparde: noun
curtainraiser

pishpardâkht: noun
prepayment

pishraft: noun
development - progression - progress - improvement - advance

pishraft kardan: verb
To prosper - To progress - To improve - To develop

pishraftan: verb
To proceed

pishrafte: adjective
advanced

pishraftegi: noun
jut - protrusion

pishravi: noun
advance - progress

pishro: adjective
forward

pishtar: adverb
before - heretofore

pishtâz: adjective
vanguard

pishvand: noun
prifix

pishvâ: adjective
leader - headman - primate

pishâhang: noun
scout

pishâmad: noun
accidence - event

pishâmad: noun
event - occurrence - accident

pishâmadegi: noun
prominence

pishâni: noun
frontal

pishâniband: noun
headband

pishâpish: noun
beforehand

piston: verb
To piston

piye: noun
suet

piyâde: adverb
pedestrian - afoot

piyâde kardan: verb
To dismount - To disembark

piyâde shodan: verb
To land - To alight

piyâderavi: noun
walk - hike

piyâdero: noun
sidewalk - peripatetic - pavement

piyâdeye shatranj: noun
pawn

piyâle: noun
cup - bowl

piyâno: noun
piano

piyâz: noun
onion

piyâz: noun
onion

piyâzche: noun
scallion

piyâze gol: noun
bulb

pizhâme: noun
nightgown - pajama

pof: noun
puff - snuff - whiff

pof kardan: verb
To puffy - To puff

pof karde: adjective
bouffant - bloat

pofak: noun
blowgun - puff

pok zadan: verb
To puff

pokht: noun
decoction

pokhtan: verb
To bake - To grill - To cook - To concoct

pokhte: adjective
ripe

pol: noun
bridge

pol bastan: verb
To span

pol sakhtan: verb
To bridge

pole havâyi: noun
skyway - overpass

pole moteharek: noun
drawbridge

polis: noun
police - cop

poliver: noun
sweater

pomâd: noun
ointment - pomade

por: noun
full - loaded

por efâde: adjective
cocksure - bigheaded - snooty - snobbish

por eltehâb: adjective
arduous

por hayejân: adjective
ebullient

por hayâhu: adjective
obstreperous - loudmouthed

por jamiyat: adjective
populous

por kardan: verb
To full - To load - To suffuse

por picho kham: noun
roundabout

por posht kardan: verb
To thicken

por posht shodan: verb
To luxuriate

por rang: adjective
chromatic

por ru: adjective
impudent - barefaced - cheeky

por saro sedâ: adjective
uproarious - loudmouthed - noisy

por zargho bargh: adjective
splendid - gaudy - gaily

por âbotâb: adjective
rotund - grandiose - ornate

por âshub: adjective
stormy - pellmell

porbahâ: adjective
valuable - invaluable

porbâr: adjective
weighty

porchâne: adjective
pernickety - talkative

porchânegi kardan: verb
To jaw

pordardesar: adjective
troublous - bothersome

porforugh: adjective
luminary

porguyi kardan: verb
To prattle

porharf: adjective
talkative - voluble - loquacious - chatty

porharfi: verb
To gash - To palaver

porharfi: noun
badinage - loquacity - yack

porharârat: adjective
steamy - spunky

porhâdese: adjective
eventful

porkharj: adjective
sumptuous - expensive

porkhatar: adjective
hazardous - dngerous

porkhor: adjective
greedy - gobbler - voracious

porkhori: noun
avidity - gut - gorge - glut

porkhori kardan: verb
To gorge

porkâr: adjective
prolific - overwrought - hardworking

pormoda'â: adjective
pretentious

porneshât: adjective
primrose

pornur: adjective
shiny

porofesor: noun
professor

porposht: adjective
steady - thick - lush - exuberant - rich

porsalâbat: adjective
rocky

porsedâ: adjective
sonorous - uproarious - loud - vociferous

porsesh: noun
inquiry - question - query

porsesh kardan: verb
To debrief

porseshgar: adjective
questioner

porseshnâme: noun
questionnaire

porshokufe: adjective
buddy

porsidan: verb
To ask - To question - To query

portalâtom: adjective
wavy

porteghâl: noun
orange - Portugal

porteghâli: adjective
Portuguese

portâghat: adjective
hardy - wiry - staminal

porz: noun
fuzz - nap

posht: noun
rear - backside - backbone

posht: noun
back

posht dard: noun
lumbago - backache

poshtak: noun
somersault - turntable

poshte: noun
hill - heap

poshte gardan: noun
nape - cervix

poshte pa: noun
instep

poshte panjare: noun
shutter

poshte sar: noun
behind - back

poshte sar gozâshtan: verb
To behind

poshte sare ham: adverb
blowbyblow - reel - consecutive

poshtekâr: noun
assiduity - perseverance

poshtekâr: adjective
diligence

poshtgarmi: noun
assurance

poshti: noun
pad - backrest - pillow

poshti: noun
dorsal

poshtibân: adjective
protector - supporter

poshtibâni: noun
patronage

poshtvâne: noun
bankroll

postchi: noun
post

poste sefâreshi: noun
registered mail

postkhâne: noun
post office

potk: noun
sledge - hammer - mallet

potk zadan: verb
To sledge

poz: noun
posture

pridan: verb
To jump - To hip - To vault

progrâm: noun
program

prozhe: noun
project

prozhektor: noun
projector

puch: adjective
empty - nude - inane - hollow - vacuous

puch kardan: verb
To void

puchi: noun
absurdity - vapidity - vanity

pud: noun
stamen

pudr: noun
powder

pudr kardan: verb
To pulverize

pudr shodan: verb
To flour

pudr sâkhtan: verb
To pestle

puk: adjective
hollow

pul: noun
money

pul: noun
money

pul dâdan: verb
To pay

pul tu jibi: noun
spendingmoney

pulak: noun
tinsel - shale - sequin

pulakdâr: adjective
scaly - scaled

pulaki: adjective
mercenary

puldâr: adjective
plutocrat

pule khord: noun
change - coin

pule naghd: noun
cash

puli: noun
monetary

pulâd: noun
steel

pulâdi: adjective
steely

pulâdin: adjective
steely - steel

pune: noun
beebalm

punez: noun
thumbtack - tack

pure: noun
tendon

push: noun
sheathe - sheath

pushe: noun
jacket - membrane - wrapper

pushesh: noun
shroud - shield - coating - cover

pushidan: verb
To don - To overlay - To wear - To hide

pushide: adjective
impenetrable - recondite - covert - secret

pushide az chaman: adjective
grassy

pushide az chub: adjective
woody

pushide az yakh: adjective
icy

pushide shodan: verb
To beetle

pushidegi: noun
secrecy - privacy

pushâk: noun
garment - clothing

pushâl: noun
chaff

pushândan: verb
To mask - To envelop - To cover - To camouflage

pushândan: verb
To shingle

pushânidan: verb
To gear - To wrap

pusidan: verb
To putrefy - To decay - To corrode

puside: adjective
musty - frowzy - ruttish - rotten

puside: verb
To spoil

pusidegi: noun
decay - putrefaction

pust: noun
peel - skin

pust kandan: verb
To peel - To hull - To hide - To skin

pust kande: adjective
picked - aboveboard

pust ârâyi: noun
taxidermy

pustdâr: adjective
husky

puste: noun
shuck - cod - chaff - case - cortex - membrane

puste mânand: adjective
crusty

pustedar: adjective
rinded

pusti: noun
cutaneous - pelting - skinny

pustin: noun
sheepskin - fur

pustkan: noun
skinner

puyidan: verb
To seek

puyâ: adjective
dynamic

puyân: adjective
snoopy - prowler

puyâyi: noun
mobility - dynamism

puze: noun
snout - rostrum - nozzle - muzzle - beak

puzeband zadan: verb
To muzzle

puzesh: noun
pardon - apology

puzesh khâstan: verb
To apologize

puzkhand: noun
snicker - sneer - smirk - grin

puzkhand zadan: verb
To titter - To snicker - To sneer

pâ: noun
leg - pod - peg - paw - foot

pâ barjâ: adjective
stable - true - resolute - firm - indefeasible - immutable

pâ barjâ kardan: verb
To fix

pâ berehne: adjective
discalced - barefoot

pâ gozâshtan: verb
To inculcate - To tread

pâband: adjective
trammel - jess - shackle - clog - clog - anklet
- hobble

pâche: noun
foot - leg

pâcheye shalvâr: noun
leg

pâdari: noun
mat

pâdegân: noun
garrison - presidio

pâdeshâh: noun
shah - king - rial - rex - potentate - monarch

pâdeshâhi: adjective
imperial - regal - kingdom - sovereignty

pâdo: noun
page

pâdtan: noun
antibody

pâdzahr: noun
antidote

pâdzahr: noun
antidote

pâdâsh: noun
testimonial - back - hay - remuneration -
gratuity

pâdâsh dâdan: verb
To compensate

pâfeshâri: noun
persistence - insistence

pâfeshâri kardan: verb
To insist - To persist

pâgir: noun
obstacle

pâk: adjective
sheer - stark - pure - clean - kosher - good

pâk kardan: verb
To ventilate - To erase - To efface - To
obliterate

pâk karde: adjective
picked

pâk kon: noun
wiper

pâk nashodani: adjective
indelible

pâk shodan: verb
To refine

pâkat: noun
pocket

pâkdâman: adjective
virtuous - virgin - chaste

pâkdâmani: noun
purity - chastity - probity

pâki: noun
innocence - purity

pâkize: adjective
tidy - clean - neat - brisk

pâksâzi: adjective
purgative

pâkzâd: adjective
highborn

pâlto: noun
overcoat - topcoat

pâludan: verb
To strain - To purify - To refine

pâludegi: noun
refinement

pâlân: noun
panel

pâlân zadan: verb
To saddle

pâlâyesh: noun
purge

pâlâyeshgâh: noun
refinery

pânsemân kardan: verb
To dressing up

pânsiyon: noun
pension - boarding

pânzdah: noun
fifteen

pâp: noun
papa - pontiff

pâpirus: noun
papyrus

pâpâ: adjective
durable

pâpâ: noun
papa

pârch: noun
pitcher

pârche: noun
stuff - textile - fabric

pârche bâfi: noun
drapery

pârche nakhi: noun
cotton

pâre: noun
fragment - bit - scrap - shred

pâre kardan: verb
To cut - To rip - To rend - To lacerate - To
mangle - To shred - To tear

pâre pâre: adjective
scrappy

pâre pâre kardan: verb
To tatter - To scalpel

pâre âjor: noun
brickbat - glut - rubble

414

pâregi: noun
tear - rupture

pâresang: noun
countermeasure - counterbalance

pârk: noun
park

pârlemân: noun
parliament

pârlemâni: adjective
parliamentary

pârsi: adjective
Parsi

pârsâ: adjective
pious - votary - devotee

pârsâl: noun
yesteryear

pârsâyi: noun
piety - pietism

pârti: noun
party

pâru: noun
shovel - oar

pâru zadan: verb
To paddle - To row

pâruzan: adjective
oarsman - paddler

pârâf: noun
initials

pârâf kardan: verb
To initial

pârâfin: noun
paraffin

pârâgerâf: noun
paragraph

pârâmetr: noun
parameter

pârâzit: noun
noise - mush - parasite

pâs: noun
pass

pâs dâdan: verb
To pass

pâsdâr: adjective
watchman - watchful - guardsman - guard

pâsdâri: noun
patrol - watch

pâsdâri kardan: verb
To watch - To patrol

pâsdârkhâne: noun
guardhouse

pâsebân: noun
guard - policeman - police

pâsebâni kardan: verb
To patrol

pâsgâh: noun
post

pâshidan: verb
To strew - To sprinkle - To spray - To pour - To infusion

pâshne: noun
heel - pivot - talon

pâshneye jurâb: noun
heel

pâsiyo: noun
patio

pâsokh: noun
response - respond - reply - answer

pâsokh dâdan: verb
To answer - To respond - To reply

pâsâzh: noun
passage

pât (dar shatrang): noun
stalemate

pâtakhte: noun
treadle

pâtil: noun
caldron

pâtogh: noun
nest - resort - rendezvous - recourse - haunt - station

pâtolozhi: noun
pathology

pây kubidan: verb
To hoof

pâydâr: adjective

constant - permanent - inexhaustible - indissoluble

pâydâr mândan: verb
To stability

pâydâri: noun
stability - endurance - constancy - resistance - permanency

pâydâri kardan: verb
To resist

pâye: noun
root - pillar - phase - leg - buttress - basis - base

pâye dâr: adjective
pedunculated

pâye zadan: verb
To truss

pâygâh: noun
base - database

pâyidan: verb
To guard - To watch

pâyin: noun
underneath - low - bottom - beneath - below

pâyin raftan: verb
To comedown

pâyin rotbe: adjective
inferior - minor

pâyin âmadan: verb
To descend - To dip - To fall

pâyin âvardan: verb
To shut - To bate - To disrate

pâyini: noun
beneath - underneath

pâyintar: adjective
subordinate - beneath - lower

pâyintarin: adjective
bottommost - undermost

pâyiz: noun
autumn - fall

pâyizi: adjective
autumnal

pâykubi: noun
stomp

pâykubi kardan: verb
To stomp

pâymardi: noun
fortitude - intercession

pâymâl kardan: verb
To suppress - To inculcate - To overwhelm

pâytakht: noun
capital

pâyân: noun
end

pâyân nâme: noun
thesis - dissertation

pâyân nâpazir: adjective
unceasing - interminable - inexhaustible

pâyân yâftan: verb
To over

pâyâne: noun
terminus - terminal

pâyâyi: noun
perpetuity

pâzadan: noun
pedal - leg - foot

r

ra'd: noun
thunder

ra's: noun
top - peak - vertex - climax

ra'she: noun
paralysis - tremor - tremble

ra'y: noun
sentence - judgment - poll - verdict - vote - opinion

ra'y dahande: adjective
voter

ra'y dâdan: verb
To sentence - To election - To resolve - To vote

ra'yat: noun
cotter - citizen - vassal - peasant

ra'âyat: noun
regard - ovservation - observance

ra'âyat kardan: verb
To observe

rabi'i: noun
vernal

rabolnô': noun
godhead

rabt: noun
correlation - relevance

rabt: noun
pertinence

rabti: noun
copulative

rad: noun
rejection - refusal - denial - veto

rad gom kardan: verb
To backtrack

rad kardan: verb
To deny - To decline - To confute - To disprove

rad shodan: verb
To blowover - To pass - To percolate

rade: noun
class - category

radebandi: verb
To categorize - To subsume

radepâ: noun
vestige - track - trace

radepâ: noun
tract

radif: noun
string - tier - run - row - rank - cue

radif shodan: verb
To tier

radyâb: noun
tracer

radâ: noun
toga - mantle - cloak - robe

radâ': noun
obstacle

raf': noun
obviation - removal

raf' kardan: verb
To obviate - To resolve - To abate

raf' nemidan: verb
To abate

rafi': adjective
skyscraper - sublime - lofty

rafigh: noun
mate - friend

rafigh budan: verb
To chum

rafigh shodan: verb
To pal

raftan: verb
To go

raftani: adjective
goner

rafto âmad: noun
traffic

raftâr: noun
behavior - manner - demeanour

raftâr: noun
behavior

raftâr kardan: verb
To demean - To act - To behave - To handle - To treat

rag: noun
streak - vessel

ragbâr: noun
cloudburst - volley - spate - shower

rage: noun
grain - vein - thread - streak - strain

ragh: noun
vellum

ragham: noun
number - digit

raghami: noun
digital

raghib: noun
antagonist - adversary - rival

raghib shodan: verb
To vie

raghigh: adjective
thin - ethereal - watery - rare - attenuate

raghigh kardan: verb
To attenuate - To dilute - To extenuate

raghigh shodan: verb
To fine

raghs: noun
dance - ball

raghse tângo: noun
tango

raghsidan: verb
To dance

raghâs: noun
jigger - dancer

raghâse: noun
ballerina

rahbar: noun
leader - pilot

rahbari: noun
leadership

rahbari kardan: verb
To lead - To pilot

rahim: adjective
clement - humane - merciful

rahm: noun
compassion - mercy - pity

rahmat: noun
mercy

rahmân: adjective
clement

rahn dâdan: verb
To pawn

rahn kardan: verb
To bond

rahnavard: noun
roadster - wayfarer

rahnemud: noun
guidance

rahnemun: noun
adviser - guideline

rahro: adjective
wayfarer

rahsepâr: verb
To leave - To proceed

rahâ: adjective
free

rahâ shodan: verb
To release

rahâ sâkhtan: verb
To indulge - To redd

rahâkardan: verb
To drop - To disentangle - To release - To extricate - To leave

rahânidan: verb
To rescue

rahânidan: verb
To rescue

rahâvard: noun
gift - present - souvenir

rahâyi: noun
escape - rescue - release

rahâyi bakhshidan: verb
To save

rahâyi dâdan: verb
To rescue - To redeem

rahâyi jostan: verb
To escape

rahâyibakhsh: adjective
redeemer

raj: noun
row

rajaz: noun
warcry - epopee - paean

rajazkhâni: noun
warcry

rajazkhâni kardan: verb
To declaim

rajim: noun
cursed

rajole siyâsi: noun
diplomat - statesman

rajâz khândan: verb
To brag - To boast

rakht: noun
clothes - garment - apparel

rakhtekhâb: noun
bed

rakhtkan: noun
cloakroom - vestry

rakhtshuyi: noun
wash

rakhtân: noun
commode

rakik: adjective
vulgar

ram: noun
scare - stampede - breakaway - rum

ram dâdan: verb
To fright - To rouse - To hare - To startle

ramagh: noun
spirit

rame: noun
herd - drove - flock

ramidan: verb
To wince - To stampede

ramz: noun
mystery - secret - symbol

ramzi: adjective
mysterious

ramâl: noun
novel - romance

rande: noun
shaver

rande kardan: verb
To plane - To bevel - To grate - To chip - To shave

rang: noun
paint

rang zadan: verb
To tincture - To dabber - To complexion

range banafsh: noun
mauve

range kamrang: noun
undertone

range roghani: noun
oilcolor - oil

range sabz: noun
green

range siyah: noun
sable - smut

range surati: noun
pink

range zard: noun
caramel

rangi: adjective
colored - chromatic

rangin: adjective
colored

rangparide: adjective
pallid - pale - lurid

rangârang: adjective
colorful

ranj: noun
agony - pain

ranj bordan: verb
To suffer - To travail - To toil - To rack

ranjbar: noun
toiler - durdge - painstaking

ranjesh: noun
irritation - vexation - bother - annoyance

ranjidan: verb
To huff - To miff

ranjidan az: verb
To resent

ranjide: adjective
sulky - angry - indignant - glum

ranjur: adjective
wretched - painful - infirm

ranjuri: noun
undernutrition

ranjândan: verb
To offend - To annoy - To irritate - To mortify

ranjânidan: verb
To pinprick - To displease

ranjâvar: adjective
painful - troublesome

rasad kardan: verb
To ovservation

rashid: adjective
high - adolescent

rashk: noun
jealousy

rasm: noun
tradition - custom - mode

rasmi: adjective
formal - official

rastan: verb
To escape - To grow

rastani: adjective
herb - plant - vegetable

rasul: noun
apostle - messenger

ravand: noun
process - procedure

ravesh: noun
style - vein - method - manner

raviye: noun
cover - upper - procedure - vamp

ravâ: noun
admissible - permissive - lawful

ravâ kardan: verb
To permit

ravâbet: noun
term

ravâdid: noun
visa

ravâdâshtan: verb
To approve

ravâj: noun
propagation - currency - vogue - prevalence

ravâj dâdan: verb
To issue

ravâj dâshtan: verb
To having spoken

ravân: adjective
smooth - voluble - versatile - fluent

ravân shodan: verb
To trill - To gush - To flow

ravân sâkhtan: noun
pour

ravâne kardan: verb
To send - To launch - To dispatch

ravâne shodan: verb
To depart

ravâne sâkhtan: verb
To fling - To send - To launch - To dispatch

ravâni: adjective
psychic

ravânkâvi: noun
psychoanalysis

ravânpezeshk: noun
psychiatrist

ravânpezeshki: noun
psychiatry

ravânshenâs: noun
psychologist

ravânshenâsi: noun
psychology

ravâyat: noun
story - narrative

razl: adjective
scoundrel

razm: noun
war - combat - battle

razmgâh: noun
battlefield

razmi: noun
epic

razmju: adjective
warrior - warlike

razmâra: noun
strategist - tactician - tactic

re'is: noun
boss - ruler

re'ise jomhur: noun
president

refrândom: noun
referendum

refâghat: noun
amity - camaraderie

refâh: noun
welfare - quiet

reghat: noun
sympathy

reghat angiz: adjective
pitiful - piteous - pathetic - deplorable

reghat âvar: adjective
lamentable

reghatbâr: adjective
pitiable - piteous

reghbat: noun
relish - propensity - zest

reghâbat: noun
contest - rivalry

reghâbat kardan: verb
To compete

rehlat kardan: verb
To pike

reihân: noun
basil

rej'at: noun
throwback - return

rejhân: noun
privilege - preference - predominance

rejhân dâdan: verb
To prefer

rekhne: noun
crack - gap - leak

rekhne kardan: verb
To transpire - To penetrate

rekhvat: noun
lethargy - lassitude - indolence - paralysis

rekord: noun
record

rekâb: noun
stirrup - step

rekâbzadan: verb
To pedal

rend: adjective
rogue - knave

rendâne: adverb
roguish

reshim gereftan: verb
To diet

reshte: noun
branch - thread - sequence - string

reshte: noun
string - field - thread

reshteye asabi: noun
nerve

reshve: noun
bribery - bribe

reshve dâdan: verb
To bribe

reshvekhâr: adjective
venal - barrator

reshvekhâri: noun
bribery

reshâdat: noun
gallantry - courage

resid: noun
receipt

residan: verb
To arrive - To achieve - To gain

residan be: verb
To reach - To overtake

reside: adjective
consummate - grown - ripe

residegi: noun
scrutiny - audit - probe - consideration

residegi kardan: verb
To audit - To inspect - To inquire

resturân: noun
restaurant

resâ: adjective
stentorian - audible - adequate

resâlat: noun
prophecy

resâlat kardan: verb
To message

resâle: noun
dissertation - handbook - booklet

resâm: noun
tracer

resândan: verb
To give - To extend - To convey

resâne: noun
vehicle - medium

resânâ: adjective
conductor - conductive

revâl: noun
zeitgeist - rubric

rezhe: noun
parade - pageant - array - review

rezhe raftan: verb
To troop - To defile - To parade

rezhim: noun
regime

rezâlat: noun
blackguardism

rezâyat: noun
satisfaction

rezâyat dâdan: verb
To consent - To assent - To acquiesce - To
accede

rezâyatbakhsh: adjective
satisfactory

rezâyatmandi: noun
satisfaction

rezâyatnâme: noun
testimonial

reâktor: noun
reactor

ridan: verb
To Shit

rig: noun
grit - gravel - pebble - sand

rikhtan: verb
To shed - To strew - To dust - To disgorge -
To pour

rikhtegari: noun
casting

rikhto pâsh: noun
splurge

risande: adjective
spinner

rish: noun
beard

rish sefid: adjective
dean

rishe: noun
theme - tassel - stub - stem - germ -
pedigree

rishe: noun
root

rishe'i: adjective
thematic - comate - rooty

rishedâr: adjective
stubby - rooty

rishedâr kardan: verb
To root

rishi: adjective
ulceration

rishkhand: noun
scoff - sarcasm - jeer - ridicule

rishkhand: noun
cajolery

risidan: verb
To spin

risk: noun
venture - risk

rismân: noun
string - thread - line - cord - warp - chord - rope

rivâs: noun
rhubarb

riyavi: noun
pulmonary

riye: noun
lung

riyâ: noun
duplicity - hyporisy

riyâkâr: adjective
insincere - hypocritical

riyâkâri: noun
sham - hyporisy

riyâsat: noun
presidency

riyâsat kardan: verb
To superintend - To chairman

riyâzat: noun
penance - austerity - abstinence

riyâzat: noun
austerity

riyâzidân: noun
mathematician

riyâziyât: noun
mathematics

riz: adjective
tiny - small - shred

riz riz kardan: verb
To mince - To comminute - To chop

rizandâm: adjective
midget

rizekâri: noun
elegance - intricacy

rizesh: noun
spray - slide - downfall - diffusion

rizesh: noun
inset

rizriz shodan: verb
To crash

ro'use matâleb: noun
outline

ro'âyâ: noun
peasantry

rob: noun
sauce

rob': noun
quarter - redundancy

robudan: verb
To grab - To rob - To steal

robâ: noun
gavel

robâ'i: noun
quatrain

robâkhâr: adjective
usurious - usurer

robâkhâri: noun
usury

robât: noun
sinew - ligature - ligament

robâyande: adjective
snatcher

robâyesh: noun
snatch - seizure - rapture - grab

roftegar: noun
sweeper - dustman

rofu: noun
darn

rofu kardan: verb
To mend - To darn

roju': noun
reversion - respect - referral - reference

roju' kardan: verb
To revert

roju'i: noun
reversional

rok: adjective
frank - straightforward - straight

rok: adjective
rack - frank

rokgu: adjective
frank

rokguyi: noun
candour - candor

rokh: noun
face - cleavage

rokh: noun
rook

rokh dâdan: verb
To befall - To arise - To pass - To outcrop - To occur

rokhdâd: noun
occurrence

rokhsat: noun
respite - reprieve - leave - permission

rokhsat dâdan: verb
To allow

rokhsâr: noun
visage - face

rokn: noun
column - pillar

rokud: noun
slump - stagnancy - inactivity - inaction

rol: noun
role

rolet: noun
jellyroll - roulette

român nevis: noun
novelist

româtism: noun
rheumatiz

ronesâns: noun
renaissance

ros: noun
clay

roshd: noun
growth

roshd: noun
growth - development

roshd kardan: verb
To grow - To mature

rosub: noun
sediment - tartar

rosub kardan: verb
To sediment

rosukh: noun
transfusion - sink - seepage - seep

rosukh kardan: verb
To pierce - To perforate - To soak

rosum: noun
mores - manner

rosvâ: adjective
blatant - ignominious - infamous

rosvâyi: noun
notoriety

rosvâyi: noun
scandal - disrepute - dishonor - disgrace

rotbe: noun
degree - rank - grade

roteyl: noun
tarantula

rotubat: noun
moisture - humidity - wet - damp

ru: noun
top - face - uppermost - visage

ruandâz: noun
coverlet

ruband: noun
mask

ruberu: noun
adverse - opposite

ruberu shodan: verb
To cross - To envisage - To encounter

rubâh: noun
reynard - fox

rud: noun
stream - kil

rud: noun
river - stream

rude: noun
bowel - gut - garbage

rude derâzi: noun
yak

rudel: noun
indigestion

rudkhâne: noun
river - strand

rudâdan: verb
To spoil

ruftan: verb
To sweep

ruh: noun
sprite - ghost

ruhe palid: noun
devil

ruheham rafte: adverb
altogether - overall

ruhi: adjective
psychic - spiritual - intrinsic - inner - mental

ruhiye: noun
morale - moral - mentality - spirit - tuck

rukafshi: noun
galosh - overshoe

rukesh: noun
crowns

rukesh kardan: verb
To face - To coat - To plate

rukesh zadan: verb
To recap

rukeshe mota'kâ: noun
slipover

rumizi: noun
tablecloth

runevesht: noun
counterpart - copy - transcript

runevesht bardâshtan: verb
To transcribe

runevis kardan: verb
To transcribe

runevisi kardan: verb
To copy

rupush: noun
gown - topcoat - cortex

rus: noun
Russia

rusari: noun
scarf - headgear - kerchief

rusari: noun
scarf

rusefid kardan: verb
To exonerate - To acquit

rusi: adjective
russian

rustâ: noun
village

rustâyi: adjective
rustic - rural - boor

rutakhti: noun
counterpane

ruy dâdan: verb
To befall - To happen

ruydâd: noun
event

ruye: noun
upon - over - on

ruye pâ istâdan: verb
To standup

ruyeham: adverb
sum

ruyeham: noun
overhand - wholly

ruyidan: verb
To vegetate - To grow

ruyintan: adjective
invulnerable

ruyâruyi: noun
encounter

ruyôndan: verb
To grow

ruz: noun
daytime - day

ruze: noun
fast

ruze ba'd: noun
tomorrow

ruze gereftan: verb
To fast

ruze ghiyâmat: noun
doomsday

ruze pish: noun
yesterday

ruze ta'til: noun
holiday

ruzegâr: noun
time - world - period

ruzi: noun
someday

ruzmare: adjective
routine

ruznâme: noun
journal - paper - newspaper - gazette

ruznâme forushi: noun
newsstand

ruznâme negâr: adjective
journalist

ruznâme negâri: noun
journalism

ruzâne: adverb
daily

râbet: noun
liaison - gobetween - copulative

râbete: noun
relation - linkage - liaison

râbete: noun
relevance

râbete dâshtan: verb
To correspond

râbeteye nâmashru': noun
liaison

râd: adjective
upright - magnaimous - honest

râdio aktiv: noun
radioisotope - radioactive

râdio'i: noun
radio

râdiolozhi: noun
radiology

râdioterâpi: noun
radiotherapy

râdiyo: noun
radio

râdiyâtor: noun
radiator

râdmardi: noun
magnanimity

râdâr: noun
radar

râfe': adjective
ablative

râh: noun
path - highway - manner - entry - road - way

râh dâdan: verb
To admit

râh raftan: verb
To walk

râh yâftan: verb
To accede

râh'âhan: noun
railway - railroad - road

râhat: adjective
convenient - comfortable - comfort

râhat: adjective
snug - homey

râhat talabi: noun
indolence

râhband: noun
hedge

râhbandân: noun
blockade

râhbord: noun
guideline

râhdâri: noun
toll

râhe hal: noun
solution - out

râhe obur: noun
transit

râheb: noun
monk

râheb: noun
monk - cowl

râhebe: noun
nun - cloistress

râhi shodan: verb
To go - To depart

râhnamâ: noun
leader - conductor - guideline - guidance

râhnamâyi: noun
lead - help - guidance

râhnamâyi kardan: verb
To guide - To lead - To instruct

râhpeimâyi: noun
march

râhpeimâyi kardan: verb
To march

râhpele: noun
staircase

râhpeymâ: adjective
marcher - marching

râhzan: noun
brigand - bandit - robber

râhzani: noun
banditry

râje' be: noun
about - regarding

râked: adjective
stagnant - dull - resting

râked shodan: verb
To statgnate

râket: noun
rocket - racket

râkete tenis: noun
racket

râm: adjective
tame - meek - inward - obedient - domestic

râm kardan: verb
To daunt - To gentle - To bridle - To master - To subdue

rân: noun
leg

rân: noun
thigh - leg

rânande: adjective
helmsman - driver - repellent

rânandegi kardan: verb
To drive - To chauffeur

rând: noun
osmosis

rândan: verb
To steer - To pilot - To drive

rânde: adjective
outcast - castaway

rândegi: noun
expultion

rânesh: noun
buoyancy

râsekh: adjective
firm

râst: noun
straightforward - right

râst kardan: verb
To unbend - To erect - To straighten

râste: noun
row - phylum

râstgu: adjective
true - sooth - veracious

râstguyi: noun
veracity

râsti: noun
truth - veracity - probity

râstin: adjective
real - true

râstnamâ: adjective
sincere

râsu: noun
weasel

râvi: adjective
storyteller - narrator

râyegân: adjective
free - gratuitous - gratis

râyehe: noun
smell - scent - aroma

râyej: noun
current - brisk - prevalent

râyej shodan: verb
To pass

râygâni: noun
gratuity

râyzan: adjective
adviser - counselor - consultant

râyzani: noun
counsel - advice

râyzani kardan: verb
To advise - To consult

râz: noun
secret - mystery - covert

râzdâr: adjective
secretary - confident

râzdâri: noun
secrecy

râzi: adjective
content - happy - acquiescent

râzi kardan: verb
To satisfy - To sate - To content - To bate

râzi shodan: verb
To supple - To acquiesce - To consent

râzi sâkhtan: verb
To reconcile

rô'yat: noun
seeing

rôghan: noun
ointment - oil - butter

rôghandân: noun
saucepan

rôghani: adjective
unctuous - greasy - oily

rôhâni: adjective
priest - clergyman - sacred

rôhâniyun: noun
clergy

rônagh yâftan: verb
To thrive - To prosper

rôshan: adjective
serene - sunny - perspicuous - lucid - bright

rôshan kardan: verb
To brighten - To lighten - To ignite - To clarify - To explain

rôshan shodan: verb
To shine - To kindle - To open

rôshan sâkhtan: verb
To picture

rôshanbin: adjective
clairvoyant

rôshanfekr: adjective
illuminate

rôshanfekr: adjective
highbrow - liberal - intellectual

rôshanfekr: adjective
intellectual

rôshangar: adjective
explanatory

rôshani: adjective
shine - lucidity - glim - clarity

rôshanibakhsh: adjective
luminous

rôshanizâ: adjective
photogenic

rôshanâyi: noun
light - ray

rôyâ: noun
vision

rôyâyi: adjective
dreamy - visionary

rôzane: noun
hatch - peephole - loophole - outlet

S

sa'b: adjective
unwieldy - difficult

sa'bol obur: noun
impassable

sa'id: adjective
jovial - blest - auspicious - happy

sa'y: noun
endeavor - effort

sa'y kardan: verb
To try - To hear

sa'âdat: noun
welfare - paradise

sa'âdatmand: adjective
happy - blissful

sabab: noun
reason - cause

sabad: noun
basket - kist

sabad: noun
basket

sabet: noun
immovable - immobile - firm - stable

sabk: noun
style - structure - mode

sabok: noun
soft - thin - levity - levigate - volatile

sabok: adjective
way

sabokdasti: noun
dexterity

saboki: noun
stylist - buoyancy

sabokmaghz: adjective
silly - idiot

sabr: noun
patience

sabr kardan: verb
To wait

sabt: noun
registration

sabt: noun
record

sabt kardan: verb
To register - To record

sabu: noun
crock - jar

sabur: adjective
patient

sabus: noun
slough - shuck

sabuse: noun
scruff

sabz: adjective
green

sabz kardan: verb
To green

sabze: noun
greenery - green - grass - vegetable

sabzi: noun
legume - vegetable - greenery

sabzijât: noun
green

sabât: noun
constancy - fortitude - permanency - stability

sabâte ghadam: noun
perseverance

sad: noun
hundred

sad: noun
barrier

sad: noun
dam - dike - dyke - barrier - block - stoppage

sad kardan: verb
To stop

sadaf: noun
shard - shale - pearl

sadaghe: noun
dole - charity - alms

sadame: noun
injury - hurt - harm

sadame didan: verb
To miscarry

sadame zadan: verb
To offend - To harm

sade: noun
century - centennial - centenary

saderâh: noun
blockade

sadre'azam: noun
chancellor

sadsâle: adjective
centennial - centenary

saf: noun
queue - array - rank - row

saf bastan: verb
To cue

safar: noun
voyage - journey - trip - tour

safarnâme: noun
itinerary

safhe: noun
leaf - page - sheet

safhe: noun
disk - page

safine: noun
ship

safir: noun
whistle - whish

safir: noun
ambassador

safrâ: noun
bile - gall - yellowbile

safsate: noun
idol - sophistry - sophistication - sophism

saftebâzi: adjective
speculator

safâ: noun
ingenuity - candour - candor - serenity -
purity

safârâyi: noun
embattle

sag: noun
dog

sagak: noun
tach - buckle

sage âbi: noun
beaver

saghez: noun
turpentine - galipot

saghf: noun
soffit - ceiling - roof - loft

saghf: noun
roof

saghir: verb
To underage - To lowly - To lesser

sahar: noun
charm - wizardry

saharkhiz: adjective
riser

sahih: adjective
valid - right - correct - true

sahim: noun
sharer - participant

sahiyebandi kardan: verb
To lot - To portion

sahl: adjective
eath - easy

sahlengar: adjective
nonchalant - inconsiderate - lax

sahlengâri: noun
indifference - nonchalance

sahm: noun
share - proportion - ration - ratio

sahm bordan: verb
To impart - To share

sahmgin: adjective
horrible - hideous

sahmiye: noun
scantling - quota - ration

sahmnâk: adjective
terrible - redoubtable - horrid

sahn: noun
apron

sahne: noun
scene - arena

sahnesâzi: noun
histrionics - scenery

sahneârâ: noun
scenarist

sahrâ: noun
desert - wilderness

sahrâyi: adjective
outdoor

sahv: adjective
inadvertent - wrong - goof

sahyonist: adjective
Zionist

sahâf: noun
bookmaker - bookbinder

sahâm: noun
portfolio - liquidate - stock

sahâmi: noun
jointstock

sakane: noun
population - populace - habitancy

sakhre: noun
cliff - rock - roach

sakht: adjective
difficult - hard

sakht kardan: verb
To intensify - To harden - To ossify

sakhtgir: adjective
strict - intransigent

sakhtgir: adjective
taskmaster - stringent

sakhtgiri: noun
severity - stricture

sakhtgiri: noun
rigor - stringency

sakhti: adjective
solidity - severity - hardship - violence

sakhti: noun
intensity

salb kardan: verb
To devest

salbe mâlekiyat: noun
dispossession

salib: noun
cross

salighe: noun
taste - tact

salis: adjective
fluent - voluble

salis budan: verb
To flow

salite: noun
jezebel - shrew

salmâni: noun
barber - haircut

salmâni kardan: verb
To barber

saltanat: noun
sultanate - reign - majesty

saltanati: adjective
royal - rial - regnal

salâhdid: noun
discretion - government

salâhdid: adjective
capable

salâhiyat: noun
ability - qualification - competence -
capacity - capability

salâm: noun
hello - salute - salutation

salâm kardan: verb
To hello - To hail

salâmat: noun
safety - health

salâmati: noun
peace

sam: noun
poison

sam'ak: noun
earphone

samand: noun
dun

samandar: noun
salamander

samar: noun
fruit

samar dâdan: verb
To yield

samfoni: noun
symphony

samgh: noun
resin - gum

sami: adjective
toxic - poisonous - venomous

samimi: adjective
sincere - warm - chummy

samimi: adjective
friendly

samimiyat: noun
sincerity - devotion - confidence - intimacy

samimâne: adverb
hearty - earnest

samimâne: adverb
inmost

sampâsh: noun
sprayer

440

sampâshi: noun
spray

sampâshi kardan: verb
To spray

samt: noun
side

samur: noun
sable - zibelline

san'at: noun
industry

san'atgar: noun
artist - artisan

san'ati: adjective
industrial

sanad: noun
document

sanadiyat: noun
authenticity

sanam: noun
idol - idol

sanbole: noun
cluster - virgin

sandal: noun
sandal

sandali: noun
chair - seat

sandaliye râhati: noun
lounge - armchair

sandaliye tâsho: noun
jumpseat

sandoghche: noun
ark - kist

sandoghdâr: noun
cashier - bursar - purser - treasurer

sandoghkhâne: noun
closet

sandugh: noun
box

sandughe post: noun
mailbox

sandân: noun
anvil

sang: noun
rock - stone

sangar: noun
trench - stronghold - parapet - citadel

sangdel: adjective
cruel

sangdel: adjective
callous

sangepâ: noun
pumice

sangfarsh: noun
pavement - cobblestone

sangfarsh kardan: verb
To flag - To hardsurface - To pave

sangi: adjective
stone

sangi: noun
stony

sangin: adjective
sober - weighty - heavy

sangin kardan: verb
To encumber - To gravitate - To load

sangini: noun
weight - gravity

sanglâkh: adjective
stony - rocky

sangrize: noun
slither - grit - gravel

sangsâr kardan: verb
To stone

sangtarâsh: noun
stonemason - stonecutter

sangvâre: noun
fossil

sanjesh: noun
evaluation - assessment

sanjidan: verb
To evaluate - To measure

sanjide: adjective
weighty

sanjâgh: noun
pin - ouch

sanjâghak: noun
dragonfly

sar: noun
apex - top - head

sar boridan: verb
To behead - To decollate

sar reshte: noun
scent - competence

sar resid: noun
maturity - usance

sar tekân dâdan: verb
To beck - To nod

sar zadan: verb
To rise - To amount

sar'râst: adjective
straightforward - upstanding

sarafkande: adjective
ashamed - abject

sarafkandegi: noun
dejection

sarak: noun
slippage

saranjam: noun
upshot

saratâni: noun
cancerous

sarberâh: noun
tractable - docile

sarbesar: noun
endwise - endways

sarboland: adjective
proud - elate

sarboland: adjective
snood

sarbolandi: noun
pride

sarbâz: noun
soldier - private

sarbâz zadan: verb
To refuse

sarbâzi: noun
military

sarcheshme: noun
fountain - source

sarcheshme gereftan: verb
To emanate

sard: adjective
raw - fresh - distant - cool - arctic

sard: adjective
chilly

sard kardan: verb
To refrigerate

sardabir: noun
redactor

sardamâgh: noun
mood

sardar: noun
portal

sardard: noun
headache

sardargom: noun
amaze

sardast: noun
wristband

sardaste: noun
protagonist - marshal - chieftain

sardasti: noun
sketchy

sardi: noun
ice

sardkhâne: noun
springhouse - fridge

sardkon: noun
cooler

sardâb: noun
basement - cellar

sardâr: noun
headed

sarehambandi: noun
tinker - shakeup

sarehâl: noun
cheery

sarekeyf: adjective
jolly - gay

443

sarekhar: adjective
killjoy

sarekâr: noun
overseer - taskmaster

sarepâyi: noun
sandal

sareshab: noun
evening

saresid: noun
calendar - maturity

saretân: noun
cancer

saretânzâ: adjective
carcinogen

sarf: noun
expenditure

sarf shodan: verb
To spend

sarfe: noun
gain - advantage

sarfe nazar: verb
To withdraw - To withdrawal - To calloff - To forget - To betake

sarfeju: adjective
thrifty - inexpensive - parsimonious

sarfejuyi: noun
savings

sarfenazar: noun
surrender - waiver

sargardân: adjective
straggle - wanderer - adrift

sargardân budan: verb
To traipse - To straggle - To wander - To moon

sargardân shodan: verb
To stray

sargardâni: noun
wandering

sargarm kardan: verb
To entertain - To occupy - To inveigle

sargarmi: noun
recreation - fun - pastime - avocation - hobby

sargashtegi: noun
amazement - perplexity

sargije: noun
vertigo

sargord: noun
major

sargozasht: noun
adventure - memoir - story - destiny

sargozasht: noun
case

sarhad: noun
demarcation - bound - border - mete

sarhang: noun
colonel

sari': adjective
swift - speedy - prompt - quick - rapid

sari'tar: adjective
faster

sarian: adverb
apace - pronto

sarih: adjective
frank - clear - explicit - abstract -
unequivocal - straight

sarihan: adverb
expressly

sarir: noun
throne

sarjam': noun
total - tot - overhead

sarjukhe: noun
corporal

sarkarde: adjective
commander - captain

sarkardegi: noun
command

sarkesh: adjective
turbulent - malcontent - irrepressible - rebel

sarkeshi: noun
recalcitrance - rebellion - contumacy

sarkeshi kardan: verb
To inspect - To visit

sarkeshidan: verb
To swill - To quaff - To lap - To guzzle

sarkubi: noun
squelch - repression

sarkuft: noun
rail

sarkârgar: noun
joss

sarlôhe: noun
caption - epigraph - signboard

sarmaghâle: noun
editorial

sarmashgh: noun
example - lead - model - pacemaker

sarmast: adjective
maudlin

sarmâ: noun
cold

sarmâ zadan: verb
To frost

sarmâkhordegi: noun
cold - flu

sarmâye: noun
turnover - stock - asset - capital

sarmâyedâr: adjective
capitalist

sarmâyegozâr: adjective
investor

sarmâzadegi: noun
chilblain

sarneguni: noun
debacle

sarnevesht: noun
fate - destiny

sarneyze: noun
bayonet

saro sedâ: noun
explosion - clamor - noise

sarparast: noun
supervisor - protector - caretaker

sarparasti kardan: verb
To oversee - To preside - To superintend

sarpichi: noun
refusal - disobedience - transgression

sarpichi kardan: verb
To disobey - To challenge

sarpush: noun
lid - valve - cover - casquet - capsule - cap

sarpushide: adjective
porch

sarsafhe: noun
headline - head

sarsakht: adjective
stubborn - obstinate - intransigent

sarsakhti: noun
tenacity - obstinacy - pertinacity

sarsari: noun
perfunctory - cursory - superficial

sarsarâ: noun
gallery - hall - portico

sarsepordan: verb
To commit

sarsepordegi: noun
commitment

sarshir: noun
butterfat - cream

sarshomâri: noun
census - capitation - statistic

sarshâr: adjective
profuse - alive - opulence - galore

sarshâr sâkhtan: verb
To profuse

sarshâri: noun
profusion

sarsâm: noun
delirium - maze

sartâpâ: noun
capapie

sartâsar: noun
through - overall - across

sarv: noun
cedar

sarvar: noun
overlord - joy

sarvari kardan: verb
To prince

sarvân: noun
captain

sarzade: adjective
uninvited

sarzamin: noun
territory - land

sarzanesh: noun
snub - obloquy - demerit - blame

sarzanesh kardan: verb
To scold - To blame - To berate - To chide -
To censure

sarzende: adjective
spirituous - alive - vivacious - lively

sarzendegi: noun
vivacity - esprit

sarâb: noun
mirage

sarâf: adjective
banker - usurer - moneychanger

sarâf: noun
changer

sarâfi: noun
exchange

sarâfkhâne: noun
exchange

sarâghâz: adverb
preface - prologue

sarâmad: noun
perfect - pre-eminent - master

sarâne: noun
capitation

sarâriz shodan: verb
To top - To slope - To plummet - To ramp

sarâsar: noun
throughout - quite - whole

sarâshibi: noun
abrupt - slide

sarâshpaz: noun
chef

sarâsime: adjective
headfirst - pellmell

sarâsimegi: noun
scurry

sarây: noun
home - house

sarâzir: noun
steep - ramp

sarâziri: adjective
slope - slide - downhill

sath: noun
surface - sheet - external

sathe zamin: noun
earth

sathi: adjective
surface - superficial

sathi: noun
superficiality

satl: noun
kit - pail - bucket - bail

satle zobâle: noun
ashcan

satr: noun
line

savâ: noun
separate - segregate - asunder - apart

savâ kardan: verb
To detach - To disassemble - To unlink - To separate

savâbegh: noun
record - dossier - information

savâd: noun
literacy

savâr: noun
trooper - horseback

savâr kardan: verb
To saddle - To jumble - To drive

savâr kardan: verb
To set - To assemble - To mount - To enchase

savâr shodan: verb
To mount

savâri: adjective
ride - cavalcade

savârkâr: noun
rider - horseman

sayâd: noun
hunter

sayâl: adjective
fluor - mobile

sayâr: adjective
ambulatory - migrant - itinerant - wanderer

sayârak: noun
asteroid

sayâre: noun
planet

se: noun
three

se jânebe: adjective
tripartite - trilateral

sebarâbar: adjective
threefold - triplicate - triple - treble

sebghat: noun
antedate

sebghat gereftan: verb
To outpace - To outpoint - To outgo

sebghat gereftan az: verb
To pass

sebghat jostan: verb
To transcend - To outguess

sebil: noun
mustache

sedgh: noun
truth - verity

sedâ: noun
sound - tone - noise - voice - vocal

sedâ kardan: verb
To cry - To click - To clang - To rustle

sedâ khafekon: noun
muffler - silencer

sedâ zadan: verb
To hail - To call

sedâdâr: adjective
vowel - phonetic - sonorous - sonant

sedâghat: noun
truth - loyalty - honesty - veracity

sefat: noun
quality - qualification - adjective

sefid: adjective
snowy - hoary

sefid kardan: verb
To tin - To bleach - To whiten

sefid shodan: verb
To whiten

sefidi: noun
blank

sefidpust: adjective
caucasian

sefr: noun
zero - null - nothing

seft: adjective
tough - tight - tense - concrete - hard

seft kardan: verb
To stiff - To toughen - To tighten - To firm

seft shodan: verb
To toughen - To tighten

sefâhat: noun
idiotism

sefârat: noun
legation

sefâratkhâne: noun
embassy

sefâresh: noun
indent

sefâreshi: adjective
bespoke

segholu: adjective
triplet

seghr: noun
imfancy

seght kardan: verb
To abort

segâl: noun
intention

449

segâne: adjective
threefold - triplet - triple

sehat: noun
rectitude - authenticity - accuracy

sehe: noun
signature

sehrâmiz: adjective
magical - magic - sorcerous

seid: noun
quarry - prey - predatin - raven

seighal: noun
burnish - varnish

seil: noun
overflow - flood - torrent

seke: noun
coin - money

seke zadan: verb
To mint - To poke - To coin

sekhâvat: noun
generosity - bounty

sekhâvatmandi: noun
benevolence

sekhâvatmandâne: adverb
handsome - free

seks: noun
sex

sekseke: noun
hiccup

sekseke kardan: verb
To hiccough - To hiccup

sekte: noun
apoplexy - halt - caesura

selahshur: adjective
warrior - knight

selsele: noun
string - chain

selul: noun
cell

selâh: noun
weapon - armament - arm

semat: noun
position - job

semej: adjective
stubborn - stickler - pertinacious

seminâr: noun
seminar

semsâr: noun
broker

semâjat: noun
pertinacity - persistence - insist

semâjat kardan: verb
To dun - To persist - To importune

sen: noun
age

sendikâ: noun
syndicate

senf: noun
order - guild - caste

senjed: noun
service

senkhiyat: noun
congruity

senobar: noun
spruce - pinon - pine

sent: noun
cent

senâtor: noun
senator

sepahlu: adjective
triangle

separ: noun
parapet - buffer - shield

separi kardan: verb
To serving - To survive

sepas: adverb
therefore - thenceforth - then - afterwards - next

sepehr: noun
heaven

sepide dam: noun
daybreak - dawn

sepidâr: noun
poplar

sepordan: verb
To deposit - To confide - To entrust

seporde: noun
deposit

septâmbr: noun
september

sepâh: noun
army - host - corps

sepâs: noun
thank

sepâsgozâr: adjective
thankful

sepâsgozâri: noun
gratuity - gratitude - thanksgiving - thank

sepâsgozâri kardan: verb
To thank

sepâye: noun
andiron - trivet - tripod

ser: noun
secret - mystery

serang: adjective
tricolor

sereshk: noun
tear

seresht: noun
temperament - make - nature

serfan: adverb
alone - downright - only

451

serghat: noun
thievery - theft - robbery

serghat kardan: verb
To lift - To rob - To steal

seri: adjective
undercover - esoteric - crypt - occult

seri budan: verb
To secrecy

serish: adjective
paste - glue

serke: noun
pickle - vinegar

serom: noun
serum

servat: noun
wealth - money

servatmand: adjective
wealthy

servis: noun
service

seryâl: noun
serial

seryâyat: noun
transmittal - transmission - contagion

serâhat: noun
speciosity - precision

serâyat kardan: verb
To transmit - To permeate - To infect

serâyedâr: noun
janitor - caretaker - custodian

setabr: adjective
sturdy - stalwart - thick - robust

setam: noun
oppression - cruelty - injustice - tyranny

setam kardan: verb
To tyrannize

setamgar: adjective
tyrant - cruel

setamgari: noun
ravage - tyranny

setamgarâne: adverb
tyrannous - tyrannical

setamkâr: adjective
cruel

setarvan: noun
sterile - barren

setiz: noun
struggle - battle - warfare - combat

setize: noun
strife - quarrel - dispute - controversy - conflict

setizegar: adjective
contentious - warlike - militant - quarrelsome

setizeju: adjective
querulous

setizeju: adjective
contestant - quarrelsome

setizejuyi: noun
pugnacity

setorg: adjective
large - huge

setork: adjective
boisterous - big

setudan: verb
To extol - To glorify - To applaud - To adore
- To praise

setudani: noun
laudable - praiseworthy - admirable -
commendable

setude: adjective
exemplary - honorable - laudable

setâk: noun
stem

setândan: verb
To take - To get

setâre: noun
star

setâre shenâs: noun
astronomer - astrologer

setâre shenâsi: adjective
uranology - astronomy - astrology

setâreye ghotbi: noun
northstar

setâyesh: noun
worship - praise

setâyesh kardan: verb
To glorify - To eulogize - To worship

setâyeshgar: adjective
ilolater - praiser

sevom: noun
third

sevomi: adjective
third

sevomin: adjective
tertiary

seyd kardan: verb
To hunt - To prey

seyghal: noun
polish

seyghal dâdan: verb
To gloss - To burnish - To polish

seyghali kardan: verb
To varnish

seylâb: noun
syllable - spate

sezâ: noun
punishment - retribution

sezâvar: noun
worthy - worth

sezâvâr budan: verb
To deserve

sha'n: noun
dignity - grandeur - status

shab: noun
eve - night

shab hengâm: adverb
nightfall - night

shabah: noun
sprite - ghost

shabah: noun
quasi

shabah: noun
specter - ghost

shabake: noun
network - net

shabake sâkhtan: verb
To mesh

shabakeye ertebâti: noun
network

shabdar: noun
clover

shabgard: noun
hobgoblin

shabih: noun
similar - alike - likeness

shabihsâzi: noun
imagery

shabnam: noun
dew - frost

shabneshini: noun
wake

shabâhat: noun
resemblance - equality

shabâhat dâshtan: verb
To resemble

shabân: noun
pastor - looker

shabâne: adjective
overnight - nocturnal - nightly

shabângâh: noun
nightfall

shabâni: noun
pastoral

shadid: adjective
drastic - chronic - rigorous - hard - intense - tough

shadid kardan: verb
To keen - To heighten

shadid shodan: verb
To intensify

shadidolahn: adjective
overtone

shafagh: noun
twilight

shafagh: noun
crepuscule

shafeghat: noun
mercy - compassion - ruth

shafi': adjective
propitious

shafigh: adjective
sympathetic

shaftâlu: noun
peach

shafâ: noun
cure

shafâ dâdan: verb
To cure - To heal - To mend - To medicate

shafâ yâftan: verb
To over

shafâ'at: noun
intervention - intercession

shafâbakhsh: adjective
medicinal - medic - remedial - curative

shafâd dahande: adjective
healer

shafâf: adjective
transparent - elucidate - lucid

shafâf budan: verb
To lucidity

shafâhi: noun
oral - verbal - unwritten

shagh shodan: verb
To erect

shaghe: noun
hew

shahbânu: noun
empress - queen

shahd: noun
honey - molasses - ambrosia

shahid: noun
martyr

shahmât kardan: verb
To checkmate

shahr: noun
town - city - parish - home

shahrak: noun
town

shahrdâr: noun
municipality - mayor

shahrestân: noun
township - county - parish

shahri: adjective
urban - civic

shahriye: noun
tuition

shahriyâr: noun
sovereign - king - monarch

shahrneshin: noun
urbanite - urban

shahrsâzi: noun
urbanization

shahrvand: noun
national - citizen

shahvat: noun
lust - flesh - rut

shahvatangiz: adjective
sexy - lascivious - luscious

shahvatrân: adjective
oversexed - voluptuous - licentious - lecher

shahvatrâni: noun
pleasure - lechery

shahvâni: adjective
sensual

shahâb: noun
meteor

shahâdat: noun
testimony - evidence - martyrdom

shahâdat dâdan: verb
To attest - To affirm - To voucher - To
evidence - To testify

shahâmat: noun
dare

shajarenâme: noun
pedigree - genealogy

shak: noun
skepticism - doubt - uncertainty

shak dâshtan: verb
To doubt - To suspect

shakhs: noun
individual - person

shakhsi: adjective
personal - someone

shakhsiyat: noun
character - personality

shakib: adjective
patience

shakibâ: adjective
tolerant - patient

shakibâyi: noun
fortitude - patience - sufferance

shakil: adjective
shapely - pretty

shakâk: adjective
sceptic

shakâki: noun
incredulity

shalgham: noun
turnip

shalil: noun
nectarine

shalvâr: noun
pants

shalâgh: noun
lash - lambaste

shalâgh zadan: verb
To leather

sham': noun
candle

sham'dân: noun
candlestick

shamshir: noun
sword

shamshir bâzi kardan: verb
To fence

shamshirbâz: noun
swordsman

shamshirbâzi: noun
fence

shamshirmâhi: noun
swordfish

shamshirzan: noun
swordsman

shamâyel: noun
icon - image

shanbe: noun
Saturday

shangul: adjective
sprightly

shani': adjective
nefarious - hideous

shar'i: adjective
legal - canonical - juridical

shar'i kardan: verb
To canonize

sharbat: noun
juice - beverage - nectar

sharbat: noun
syrup

shargh: noun
east - orient

sharghi: adjective
eastern

sharh: noun
description - explanation - recitation - statement

sharh dâdan: verb
To explain - To describe - To illustrate

sharhe hâl: noun
memoir

sharif: noun
honor

sharif: adjective
patrician - honorable - noble

sharik: adjective
share

sharik shodan: verb
To participate - To partake

sharir: noun
villainous - villain - wicked - nefarious - naughty

shariyân: noun
artery

shariyâni: adjective
arterial

sharkat kardan: verb
To participate - To partake

sharkati: adjective
joint

sharm: noun
shame

sharmande: verb
To blush - To bash

sharmande: adjective
ashamed

sharmande kardan: verb
To shame - To abash

sharmgin: adjective
hangdog

sharmsâr: adjective
ashamed

sharmsâr shodan: verb
To embarrass

sharmsâri: noun
shame

sharmâvar: adjective
shameful

shart: noun
condition - reservation - clause

shart: noun
bet

shart bastan: verb
To bet

shartbandi kardan: verb
To gamble - To stake

sharti: adjective
provisional - eventual - conditional

sharâb: noun
wine

sharâbkhâri: noun
binge

sharâbshenâs: noun
gourmet

sharâyet: noun
term - qualification

shast: noun
thumb

shast: noun
threescore - sixty

shastom: adjective
sixtieth

shastomin: adjective
sixtieth

shate: noun
louse

shatranj: noun
chess

shatranji: adjective
plaid - checker

458

shatranji kardan: verb
To checker

shayâd: adjective
trickster

shayâdi: noun
abusive - juggle

she'r: noun
poetry - poem

shebhe ghâre: noun
subcontinent

shedat: noun
severity - intensity - violence - extremity

shedat dâshtan: verb
To rage

shedate amal: noun
arrogance - force

shefte: adjective
vexatious - mortar

shegarf: adjective
wondrous - prodigious - tremendous

shegeft: noun
surprise - prodigious - wonder

shegeftangiz: adjective
phenomenal - stupendous

shegefti: noun
amazement - prodigy - portent - marvel

shegeftâvar: adjective
extraordinary - exclamatory

shegh: noun
prick - inelastic - tough - stiff

sheidâ: adjective
manic - lovelorn

sheighali: adjective
smooth - shiny - glossy - reflective

sheikh: noun
patriarch

sheipur: noun
trumpet - bugle - horn - clarion

sheitanat: noun
mischief - shenanigan

sheitanat kardan: verb
To monkey

sheitanatâmiz: adjective
mischievous - sly

sheitân: noun
devil - impish

shekam: noun
abdomen

shekamband: noun
truss

shekambe: noun
tripe

shekamdard: noun
bellyache

shekami: adjective
gastric - uterine - ventral

459

shekamparast: adjective
gourmand - glutton

shekan: noun
plica - crease

shekanande: adjective
brittle - plucky - frail

shekanandegi: noun
frangibility

shekanje: noun
torture - torment

shekanje kardan: verb
To excruciate

shekast: noun
break - refraction - fracture

shekast: noun
failure

shekast dâdan: verb
To smash - To defeat - To vanquish

shekast khordan: verb
To fail

shekast nâpazir: adjective
invulnerable - invincible - insuperable -
unbeatable

shekastan: verb
To break - To crackle - To cleave - To chop -
To fracture

shekastan: verb
To break

shekastani: noun
breakage - breakable

shekaste: adjective
zigzag

shekaste fâhesh: noun
lurch

shekaste nafsi: noun
modesty

shekastegi: noun
fracture

shekl: noun
shape - schema - configuration - form

shekl gereftan: verb
To form

sheklak: noun
grimace

shekoftan: verb
To burst - To nip - To open - To dehisce

shekoftegi: noun
efflorescence

shekufe: noun
blossom - bloom

shekufe dâdan: verb
To flower

shekufe kardan: verb
To bud - To bloom

shekve kardan: verb
To gripe - To plain

460

shekve âmiz: adjective
plaintive

shekâf: noun
crack - break - split

shekâf dâdan: verb
To slash - To shear - To chap

shekâfande: adjective
ripping - cleaver

shekâftan: verb
To split - To slat - To pierce - To fracture

shekâftegi: noun
cleavage

shekâr: noun
predatin - hunt

shekâr kardan: verb
To hunt

shekârbân: adjective
gamekeeper

shekârchi: adjective
hunter - woodman

shekârgâh: noun
preserve

shekâyat: noun
grievance - complaint

shekâyat kardan: verb
To bitch - To complain

shelakhte: adjective
sloppy - slipshod - blowzy

shelang: noun
hose

shelik: noun
fire - shoot

shelik kardan: verb
To fire - To shoot

shemordan: verb
To enumerate - To count - To reckon

shemsh: noun
bullion - bar

shemâtat kardan: verb
To taunt

shen: noun
sand - grit - gravel

shen pâshidan: verb
To gravel - To sand

shenavande: noun
listener - auditor

shenavandegân: noun
grandstand - listeners

shenavâ: adjective
receptive

shenavâ'i: noun
audition - hearing

shenel: noun
cape

sheni: noun
sandy - gravel

shenidan: verb
To hear - To listen

shenidani: adjective
audible

shenzâr: noun
beach

shenâ: noun
swim

shenâ kardan: verb
To swim

shenâ konande: adjective
swimmer

shenâgar: adjective
swimmer

shenâkht: noun
cognition - recognition

shenâkhtan: verb
To identify - To notice - To know - To
recognize

shenâsâyi: noun
identity - cognizance - reconnaissance -
recognition

shenâvar: adjective
afloat - adrift - buoyant

shenâvar shodan: verb
To swim - To float

shepesh: noun
louse

shepesh hâ: noun
lice

shepeshu: adjective
lousy

sherik: adjective
partner

sherik kardan: verb
To associate

sherkat: noun
corporation - firm - company - institution

sherkat jostan: verb
To assist

sherâfat: noun
honor

sherâfatmand: adjective
upstanding

sherâfatmandâne: adverb
honorable

sherârat: noun
iniquity - villainy - mischief - malfeasance -
depravity

shesh: noun
six

sheshdâng: noun
soprano

sheshgushe: adjective
hesagonal

sheshgâne: adjective
sextet

sheshmâhe: adjective
semiannual

sheshom: adjective
sixth

sheshomin: adjective
sixth

shetâ: noun
winter

shetâb: noun
velocity - hustle - haste

shetâb: noun
expediency

shetâb dâdan: verb
To accelerate

shetâbzade: adjective
hasty

shetâbzade: adjective
precipitant

shetâbzadegi: adverb
snap

shetâbân: noun
expedite

shetâftan: verb
To hasten

shevid: noun
dill

sheyhe: noun
hinny

sheyhe keshidan: verb
To hinny

sheypur zadan: verb
To trumpet

sheypurchi: noun
trumpeter - trumpet

sheytân: noun
devil

shib: noun
inclination - dip - slope - slant

shib dâshtan: verb
To tilt

shibdâr: adjective
gradient - slope - shelvy

shibe molâyem: noun
espianade

shiftan: verb
To charm - To captivate - To allure - To
mash

shifte: adjective
amorous - fond - captive

shifte kardan: verb
To enthral

shiftegi: noun
preoccupation

shik: adjective
snappy - dapper - dinky

shik: noun
swagger

shikpush: adjective
ritzy - dandy

shimidân: noun
chemist

shimiyâyi: noun
chemical

shir: noun
sop - lion - milk

shir dâdan: verb
To feeding - To foster

shirbâ: noun
cullis - porridge

shire: noun
juice - extract - molasses

shire'i: adjective
junkie

shiri: adjective
milky

shiri rang: adjective
milky

shirin: adjective
sweet

shirini: noun
sugar - cookie - pastry - amiability

shirinipazi: noun
pastry

shirinzabân: adjective
sugary - mealymouthed

shirje: noun
dive - plunge

shirje: noun
diving

shirje raftan: verb
To dive

shirmâhi: noun
walrus

shirzan: adjective
heroine

shirâb: noun
tap - spout - spigot

shirâbe: noun
emulsion - latex

shirâze: noun
headband

shishe: noun
weevil - louse

shishe: noun
glass - bottle

shishe'âlât: noun
glass

shishebor: noun
glazier

shivan: noun
whimper

shivan kardan: noun
wail

shive: noun
method - pace - device - style - technique

shivâ: adjective
eloquent

shiyâf: noun
suppository

shiyâr: adjective
thread - ruck - rake - groove

sho'bade: noun
juggle - legerdemain

sho'badebâz: adjective
juggler

sho'be: noun
branch

sho'le: noun
flame

sho'le zadan: verb
To flame

sho'levar: adjective
inflammable - aflame - afire

sho'ur: noun
sense - reason

sho'â': noun
ray - radius - beam

sho'â'i: adjective
radiant - radial

sho'âr: noun
slogan - motto

shobhe: noun
doubt - misgiving

shodan: verb
To become - To grow - To be

shodani: adjective
possible

shoghl: noun
profession - occupation - work - job

shoghâl: noun
reynard

shogun: noun
presage - auspices - augur

shohrat: noun
esteem - fame - reputation - renown

shohrat dâshtan: verb
To repute

shohud: noun
intuition

shojâ': adjective
brave

shojâ'at: noun
courage - bravery

shok: noun
thistle

shokhm: noun
plough - plow

shokhm kardan: verb
To plough - To plow

shokhm zadan: verb
To plough - To plow

shokr: noun
sugar

shokr: noun
thank

shokrgozâri: noun
eucharist - thanksgiving

shokufâyi: noun
efflorescence

shokuh: noun
glory - magnitude - pomp

shol: adjective
ramshackle - loose

shol: adjective
sleazy

shol kardan: verb
To slack - To relax - To unloose - To loosen

sholi: adjective
slack

sholugh: adjective
noise - busy - tumult

sholughi: noun
jumble - crowd - bustle

shomul: noun
incurrence - inclusion - liability

shomâ: noun
you

shomâl: noun
north

shomâle bâkhtari: adjective
northwest

shomâle gharb: noun
northwest

shomâle gharbi: adjective
northwest

shomâle khâvari: adjective
northeast

shomâle shargh: noun
northeast

shomâle sharghi: adjective
northeast

shomâli: adjective
northern

shomâr: noun
unit

shomâre: noun
issue - numeral - number

shomâresh: noun
computation - tab

shomâreshgar: noun
numerator

shorshor: adjective
gurgle

shoru': noun
start - alpha - inception - resumption - onset

shoru' kardan: verb
To start - To launch - To begin - To embark

shosh: noun
lung

shoshte shodan: verb
To tub - To launder

shostan: verb
To wash - To leach - To launder

shostani: adjective
washable

shostoshu: noun
wash - rinse - bathe - bath

shostoshu dâdan: verb
To wash

shotor: noun
camel

shotormorgh: noun
ostrich

shovâliye: noun
knight - cavalier

shoyu': noun
prevalence - outbreak

shoyu' yâftan: verb
To breakout

shufer: noun
driver - chauffeur

shukh: adjective
joker - jester

shukh budan: verb
To joviality

shukh tab'i: noun
prank - jocundity

shukhi: noun
joke - humor - fun

shukhi kardan: verb
To josh - To joke - To jest - To fun

shum: adjective
unlucky - ghastly - ominous

shur: adjective
salty

shur kardan: verb
To salt

shurangiz: adjective
sensational

shurbakht: adjective
unhappy

shuresh: noun
riot - revolt - rebellion

shureshi: adjective
insurgent - rioter - rebel

shureye sar: noun
shale - scruff - dandruff - dander

shuri: noun
salinity

shuridan: verb
To revolt - To rebel

shuride: adjective
fool - berserk - distraught - crazy

shuridegi: noun
snarl

shuy: noun
husband

shâ'ebe: noun
alloy

shâ'eri: adjective
poesy

shâd: adjective
joyful - merry - happy - cheery - glad

shâdemân: adjective
upbeat

shâdi: noun
joyance - curvet

shâdi kardan: verb
To joy - To revel

shâdibakhsh: adjective
breezy

shâdkâm: adjective
upbeat - merry

shâdkâmi: noun
welfare

shâdâb: adjective
lush - succulent - juicy

shâdâbi: noun
succulence

shâer: noun
poet - bard

shâerâne: adverb
poetic

shâgerd: noun
pupil - student - disciple - mate

shâgerdi: adjective
journeywork

shâgh: adjective
astringent - severe - stark

shâghel: noun
practitioner

shâh: noun
sceptered - king

shâh: noun
king

shâhanshâhi: adjective
imperial

shâhdokht: adjective
princesse

shâhed: noun
theme - testimonial - instance - voucher

shâhi: noun
cress

shâhin: noun
hawk

shâhkâr: adjective
masterwork - mesterpiece

shâhnâme: noun
epopee

shâhrag: noun
artery - aorta

shâhrâh: noun
superhighway - thoroughfare - freeway - highway

shâhtut: noun
blackberry

shâhzâde: noun
lord - prince

shâhâne: adverb
sceptered - royal - majestic

shâker: adjective
thankful

shâkh: noun
horn - branch

shâkh zadan: verb
To push - To butt - To gore

shâkhak: noun
antenna

shâkhdâr: adjective
cuspidate - cornuted

shâkhe: noun
sprout - tributary

shâkhe zadan: verb
To truncate

shâkhes: noun
tyupical - indicator - index - dial

shâkho barg: noun
bush

shâki: adjective
complainant - plaintiff

shâl: noun
wraparound - shawl

shâli: noun
camlet

shâlude: adjective
infrastructure - skeleton

shâm: noun
supper - meat - dinner

shâmel: noun
inclusive - in

shâmel budan: verb
To comprise - To contain - To consist - To encompass

shâmgâh: noun
eventide - eve

shâmpânze: noun
chimpanzee

shâne: noun
shoulder - comb - pitchfork - heckle

shâne: noun
shoulder - comb - heckle

shâne kardan: verb
To comb

shâns: noun
chance - fortune - fortuity - luck

shânsi: adjective
lottery

shânzdah: noun
sixteen

shânzdahom: adjective
sixteenth

shânzdahomin: adjective
sixteenth - sixteen

shâre': noun
lawyer

shârlâtan bâzi: noun
sciolism - quackery

shârlâtân: adjective
charlatan

shâsh: noun
piss - urine

shâshidan: verb
To piss - To urinate

shâyad: adverb
maybe - may - perhaps

shâye': adjective
prevalent - rampant - widespread

shâye' shodan: verb
To prevail

shâye'e: noun
rumor

shâye'ât: noun
canard - murmur

shâyeste: noun
proper - suitable - worthy - competent

shâyeste budan: verb
To adequate - To merit

shâyestegi: noun
competence - eligibility - merit

shâyestegi dâshtan: verb
To able - To deserve

shâyestetarin: adjective
best

shâyân: noun
worthy - considerable

shôgh: noun
zeal - ardor - delight - craze

shôhar: noun
husband

shôhar dâdan: verb
To espouse

shôhardâr: adjective
married

shôkarân: noun
hemlock

shôravi: noun
Soviet Union

shôrâ: noun
diet - council - moot

si: noun
thirty

sib: noun
apple

sibak: noun
tuber

sifun: noun
siphon

sighe: noun
concubine

sigâr: noun
cigarette - cigar

sigâr keshidan: verb
To smoke

sikh: noun
stiff - grid - gad

sikh zadan: verb
To yerk - To prod - To poke - To gig

sikhak: noun
steeve - goad - gaff - gad

sikhunak: noun
prick - poke - jag

silandr: noun
cylinder

sili: noun
slap

sili zadan: verb
To slap

silikon: noun
silicon

silikâ: noun
silica

silis: adjective
silica

silisiyom: noun
silicon

sim: noun
wire - cord - line - string - silver

simkesh: noun
wirepuller

simorgh: noun
roc

simâ: noun
visage - countenance - feature - face

simâb: noun
mercury

simân: noun
cement

sinamâ: noun
picture - movie - cinema

471

sine: noun
bust - breast - bosom - heart

sine jolô dâdan: verb
To perk

sineband: noun
napkin

sinemâ: noun
cinema

sinepahlu: noun
pneumonia

sini: noun
tray - paten - dish

sir: noun
garlic

sir kardan: verb
To feed - To roam

siri: adjective
amplitude - full

sirk: noun
circus

sirâbi: noun
tripe

siyom: adjective
thirtieth

siyomin: adjective
thirtieth

siyâh: adjective
jetty - sooty - black - negro - grimy

siyâh kardan: verb
To blacken - To black - To denigrate

siyâhat: noun
journey - tourism - tour

siyâhat kardan: verb
To rubberneck - To explore - To tour - To safari

siyâhe: noun
invoice - inventory

siyâhi: adjective
black

siyâhi: noun
soldier - trouper - trooper - corpsman

siyâhpust: adjective
negro - ethiopian

siyâhpust: adjective
blackamoor

siyâhrag: noun
vein

siyâhrang: adjective
black

siyâsat: noun
diplomacy - policy

siyâsatmadâr: noun
statesman - politician - diplomat

siyâsi: adjective
politic

siyâtik: noun
sciatica

sizdah: noun
thirteen

sizdahom: adjective
thirteenth

sizdahomin: adjective
thirteenth

skhel dâdan: verb
To crystallize - To model

so'ud: noun
rise - bulge - ascent - ascension - mount

so'ud kardan: verb
To soar - To mount - To ascend - To climb -
To rise

sobh: noun
morning - daybreak

sobhâne: noun
breakfast

sobât: noun
consistency

sodur: noun
emission - issuance

sodyom: noun
sodium

sofre: noun
tablecloth - table

sofâl: noun
clay - earthenware

sofâlgari: noun
pottery

sofâli: adjective
earthen - bat

sofâlin: adjective
earthenware

soghrâ: adjective
minor

soghut: noun
crash - elapse - downfall - fall

soghut: noun
fall - crash - drop

soghut kardan: verb
To slump

sohbat: noun
talk - speech - dialogue - converse

sohulat: noun
ease

sokhan: noun
speech - word - redundancy

sokhan: noun
speech

sokhan parâkani: noun
transmission - broadcast

sokhanchin: noun
telltale - informer

sokhanchin: noun
gossip

sokhane tond: noun
vitriolic

sokhangu: noun
talker - spokesman - speaker

sokhanrân: adjective
lecturer - orator - spokesman

sokhanrâni: noun
lecture - oration

sokhansârâyi: noun
elocution

sokhanvar: adjective
eloquent

soknâ: noun
habitancy - occupancy

soknâ kardan: verb
To dwell

sokun: noun
quiet - inaction - inertia

sokunat: noun
habitancy - occupancy

sokut: noun
calm - silence

sokân: noun
steerage - helm

sokân: noun
rudder

solh: noun
peace

solh dâdan: verb
To reconcile

solhju: adjective
pacifier - pacific

solhâmiz: adjective
peaceful

sols: adjective
third

solte: noun
ascendency - mastery

solte: noun
sovereignty

solteju: adjective
aggressive

soltân: noun
king - monarch - sultan

soluk: noun
demeanour - conduct - behavior

sonat: noun
tradition - custom

sonbe: noun
piston - ramrod

sonbe zadan: verb
To ram - To swab

sor khordan: verb
To skid - To skate - To glide

474

sor'at: noun
speed

sorang: noun
artery

sorang: noun
syringe

soranj: noun
putty

sorb: noun
plumb

sorb: noun
plumbum

sorbi: adjective
leaden

sorfe: noun
cough

sorfe kardan: verb
To cough

sorgh kardan: verb
To fry - To rose

soridan: verb
To coast - To glide - To slither - To slide - To skid

sorkh: adjective
sanguine - rosy - red

sorkhak: noun
measles

sorkhak: noun
rubeola

sorkhje: noun
rubeola

sorkhjâme: adjective
scarlet

sorkhshodegi: noun
scarlet

sorkhâb: noun
rouge

sorsore: noun
slide

sorud: noun
song - sing - hymn - anthem - chant

sorud: noun
carol

sorudan: verb
To sing - To compose

sorush: noun
oracle - gabriel

sorâgh: noun
scent

sorâyande: adjective
singer - vocalist - warbler - composer

sorâyidan: verb
To troll - To intone - To warble

sos: noun
sauce

sosis: noun
sausage

sost: adjective
tardy - loose - inactive

sost budan: verb
To lazy

sost kardan: verb
To enervate - To discourage - To weaken -
To loosen

sost shodan: adjective
unclinch - unclench - weaken

sosti: noun
lassitude - indolence - inaction

sosti: noun
phlegm - asthenia

sotfân: noun
lieutenant

sotun: noun
column - pillar - pile

sotune fagharât: noun
spine - backbone

soâl: noun
question - query

su: noun
side

su'e tafâhom: noun
gaingiving - imbroglio - misapprehension

su'e tafâhom: noun
embroglio

su'ezan: noun
suspicion

sud: noun
interest - profit - advantage

sud bordan: verb
To gain - To profit

sudesahâm: noun
dividend - revenue

sudju: adjective
jobber

sudjuyi: noun
jobbery

sudmand: adjective
useful - lucrative - beneficial

sudmand budan: verb
To advantage

sudmandi: noun
efficacy - productivity - utilization

sudâvar: adjective
profitable

sue zan: noun
suspicion - distrust

sug: noun
sorrow

sugnâk: noun
lamentable

sugnâme: noun
jeremiad

sugvâr: adjective
rueful - mournful

sugvâr: adjective
mournful - plaintful

sugvâri: noun
jeremiad - lament

sukhgir: noun
refuelling

sukht: noun
stoker - fuel - combustion

sukhtan: verb
To consumption - To combustion - To burn -
To broil - To singe

sukhtegi: noun
scorch - scald

sukhto sâz: noun
metabolism

sup: noun
soup

supâp: noun
valve

sur: noun
banquet

sur dâdan: verb
To regale

sur zadan: verb
To junket

surat: noun
face - aspect - visage - list

surat gereftan: verb
To accomplish

surat jalase: noun
proceedings - record

surat kardan: verb
To invoice

surat tarâsh: noun
shaver

surate ghazâ: noun
menu

surate kasr: noun
numerator

surathesâb: noun
bill - tab

suri: noun
superficial - simulate - nominal - ostensible

suriye: noun
syria

suriye'i: adjective
syrian

surâkh: noun
puncture - leak - hole

surâkh kardan: verb
To delve - To puncture - To punch

surâkhe bini: noun
snuffer - nostril

susk: noun
beetle - dorbeetle

susmâr: noun
lizard - crocodile - worm

susu: noun
gleam - flicker

susu zadan: verb
To shimmer - To blink - To flicker - To glimmer - To gleam

susyâlist: noun
socialist

susyâlizm: noun
socialism

sut: noun
whistler - whistle

sut zadan: verb
To whistle

suye: noun
to - unto

suz: noun
blast

suzan: noun
stylus - needle

suzesh: noun
twinge - irritation

suzeshe me'de: noun
heartburn

suzeshâvar: adjective
caustic - abrasive - irritant

suznâk: adjective
pungent - pathetic - plaintive

suzân: adjective
scathing - ardent - alight - acrimonious

suzânande: adjective
torrid - acrid

suzândan: verb
To fry - To cauterize - To burn

sâ'at: noun
hour - watch

sâ'at sâz: adjective
watchmaker

sâ'ate sheni: noun
hourglass

sâ'eghe: noun
thunderbolt

sâ'i: noun
assiduous - laborious - diligent

sâat: noun
clock - hour

sâbegh: adjective
previous - former - predecessor

sâbeghan: adverb
previously - once - heretofore

sâbeghe: noun
background - precedence - history - record

sâbeghi: adjective
old - previous

sâbet ghadam: adjective
steadfast - constant - consistent

sâbet kardan: verb
To prove - To evidence - To immobilize

sâbet mândan: verb
To fix

sâbun: noun
soap

sâbun zadan: verb
To lather - To scour - To soap

sâchme: noun
shot

sâde: adjective
simple - explicit - plain - idiot

sâde: adjective
simple - easy - plain

sâde del: adjective
simple - sheepish

sâdegh: adjective
sincere - honest - loyal

sâdeghâne: adverb
loyal - truly

sâdegi: noun
unreserve - naivete - spartanism - simplicity

sâdeloh: adjective
dupe

sâder kardan: verb
To export

sâder konande: adjective
exporter

sâderât: noun
export

sâf: adjective
serene - plain - explicit - clear

sâf kardan: verb
To strain - To smooth - To clear

sâf shodan: verb
To fine - To smooth

sâfi: noun
gloss - leach - purity - strainer

sâfi: verb
To leach

sâgh: noun
stalk

sâgh: noun
peduncle

sâghar: noun
goblet - cup

sâghdush: noun
groomsman

sâghe: noun
stem - stalk - shank

sâghe pâ: noun
shin - shank - leg

sâgheye gol: noun
peduncle

sâghi: noun
drawer - bung

sâghpush: noun
legging - jambeau

sâheb: noun
padrone - lord

sâhebe emtiyâz: adjective
grantee

sâhebkhâne: noun
host - landlord

sâhel: adjective
righteous

sâhel: noun
shore - coast - beach - bank - littoral

sâhele daryâ: noun
seashore - seacoast

sâher: noun
sorcerous - conjurer - necromancer - hex

sâhere: adjective
hellcat - hag - witch

sâk: noun
bag

sâken: adjective
inmate - inhabitant - occupant - calm

sâken budan: verb
To dwell

sâket: noun
silent - calm - acquiescent

sâket budan: verb
To mum

sâket shodan: verb
To stanch - To lull - To shut up

sâkht: noun
manufacture - production

sâkhtan: verb
To establish - To build - To invent - To
manufacture - To make

sâkhtegi: adjective
imitation - false

sâkhtemân: noun
construction - frame

sâkhtâr: noun
structure

sâl: noun
year

sâlek: adjective
peripatetic - gradient

sâlem: adjective
healthy - valid - safe

sâlem: noun
amphitheater - coliseum - gallery

sâles: adjective
third - tertiary

sâlgard: noun
jubilee

sâliyâne: adverb
yearly - annual

sâlkhorde: adjective
elderly - hoary

sâlkhordegi: noun
senility

sâlnâme: noun
calendar

sâlâd: noun
salad

sâlâr: noun
chieftain - chief

sâmet: noun
silent - speechless - mute - consonantal

sâmân: noun
order - repose

sânavi: adjective
peripheral - secondary

sândevich: noun
sandwich

sânehe: noun
accident

sâni: adjective
second

sâniye: noun
second

sânsur: noun
censorship

sântigerâd: noun
centigrade

sântimetr: noun
centimeter

sâr: noun
camel

sârebân: noun
cameleer

sâregh: noun
thief - robber

sâs: noun
bug

sâsur: noun
hatchet

sâte': noun
diffusive - radiant

sâte' shodan: verb
To scintillate

sâtur: noun
masher - whittle - cleaver - chopper

sâyande: adjective
grating - abrasive

sâye: noun
sunshade - shadow - shade - auspices

sâye afkandan: verb
To shade

sâye andâkhtan: verb
To overcast - To umber

sâyebân: noun
sunshade

sâyebân: adjective
shade

sâyemânand: adjective
shadowy

sâyerin: noun
rest

sâyesh: noun
abrasion - erosion - friction

sâyidan: verb
To grind - To levigate

sâyide shodan: verb
To rub

sâyidegi: noun
attrition - abrasion - gall - chafe - erosion

sâyz: noun
size

sâz zadan: verb
To tune

sâzande: adjective
composer - constituent - maker

sâzdahani: noun
harmonica

sâzegar: adjective
salubrious - compatible

sâzegâr kardan: verb
To adjust

sâzemân: noun
structure - infrastructure - organization

sâzemân dahande: adjective
catalyst

sâzemân dâdan: verb
To organize

sâzesh: noun
collusion - agreement

sâzo âvâz: noun
concert

sâzobarg: noun
outfit - ordnance - equipment

sôdâ: noun
trade

sôdâgari: adjective
tradesman - trader - merchant

sôf: noun
camlet

sôgand: noun
oath - sanction - sacrament

sôgand dâdan: verb
To sworn - To conjure

sôgand khordan: verb
To swear - To oath

sôgandnôme: noun
affidavit

sôghât: noun
souvenir

sôghât: noun
sovenior

sôgoli: noun
favorite

sôhân: noun
rasp

sôhân zadan: verb
To rasp - To float

sôme'e: noun
monastery - abbey - convent - cloister

sôt: noun
phoneme - voice

sôt: noun
phone

sôti: adjective
sonic - sonant - vowel - vocal - phomenic

sôyâ: noun
soya

t

ta'adi: noun
oppression - abusive - inroad - infringe -
incursion

ta'adi kardan: verb
To trepass - To ingrate - To oppress

ta'adod: noun
multiplicity - plurality

ta'afon: noun
putrefaction - stink - stench

ta'ahod: noun
onus - warranty - guarantee - committal -
commitment - assurance - mandate

ta'ahod dâdan: verb
To plight

ta'ahod kardan: verb
To guarantee - To underwrite - To
undertake

ta'ahod pardâkhtan: noun
subscription

ta'ajob: noun
marvel - wonder

ta'ajob: noun
surprise

ta'ajob kardan: verb
To wonder

ta'alogh: noun
dependency

ta'alogh dâshtan: verb
To belong

ta'alol: noun
delay

ta'alom âvar: adjective
grievous

ta'amod: noun
witting

ta'amodan: adverb
deliberate

ta'amodi: adjective
studied

ta'amogh: noun
cud

ta'amogh kardan: verb
To turnover - To ponder - To deliberate

ta'amol: noun
indecision

ta'amol kardan: verb
To hesitate

ta'aroz: noun
remonstrance - agression - invasion

ta'aroz kardan: verb
To remonstrate

ta'asob: noun
bias - zealotry - zeal - intolerance - prejudice

ta'asof: noun
ruth - regret - greet

ta'asof khordan: verb
To sorrow

ta'asof khordan: verb
To lament - To sorrow

ta'asof âvar: adjective
wretched

ta'asor: noun
regret - greet

ta'asor pazir: adjective
impressionable - passive

ta'asor âvar: adjective
pathetic - heinous

ta'bir: noun
phrase - comment - explanation

ta'bir kardan: verb
To construe - To comment - To phrase

ta'biye: noun
appliance - improvisation - shift - shebang

ta'biye kardan: verb
To workout - To contrive - To improvise

ta'dib: noun
discipline - correction

ta'dib kardan: verb
To correct - To discipline

ta'dil kardan: verb
To adjustment

ta'dil kardan: noun
modify - moderate - adjust - adapt

ta'dil konande: adjective
regulator

ta'ghib: noun
chase-chace - pursuit

ta'ghib kardan: verb
To tail - To pursue - To suit - To follow - To chase

ta'jil: noun
hasten

ta'khir: noun
delay - demur

ta'khir kardan: verb
To linger - To lag - To delay - To defer

ta'kid: noun
emphasis - stress

ta'kid kardan: verb
To stress - To underline

ta'lif: noun
essay - compilation

ta'lif kardan: verb
To write - To compile

ta'ligh: noun
suspension - abeyance - precipitant - hang

ta'lim: noun
tuition - edification - doctrine

ta'lim dâdan: verb
To guide - To educate - To teach

ta'm: noun
taste - flavor

ta'mid: noun
baptism

ta'mim: noun
popularization - universalization

ta'mim dâdan: verb
To generalize - To distribute

ta'min: noun
security - secure

ta'mir: noun
reparation - renovation - maintenance - upkeep

ta'mir kardan: verb
To patch - To mend - To repair

ta'mir pazir: adjective
reparable

ta'mirgâh: noun
shootinggallery

ta'mirkâr: noun
serviceman

ta'ne: noun
scoff - satire

ta'ne zadan: verb
To taunt - To quip

ta'ne âmiz: adjective
sardonic - sarcastic

ta'rif: noun
quantification - compliment - explanation - description - definition

ta'rif kardan: verb
To praise - To recount - To define

ta'sir: noun
effect - influence

ta'sirpazir: adjective
impressible

ta'sis kardan: verb
To establish - To constitute - To invent - To institute

ta'sisât: noun
installation

ta'til: noun
holiday - vacation

ta'til kardan: verb
To vacate - To stop - To shut

ta'til shodan: verb
To shut

ta'tiliye movaghati: noun
recess

ta'vigh: noun
procrastination - deferment

ta'vil: noun
gloss - paraphrase

ta'viz: noun
replacement - refill - switch - substitute - shift - turnover

ta'viz kardan: verb
To shift - To supplant - To substitute

ta'yid: noun
support - endorsement - grace

ta'yin: noun
nomination - avow - appointment

ta'yin kardan: verb
To determine - To prescribe - To qualify - To appoint

ta'yin konande: adjective
determinant

ta'yine gheimat: noun
appraisal

ta'zim: noun
bow - curtsy - obeisance

ta'zim kardan: verb
To bow - To bend - To beck

ta'âdol: noun
equilibrium - parity - par

ta'âli: noun
sublimity - ascendency - eminence

ta'ârof: noun
salutation - compliment - comity - chivalry

ta'âvon: noun
cooperation

tab': noun
impression - impress

tab'id: noun
expultion - exile

tab'id kardan: verb
To abandon - To deport - To exile

tab'iz: noun
prejudice

tab'iz âmiz: adjective
prejudicial

tab'ize nezhâdi: noun
segregation - racism

taba'e: noun
citizen

taba'eye yek keshvar: noun
citizen

taba'iyat: noun
allegiance - adherence

tabaghe: noun
category - class

tabaghe bandi: noun
classification

tabah kâr: adjective
wicked - untoward - villain

tabah kâri: noun
villainy - crime

tabar: noun
ax - chopper

tabasom: noun
smile

tabdil: noun
conversion

tabdil kardan: verb
To transmute - To transform - To convert

tabi'at: noun
nature

tabi'i: adjective
natural - normal

tabib: noun
leech - medico - medic

tabkh kardan: verb
To bake

tabkhir kardan: verb
To vaporize - To evaporate

tabkhir shodan: verb
To evaporate - To vaporize

tabl: noun
drum

table: noun
belly

tabligh: noun
advertisement - propagation - propaganda

tabligh kardan: verb
To advertise

tablighât: noun
advertisement - publicity - propaganda

tablighât kardan: verb
To proselyte - To propagandize

tabotâb: noun
flame - ardor

tabrik goftan: verb
To greet - To congratulate

tabâdol: noun
exchange

tabâdol kardan: verb
To interchange - To exchange

tabâh kardan: verb
To destroy - To ruin

tabâh shodan: verb
To vitiate

tabâhi: noun
spoil - destruction - depravity - decay

tabâhkonande: adjective
corrosive

tabâl: noun
beater

tabâni: noun
collusion - cahoot

tabâr: noun
tribe - race

tadbir: noun
plan - machination - scheme

tadfin: noun
interment

488

tadlis kardan: verb
To dissemble

tadrij: noun
gradually

tadriji: adjective
slow - imperceptible - piecemeal - gradual

tadris: noun
teaching - training

tadris kardan: verb
To profess - To lesson - To teach

tadârok: noun
preparation - provision

tadârok didan: verb
To supply

tadârokât: noun
munition

tafahos: noun
disquisition

tafahos kardan: verb
To hunt - To dive

tafakor: noun
thought - cud

tafakor kardan: verb
To ponder - To consider - To speculate

tafanoni: noun
fancy

tafaroj: noun
promenade - outing

tafaroj kardan: verb
To promenade

tafarojgâh: noun
promenade

tafavogh: noun
supremacy - advantage - prevalence - vantage

tafavogh jostan: verb
To surpass

tafhim: noun
realization

tafkik: noun
segregation - segregate

tafkik kardan: verb
To separate - To centrifuge - To partition

tafkik konande: adjective
diacritic

tafkik shodan: verb
To part

tafkikpazir: adjective
severable

tafraghe: noun
division - sequester - schism

tafraghe andâz: adjective
divisive

tafre: noun
procrastination - evasion

tafre raftan: verb
To dodge - To evade - To avoid

tafrigh kardan: verb
To deduce

tafrih: noun
recreation - diversion

tafrih kardan: verb
To game - To recreate

tafrihgâh: noun
playground

tafrihi: adjective
social - sport - sport

tafsil: noun
gloss - circumstance - detail

tafsili: adjective
formal

tafsir: noun
commentary - comment - exposition -
explanation

tafsir: noun
interpretation

tafsir kardan: verb
To interpret

taftish: noun
detection

taftish kardan: verb
To inspect

tafviz: noun
submission - investiture - resignation

tafviz kardan: verb
To vouchsafe - To lodge - To resign - To
abdicate

tafâkhor kardan: verb
To pride

tafâsil: noun
detail

tafâvot: noun
difference - diversity - discrepancy

tafâvot: noun
difference

tafâvot dâshtan: verb
To differ

tagarg: noun
hailstone

tagarg: noun
hail

tagh tagh: adverb
clack - rattle

tagh'yir: noun
change

tagh'yir dahande: noun
transformer - changer

tagh'yir dâdan: verb
To alter - To interchange - To modify - To
change

tagh'yir kardan: verb
To revolve - To change

tagh'yir nâpazir: adjective
unalterable - immutable - ireversible -
inelastic

tagh'yire alâmat: noun
duff

tagh'yire fasl: noun
season

tagh'yire fekr: noun
quirk

tagh'yire fâhesh: noun
upheaval

tagh'yire jahat: noun
turquoise - shift

tagh'yire jahat dâdan: verb
To veer - To shunt

tagh'yire makân: noun
movement - move - shift

tagh'yire nâgahâni: noun
quirk - revulsion - mutation

tagh'yire shekl: noun
transiguration - paramorphic

tagh'yire shekl dâdan: verb
To misshape - To transform - To transfigure

tagh'yirpazir: adjective
convertible - changeable - variable

tagh'yirpaziri: noun
variation

taghabol kardan: adjective
undertake

taghadom: noun
primacy - preference - lead

taghados: noun
sanctity - sacrosanctity - holiness -
venerability

taghalob: noun
slur - skulduggery - cross

taghalob kardan: verb
To sharpen

taghalobi: adjective
unfeigned - unfathered

taghalâ: noun
wrestle - effort - scrabble - tug

taghalâ kardan: verb
To struggle - To wrestle - To attempt - To
labor

taghayor: noun
huff

taghbih kardan: adjective
denounce - decry

taghdim: noun
offer - proffer - presentation

taghdim kardan: verb
To tender

taghdir: noun
thank - fate - ordinance - destiny -
destination

taghdir kardan: verb
To appreciate

taghdis: noun
edification - canonization - veneration

taghdis kardan: verb
To sancify - To bless - To hallow - To
enshrine - To edify

taghir yâftan: verb
To alter

taghiye: noun
reservation

taghlid: noun
fake - mimicry - mime - imitation -
burlesque

taghlidi: adjective
imitative

taghlil: noun
depletion - cutback - diminution - reduction

taghlil dahande: adjective
reducer

taghlil dâdan: verb
To lessen - To weaken - To cutdown

taghlil yâftan: verb
To lessen - To diminish

taghliz: noun
condensation - concentrate

taghrib: noun
access

taghriban: adverb
almost

taghribi: adjective
approximate - proximate

taghrir: noun
statement - emprise

taghsim: noun
division - cleavage

taghsim kardan: verb
To divide - To distribute - To compartment

taghsim konande: adjective
denominator - divisive

taghsim shodan: verb
To devide

taghsir: noun
guilt - delinquency - crime

taghvim: noun
calendar

taghvim kardan: verb
To appraise

taghviyat: noun
nutrition - reinforcement - amplification -
abet

taghviyat dâdan: verb
To strengthen

taghviyat kardan: verb
To reinforce - To bolster

taghviyat konande: adjective
reinforcer - booster - amplifier

taghviyat shodan: verb
To invigorate

taghvâ: noun
piety - pietism - virtue

taghziye: noun
nutrition - nurture - nourishment - nourish - sustenance

taghziye kardan: verb
To pasture

taghâbol: noun
contrast

taghârob: noun
convergence

taghâron: noun
symmetry - polarity - parallelism

taghâza: noun
request - plea

taghâzâ kardan: verb
To demand

taghâzâ konande: adjective
applicant

tah: noun
bottom - base

tah chek: noun
stub

tah keshidan: verb
To peter

tahadob: noun
bulge

tahaghogh: noun
realization

tahaghogh yâftan: verb
To comeoff - To realize

tahajor: noun
calcification

tahakom kardan: verb
To domineer

tahakom âmiz: adjective
imperious

tahamol: noun
tolerance - endurance

tahamol kardan: verb
To undergo - To bear - To withstand - To endure - To tolerate

tahamol pazir: adjective
endurable

tahamole khesarat: noun
toll

taharok: noun
stimulus - mobility

tahason: noun
refuge

tahavo' âvar: adjective
queasy - nauseous

tahavol: noun
upheaval - evolution - change

tahavole shadid: adjective
upthrow

tahavor: noun
impetuosity - temerity

tahdid: noun
limitation - restriction

tahdid: noun
threat - blackmail - menace

tahdid âmiz: adjective
minatory - black

tahghigh: noun
scrutiny - scholarship - research

tahghigh: noun
disquisition

tahghigh kardan: verb
To investigate - To inquire - To research

tahghir: noun
scorn - humility - disdain - contempt

tahghir âmiz: adjective
contemptuous - pejorative

tahiye: noun
provision - procurement

tahiye kardan: verb
To cater - To produce

tahkim kardan: verb
To strengthen - To bully - To prestress

tahlil: noun
resolution - corrosion - erosion - analysis

tahlil bordan: verb
To stub - To imbibe - To useup - To undermine - To absorb

tahlil kardan: verb
To analyze

tahlil raftan: verb
To dwindle - To consume - To gnaw - To assimilate

tahmil: noun
protrusion - incurrence - imposition

tahmil kardan: verb
To constrain - To inflict - To protrude

tahmânde: noun
scrap - silt - riffraff

tahniyat: noun
salutation

tahniyat goftan: verb
To salute

tahrif: noun
anagram - distortion - garble - sophistication

tahrif kardan: verb
To distort - To agonize

tahrif shodan: verb
To mutilate

tahrik: noun
incitement - provacation - stimulus

tahrik kardan: verb
To provoke - To stimulate - To arouse - To instigate

tahrik pazir: adjective
irritable

tahrik shodan: verb
To induce

tahrim: noun
prohibition - embargo - interdict - boycott

tahrim kardan: verb
To boycott - To blackball - To ban - To proscribe - To prohibit

tahrir kardan: verb
To write - To redact

tahrirdâr: adjective
tremulous

tahriri: adjective
scribal

tahrish: noun
stubble - tuft

tahsigâr: noun
snip - stump - stub

tahsil: noun
study

tahsil kardan: verb
To study

tahsin: noun
praise - applause

tahsin: noun
sanctuary

tahsin kardan: verb
To applaud - To admire

tahte feshâr: adjective
impacted - beneath

tahte mohâsere: adjective
enclave

tahte nofuz: adjective
beneath

tahte ta'sir gharâr dâdan: verb
To influence

tahte ta'sir vâghe shodan: verb
To react

tahte tasalot: adjective
subject - under

tahtol'lafzi: noun
verbatim - verbal - literal

tahtâni: noun
beneath

tahvil: noun
transfer - delivery

tahvil dâdan: verb
To deliver

tahvil dâr: noun
cashier

tahvildâr: noun
teller

tahviye: noun
ventilation

tahviye kardan: verb
To ventilate

tahyij: noun
excitement - fry - incitement

tahyij kardan: verb
To stimulate - To motivate

tahzib: noun
polish - edification - reformation -
refinement

tahâjom: noun
invasion - inroad - agression

tahâl: noun
spleen

tahârat: noun
purity

tahâtor: noun
cambium - dicker

tajali: noun
expression - influence - phenomenon

tajali kardan: verb
To transfigure - To emanate

tajamo': noun
aggregation

tajamol: noun
pomp - luxe

tajamoli: noun
fancy

tajarod: noun
bachelorhood

tajasom: noun
portrayal - incarnation - projection - shape

tajasome ruh: noun
ghost

tajasos: noun
search - research

tajdid: noun
renewal - resumption - restoration -
repetition

tajdide banâ: noun
reconstruction

tajdide ghovâ: noun
rest - refection

tajdide hayât: noun
resurgence - renascence - rebirth

tajdide khâtere: noun
recollection

tajdide nazar: noun
revision - revisal - review - reconsideration

tajhiz: noun
outfit

tajhiz kardan: verb
To outfit

tajhizât: noun
materiel - equipment

tajlil: noun
homage - celebration - kudos

tajlil kardan: verb
To exalt - To ennoble - To glorify - To celebrate

tajlili: adjective
honorific

tajrobe: noun
experiment - experience

tajrobe kardan: verb
To experiment - To experience

tajrobi: adjective
tentative

tajviz: noun
prescription - approval

tajviz kardan: verb
To prescribe

tajyinât: noun
decorations

tajziye: noun
analysis - breakup

tajziye kardan: verb
To decompose - To breakdown - To analyze - To abstract

tajziye nâpazir: adjective
irresolvable - indissoluble

tajziye pazir: adjective
dissoluble

tajziye shodan: verb
To parse - To disintegrate

tajziye talab: adjective
secessionist

tajziye talabi: noun
secessionism - secession

tajâhol: noun
evasion

tajânos: noun
congruity - congruence

tajâvoz: noun
violation - assault - agression - offense

tajâvoz kardan: verb
To invade - To impinge - To molest - To trepass

tajâyike: preposition
insofaras

tak: noun
solo - solitaire - singular - single - one - odd

tak khân: adjective
soloist

tak navâz: adjective
soloist

tak tak: adverb
sporadic

tak yâkhte: noun
protozoan

takadi kardan: verb
To panhandle

takafol: noun
sponsorship

takalom: noun
language

takalom kardan: verb
To speak

takbir: noun
insolence - height - pride - arrogance - ruffe

takfir: noun
commination

takfir kardan: verb
To excommunicate

takh kardan: verb
To embitter

takhalof: noun
trepass - transgression - delinquency

takhalof kardan: verb
To infract

takhalos: noun
pseudonym

takhasos: noun
proficiency - specialty

takhati: noun
outrage - trepass

takhati az ghânun: noun
misdemeanor

takhati kardan: verb
To offend - To impinge

takhayol: noun
specter

takhayolât: noun
vagary

takhdir: noun
stupefaction

takhdir kardan: verb
To drug - To dope - To stupefy

takhfif: noun
discount - remission - refraction - rebate

takhfif dâdan: verb
To abate - To discount

takhfif yâftan: verb
To scant - To lessen

takhfife dard: noun
analgesia

takhliye kardan: verb
To vacate

takhmin: noun
estimate - approximation

takhmin zadan: verb
To estimate

takhmir: noun
fermentation - zymosis

takhmir kardan: verb
To quicken

takhmir shodan: verb
To yeast

takhrib: noun
subversion - destruction - demolition

takhsis: noun
devotion - designation

takhsis dâdan: verb
To designate - To allot

takht: noun
sole - throne - couch

takhte: noun
sheet - tablet - gob - board

takhte nard: noun
backgammon

takhte sang: noun
cliff - roach - boulder

takhte siyâh: noun
blackboard

takhte'I: adjective
board

takhtekhâb: noun
hay

takhteye shatranj: noun
chessboard

takhtân: noun
terrace

taklif: noun
task - imposition - duty

takmil: noun
replete - compietion

takmil kardan: verb
To supplement - To perfect - To round

takmili: adjective
supplementary

takrim: noun
tribute - reverence - veneration

takrim kardan: verb
To venerate - To dignify - To glorify

taksir: noun
propagation - reproduction

takvin: noun
development - genesis

takvini: adjective
developmental - genetic

takzib: noun
disproof - denial - refutation - rebuttal

takzib kardan: verb
To impugn - To refute - To deny

takâfu: noun
adequacy

takâpu: noun
search - prowl - roam

takâpu kardan: verb
To scour

takâvar: noun
commando

tal: noun
plume - hill

tala'lo: noun
sparkle - glitter - glint

talab: noun
demand - quest

talab kardan: verb
To invoke - To fish

talabidan: verb
To seek - To ask - To invite - To crave

talabkâr: adjective
creditor

talaf kardan: verb
To squander - To lose - To misspend

talaf shodan: verb
To perish

talafoz: noun
pronunciation - accent - intonation

talafoz kardan: verb
To enunciate - To vocalize - To pronounce

talafât: noun
casualty - victim

talagh talagh: noun
jolt

talake kardan: verb
To mooch

talamoz: noun
pupilage

tale: noun
trap - hook - noose - snare

tale: noun
trap

tale andâkhtan: verb
To entrap

tale mush: noun
rattrap

talgh: noun
talc - isinglass

talghin: noun
compilation - reconciliation - incorporation

talghin kardan: verb
To inculcate - To insinuate - To indoctrinate

talkh: noun
bitter - virulent

talkhi: noun
poignancy - virulence - gall

talkhis: noun
precis

talkho shirin: adjective
bittersweet

talvihan goftan: verb
To mince

talâ: noun
gold

talâfi: noun
retribution - retort - restitution - reprisal - repay

talâfi kardan: verb
To meet

talâfi kardan: verb
To retaliate - To reprisal - To reciprocate - To avenge

talâgh: noun
divorce

talâkubi: noun
inlay

talâsh: noun
endeavor - effort

talâsh kardan: verb
To endeavor - To effort

talâsâz: noun
goldsmith

talâtom: noun
turbulence - toss

talâtom dâshtan: verb
To roll

talâyi: adjective
auburn - golden - gilt

tam'mâ': noun
greedy - avaricious

tama': noun
greed - avidity - avarice

tamadon: noun
culture

tamanâ kardan: verb
To request

tamarkoz: noun
centralization

tamarkoz yâftan: verb
To centennial - To center

tamarod: noun
contumacy - recalcitrance - rebellion

tamarod: noun
insurgency

tamarod kardan: verb
To rebel

tamaskhor: noun
sneer - scorn - scoff

tamaskhor kardan: verb
To ridicule - To deride - To scoff

tamavoj: noun
undulation

tamavol: noun
wealth

tamdid: noun
revival - extension

tamdid kardan: verb
To extend

tameshk: noun
razz - raspberry

tamhid: noun
scheme - appliance - device - contrivance

tamhid: verb
To vamp

tamiz: noun
clean - neat - pure

tamiz: adjective
spiffy - clean

tamiz dâdan: verb
To distinguish - To discern

tamiz kardan: adjective
scourer

tamiz kardan: verb
To cleanse - To clean - To scrub - To scavenge

tamjid: noun
plaudit - stratagem

tamjid: noun
ploy

tamjid kardan: verb
To exalt - To laud

tamkin: noun
deference - stoop

tamkin kardan: verb
To deign - To condescend

tamr: noun
stamp

tamr: noun
stamp

tamrin: noun
practice - exercise - rehearsal

tamrin dâdan: verb
To experience - To exercise

tamsil: noun
parable - allegory

tamsil: noun
allegory

tamâm: noun
entire - complete - full - whole

tamâm ayâr: adjective
sterling - hipandthigh - perfect

tamâm kardan: verb
To end - To die

tamâm shodan: verb
To finish

tamâman: adverb
altogether - all - wholly - throughout

tamâmiyat: noun
totality - integrity - entirety

tamâmo kamâl: adjective
thoroughgoing - consummate - wholly

tamâroz kardan: verb
To malinger

tamâs: noun
contact

tamâs yâftan: verb
To contact

tamâshâ: noun
spectacle - sight

tamâshâchi: noun
bystander - onlooker

tamâshâchi budan: verb
To spectate

tamâshâgar: adjective
spectator - viewer - bystander

tamâshâkhâne: noun
opera - theater

tamâshâyi: adjective
spectacular

tamâyol: noun
tendency

tamâyol dâshtan: verb
To desire

tan: noun
body

tan dar dâdan: verb
To acquiescence - To acquiesce - To accede

tanafor: noun
abhorrence - hatred - hate - disgust

tanafor dâshtan: verb
To abhor - To mislike - To detest

tanafor âvar: adjective
revulsive - repulsive

tanafore shadid: noun
revulsion

tanafos: noun
intake - respiration - recess

tanafos kardan: verb
To inhale

tanavo': noun
variety - diversity

tanazol: noun
depression - setback

tanazol dâdan: verb
To reduce - To playdown - To lower

tanazole gheimat: noun
cutrate

tanazole gheimat: verb
To fall - To decline - To decay

tanazole rotbe: noun
demotion

tanbal: adjective
lazy - inactive - idle

tanbali: noun
indolence - inaction - sloth

tanbali kardan: verb
To laze

tanbih: noun
punishment

tanbihi: adjective
pnitive

tanbâku: noun
tobacco

tandis: noun
statue

tandis: noun
tennis

tandisgar: adjective
sculptor

tandorost: adjective
healthy - well

tandorosti: noun
health

tane zadan: verb
To shove - To jostle - To hunch

taneye derakht: noun
bough

tanfiz kardan: verb
To validate

tang: adjective
tight

tangdast: adjective
indigent - underprivileged

tangdasti: noun
distress

tangdasti: noun
poverty

tange: noun
strait - neck - gut - canyon - bottleneck

tangi: noun
stricture - drouth

tangiye nafas: noun
asthma

tangnazar: adjective
insular

tangnâ: noun
impasse - hairbreadth - bottleneck

tangrâh: noun
bottleneck

tanhayi: noun
privacy - solitude

tanhâ: adjective
single - alone - lonely

tanhâ gozashtan: verb
To strand

tanidan: verb
To spin

tanin: noun
sonance - ring - resonance - noise

tanin: noun
tingle

tanin afkandan: verb
To din

tanin andâkhtan: verb
To ting - To reverberate

tanumand: adjective
sturdy - stalwart - rugged - robust - corpulent

tanur: noun
oven

tanz: noun
scoff - satire - quip

tanzil: noun
interest

tanzim: noun
alignment - adjustment

tanzim kardan: verb
To modulate - To adjust

tanâb: noun
tow - line - rope - reeve

tanâbe: noun
humor

tanâghoz: noun
incoherence - antithesis - repugnance - inconsistency

tanâsob: noun
cooridnation - congruence - proportion

tanâsoli: noun
sexual - genie

tanâvob: noun
shift - alternation - frequency

tanâvobi: adjective
alternative - alternating

tanâz: adjective
coquette

tanâzi kardan: verb
To coquette

tanâzo': noun
struggle

tapande: verb
To palpitant

tape: noun
mount - hill

tapesh: noun
beat - pant - pitterpatter - tremor - throb - pump

tapeshe del: noun
heartbeat

tapidan: verb
To throb - To pulse - To beat

tapânche: noun
pistol

tapândan: verb
To stuff

tar: adjective
humid - moist - rainy - wet

tar kardan: verb
To moisten - To wet - To dab

tar shodan: verb
To moisten

tarab: noun
joviality - jollification - jocularity

tarabangiz: adjective
jovial

taradod kardan: verb
To traffic

taraf: noun
face - opponent - side

tarafdâr: adjective
fan - advocate

tarafdâr budan: verb
To adhere

tarafdâri: noun
adhesion - devotion

tarafe moghâbel: noun
obverse

taragh torugh: noun
crack

taraghe: noun
cracker

taraghi: noun
promotion - progress - boost - ascent - development

taraghi dâdan: verb
To advance - To boost - To promote

taraghi kardan: verb
To climb - To remunerate - To grow - To upwell

tarahom: noun
pathos

tarahom kardan: verb
To pity

tarak: noun
crack - chap - fracture

tarak khordegi: noun
fraction

tarakidan: verb
To explode - To burst

tarakidegi: noun
bust

tarakândan: verb
To chap - To pop - To blowup - To blast

tarashoh: noun
discharge - sprinkle - splutter

tarashoh kardan: verb
To sprinkle - To plash - To discharge

tarbiyat: noun
upbringing - pedagogy - gentry

tarbiyat kardan: verb
To train - To educate

tarbiyati: adjective
cultural

tard: noun
ostracism

tard krdan: verb
To excommunicate

tardasti: noun
swiftness

tardid: noun
suspicion - skepticism - uncertainty - doubt

tardid dâshtan: verb
To scruple - To stagger - To vacillate

tardid kardan: verb
To stick - To totter - To doubt

tarekânidan: verb
To detonate - To crack

tarfi': noun
raise - upgrade - preferment - preference -
promotion

targhib: noun
persuasion

targhib kardan: verb
To persuade

targhigh: noun
rarefaction

targhikhâh: adjective
progressive

targhove: noun
clavicle

tarh: noun
pattern - plot - plan - draft - - skeleton -
proposal

tarh kardan: verb
To draft - To frame - To chart - To cast

tarh rikhtan: verb
To model

tarhrizi: noun
skeleton - schematization - projection

tarigh: noun
way - method

tarighat: noun
path

tarighe: noun
method

tarjihan: adverb
rather

tarjome: noun
version - rendition

tarjome kardan: verb
To translate - To interpret

tarjomân: noun
translator - dragoman

tark goftan: verb
To abdicate - To walkouton

tark goftan: verb
To abandon

tark kardan: verb
To relinquish - To disuse - To leave

tark khorde: adjective
clef

tarkdâr: adjective
rimose

tarke: noun
twig

tarke aghide: noun
apostasy

tarke khedmat: noun
desertion

tarke'l: adjective
wicker

tarkesh: noun
quiver

tarkhis: noun
release

tarkhis kardan: verb
To release

tarkib: noun
syntax - blend - mixture - compound

tarkib kardan: verb
To constitute - To incorporate - To merge

tarmim: noun
relief

tarmim kardan: verb
To amend - To rehabilitate - To reform

taro tamiz: adjective
trim - shipshape

taro tâze: adjective
pristine - green - fresh - spannew

tars: noun
fear - dread - horror - awful

tarsidan: verb
To abhor - To scare

tarside: adjective
afraid

tarsim kardan: verb
To trace - To map

tarsim nemudan: verb
To delineate

tarsimi: adjective
graphic

tarsnâk: adjective
terrific - terrible - tremendous - horrid - hideous - nightmarish

tarsnâk: adjective
scary

tarsu: adjective
skittish - shy - sheepish - shamefaced - timorous - timid

tarsu: adjective
timid

tarsânande: adjective
deterrent - scaremonger - scarer

tarsândan: verb
To threat - To scare - To daunt - To fright -
To fray - To intimidate - To horrify

tarsânidan: verb
To threat - To scare - To daunt - To fright -
To fray - To intimidate - To horrify

tarsâvar: adjective
phobic - fearful - horrible - bloodcurdling -
awesome

tartib: noun
layout - collocation - rank - discipline - setup

tartib dâdan: verb
To arrange

tartibi: adjective
serial - ordinal

tarvij: noun
promotion

tarvij kardan: verb
To cultivate - To promulgate - To promote

taryâk: noun
opium

tarz: noun
method

tarze barkhord: noun
front - attitude

tarze fekr: noun
ideology

tarze fekr: noun
mentality

tarzekâr: noun
workmanship

tarâbari: noun
transport

tarâh: noun
designer - sketcher

tarâhi kardan: verb
To contour

tarâkom: noun
density - congeries - compression

tarâshe: noun
chip - excelsior - splint - slither

tarâshidan: verb
To shave - To raze - To erase

tarâshidegi: noun
erasure

tarâvat: noun
effervescence

tarâz: noun
even - level - balance - slight

tarâzu: noun
balance

tarâzu: noun
scale

tasadi: noun
tenure - incumbency - commission

tasali dahande: adjective
comforter

tasali dâdan: verb
To solace - To relieve - To cherish - To console

tasalot: noun
gripe - dominance

tasalsol: noun
progression - sequence - continuity

tasano'l: noun
sophisticated - mannered

tasarof: noun
seizure - tenure - occupation - occupancy - possession

tasarof kardan: verb
To grab - To hold

tasavor: noun
supposition - image - idea - vision

tasavor kardani: adjective
conceivable

tasavor nakardani: adjective
inconceivable

tasavore ghalat: noun
misconception

tasavore koli: noun
concept

tasavorât: noun
imagery

tasbih: noun
hallelujah - rosary

tasbit kardan: verb
To stabilize - To confirm - To reinstate

tasdigh: noun
ratification - acknohledgement - testimony

tasdigh kardan: verb
To justify - To affirm - To confirm - To recognize - To certify

tasdigh nâme: noun
testimonial

tasfiye: noun
catharsis - infiltration - administration - settlement - settle

tasfiye khâne: noun
refinery

tasfiye konande: adjective
cathartic

tasha'sho: noun
glare - refulgence - ray - radiance - flash

tasha'sho' dâshtan: verb
To ray

tashakor: noun
thank

tashakor kardan: verb
To thank

tashanoj: noun
tension - convulsion

tashar zadan: verb
To browbeat

tashar zadan: verb
To intimidate

tashbih: noun
metaphor - comparison - simile

tashdid: noun
accent - intensification

tashdid: noun
resonance

tashdid kardan: verb
To intensify - To exasperate - To exacerbate

tashdid konande: adjective
booster

tashghis: noun
diagnosis

tashig: noun
correction - rectification - amendment

tashih kardan: verb
To emendate - To emend - To refine - To rectify

tashim kardan: verb
To whack - To portion

tashkhis: noun
recognition

tashkhis: verb
To recognize - To distinguish - To discern

tashkhishe hoviyat dâdan: verb
To identify

tashkhishi: adjective
diagnostic

tashkil dahande: adjective
constitutive - fundametal - former

tashkil dâdan: verb
To form - To constitute

tashkil shode: adjective
wrought

tashkilât: noun
organization - brigade

tashrifât: noun
ritual - ceremony - ceremonial

tashrifâti: adjective
ceremonial

tashrih: noun
surgery - description - dissection - anatomy

tashrih: noun
innuendo

tashrihi: noun
explanatory - interpretive

tashrike masâ'l: noun
cooperation - collaborate

tasht: noun
tub

tashvigh: noun
eulogy - abet - persuasion

tashvigh kardan: verb
To cheer - To countenance - To encourage

tashvigh va targhib kardan: verb
To exhort

tashvighi: adjective
persuasive

tashvish: noun
phobia - anxiety

tashâboh: noun
similarity - resemblance

taskhir: noun
capture

taskhir kardan: verb
To conquer

taskhir nâpazir: adjective
unconquerable - indomitable

taskin: noun
solace - sedation - relief

taskin dahande: adjective
sooth - sedate - pacifier

taskin dâdan: verb
To pacify - To appease - To placate - To smooth

taslihât: noun
armament - weaponry

taslim: noun
submission - resignation - rendition

taslim kardan: verb
To lodge - To cede - To consign

taslim shodan: verb
To surrender - To succumb - To capitulate

tasliyat: verb
To solace

tasliyat: noun
condolence

tasliyat dâdan: verb
To console - To condole

tasme: noun
lash - belt - bail

tasme: noun
strap

tasmim: noun
pluck - avow - decision - resolution - canon

tasmim gereftan: verb
To determine - To decide - To resolve

tasnif: noun
song - sing - ballad - impromptu

tasnif kardan: verb
To compose - To make

tasri': noun
speedup - expedition

tasri' kardan: verb
To precipitate - To accelerate

tasrih: noun
speciosity - specification

tasrih kardan: verb
To specify - To affirm - To reiterate

tastih kardan: verb
To surface - To grade

tasvib: noun
sanction - resolution - ratification - approval

tasvib kardan: verb
To approve - To resolute - To ratify

tasvibnâme: noun
resolution

tasvibnâme: noun
canon

tasvir: noun
portrait - vignette - image

tasvir kardan: verb
To figure - To portrait

tasvir keshidan: verb
To portray

tasvirbardâr: noun
cameraman

tasvirbardâri: noun
xerography

tasviri: adjective
figurative - pictorial

tasviye: noun
solution - settlement - settle - adjustment

tasviye kardan: verb
To defray - To compromise - To liquidate -
To payoff

tasviye nemudan: verb
To adjust

tasâdof: noun
occasion - coincidence - encounter -
accidence

tasâdof: noun
accident

tasâdof kardan: verb
To jar - To hurtle - To bop

tasâdofan: adverb
peradventure

tasâdofi: adjective
accident - random - chanceful

tasâdofât: noun
casualty

tasâdom: noun
smash - shock - collission - clash -
concussion

tasâhob kardan: verb
To seis

tasâod: noun
progression

tasâodi: adjective
progressive

tasâvi: noun
parity - par - equality

tasâviye hoghugh: noun
equity

513

tatame: noun
remanence

tatbigh: noun
comparison - collation - harmony -
adjustment

tatbigh kardan: verb
To tally - To reconcile - To fit

tatbigh nemudan: verb
To accommodate

tatbighi: adjective
comparative

tathir: noun
catharsis - purge

tathir: noun
auspices

tathir kardan: verb
To sancify - To purge - To expurgate - To
cleanse

tatmi': noun
lure - entice

tatmi' kardan: verb
To bribe - To allure

tatvil: noun
prolongation

tatâbogh: noun
accordance

tavagho': noun
expectancy

tavaghof: noun
stop - stay - pause - cessation - cease

tavaghof kardan: verb
To stop - To stay - To stand

tavaghofgâh: noun
stay

tavajoh: noun
tendency - consideration - remark - regard

tavajoh kardan: verb
To attend - To assist - To mark - To ward

tavajohât: noun
auspices

tavakol: noun
trust - reliance

tavalod: noun
get - geniture - birth

tavarogh: noun
slate

tavarom: noun
inflation

tavasol: noun
recourse

tavasot: noun
per - via

tavil: adjective
major - long - lengthy

tavile: noun
stable - barn

tavâbe': noun
environs

tavâfi kardan: verb
To hawk - To vend - To peddle

tavâfogh: noun
understanding - agreement - accordance -
accord - rapport

tavâfogh dâshtan: verb
To adhere

tavâfoghi: adjective
adaptive

tavâli: noun
subsequence - sequence - progression

tavân: noun
vigor - power - potency - exponent

tavânbakhsh: noun
rehabilitation

tavângar: adjective
wealthy - rich

tavângari: noun
opulence

tavânâ: adjective
mighty - authoritative - able - capable

tavânâyi: noun
strength - authority - ability

tavâzo': noun
obeisance - courtesy - humility

tavâzo' kardan: verb
To condescend

tavâzon: noun
balance - poise - harmony

tayâre: noun
aircraft - aeroplane

taz'if kardan: verb
To unbrace - To castrate

taz'ife ruhiye kardan: verb
To demoralize - To cow

taz'yi': noun
wastage

tazakor: noun
hint - mention - remembrance - notification

tazakor dâdan: verb
To warn - To callup

tazalom: noun
plaint - petition

tazalzol: noun
shake - insecurity

tazalzol nâpazir: adjective
adamant - imperturbable

tazaro': noun
imprecation

tazkiye: noun
refinement

tazmin: noun
guaranty - warranty - collateral - assurance

tazmin kardan: verb
To bond - To ensure - To certify - To warrant

tazmin konande: adjective
voucher

tazrigh: noun
infusion - shot - transfusion

tazrighe khun: noun
transfusion

tazvir: noun
artifice - wile - duplicity

tazvir kardan: verb
To fox

tazyin kardan: verb
To decorate

tazyini: adjective
complement

tazâd: noun
confliction - conflict - opposition

tazâhor: noun
ostentation - display - pretension - pretense

tazâhor kardan: verb
To sham - To assume

tazâhorât: noun
parade

tazâhorât kardan: verb
To demonstrate

te'dâd: noun
some

teb: noun
medicine - physic

tebghe: noun
tray

tebi: adjective
medico

tebâbat kardan: verb
To doctor

tefl: noun
baby - babe - infant - child

tegh kardan: verb
To crack

tei: noun
duration

tei kardan: verb
To traverse - To negotiate - To cover

tei shodan: verb
To blowover

teif: noun
spectrum

tejarat: noun
commerce - trade

tejârat kardan: verb
To commerce - To trade

tejârati: adjective
mercantile - commercial

tejâratkhâne: noun
firm

tejâri: adjective
commercial

teke: noun
slice - loaf - item - portion

teke felez: noun
nugget

teke kâghaz: noun
slip

teke teke: adjective
patchy - piecemeal - scrappy

teke teke kardan: verb
To slab

tekrâr: noun
repetition - renewal

tekrâr kardan: verb
To repeat - To renew - To rehearse - To reduplicate

tekrâr konande: adjective
repeater

tekrâr shodan: verb
To recur

tekrâre mokararât: noun
rehash

tekrâri: adjective
repetitive - repetitious

tekye: noun
lean - reliance

tekye dâdan: verb
To rest - To bolster

tekye kalâm: noun
slogan

tekye kardan: verb
To recline - To lean

tekye zadan: verb
To lean

tekyegâh: noun
base - backrest - back

tekân: noun
shake - jostle - jolt - movement - move - motion

tekân dâdan: verb
To move - To shake

tekân khordan: verb
To vibrate - To quake

tekândahande: adjective
jolter - shaker - mover

tekâne sar: noun
nod

tekâne tond: adjective
jerk

tele sheni: noun
dune

telefon: noun
telephone - phone

telefon kardan: verb
To call

telefon zadan: verb
To call

telefonchi: noun
operator

telefoni: adjective
telephonic

telegrâf: noun
telegraphy - telegraph - telegram

telegrâm: noun
telegram

teleskob: noun
telescope

telesm: noun
charm - talisman - spell

telesm kardan: verb
To glamorize

telo telo khor: verb
To tipsy

telvezion: noun
television - video

telô telô khordan: verb
To dodder - To reel - To wobble - To
vacillate - To teeter

temsâh: noun
alligator - crocodile

temsâl: noun
effigy - representation - image - statue

terekidan: verb
To bust

teror kardan: verb
To terrorize

terâs: noun
terrace

terâvat bakhsh: adjective
refresher

teshne: adjective
thirsty

teshne budan: verb
To thirst

teshne shodan: verb
To dry

teshnegi: noun
thirst

tez: noun
dissertation - thesis

that: noun
subject - sub - under

tifus: noun
typhus

tigh: noun
thorn - bur - prick

tighe: noun
blade - knife

tighe âftab: noun
sunrise - sunbeam - streamer

tik: noun
click

tile: noun
marble - dib

tile bâzi: noun
dib - marble

tim: noun
team

timâr: noun
attendance - care

timâr kardan: verb
To groom

timârestan: noun
lunatic asylum

tip: noun
brigade

tir: noun
shot - dart - gunshot - arrow - bar

tir andâkhtan: verb
To shaft

tir keshidan: verb
To prickle

tir'ras: noun
range - gunshot

tirandâzi kardan: verb
To gun

tire: adjective
lurid - ilk - murky - dark - gloomy - turbid

tire: adjective
dark

tire kardan: verb
To gloom - To overcast - To obscure - To fog

tire rang: adjective
dingy - austere

tire ruz: adjective
miserable

tirebakht: adjective
miserable - unlucky

tiregi: noun
obscurity - gloom - fog - muddle - blur

tireotâr: adjective
bleary

tirâhan: noun
beam

tishe: noun
hatchet

tiz: adjective
sharp - incisive - acute - brisk - bitter - keen

tiz hush: adjective
perspicacious - sitted

tiz kardan: verb
To sharpen - To sharp - To whet - To keen

tiz shodan: verb
To sharpen

tizhush: adjective
clever

tizi: noun
pharpness

tizrô: adjective
acute

to'me: noun
prey - victim

to'meye shekâr: noun
hank

tobe: noun
penitence - contrition - repentance

tobe kardan: verb
To repent

tobikh: noun
snuff - reproach - rail - vituperation

tobikh kardan: verb
To reprehend - To rebuke - To rail

tof: noun
spit

tof andâkhtan: verb
To spit

tofang: noun
gun - rifle

tofangdâr: noun
gunman

tofange bâdi: noun
blowgun

tofigh: noun
success

tofuliat: noun
childhood

tofâle: noun
slop - slag - scum - ross - dross - crap - bagasse

toghif kardan: verb
To seize - To detain - To confiscate - To arrest - To apprehend

toghyân: noun
tornado - rebellion - outflow

toghyân kardan: verb
To overflow - To flood

toghyângar: adjective
rebel

tohfe: noun
curio - rarity - trove

tohi: adjective
empty - hollow - vacuous

tohi kardan: verb
To purge - To vacate - To deplete - To exhaust - To evacuate

tohi shodan: verb
To empty

tohid: noun
theism - monotheism

tohidast: adjective
poor - impecunious - indigent

tohin: noun
vituperation - insult - insolence - offense

tohin âmiz: adjective
abusive

tohmat: noun
scandal - defamation - abusive

tohmat zadan: verb
To accuse - To slander - To scandal

tojih kardan: verb
To legtimize - To vindicate - To justify

tojih konande: adjective
justifier

tojihpazir: noun
justification - rationalization

tojihpazir: adjective
justifiable

tokhm: noun
semen - seed - testicle - egg

tokhm dâdan: noun
cyst

tokhm gozâshtan: verb
To hatch

tokhmak: noun
ovum

tokhmdân: noun
ovary - pod

tokhme morgh: noun
egg

tokhmemorghi shekl: noun
oval

tolid kardan: verb
To generate - To produce - To manufacture

tolid konande: adjective
productive - producer - genie

tolombe: noun
ram - pump

tolombe zadan: verb
To pump

tolu': noun
dawn - rise - break - peep

ton: noun
ton

tond: adjective
spicy - fast - keen

tond mezâj: adjective
hot - irritable - peevish

tond raftan: verb
To fleet

tond shodan: verb
To accelerate

tond tond harf zadan: verb
To chatter - To patter

tondar: noun
thunder

tondbâd: noun
hurricane

tondi: adjective
speed - acrimony - rigor - rapidity

tondkhu: adjective
acrid - fierce

tondo tiz: noun
stringent - nippy - astringent - ardent -
peppery

tondrah raftan: verb
To scud

tondro: adjective
swift - speedster - extrimist - fast - rapid -
racer

tong: adjective
narrow - disgrace

tonok: adjective
sparse

topol: adjective
rotund

topoli: noun
squab - rondure

toranj: noun
bergamot

tord: adjective
brittle - crisp

tore: noun
crimp - ringlet - whisker

torki: adjective
Turkish

tormoz: noun
brake

tormoz kardan: verb
To brake

torobche: noun
radish

toroshru: adjective
moody

toroshruyi: noun
scowl - sulk - lower

toroshruyi: noun
austerity - glower

torsh: adjective
sour - tart - acid - acetic

torsh budan: verb
To sour

torshi: noun
pickle - acidity - acerbity - souse

torshi andâkhtan: verb
To pickle

torshide: adjective
overripe - reechy - rancid - frowzy

torshmaze: adjective
tart - sour

torshruyi kardan: verb
To hump

torâ: noun
thee - you

tose' yâftan: verb
To develop

tose'e: noun
extension - development

tose'e dâdan: verb
To develop - To expand - To enlarge

toshak: noun
panel - pad - mattress

toshih: noun
signature

tosif: noun
description

tosif kardan: verb
To portray - To characterize - To describe

tosifi: adjective
descriptive

tosiye: noun
recommendation

tosiye kardan: verb
To advise

tote'e: noun
plot - conspiracy

tozih: noun
statement - comment - explanation -
paraphrase

tozih dâdan: verb
To illustrate - To explain - To elucidate - To
clarify

tozihât: noun
preamble

tu: noun
inside - thou

tu'âlet: noun
toilet

tudahani: noun
slap

tude: noun
bulk - mass - heap - volume

tude: noun
ruck

tude shodan: verb
To drift

tudeye shen: noun
sandpile

tufân: noun
tornado - storm

tufân: noun
flood - hurricane

tufân: noun
slat - shingle - lath

tufâni: adjective
stormy

tufâni: adjective
windy

tughigh: noun
constraint - arrest - suppression

tukhâli: adjective
gash

tul: noun
abscissa - length

tul keshidan: verb
To last

tule: noun
cub - whelp

tule: noun
yelper

tule sag: noun
whelp - puppy - pup

tuli: noun
linear

tulâni: adjective
prolix - long - great

tumur: noun
tumor - growth

tumâr: noun
roll - role - scroll

tunel: noun
tunnel - tube

tup: noun
bluff - artillery - gun

tup bâzi: noun
ball

tupkhâne: noun
ordnance - gunnery - artillery

tur: noun
saveall - net - gauze

tur sâkhtan: verb
To mesh

turaftan: verb
To enter - To retract

turbin: noun
turbine

turi: noun
net - lace

tus: noun
birch

tushe: noun
luggage - provision

tuti: noun
parrot

tutivâr: adverb
parrot

tutun: noun
tobacco

tuye: noun
within - aboard - in - into

tâ: preposition
than - until - to

tâ: preposition
till

tâ abad: adverb
forever

tâ hadike: preposition
to the extent

tâ injâ: adverb
hitherto - here

tâ inke: preposition
till - than - until

tâ kardan: verb
To limber

tâ moghe'i ke: adverb
while

tâ vaghti ke: adverb
till

tâ vaghtike: preposition
until

tâ ândâze'I: adverb
to an extend

tâ ânke: preposition
till

tâ ânvaght: adverb
yet

tâ'un: noun
plague - pest

tâb: noun
glow - patience - swing - sway - twist

tâb: noun
taboo

tâb bardâshtan: verb
To warp

tâb âvardan: verb
To abide - To bear - To withstand

tâbande: adjective
spinner - phosphorous - phosphoric

tâbe': noun
subsidiary - submission - citizen

tâbe' gharâr dâdan: verb
To subordinate

tâbe'e khod kardan: verb
To govern

tâbe'iyat: noun
sequence - nationality - allegiance

tâbehâl: adverb
hitherto

tâbesh: noun
flame - glow - glitter - glint - brilliance - shine

tâbeshdâr: adjective
radioactive

tâbeshi: adjective
radial

tâbestân: noun
summer

tâbidan: verb
To shine - To glow - To glint - To radiate

tâbkhordegi: noun
ruga

tâblo: noun
tableau - sign

tâbnâk: adjective
radiant - bright - sunny

tâbut: noun
coffin

tâbân: adjective
shiner - light - bright - luminous

tâbânidan: verb
To glint

tâfi: noun
caramel - butterscotch - taffy

tâgh: noun
roof - arch - arc - azygos - vault

tâgh zadan: verb
To roof

tâghat: noun
lip - patience - nerve - gut - sufferance -
stamina

tâghat dâshtan: verb
To tolerate

tâghatfarsâ: adjective
severe - troublous - tiresome

tâghbâz: adjective
supine

tâghche: noun
shelf

tâghche: noun
niche - ledge

tâghchedâr kardan: verb
To shelve

tâhadi: adverb
cretain - kindof - pretty - partly - somewhat

tâher: noun
clean

tâhodudike: adverb
somedeal

tâj: noun
crown

tâjegol: noun
wreath - garland

tâjer: noun
businessman - merchant

tâjâyike: preposition
as far as

tâk: noun
grapevine - vine

tâkestân: noun
arbor - vineyard

tâkht kardan: verb
To attack

tâkhto tâz: noun
ravage - raid - invasion - attack

tâkonun: adverb
yet - hitherto - heretofore

tâksi: noun
taxi - cab

tâle': adjective
horoscope - fortune

tâle' bini: noun
astronomy - astrology

tâleb: adjective
wishful - applicant

tâlebi: noun
cantaloupe

tâlâb: noun
lagoon - pond

tâlâr: noun
chamber - amphitheater - hall

tâlâr: noun
saloon

tâm: adjective
total

tânk: noun
tank

târ: adjective
dim - obscure - blear

târek: adjective
apex

târek donyâ: adjective
hermit - monk - ascetic

târi: noun
umbrage - obscurity

târik: adjective
dark - dim - dusky

târik kardan: verb
To gloom - To overshadow - To obscure - To dark

târikh: noun
history - date - era

târikhche: noun
record - chronicle - annals - memoir - history

târikhdân: noun
historian

târikhi: adjective
historic

târki: noun
vertical

târkonande: adjective
dimmer

târopud: noun
sinew - texture - warpandwoof

târâj: noun
spoil - loot - booty - plunder - pillage

târâj kardan: verb
To devastate - To overrun

tâs: noun
bald

tâs kabâb: noun
stew

tâsho: adjective
jackknife - slipper - pliant - lissome - limber

tâto: noun
pony

tâtâr: noun
tatar - tartar

tâval: noun
gall - welt - blister

tâval zadan: verb
To scorch - To breakout - To blister

tâvus: noun
peacock

tâvân: noun
penalty - indemnity - fine

tâvân dâdan: verb
To compensate - To remunerate - To penalize

tâyefe: noun
tribe

tâzamânike: preposition
pending

tâze: adjective
fresh - uptodate

tâze bedorân reside: adjective
upstart

tâze dâmâd: adjective
birdegroom - newlywed

tâze kardan: verb
To refresh - To fresh

tâzegi: noun
recency - novelty

tâzekar: adjective
tyro - novitiate - novice - beginner

tâzenafas: adjective
fresh

tâzetar: adjective
newest

tâzevâred: adjective
immigrant - newcomer

tâzi: noun
greyhound - arabic

tâzidan: verb
To gallop

tâziyâne: noun
scourge - lash - rawhide - whip

tâziyâne zadan: verb
To stripe - To scourge - To lambaste

tôam: noun
conjugate - geminate - joint

tôgh: noun
torque

tôghe: noun
torque - ring

tôghi: noun
torpid

tôhidgarâyi: noun
unitarianism

tôlid: noun
manufacture - production

tôr: noun
sort

tôsan: noun
steed

tôshih kardan: verb
To autograph

tôsiye kardan: verb
To counsel - To recommit

tôte'egar: adjective
subversive - plotter

u

u: pronoun
she - he

urâ: verb
him - her

V

va'de: noun
promise

va'de dâdan: verb
To invite

va'z: noun
sermon

va'z kardan: verb
To preach - To admonish

vabâ: noun
cholera

vadi'e: noun
trust

vafatn vafatnâme: noun
epitaph

vafâ: noun
troth

vafâ kardan: verb
To pass

vafâ kardan: verb
To adhere - To abide

vafâ kardan: verb
To accomplish

vafâdâr: adjective
loyal

vafâdâri: noun
loyalty

vagarna: noun
otherwise

vaghf: noun
devotion

vaghf kardan: verb
To devote - To dedicate - To bequeath

vaghfe: noun
suspension - pause - break - cease

vaghih: adjective
hideous

vaght: noun
time

vaghtike: preposition
when

vaghtshenâs: adjective
punctual

vaghâr: adjective
solemnity - serenity - elegance - dignity

vah'y: noun
inspiration - revelation

vahdat: noun
unity - unification

vahle: noun
stage - place - instance - heat - onset -
occasion

vahm: noun
delusion - mirage

vahshat: noun
dread - fray - horror

vahshatnâk: adjective
dreadful - bloodcurdling - terrible

vahshatzade: adjective
aghast

vahshatzadegi: noun
startle - dismay

vahshatâvar: adjective
awesome - terrible

vahshi: adjective
savage - harebrained - brutal - ferocious

vahshigari: noun
savagery - brutality - barbarism

vahshigari: noun
truculence

vahshigari kardan: verb
To rampage

vahshiyâne: adverb
savage - barbaric

vajab: noun
span - palm

vajab kardan: verb
To span

vajh: noun
payment - face - mode - form

vajin kardan: verb
To weed

vakhim: adjective
worse

vakhim: adjective
serious - tense - crucial - critical - fatal

vakil: noun
attorney - lawyer

vakil: noun
attorney

vakil modâfe': noun
counselor - attorney - advocate

valad: noun
son

vali: preposition
but - yet

valiahd: noun
crown prince

var raftan: verb
To twiddle

varagh: noun
sheet - leaf - card

varagh zadan: verb
To leaf - To turnover

varaghe: noun
sheet - paper - form

varam: noun
tumor - welt - dropsy - bunny

varam: adjective
edema

varid: noun
vein

varidi: noun
venous

varshekast: noun
broke

varshekast shodan: verb
To smash - To bust

varshekaste: adjective
broke - bankrupt

varshô: noun
nickel - Warsaw

varzesh: noun
sport - exercise

varzesh: noun
blast - guff - whop - whiff

varzesh kardan: verb
To exercise

varzeshgâh: noun
stadium

varzeshi: noun
sporty - athletic

varzeshkâr: adjective
athlete - sportsman

varzidan: verb
To ompliments - To knead

varzidegi: noun
mastery

vasat: noun
amidst - amid - middling - mediocre

vasati: noun
meddle - mid - median

vasf: noun
description - picture

vasfi: adjective
descriptive - adjective

vasi: noun
successor

vasi': adjective
spacious - comprehensive - extensive -
abroad

vasi' kardan: verb
To broaden - To enlarge

vasighe: noun
bail - deposit - guarantee

vasighe: noun
collateral

vasile: noun
instrument - handle

vasileye naghliye: noun
transport - conveyance - vehicle

vasiyat: noun
wills

vasiyat kardan: verb
To testate

vasiyatnâme: noun
testament - devise - will

vasl kardan: verb
To connect

vaslat: noun
union

vaslat dâdan: verb
To match - To adjoin - To unite

vasle: noun
splotch - patch - inset

vasvase: noun
temptation

vasvase kardan: verb
To solicit

vasvâs: noun
freak - obsession

vasvâs dâshtan: verb
To scruple

vasâyel: noun
utensil

vatan: noun
home

vatar: noun
sinew - tendon - hypotenuse - cord - nerve

vatar: noun
chord - hypotenuse

vaz': noun
situation - status - position

vaz'iyat: noun
status - situation - condition - position

vazagh: noun
toad - frog

vazidan: verb
To puff - To whiff - To blow

vazidan: verb
To breeze

vazife: noun
task - duty - function - assignment

vazife dâshtan: verb
To function

vazifeshenâs: adjective
loyal - conscientious - dutiful

vazin: adjective
weighty - heavy - ponderous

vazir: noun
queen

vazn: noun
weight

vazn: noun
weight

vazn kardan: verb
To weigh

vazne: noun
sinker

vazândan: verb
To whiff

vefgh: noun
accordance

vefgh dâdan: verb
To reconcile - To assimilate - To adjust - To adapt

vefâgh: noun
consensus

veghâhat: noun
obscenity

vejhe: noun
phase

vekâlat: noun
attorney - advocacy

vekâlat dâdan: verb
To empower - To delegate

vekâlatnâme: noun
proxy

vel: adjective
loose - baggy

vel gashtan: verb
To traipse - To putter - To slosh - To hangaround

vel kardan: verb
To leave - To lax - To relinquish - To quit

velarm: adjective
lukewarm - tepid

velgard: adjective
tramp - rambler - vagabond - hooligan

velgardi: noun
tramp - profligacy - vagrancy

velkharj: adjective
spendthrift - profligate - wasteful - prodigal

velkharji: noun
lavish - prodigality - profligacy - squander

velkharji kardan: verb
To lavish - To indulgence

velâyat: noun
province

verd: noun
abracadabra - jaber - slogan

verâj: adjective
talkative - chatty - loquacious

verâji: noun
palaver - cackle - yack - jaw

verâji kardan: verb
To rattle - To verbalize - To blab

verâsat: noun
heredity - inheritance

vesâl: noun
joiner

vesâl: noun
tinker

vesâtat: noun
intermediary - intercession

vezvez: noun
zoom - buzz - drone

vezvez kardan: verb
To drone - To hum - To buzz - To bombinate

vezârat: noun
ministry

vezâratkhâne: noun
ministry

vietnâmi: adjective
vietnamese

vilâ: noun
villa

virgul: noun
comma

virus: noun
virus

virân: noun
subversive - ruinous - desolate

virân kardan: verb
To destroy - To demolish - To gaunt

virân shodan: verb
To fall - To wrack

virâne: adjective
ruin

virângar: adjective
ruinous - destroyer

virâni: noun
destruction - demolition - ravage - ruination

virâstan: verb
To edit

virâyesh: noun
edition

viski: noun
whiskey

vitrin: noun
showcase - window

viyolon: noun
violin

vizhe: adjective
net - particular - adhoc - peculiar - specific

vizhe: adjective
special

vizhegi: noun
trait

vizitor: noun
salesman

vizâ: noun
visa

vofur: adjective
superabundance - affluence - abundance - plurality

voghu': noun
incidence - occurrence

voghuf: noun
knowledge - liegemen

536

vojdân: noun
breast - conscience

vojub: noun
incumbency

vojud: noun
existence - personality - person

vojud dâshtan: verb
To be - To exist

voltâzh: noun
voltage

vorud: noun
entry - entrance - arrival

vos'at: noun
extent - expanse - latitude

vos'ate nazar: noun
breadth

vosul: noun
recovery

vosul kardan: verb
To collect - To cash - To receive - To receipt

vozuh: noun
speciosity - lucidity - light - clarity

vâ: preposition
oh - voice

vâ: preposition
pshaw

vâ kardan: verb
To unwreathe

vâ raftan: verb
To wane

vâ'ez: noun
preacher

vâbaste: adjective
subordinate - dependent - relevant - affiliate

vâbastegi: noun
relationship - coherency - contiguity - interdependence

vâbastegi: noun
relation - dependence

vâdbud: noun
souvenir - memorial - reminiscent

vâdi: noun
valley

vâdâshtan: verb
To stand - To cause - To wrest - To appoint

vâfer: adjective
opulent - abundant - luxuriant - profuse

vâgh: noun
waterfowl

vâghe' bini: noun
realism

vâghe' budan: verb
To stand

vâghe'bin: adjective
pragmatic

vâghe'e: noun
event - occurrence - incident

vâghe'garâyi: noun
realism

vâghe'i: adjective
true - real - essential - actual

vâghe'i: adjective
concrete - real

vâghe'iyat: noun
reality - verity

vâghe'ye nâgovâr: noun
accident

vâghean: adverb
indeed - quite - really

vâghef: adjective
benefactor

vâghvâgh: noun
yip - yelp

vâghvâgh kardan: verb
To yelp

vâgir: noun
contagious - epidemic - infectious

vâgirdâr: adjective
zymotic - contagious

vâgiri: noun
contagion

vâgon: noun
wagon

vâgozari: noun
surrender - assignment - abandonment -
abandon - resignation

vâgozâr kardan: verb
To yield - To admit - To abdicate - To
abandon - To concede

vâgozârdan: verb
To devolve - To betake

vâgozâri: noun
abalienate

vâgozâshtan: verb
To setup - To subside

vâhed: noun
single - one - univalent - unity

vâhi: noun
unsubstantial - unrealistic - unreal -
romantic

vâjeb: adjective
essential - fundametal - necessary -
obligatory

vâjeb kardan: verb
To necessitate

vâjebi: noun
depilatory

vâjedesharâyet: adjective
eligible - bonafide

vâkonesh: noun
response - repercussion - reflex - rebound

vâks: noun
shiner

vâks zadan: verb
To polish

vâksan: noun
vaccine

vâl: noun
voile - whale

vâled: noun
father

vâlede: noun
mother

vâledein: noun
parent

vâledeyn: noun
parent

vâlâ: adjective
sublime - otherwise - haughty

vâlâmaghâm: adjective
eminent

vâm: noun
debt - loan

vâm dâdan: verb
To lend

vâm gereftan: verb
To borrow

vâmândan: verb
To overweary

vâmândegi: noun
lag

vân: noun
tub - bath

vâne hamâm: noun
receptor - bathtub

vânemud: noun
pretension

vânemud kardan: verb
To pretend - To simulate

vânet: noun
watt

vângahi: noun
besides - beside

vânil: noun
vanilla

vârasi kardan: verb
To sift - To investigate

vâraste: adjective
pious - light

vâred: noun
conscious - relevant - comer

vâred bekâr: adjective
pundit

vâred shodan: verb
To enter - To arrive

vâred âmadan: verb
To incur

vâredkonande: adjective
importer

vâredât: noun
imports

vâres: adjective
heir

vâriz: noun
settlement - settle

vâriz kardan: verb
To square - To settle - To even

vârune: adjective
converse - reverse - opposite - inverse -
upsidedown

vârune shodan: verb
To keel

vâsete: noun
middleman

vâsher: noun
washer

vâzeh: adjective
lucid - explicit - clear - obvious

vâzelin: noun
vaseline

vâzhe: noun
word - vocabulary

vâzhegun: noun
converse - upsidedown - subversive

vâzhegun kardan: verb
To topple - To upset - To overturn - To
reverse

vâzhegun shodan: verb
To capsize - To purl

vâzhegun sâkhtan: verb
To subvert

vâzheguni: noun
overturn - reversal - upset

vâzhegunsâzi: noun
reversal

vâzhegân: noun
terminology - vocabulary

vâzhenegâri: noun
lexicography

vâzhenâme: noun
dictionary - lexicon

y

ya'ni: noun
nee - namely - innuendo

ya'ni: noun
nee - namely - innuendo

yadak: noun
trailer

yadak: noun
trailer

yadak kesh: adjective
tug - tow

yadaki: adjective
extra - reserve - refill - spare

yadaki: noun
extra - reserve - refill - spare

yadi: noun
handmade

yaghe: noun
collar

yaghe: noun
collar

yaghin: noun
sure - positive - certitude - certainty

yaghin: noun
sure - cerainty

yaghmâ: noun
spoil - booty - plunder - pillage -
despoliation

yaghmâ: noun
spoil - pillage - despoliation - ravage

yaghmâgar: adjective
predatory

yaghmâgari: noun
rapacity

yahova: noun
yahveh

yahudi: adjective
hebrew - jewish - jew

yahudi: adjective
Hebrew - Jewish - Jew

yahudiyat: noun
judaism - jewry

yahyâ: noun
john

yakh: noun
ice

yakh: noun
ice

yakh bastan: verb
To ice - To congeal - To freeze

yakh bastan: verb
To ice - To congeal - To freeze

yakhbandân: adjective
glacial

yakhchâl: noun
refrigerator

yakhchâl: noun
refrigerator

yakhdân: noun
freezer

yakhzadegi: noun
freeze

yaraghân: noun
jaundice

yaraghân: noun
jaundice

yarâgh: noun
trapping - stripe

yashm: noun
jasper

yashmi: adjective
jaspery

yatim: adjective
orphan

yatimkhâne: noun
orphanage

yavâsh: adjective
slow

yavâsh: adjective
slow

yavâshaki: noun
stealthy

yavâshaki: adverb
stealthy

yazdân: noun
god

yazdân: noun
god

yegân: noun
unitage - unit

yegâne: adjective
sole - unique

yegâne: adjective
sole - only - one - unique

yegânegi: noun
oneness - unity

yegânegi: noun
oneness - marriage - unity - unification

yeilâgh: noun
summer

yek: noun
one

yek: noun
one

yek râst: adjective
sheer - right

yekbâre digar: noun
again - once

yekdande: adjective
strict

yekdande: adjective
adamant - dogged

yekdande: adjective
adamant - dogged

yekdarmiyân: noun
alternate

yekdeli: noun
empathy - unanimity

yeke: noun
jolt - lone - univalent

yeke khordan: verb
To upstart

yeketâz: adjective
totalitarian

yeketâz: adjective
totalitarian

yeki: verb
To one

yeki shodan: verb
To coalesce - To unify

yekjur: noun
homogeneous - alike

yekjâ: noun
together

yekjâ: adjective
lump

yekjânebe: noun
unilateral

yeklâ: adjective
unifilar

yekmartabe: adjective
once - sudden

yekmâhe: adjective
monthly

yeknavâ: adjective
univocal

yeknavâkht: adjective
singsong - level

yeknavâkht: adjective
same - steady - monotonous

yeknavâkht kardan: verb
To uniform

yeknavâkhti: noun
tedium - humdrum - monotony - uniformity

yekom: adjective
first

yekpâ: noun
unipod

yeksare: noun
indiscriminate - hipandthigh - altogether -
nonstop

yeksare: adjective
indiscriminate - hipandthigh - altogether -
nonstop

yeksedâ: noun
univocal

yeksedâyi: noun
unison

yekshanbe: noun
sunday

yekshanbe: noun
sunday

yeksu: adjective
one side

yeksu: noun
side

yeksâle: adjective
yearlong

yeksân: noun
equal - alike - akin - similar - same

yeksân: adjective
equal - alike - akin - similar - same

yektarafe: adjective
sideway

yektarafe: adjective
overhand - unilateral

yektarafe: adjective
overhand - unilateral

yektâ: adjective
alone - unique

yektâ: adjective
alone - unique

yektâparast: adjective
unitary - unitarian

yektâparast: adjective
unitary - unitarian

yektâparasti: noun
monotheism - unitarianism

yekvari: noun
lopsided - sidle

yekân: adjective
unit

yeylâgh: noun
country - summer

yobusat: noun
constipation

yod zadan: verb
To iodize

yonje: noun
alfalfa

yonje: noun
alfalfa

yugh: noun
yoke

yugh: noun
yoke

yunân: noun
Greece

yunâni: adjective
Greek

yuresh: noun
attack - rush - raid - offense

yuresh: noun
attack - assault - raid - offense

yuresh bordan: verb
To push

yuresh âvardan: verb
To sally - To storm - To sortie - To raid

yurtem raftan: verb
To trot

yurtme: noun
trot

yurtme: noun
trot

yurtme raftan: verb
To trot

yuzpalang: noun
panther

yuzpalang: noun
panther

yâ: preposition
or

yâ: noun
or

yâ al'lâh: noun
hallo

yâ'isegi: noun
menopause

yâbu: noun
workhorse

yâbu: noun
tit - nag - workhorse

yâd: noun
memory

yâd: noun
memory

yâd dâdan: verb
To instruct - To teach

yâd gereftan: verb
To learn

yâd gereftan: verb
To learn

yâd kardan: verb
To reminisce

yâd kardan: verb
To reminisce

yâd âvardan: verb
To remember

yâd âvardan: verb
To remember

yâd âvari: noun
reminiscence - remembrance

yâd âvari kardan: verb
To remind

yâdbud: noun
souvenir - memorial

yâdegâr: noun
souvenir - memorial - relic

yâdegâr: noun
souvenir - memorial

yâdegâri: noun
remembrance - memento

yâdegâri: noun
remembrance - memento - token

yâdâsht: noun
note

yâdâsht kardan: verb
To note

yâdâvar: adjective
memento - reminiscent - reminder

yâdâvari: noun
mention - reminder - remembrance

yâesegi: noun
menopause

yâftan: verb
To discover - To find

yâftan: verb
To discover - To meet

yâghi: adjective
turbulent - rebel - outlaw - mutinous

yâghi: adjective
turbulent - rebel - brigand - lawbreaker

yâghigari: noun
muitiny

yâghigari: noun
insurgency - insurgence

yâghigari kardan: verb
To rebel

yâghut: noun
ruby

yâghut: noun
ruby

yâkhte: noun
cell

yâkhte: noun
cell

yâl: noun
mane - crest

yâr: noun
sweetheart - friend - partner - pal - buddy

yâri: noun
help - aid - companionship

yâri: noun
help - aid - companionship

yâri kardan: verb
To aid - To help

yâri kardan: verb
To aid - To help

yâri nemudan: verb
To help

yâri nemudan: verb
To help - To aid

yâru: noun
guy - skate

yâs: noun
letdown - despair

yâs: noun
Jasmine

yâsaman: noun
gardenia

yâsamin: noun
jasmine

yâvar: adjective
assistant - assist - aid - adjutant - helper

yâve: noun
tattle - nonsense - babble - absurd

yâve: adjective
tattle - nonsense - babble - absurd

yâve goftan: verb
To babble

yâvesarâyi: noun
rant

yâvesarâyi: noun
rant

yâzda: noun
eleven

yâzdah: noun
eleven

yôm: noun
day

yôm: noun
day

yôyo: adverb
yoyo

yôyô: noun
yoyo

Z

za'f: noun
infirmity - depauperation

za'ferân: noun
saffron

za'ferân: noun
saffron - crocus

za'if: adjective
weak - lean

za'if shodan: verb
To weaken

zabt: noun
retention - record - seizure

zabt kardan: verb
To tape - To record

zabun: adjective
despicable - humble

zabân: noun
tongue - language

zabânbâz: adjective
sophist

zabâne: noun
tongue - prong - finger

zabâne keshidan: verb
To low - To lick - To flame

zabânedâr: adjective
tangy

zadan: verb
To beat - To shoot

zado khord: noun
warfare - combat - battle

zado khord kardan: verb
To skirmish - To combat - To battle

zafar: noun
victory

zaftebâzi kardan: verb
To kite - To speculate

zah'gin: adjective
toxic

zahmat: noun
discomfort - inconvenience - pain - torment
- trouble

zahmat dâdan: verb
To trouble - To bother

zahmat keshidan: verb
To toil - To plod - To muck - To labor

zahmatkesh: adjective
sufferer - studious - toiler - workingman

zahmatkesh: adjective
durdge - hardworking - laborious -
painstaking

zahr: noun
poison - venom

zahr: noun
poison

zahrdâr: adjective
venomous - poisonous

zahrâb: noun
urine

zahrâlud: adjective
baneful - poison

zajr: noun
torture - torment

zajr dâdan: verb
To torture - To torment

zakhim: adjective
squatty - russeting - russet - gross

zakhire: noun
reservoir - reservation - stock

zakhire sâzi: noun
storage

zakhm: noun
wound - scotch

zakhm: noun
wound - lesion - ulcer - sore

zakhm zadan: verb
To slash - To wound

zakhme me'de: noun
ulcer

zakhmi: adjective
traumatic - ulcerous

zakhmi kardan: verb
To scotch

zal: noun
shadow - aegis

zalil kardan: verb
To smite - To oppress

zamime: noun
supplement - enclosure - appendix - annex

zamin: noun
territory - soil - earth - ground - land

zamine: noun
background - context

zamine râ mohayâ sâkhtan: verb
To predispose

zamingir: adjective
cripple

zamini: adjective
earthy - territorial - terrestrial

zaminkhâri: noun
geophagy

zaminlarze: noun
earthquake

zaminshenâs: noun
geologist

zaminshenâsi: noun
geology

zamir: noun
conscience - ego

zamzame: noun
murmur - croon

zamzame kardan: verb
To croon - To hum - To murmur

zamâ'em: noun
paraphernalia - enclosure

zamân: noun
date - moment - time - zeitgeist

zamâne: noun
time - era

zamâni: noun
time

zan: noun
woman - wife

zan: noun
conjecture - guess - hunch - surmise

zan dâshtan: verb
To mistrust

zanande: adjective
nasty - acrimonious - acrid - beater -
hideous - harsh

zanbagh: noun
flag - lily

zanbil: noun
basket

zanbil: noun
basketry

zanbur: noun
bee

zanbure asal: noun
bumblebee - bee

zanbâz: adjective
philander - gallant

zane barâdar: noun
sisterinlaw

zane fâsed: noun
peat

zane pedar: noun
stepmother

zang: noun
rust

zangi: adjective
negro

zangule: noun
urceolate

zangzadan: verb
To stain - To rust - To ringer

zangzade: adjective
rusty - rotten

zangzadegi: adjective
corrosion - stain

zanin: adjective
suspicious

zanjabil: noun
ginger

zanjir: noun
chain

zanjir: noun
chain

zanjir kardan: verb
To manacle

zanjire: noun
continuum

zanparast: adjective
uxorious

zanân: noun
feminine - womankind

zanâne: adverb
womanly - womanish - wifely

zanânegi: noun
woman

zanâshuyi: noun
wedlock - matrimony - marriage

zar: noun
gold

zarabân: noun
beat - pulse - pitter-patter - throb

zarabâne ghalb: noun
heartbeat

zarar: noun
harm - loss

zarb: noun
stroke - contusion - beat

zarb kardan: verb
To muliply

zarbat: noun
slap - yerk - jolt

zarbat: noun
bump - hit - strike

zarbe: noun
impact - lash - tit - strike

zarbe zadan: verb
To dabber - To layon - To butt

zarbeye fani: noun
knockout

zarbo jarh: noun
maim - battery

zarbolajal: noun
deadline

zarbolmasal: noun
proverb - sooth - byword

zard: adjective
wan - aquamarine - yellow

zardak: noun
carrot

zardi: adjective
autumn - yellow

zardi: noun
jaundice

zardosht: noun
zoroaster

zardoshti: adjective
Zoroastrian

zardpey: noun
tendon

zardâlu: noun
apricot

zare: noun
shred - whit - grain - dust - vestige - bit

zarebin: noun
lens - microscope

zarf: noun
dish - container

zarfiyat: noun
capacity

zarfshuyi: noun
dishwasher

zargar: noun
goldsmith

zargh: noun
hyporisy

zargho bargh: noun
glamor - glamour - razzledazzle - luster - vitreous

zargin: adjective
virulent

zarib: noun
coefficient

zarif: adjective
capillary - delicate - slender - sheer

zarin: adjective
golden

zarparast: adjective
mammonite

zartosht: noun
zoroaster

zartoshti: adjective
parsi - zoroastrian

zarurat: noun
necessity - urgency

zaruri: adjective
urgent - necessary

zarâbkhâne: noun
mint - bank

zarâdkhâne: noun
arsenal - armory

zarâfe: noun
giraffe

zarât: noun
ingredient

zavâher: noun
external

zavâl: noun
decay - consumption - downfall - lapse

zavâyed: noun
excrement

zebardast: adjective
dextrous - dexterous - industrious -
proficient - adroit

zebardasti: noun
sleight - skill - proficiency - dexterity

zebh: noun
slaughter - hew

zebh kardan: verb
To slay

zebr: adjective
stubby - stark - shaggy - scaly - ragged -
coarse

zebrokhashen: adjective
burly

zed: noun
opposite - opponent - hostile - adversary

zede'sedâ: adjective
soundproof

zede'âb: adjective
waterproof

zedeyakh: noun
antifreeze

zediyat: noun
opposition

zedo naghiz: noun
antonym - antithesis

zedudan: verb
To efface - To remove - To clean - To
obliterate - To wipe

zefâf: noun
wedlock

zegil: noun
wart - tuber

zeh: noun
cord - chord - catgut - gut

zeh: noun
string

zeh keshi: noun
canalization

zehkeshi: noun
sewerage - drainage

zehkeshi kardan: verb
To drain

zehn: noun
remembrance - mind - mentality

zehni: adjective
subjective - psychic - intrinsic - intellectual

zeil: noun
appendix - addendum

zeitun: noun
olive

zekhâmat: noun
diameter

zekr: noun
recitation - citation - mention - penis

zekr kardan: verb
To cite - To mention

zekâvat: noun
sagacity - esprit - engine

zelzele: noun
earthquake

zelzeleshenâsi: noun
seismology

zemestân: noun
winter

zemestâni: adjective
hibernal - winter

zemnan: adverb
tacit - meanwhile - meantime

zemni: noun
tacit - accident - incident

zemâm: noun
helm - rein

zemâmdâr: noun
statesman

zemâmdâri: noun
statesmanship

zemânat: noun
guarantee - warranty - sponsorship

zemânat kardan: verb
To insure - To guarantee - To sponsor

zende: adjective
fresh - vivid - lively - alive

zende: noun
live

zende mândan: verb
To survive

zende shodan: verb
To revive - To quicken - To liven

zendedel: adjective
dashing - dapper

zendegi: noun
existence - life - habitancy

zendegi bakhshidan: verb
To animate - To enliven

zendeginâme: noun
biography

zendân: noun
jail - prison

zendân kardan: verb
To lockup - To prison

zendâni: adjective
prisoner - inmate - jailbird

zendâni kardan: verb
To incarcerate

zendâni shodan: verb
To imprisonment

zendâniye siyâsi: noun
political prisoners

zengâr: noun
rust - blight - legging

zenhâr: noun
quarter

zenâ: noun
adultery

zenâkâr: adjective
adulterous - wencher

zenâzâde: adjective
adulterate

zerang: adjective
agile - adroit - clever - nimble

zerangi: noun
knack - sleight - promptitude

zereh: noun
armor - armature - mail

zerehpush: adjective
ironclad

zereshk: adjective
purple

zerâ'at kardan: verb
To cultivate

zerâfat: noun
precision - grace - delicacy - elegance

zesht: adjective
ugly - bad - horrid - homely - hideous -
invidious - maladroit

zesht: adjective
ugly - obscene

zeshti: noun
opprobrium - odium - obscenity -
inelegance - homeliness

zevâl: noun
ebb

zharf: adjective
profound - unfathomable - abysmal - deep

zharfâ: adjective
depth

zhen: noun
gene

zhende: adjective
shabby - ragged

zhende push: adjective
ragamuffin - tatter

zhenerâl: noun
general

zhenerâtor: noun
generator

zhermani: adjective
germanic

zhest: noun
pose - gesture

zhest gereftan: verb
To pose

zheton: noun
chip

zhigulu: adjective
macaroni - cockscomb

zhiyân: noun
fierce - rapacious

zhuker: noun
joker

zhulide: adjective
draggy - ragamuffin - slovenly

zhulidegi: noun
plica - squalor

zhâkat: noun
sweater - pullover - jacket

zhâle: noun
dew - frost

zhâmbon: noun
ham

zhânviye: noun
january

zhâpon: noun
japan

zhâponi: adjective
nipponese - japanese

zibande: adjective
seemly - becoming

zibâ: adjective
cute - handsome - beautiful

zibâ kardan: verb
To embellish - To groom - To adorn - To beautify

zibâyi: noun
beauty

zihagh dânestan: verb
To justify

zihesâb: noun
accountant

zilu: noun
carpet

zin: noun
saddle

zinaf': noun
nominee - beneficiary

zinat kardan: verb
To decorate

zip: noun
zip

zir: preposition
bottom - beneath - under

zirak: adjective
subtle - smart - shrewd - sharp - astute - adroit - acute - brilliant - keen

ziraki: noun
cogency - cunning - brilliance - agility

zirbaghal: noun
armpit

zirbanâ: noun
infrastructure

zirin: noun
beneath - underside - underneath - under

zirnevis: noun
subscript

zirobam: noun
undulation

zirpirâhani: noun
underclothing

zirpush: noun
underwear

zirshalvâri: noun
drawer - pants - underpants - underdrawers

zirzamin: noun
basement - underground

zirzamini: adjective
suberranean

zirâ: preposition
because

zirâb: noun
drain - underwater

zirâb zadan: verb
To drain

zirâbi: noun
undersea

zirâke: preposition
for - because

zist: noun
existence

zistan: verb
To exist - To be - To live

zistgâh: noun
settlement

zistshenâs: noun
biologist

zistshenâsi: noun
biology

zivar: noun
trangam - jollity - jewel

ziyâd: adjective
very - vast - much - many

ziyâd kardan: verb
To add - To increase - To heighten

ziyâde: adjective
supernumerary

ziyâdejuyi: noun
avarice

ziyâderavi: noun
extravagance - intemperance - indulgence

ziyâdero: adjective
intemperate - indulgent

ziyâdi: noun
surplus - extra - excess

ziyâd shodan: verb
To increase - To grow - To proliferate

ziyâdtar: adjective
more

ziyâdtarin: adjective
most

ziyâfat: noun
repast - banquet - symposium

ziyân: noun
damage - disadvantage - loss

ziyân resândan: verb
To impair - To damage

ziyân zadan: verb
To damage

ziyânbakhsh: adjective
obnoxious

ziyânâvar: adjective
pernicious - nocuous - deleterious

ziyârat: noun
pilgrimage

ziyârat kardan: verb
To visit

ziyâratgâh: noun
shrine

zob kardan: verb
To found - To melt

zobde: adjective
elite - compendium

zobâle: noun
rubbish - garbage

zoghâl: noun
coal - char

zoghâl akhte: noun
blueberry - huckleberry - dogwood

zoghâlforosh: noun
charwoman

zoghâli: noun
carbonic

zoghâlsang: noun
collier

zoghâlzang: noun
coal

zohal: noun
satrun

zohr: noun
midday - noon

zohre: noun
gall - bile

zohur: noun
outburst - emersion - appearance

zohur: noun
advent

zokâm: noun
sniffle - influenza - cold

zolf: noun
hair

zolm: noun
cruelty - injustice - tyranny

zolm kardan: verb
To macerate

zolmâni: noun
tenebrific

zolâl: adjective
lucid - limpid - crystal - clear

zome: noun
conscience

zomokht: adjective
crude - coarse - clumsy - churlish - rugged - rude - rough

zomre: noun
class - category

zonbe: noun
barrow

zoruf: noun
utensil

zozanaghe: noun
trapezoid - trapze

zudbâvar: adjective
credulous - untutored

zudgozar: adjective
perishable - ephemeral - transient - temporary

zudras: adjective
unripe - hasty - precocious

zudtar: adjective
junior

zum: noun
zoom

zur: noun
hustle - vigor - might - power - strength

zurgu: adjective
unreasonable - incubus

zurmand: adjective
vigorous - mighty

zurâzmâyi: noun
match

zuze keshidan: verb
To yowl - To whimper - To howl

zâ'er: noun
pilgrim

zâbet: noun
archivist - constable

zâbete: noun
criterion - topic

zâd: noun
birth - son

zâde: adjective
offspring - nee

zâdgâh: noun
provenance - birthplace

zâdovalad: noun
bearing

zâdruz: noun
birthday

zâeghe: noun
palate - relish

zâgh: noun
alum

zâghche: noun
jackdaw

zâhed: adjective
pious - votary - ascetic - devotee

zâhedâne: adverb
ascetic

zâher: noun
appearance - manifest - outside

zâher: noun
sensation - appearance - manifest

zâher shodan: verb
To seem - To spring - To out - To look

zâheri: adjective
exterior - outwards - outward - superficial

zâhernamâ: adjective
seeming

zâhersâzi: adjective
histrionics

zâj: noun
vitriolic - alum

zâl: noun
albino

zâlem: adjective
cruel - ruthless - heinous

zâlemâne: adverb
tyrannous - burdensome

zâlu: noun
leech - bloodsucker

zâmen: adjective
sponsor - guarantee

zânu: noun
knee

zânu zadan: verb
To kneel

zâr: noun
deplorable - lamentable - vexation

zâre': noun
sharecropper - tiller - planter

zâri: noun
whimper - moan - plaint

zâri kardan: verb
To moan

zât: noun
substance - essence - nature

zâti: adjective
natural - congenital - inward - intrinsic - innate - inherent

zâtoriye: noun
pneumonia

zâviye: noun
canton - angle - in - hermitage

zâviyedâr: adjective
embowed

zâye': adjective
lost

zâye' kardan: verb
To spoil - To abuse

zâye' shodan: verb
To rot

zâye'ât: noun
culch - garble - wastage

zâyed: adjective
extra - waste - redundancy - further -
surplus - superfluous

zâyedolvasl: noun
unutterable

zâyemân: noun
throe - parturition - litter - childbirth

zâyesh: noun
birth

zâyeshgâh: noun
maternity

zâyidan: verb
To birth - To teem

zâyâ: adjective
zoogenic - germ

zôb: noun
fusion

zôgh: noun
zeal - verve - relish

zôj: noun
spouse - twin - even - couple – pair

Other Books of Interest

Learn Farsi in 100 Days

The Ultimate Crash Course to Learning Farsi Fast

The goal of this book is simple. It will help you incorporate the best method and the right strategies to learn Farsi FAST and EFFECTIVELY.

Learn Farsi in 100 days helps you learn speak Farsi faster than you ever thought possible. You only need to spend about 90-120 minutes daily in your 100-day period in order to learn Farsi language at advanced level. Whether you are just starting to get in touch the Farsi language, or even if you have already learned the basics of the language, this book can help you accelerate the learning process and put you on the right track.

Learn Farsi in 100 days is for Farsi learners from the beginning to the advanced level. It is a breakthrough in Farsi language learning — offering a winning formula and the most powerful methods for learning to speak Farsi fluently and confidently. Each contains 4 pages covering a comprehensive range of topics. Each day includes vocabulary, grammar, reading and writing lessons. It gives learners easy access to the Farsi vocabulary and grammar as it is actually used in a comprehensive range of everyday life situations and it teaches students to use Farsi for situations related to work, social life, and leisure. Topics such as greetings, family, weather, sports, food, customs, etc. are presented in interesting unique ways using real-life information.

Purchase on Amazon website:

https://goo.gl/eG2n11

Published By:

LearnPersianOnline.com

Farsi Conversations
Learn the Most Common Words and Phrases Farsi Speakers use Every Day

Learning about a new culture is always an exciting prospect and one of the best ways to get to know about another country, its people and their customs, is to learn the language.

Now, with Farsi Conversations: Learn the Most Common Words and Phrases Farsi Speakers use Every Day you can learn how to communicate in Farsi and learn more about Persian culture at the same time.

In this unique guide, you will be able to practice your spoken Farsi with FREE YouTube videos. It is an ideal tool for learners of Farsi at all levels, whether at school, in evening classes or at home, and is a 'must have' for business or leisure.

Farsi students can learn;

- How to use the right language structures and idioms in the right context
- Practice Farsi vocabulary and phrases needed in everyday situations
- Gain proficiency in written and spoken Farsi
- New ways of mastering Farsi phrases

By the end of the book you will have learned more than 2500 Farsi words, have mastered more than 300 commonly used Farsi verbs, key expressions and phrases and be able to pose more than 800 questions.

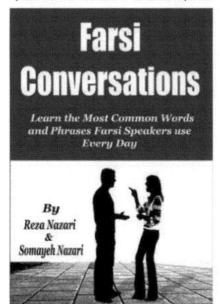

Purchase on Amazon website:

https://goo.gl/bGpVNZ

Published By:

LearnPersianOnline.com

Easy Persian Phrasebook

Essential Expressions for Communicating in Persian

Designed as a quick reference and study guide, this comprehensive phrasebook offers guidance for situations including traveling, accommodations, healthcare, emergencies and other common circumstances. A phonetic pronunciation accompanies each phrase and word.

Easy Persian Phrasebook is designed to teach the essentials of Persian quickly and effectively. The common words and phrases are organized to enable the reader to handle day to day situations. The book should suit anyone who needs to get to grips quickly with Persian, such as tourists and business travelers.

The book "*Easy Persian Phrasebook*" is incredibly useful for those who want to learn Persian language quickly and efficiently.

You'll be surprised how fast you master the first steps in learning Persian, this beautiful language!

Purchase on Amazon website:

https://goo.gl/d21Ivg

Published By:

LearnPersianOnline.com

101 Most Common Farsi Proverbs and Their Best English Equivalents

Provided specifically for Farsi learners at the advanced level, this book looks at the most colorful and entertaining area of Farsi vocabulary –proverbs. Persians love to use proverbs, phrases that are colorful and mysterious. The Essential proverbs in Persian offer an additional look at the idiomatic phrases and sayings that make Persian the rich language that it is.

This book will appeal to Farsi students at advanced level who want to understand and use the Farsi really used by native speakers. A compilation of 101 most popular Farsi proverbs widely used in Iran in everyday context with their best English equivalents are presented with illustrations so that learners using this section will have many idioms 'at their fingertips'.

Farsi proverbs in this book is a supplementary text for advanced students and professionals who want to better understand Farsi native speakers, publications and media. It's especially for those who have learned Farsi outside of Iran. If you already speak Farsi, but now would like to start speaking even better, then this book is just for you.

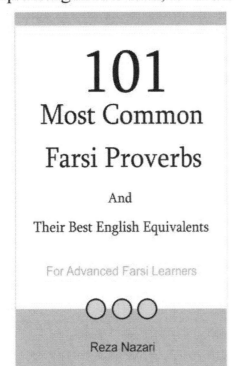

Purchase on Amazon website:

 https://goo.gl/guEmx3

Published By:

LearnPersianOnline.com

Top 1,500 Persian Words

Essential Words for Communicating in Persian

Designed as a quick reference and study guide, this reference book provides easy-to-learn lists of the most relevant Persian vocabulary. Arranged by 36 categories, these word lists furnish the reader with an invaluable knowledge of fundamental vocabulary to comprehend, read, write and speak Persian.

Top 1,500 Persian Words is intended to teach the essentials of Persian quickly and effectively. The common words are organized to enable the reader to handle day-to-day situations. Words are arranged by topic, such as Family, Jobs, weather, numbers, countries, sports, common verbs, etc. A phonetic pronunciation accompanies each word.

With daily practice, you can soon have a working vocabulary in Persian!

The book "*Top 1,500 Persian Words*" is incredibly useful for those who want to learn Persian language **quickly** and **efficiently.**

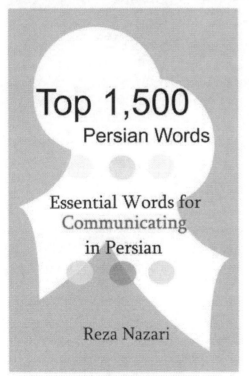

Learn Most Common Persian Words FAST!

Purchase on Amazon website:

https://goo.gl/YvhpKe

Published By:

LearnPersianOnline.com

Farsi Reading

Improve your reading skill and discover the art, culture and history of Iran:

Organized by specific reading skills, this book is designed to enhance students' Farsi reading. The entertaining topics motivate students to learn. Lively reading passages present high-interest subjects for most Farsi speakers. The short essays deepen student knowledge while strengthening reading skills.

Fifty articles in this books representing a diversity of interests intended to develop topics of central interest to Farsi language, culture, and society. Each of the book's topics is a simple essay about Iran's language, geography, culture and history.

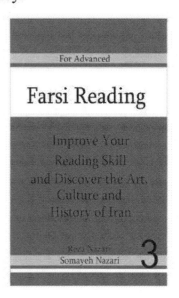

Purchase on Amazon website:

https://goo.gl/Fe5O0t   https://goo.gl/HBcNiV   https://goo.gl/U8UxMm

Published By:
LearnPersianOnline.com

Essential Idioms in Farsi

Learn The Most Common Farsi Idioms
Quickly and Effectively!

Written specifically for Farsi learners at the intermediate and advanced level, this reference book looks at the most colorful and entertaining area of Farsi vocabulary - idioms.

Persians love to use idioms, phrases that are colorful and mysterious. The Essential Idioms in Farsi offers an additional look at the idiomatic phrases and sayings that make Farsi the rich language that it is.

This book will appeal to students at advanced level who want to understand and use the Farsi really used by native speakers. Over 1,600 of the most-used Farsi idioms and phrases, which Farsi learners are likely to encounter are presented with illustrations so that learners using this book will have hundreds of idioms 'at their fingertips'.

Essential Idioms in Farsi is a supplementary text for advanced students and professionals who want to better understand Farsi native speakers, publications and media. It's especially for those who have learned Farsi outside of Iran. If you already speak Farsi, but now would like to start speaking even better, then this book is just for you.

Purchase on Amazon website:

https://goo.gl/8GEwgN

Published By:

LearnPersianOnline.com

Persian for Travel

English - Persian Travel Phrases: Start Speaking Persian Today!

This Book is for people who need to be able to communicate confidently and effectively when travelling. Typical situations covered are: at an airport, checking into a hotel, seeing a doctor, booking tickets and changing arrangements.

The emphasis is on understanding authentic Persian; on practicing the structures necessary to ask questions and check information and on extracting information from brochures, regulations and instructions. Vocabulary is clearly illustrated in context, and American English variants are provided.

"Persian for Travel" effortlessly teaches all the essential phrases you'll need to know before your trip. This book can be used as a self-study course - you do not need to work with a teacher. (It can also be used with a teacher). You don't even need to know a little Farsi before starting.

Persian For Travel

English - Persian Travel Phrases

Reza Nazari
Jalal Daie

Purchase on Amazon website:

https://goo.gl/PMfdPL

Published By:

LearnPersianOnline.com

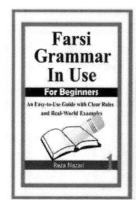    

"learn Persian Online" Publications

Learn Persian Online authors' team strives to prepare and publish the best quality Persian Language learning resources to make learning Persian easier for all. We hope that our publications help you learn this lovely language in an effective way.

Please let us know how your studies turn out. We would like to know what part of our books worked for you and how we can make these books better for others. You can reach us via email at info@learnpersianonline.com

We all in Learn Persian Online wish you good luck and successful studies!

Learn Persian Online Authors

Best Persian Learning Books

Published By:
LearnPersianOnline.com

 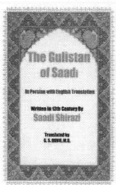 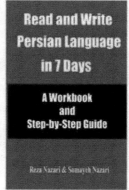  

Learn to Speak Persian Online

Enjoy interactive Persian lessons on Skype with the best native speaking Persian teachers

Online Persian Learning that's Effective, Affordable, Flexible, and Fun.

Learn Persian wherever you want; when you want

Ultimate flexibility. You can now learn Persian online via Skype, enjoy high quality engaging lessons no matter where in the world you are. It's affordable too.

Learn Persian With One-on-One Classes

We provide one-on-one Persian language tutoring online, via Skype. We believe that one-to-one tutoring is the most effective way to learn Persian.

Qualified Native Persian Tutors

Working with the best Persian tutors in the world is the key to success! Our Persian tutors give you the support & motivation you need to succeed with a personal touch.

It's easy! Here's how it works

Request a FREE introductory session
Meet a Persian tutor online via Skype
Start speaking Real Persian in Minutes

Send Email to: info@LearnPersianOnline.com

Or Call: + 1-469-230-3605

Made in the USA
Columbia, SC
22 December 2020